Praise for *Guatemala-U.S. Migration*

"Without sounding too effusive, this book is something of a 'tour de force.' While there are books and other studies about Guatemalan immigrant communities, this book is a nice combination of theory, case study, and history. I know of no other book on Guatemala or indeed about other countries that accomplishes this. The writing is superb; the book is very readable."
—ALLAN BURNS, *Professor Emeritus, University of Florida,* and author of Maya in Exile: Guatemalans in Florida

"In this in-depth, meticulous examination, Jonas and Rodríguez combine historical information, rich data, and theoretical arguments to present an impressive, nuanced overview of Guatemalan migration to the United States. Its relevance goes beyond this case, however, as it offers stimulating insights into the meanings of space and place in the study of migratory flows. It is a great contribution to the immigration scholarship, and I highly recommend it."
—CECILIA MENJÍVAR, *Cowden Distinguished Professor, Arizona State University, and author of* Enduring Violence: Ladina Women's Lives in Guatemala

"Susanne Jonas and Nestor Rodríguez's book is a major contribution to understand the recent history and contemporary features of Guatemalan and, in general, Central American migrations to the United States. In my opinion, one of its outstanding merits lies in their highlighting the regional dimension of migration dynamics. They underline the evolution of this migration region, which is embedded in a host of unfavorable circumstances and perils, as well as the ongoing difficult development of migrants' agency to fight for their rights, goals, and legitimate demands for better living conditions."
—MANUEL ÁNGEL CASTILLO, *Director of Demographic and Urban Studies, and Professor-Researcher, El Colegio de México*

*"*Guatemala-U.S. Migration *is an essential book for understanding the dynamics of Guatemalan migration to the United States over the past four decades. Jonas and Rodríguez not only examine the root causes of migra-*

*tion—political repression, social exclusion, and poverty in Guatemala—
but also illustrate how global developments and socioeconomic trends in the
United States shaped its changing policies towards the arriving migrants.
Undoubtedly, one of the book's most invaluable contributions is to demonstrate, in heretofore unavailable detail, the central role that civil society
actors, informal and formal organizations and networks, in Central
America, Mexico, and the United States have played in advocating for
and vindicating migrants' rights and influencing policies throughout the
region. This is a book for scholars, legal practitioners, and activists alike,
who will benefit from its broad and deep examination of the issues."*
—KAREN MUSALO, *Director of Center for Gender and Refugee Studies
and Professor, University of California Hastings College of the Law*

Guatemala-U.S. Migration

Guatemala-U.S. Migration

Transforming Regions

SUSANNE JONAS

AND NESTOR RODRÍGUEZ

University of Texas Press ⌁ *Austin*

Requests for permission to reproduce material from this work should be sent to:
Permissions
University of Texas Press
P.O. Box 7819
Austin, TX 78713-7819
http://utpress.utexas.edu/index.php/rp-form

♾ The paper used in this book meets the minimum requirements of ANSI/NISO
Z39.48-1992 (R1997) (Permanence of Paper).

Library of Congress Cataloging-in-Publication Data
Jonas, Susanne, 1941–
    Guatemala-U.S. migration : transforming regions / by Susanne Jonas and Nestor
Rodríguez. — First edition.
        pages   cm
    Includes bibliographical references and index.
    ISBN 978-0-292-76060-8 (cl. : alk. paper)
    ISBN 978-0-292-76826-0 (pbk. : alk. paper)
1. Guatemala—Emigration and immigration.   2. United States—Emigration and
immigration.   3. Guatemalans—United States—Social conditions.   4. Guatemalan
Americans—Social conditions.   I. Rodríguez, Nestor.   II. Title.   III. Title:
Guatemala-United States migration.
JV7416.J66   2014
304.8'7307281—dc23
                                                                    2014004655

doi:10.7560/760608

In Memory:
Frank Bonilla
Marco Antonio Chanax
Thomas Holleran
Mario Lungo
Suzanne Dod Thomas

Contents

Preface and Acknowledgments

I. By Way of Introduction

This book represents the culmination of work that we both have been doing for many years. Since the mid-1980s, Nestor has been studying and writing about the immigration and settlement of Guatemalan and other Central American immigrant communities in the Houston area. This led him to Guatemala to study the family and community origins of migration to the United States from the highland *municipio* of San Cristóbal Totonicapán. Susanne has been doing research in Guatemala and Central America since the late 1960s and writing since 1971, with a focus on the multiple dynamics of war, peace-making, and postwar uncertainties. Since the 1990s, she has explored one of those dynamics, the forced and voluntary migrations from Guatemala to Mexico and the United States, and the development of migrant communities in the United States—thereby following, in a sense, the trajectory of the Guatemalans themselves.

Both of us have developed close friendships within the Guatemalan migrant communities along the way, as well as a deep personal and intellectual commitment to understanding their lives and the forces shaping their communities. Our ongoing contact with these migrants, the advocates for their rights, and some of their families in Guatemala has inspired us; we feel privileged to present their experiences in this book. We are humbled by witnessing their daily struggles to survive, advance, and avoid deportation, and we share a commitment to seeing their lives improve and their rights respected.

As an intellectual project, our study of Guatemalan migration to the United States nationwide, beyond case studies of particular U.S. sites, is intended to expand the scope of knowledge concerning migration from peripheral to core regions of the capitalist world system—in this case, passing through the semiperiphery. In recent decades, the dominant paradigm in the U.S. migration literature has been based on Mexican migration, which is overwhelmingly labor migration. The Central American cases present a different scenario. In addition to labor migration, these particular migrant streams—particularly the largest two, Salvadoran and Guatemalan—have been driven by the dynamics of insurgencies and civil wars since the 1960s (in the Guatemalan case), most intensively during the 1980s, and by environmental disasters and multiple forms of social violence in the late 1990s and early 2000s postwar period. In short, migration has become a "normal" element of Guatemalan development since the late 1970s. Furthermore, the Central Americans' violent experiences in having to pass through Mexico to reach the United States are more exaggerated and widespread than for Mexican migrants.

Many of the immediate causes of migration from Central America can be traced to the prevalence of weak states in most Central American countries—to varying degrees within the region, but certainly in Guatemala. In addition, many Central Americans have arrived undocumented in the United States, not only as labor migrants seeking opportunities as in the Mexican case, but also for one or another reason as persons seeking protection away from home. As a result, particularly Salvadorans and Guatemalans became protagonists in organizing for the implementation of particular measures to provide relief from deportation (TPS, ABC, NACARA). In this respect, they constructed a unique history of fighting for specific immigrant rights in the U.S. context based on the notion of sanctuary, which was subsequently broadened to apply to other undocumented Latino immigrants.

Despite the similarities, there are significant differences between Salvadoran and Guatemalan migrants, as our study shows. Most important, the Guatemalan migration streams are divided ethnically between Maya and *ladino* (*mestizo*), both of which are covered in this book. The cases of Mayan migrant communities reveal specific forms of racism, violence, and discrimination to which they have been subjected in Guatemala, in transit through Mexico, and in the United States.

Our study is also intended to explain how Guatemalan migration, as part of the larger Central American migration, fostered the development of a migration region spanning from the Central American high emigration areas of El Salvador, Guatemala, and Honduras (and Nicaragua in the 1980s) through Mexico to the United States. The migration region emerged as the constant passage of migrants headed north became a social force in many local transit communities, as well as in the larger settings of Mexican states and the entire country; different social actors (individuals, groups, institutions) have reacted by restricting, exploiting, victimizing, or assisting the migrants. Our focus on the migration region enables us to conceptualize transregional social action that is grounded not in nation-states as the unit of analysis but in a larger international region of experiences concerning migrants and their interactions with other actors on the migrant trails.

II. Writing Collaboratively

This book is the product of a highly interactive collaboration over the course of many years between two social scientists with different research trajectories and prior areas of specialization. We have greatly appreciated, enjoyed, and been inspired by this collaborative process, and we both learned entirely new areas of knowledge from each other. Nestor's background as a sociologist and social demographer, with a theoretical and empirical specialization in migration studies, complemented Susanne's background as an interdisciplinary scholar on Central America, primarily Guatemala, which was subsequently extended to migration studies. Hence, although one of us took primary responsibility for each of the chapters in this book, we also incorporated in our chapters elements of each other's expertise, including some written text. We wrote, read, rewrote, and reread multiple drafts of each chapter until all of our own questions were resolved, as well as most of those noted by the reviewers of our manuscript.

During the process of writing the book, we also discovered that different chapters had to be written in different "voices," each chapter having its own story to tell. For example, while Chapter 1 is primarily theoretical, Chapter 2 is constructed around the central core of a time series chart of the phases of Guatemalan migration. Chapters 3, 4, and 5 rely heavily on primary interviews and surveys. In addition to interviews in the migrant communities in Houston and the San Francisco area, we did interviews in the sending community of San Cristóbal Totonicapán and with nationwide organizers for migrant rights in Guatemala, Mexico, and the United States. We also drew on interviews and research by Guatemalan and U.S. scholars in other venues, including Mexico.

III. Acknowledgments

As indicated above, our greatest gratitude is owed to the Guatemalan migrants, and their families and friends in Guatemala, the United States, and Mexico, who shared their stories, knowledge, wisdom, and first-hand expertise. We thank reviewers Allan Burns and James Loucky for very careful, comprehensive, and constructive reviews of our entire manuscript. We also thank the production staff at University of Texas Press. Above all, we are grateful to Theresa May, our editor at University of Texas Press, for her infinite patience, wise guidance, and constant interest during the many years that she shepherded this book through its different stages.

We are also grateful to many individuals who helped move our book project forward to completion. While it is difficult to list the names of all who helped us in our research and intellectual inspiration for this book, for Nestor the individuals who provided assistance include Milton Jamail, Margo Gutiérrez, Monty Tidwell, James Loucky, Jacqueline Hagan, Robert L. Bach, Cecilia Menjívar, Michael Olivas, Charles Munnell, Mike McMahan, Juan Chanax, Florinda Chanax, Armando Sapón, Nazario Monzón, and Benito Juárez.

Susanne expresses special gratitude to Manuel Ángel Castillo in Mexico and Irene Palma in Guatemala for collaboration over the course of two decades—and to Frank Bonilla and Mario Lungo posthumously for guidance in transitioning to migration studies. She also thanks Fabienne Venet, Jacobo Dardón, Mauro Verzeletti, Edelberto Torres-Rivas, Ricardo Falla, Carol Girón, Saskia Sassen, Karen Musalo, Mark Silverman, Catherine Tactaquin, Chester Hartman, Felix Fuentes, Nora Hamilton, Norma Chinchilla, Carlos Córdova, Elizabeth "Betita" Martínez, Suzanne Dod Thomas—as well as numerous Guatemalan and Salvadoran migration rights advocates, and colleagues in the Chicano/Latino Research Center's "Latinos in California" Cluster at the University of California, Santa Cruz. Outstanding student research assistance came from Aura Aparicio, Angela Peña, Shannon Bowman, Nadia Grosfoguel, and Esmeralda Aguilar. On a personal note, endless gratitude to my husband, Thomas Holleran, for his support during the life of this book until his untimely passing in 2011.

As always, although we gained new insights and knowledge from our colleagues, only the two of us bear responsibility for the final contents.

Susanne thanks the following institutions for financial assistance: Ford Foundation and Mexico office of Ford Foundation; Dante B. Fascell North-South Center of the University of Miami; Colegio de la Frontera Norte, Mexico; University of California Institute for Mexico and the United States (UC MEXUS); and the following units at University of California, Santa Cruz: Chicano/Latino Research Center (CLRC), Hemispheric Dialogues (a Ford Foundation–funded collaboration between CLRC and the Latin American & Latino Studies Department), Merrill College, and the Institute for Advanced Feminist Research.

Nestor thanks the following institutions for financial assistance: Ford

Foundation; Institute on Multiculturalism and International Labor, SUNY Binghamton; Open Society Foundation; University of Houston Institute for Higher Education, Law and Governance; Hogg Foundation for Mental Health; American Friends Service Committee; Joseph S. Werlin Endowment at the University of Houston; and The University of Texas at Austin Population Research Center, Lozano Long Institute of Latin American Studies, and College of Liberal Arts.

—Susanne Jonas and Nestor Rodríguez, August 2013

Guatemala-U.S. Migration

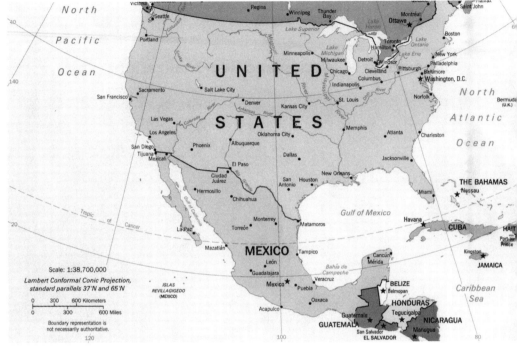

The migration region: Guatemala, Mexico, United States. Courtesy of the University of Texas Libraries, the University of Texas at Austin.

CHAPTER 1

Theoretical Perspectives:
Guatemalan Migration and Regionalization

Initially, the project of this book was defined as a study of Guatemalan migration to the United States—the first such book in English to include both *ladino* and Mayan migrant streams, and to address Guatemalan migration to the United States nationally (in contrast to the many excellent case studies of Guatemalan immigrant communities in various U.S. locales). As the book progressed, however, this study required higher levels of conceptualization, acquiring a regional lens that included Mexico as well. Although the book focuses mainly on Guatemalan migration, that focus is extended to Central American migration at times to theorize more broadly about the interaction between processes of migration and regionalization.

As a result, this book has a dual agenda: to provide an empirical study and to present broad conceptual goals.[1] The book's dual project of empirical research and broad conceptualizations and reconceptualizations has introduced intellectual challenges and tensions, insofar as the process of moving back and forth between levels of generalization requires great precision. For this reason, the book begins with this primarily conceptual introductory chapter written at several levels of generalization. Among other conceptualizations, we elaborate on the emergence of a migration region from Central America to North America and on the sociospatial developments that transpire across it, using insights gained from works on the social production of space (Gottdiener 1985; Soja 1989; Lefebvre 1991; Harvey 2006). These works focus on the construction or conversion of areas by human behavior into social environments with specific qualities of social relations (such as treatment of migrants), and often within larger political-economic frameworks such as capitalist development.

When we speak of Central America, we refer primarily to the "Northern Triangle" composed of Guatemala, Honduras, and El Salvador. With some exceptions, these countries generally have similar social, economic, and security profiles in which large segments of their populations share common conditions of poverty, unemployment, and low income in social environments replete with threats of criminal violence (CEPAL 2012; Meyer and Seelke 2012). Moreover, the migrants from the three countries share many experiences in the passage through Mexico and in their settlement in the United States (Rodriguez 2007; Hagan 2008).

Crisis and Transformation

Much of Central America was in turmoil in the late 1970s and early 1980s. Civil wars and other forms of political conflict, as well as economic deterioration, threw much of the region into crisis. This was not a new development, however. Political instability had visited the region many times before, and for the large masses of workers, especially in rural areas, economic scarcity had become a way of life. But what was new was that for the first time, large numbers of workers, families, and even whole communities migrated abroad to escape the violence and to cope with economic decline.

Guatemalan and other Central American men and women emigrated from poor *municipios* (municipalities) in rural areas, as well as from poor *barrios* (neighborhoods) in urban areas. Members of the middle classes also emigrated, or stayed longer or permanently abroad. Beginning as a trickle in the mid-1970s, the migration became a mass exodus in the 1980s (Aguayo 1985) and transformed the structural relations between Central America and the United States.[2] The migration northward also transformed sociospatial patterns of interaction from Central America to the United States and over the years created a *migration region* with new interactions and policies concerning the mass movement of Central Americans through the region.[3] Sociospatial transformations involved establishing new social behaviors within and between groups in specific localities, such as behaviors involved in providing support or resistance to passing Central American migrants.

Social crises are moments when internal or external factors threaten normal social conditions. Crises are not prerequisites for social transformations, but they often have acted as catalysts, if not actual sources, of major social change. A society can survive a crisis in an unchanged form only if it overcomes the threat, or if the threat disappears. The alternatives are that the society disappears or changes into a new social structure, or makes significant alterations of social relations while trying to maintain the original social structure. All societies are vulnerable to crises, but societies on the periphery of the capitalist world economy are the most vulnerable and least able to withstand crisis conditions. These societies often depend on foreign capital investments; face precarious external market demand for their products; have weak levels of solidarity across classes as a result of social polarization; and have minimal or no social welfare resources to sustain their populations through periods of crises. After attempts to change social conditions through collective action fail, for many members in these societies, especially in the more vulnerable sectors, migration may be the best strategy for survival during crises.

In the late 1970s and early 1980s, growing numbers of Guatemalans migrated as high levels of poverty, as well as social and political turmoil, characterized Guatemalan society. In the following years, large numbers of Guatemalan migrants headed north to the United States (Aguayo and Fagan 1988). United States government statistical records indicate that the first significant wave of Guatemalan migration to the United States began in 1977. In absolute numbers, the number of arriving Guatemalan migrants was small compared to Salvadorans or migrants from other world regions, but the percentage change from previous years was large. The 3,599 Guatemalans admitted with visas into the United States in 1977 represented an 82 percent increase from the previous year and the largest number of Guatemalans that had ever been admitted in a single year. Moreover, the 5,093 Guatemalans apprehended for undocumented entry represented a 200 percent increase from the previous year and the largest number of Guatemalans that had ever been apprehended for undocumented entry in a single year (U.S. INS 1977).

The large percentage increase also recorded in the number of Salvadoran migrants entering or attempting to enter the United States in 1977 indicated the larger scope of the crises spurring the northward migration patterns. In Central America, El Salvador as well as Guatemala and Nicaragua were caught up in civil wars that caused massive levels of death and relocation. In Guatemala alone, an estimated 200,000 persons were killed or "disappeared" during the violence of the civil war. Additionally, virtually all of Latin America was experiencing economic crises that served as the prelude to the "Lost Decade" of the 1980s, a period in which economic growth, per capita income, and investment dropped as unemployment/underemployment, inflation, and foreign debt increased (Hayes 1989).

In the context of growing economic immiseration in the 1970s in Guatemala, modernization and diversification of agricultural exports kept macroeconomic growth rates at 5–6 percent annually, but the benefits of economic growth did not reach the millions of impoverished peasants (Jonas 1991). The population of small farmers grew by 54 percent, but the land area for subsistence peasant farming increased by only 6 percent (Villacorta Escobar 1984).

In the small urban industrial sector, workers did not fare much better. Already economically stressed, industrial urban workers faced additional economic restrictions as rising oil prices increased energy costs and the slow-moving industrial export economy failed to stimulate job growth (Jonas 1991).

On Guatemala's social-political front, even in the face of military dictatorship and repression, organizing increased among agricultural and industrial workers, as well as among other popular sectors (Jonas 1991). The massive earthquake in 1976 also led to new organizing among the poor, both by those who remained in the affected Mayan highland areas and those who migrated to Guatemala City. Government political/military repression had been an integral part of Guatemalan society since the mid-1950s and throughout the 1960s and 1970s, with some periods being more intense than others. The repression escalated significantly after 1977, inflicting heavy casualties within the popular sectors opposing the government and those, such as students, workers, and peasants, who supported these sectors.

By the early 1980s, a major transformation and increase in *concientización* (self-awareness) were occurring within entire communities in the Mayan highlands, leading these communities to resist army repression. By this time, revolutionary insurgents of the Unidad Revolucionaria Nacional Guatemalteca (URNG) were based largely in that same area. The government and army responded by unleashing a genocidal, scorched-earth, military counterinsurgency offensive (1981–1983) against growing revolutionary and Mayan popular movements in the highlands (Handy 1984). These conditions of modern-day holocaust (leaving more than 150,000 civilian victims between 1981 and 1983 alone) produced massive internal displacements and migrations abroad, principally to Mexico and the United States (Aguayo and Fagen 1988). Refugees, overwhelmingly Maya from the highlands in Guatemala, began arriving in Mexico by the hundreds in mid-1980, but their numbers increased into the tens of thousands by mid-1981 and became an even larger wave by 1983 (Aguayo 1985; Falla 1994).

Crises can generate mass migration flows, but at some point, potential destination points also begin to influence the migration. Refugees fleeing political upheavals or natural disasters may select destination points that have comparative advantages, such as liberal refugee policies (Zolberg, Suhrke, and Aguayo 1989). For economic migrants, comparative advantages are a primary concern since the only resources they usually find in their migration are what they can provide for themselves beyond any initial forms of social support. Moreover, many economic migrants are pressed to generate income as soon as possible in order to help support families left back home. Every refugee is a potential economic migrant because the need for sustenance is ever present, and greater when a family migrates together. From this perspective, it is easy to understand why many Guatemalan migrants fleeing political violence and economic deterioration headed to the large job markets of the United States.

As Chapter 2 describes, the timing of mass migration out of Guatemala and the larger Central American region coincided with a major economic restructuring in the United States. Responding to rising global competition and dropping corporate profit rates, many U.S. corporations increasingly hired foreign-born migrant labor to work under scaled-down wages in labor-intensive production. At the time, there were no penalties against employers who hired undocumented migrant workers, so some corporations turned to this labor force to restructure their production activities (e.g., see Morales 1983).[4]

Seen from the perspective of individuals or families, the migration process appears to be a pure act of human agency. The migrants, or those who guide them, decide what date to leave, what roads to take, when to stop and rest, and where to attempt border crossings. But the perception of migration as pure self-activity is a misconception. Structural contours limit the choices of the migrants from the moment they start their journey. The capitalist political-economic system that frames the region through which Guatemalans and other Central Americans cross on the northward trek allows for wandering within its geography, but for most migrants, the journey ends in incorporation into a labor stratum that helps to sustain and reproduce the system. Only a relatively small number of these migrants incorporate into an entrepreneurial stratum, and they frequently do so through enterprises that cater to migrants.[5]

The autonomous migration undertaken by individuals and families in developing countries to locate more secure social environments abroad often helps the larger global or interregional system to restructure in other (far-away) settings, as the migration ultimately amounts to a labor transfer. From this broader view, what is originally seen as unique and special about the Guatemalan and the larger Central American migration merges in the aggregate outcome with a historical trend in Western societies: international migration within and between regions ultimately supplies capitalist economies with lower-wage labor, and increasingly with high-wage labor as well (Cohen 1987; Harris 1995). In manufacturing economies, an oversupply of low-wage labor is necessary from the standpoint of capital to control wages and supply cyclical demands for industrial labor. Almost ironically, the settings of advanced capitalism of professional and high-tech business services also have developed a structural need for low-wage, flexible labor, that is, low-wage workforces willing to work in wide-ranging, labor-intensive, personal/household and business services that support high-skilled service workers and firms (Sassen 1988). Migrant workers from peripheral societies are an optimal workforce for this new labor demand, since the low-paid service jobs they take in the advanced capitalist service economy actually represent transregional upward mobility for most, which increases their labor commitment (Piore 1979).

Especially in the years when the hiring of undocumented labor was not illegal, employers usually desired an oversupply of foreign-born migrant workers. The constant influx of a large number of low-wage, undocumented migrant workers enabled employers to hold wages down in the lower echelons of the labor market. An oversupply of these migrant workers also enabled employers to easily replenish their workforces when their workers moved to other labor markets in the country or were deported for being undocumented.

Transregional Migration

The large and heavily land-based migration patterns from Guatemala and other Central American countries to the United States have affected many areas throughout the expanse that the migrants travel. It is the thesis of this book that the social and spatial impacts of this migration accumulated and aggregated into a "region"; hence, we refer to the Central American migration process as transregional migration. Although the migrants are not creating new territory, they are re*socializing* preexisting regions in a continual process of sociospatial reproduction (Soja 1989; Lefebvre 1991).[6] In the history of the expanse ranging from Central America to North America, this process has been ongoing for thousands of years. For the Maya and other indigenous populations that currently live in and migrate from the southern reaches of the expanse, the sociospatial reproduction has a history of more than two thousand years (Carmack 1981; Castillo, Toussaint, and Vázquez 2006).

Capital and political powers have been major forces of regional development. Capital has created core, semiperipheral, and peripheral world regions through strategies of uneven economic development, and political powers have configured geopolitical regions through treaties, alliances, and domination (Wallerstein 1974). In addition to these sources of macro spatialization, popular agency by common people, including workers and peasants, as well as by local institutional builders, also has produced broad regions that serve to sustain the populations that generate them. Yet, although popular action molds these regions, the eventual involvement of other sectors, including the state, develops the regions into broad social domains. This is true of migration regions as well. There is a special feature of these regions that needs to be considered within the world divisions of capital. Migration regions serve capital as conduits of labor flows, but they contradict the uneven-development, geographical strategy of capital. The contradiction lies in the attempt by labor (even in its potential form) to emigrate from peripheral regions in order to find work in the more prosperous core regions of capital. The commitment of migrants to succeed in their journeys keeps migration regions in a dynamic state as a multitude of nonmigrant actors attempt to counter, exploit, control, or assist the migration process (Urrea 2005; Rodriguez 2007; Hagan 2008).

The regionalization produced by Guatemalan and other Central American migration involves more than giving new social qualities to a social environment. Regionalization amounts to a "duality of structure" (Giddens 1986) in which migrants imbue environments with new social qualities, and in which environments in turn shape migrants with new spatial experiences. From this perspective, the land-based migration of thousands of Guatemalans and other Central Americans is much more than simply trekking through an expanse; it is the mutual interaction between the social and the spatial with developmental consequences for both. The migrant passages give new identities and social relations to the settings through which the migrants pass, and the settings give migrants new experiences that become part of their migration knowledge. This knowledge becomes a resource for enhancing their probability of migrating successfully, and for sharing with others who are planning to migrate. For this reason, the large-scale terrestrial flow of Central Americans cannot be fully understood without understanding the socioregional/spatial dynamics involved in their migration.

Given that migration research has generally underemphasized the spatial dimension, the spatial qualities of Guatemalan and other Central American migration need to be explained further. During their northward migration, Central American migrants interact with specific qualities of the expanse through which they travel, and some spatial features of the expanse affect the interaction among migrants and between migrants and other actors. These interactions transpire as migrants collectively maneuver across difficult or dangerous spaces and as they encounter other beneficent or threatening actors on the trail. These levels of social interaction produce space as a social environment with a symbolic system of assistance or danger that helps to frame the social interaction of the migrants.

The types, forms, and levels of social interaction during migration create textured social spaces that frame the migration process and experience. Migration becomes a collection of sociospatial experiences. From this perspective, space is not simply an inanimate, physical object through which migrants cross; on the contrary, it is a transformative source affecting social interaction during migration. The spatial-symbolic qualities of the migration region predispose certain types of social interaction: migrants trek in groups to known *more secure crossing areas*; smugglers wait in known *trails where migrants are in greater need of assistance* to continue the journey; bandits, gangs, and sexual predators lie waiting in known *secluded places where migrants (especially women) are most vulnerable*; religious and human rights workers prepare migrant shelters in known *intermittent localities*; and state security agents set up checkpoints in known *crossing areas.*[7]

Other factors also contribute to the social production of space in the regions of Guatemalan and other Central American migration. These factors include coping knowledge, that is, the lore of migration survival and norms of migrant behavior associated with particular spatial conditions. The social production of space also occurs as migrants take advantage of some spatial qualities (e.g., roads that facilitate travel), resist other geographical features (e.g., dangerous crossing points), and accommodate to yet other spatial conditions (e.g., temporary resting areas).

Sociospatial contours delineate the migration region produced by Guatemalan and other Central American migrants. Although Central American migrants carry national identities, their nationalities are not the primary markers in all moments of the migration. National identity affects the migration region, but it does not organize it. Nor does regionalization conform to national boundaries. Extending from Central America to migrant settlements in Mexico, the United States, and beyond to Canada, the sociospatial contours of the migration region transcend national boundaries.[8] The contours reflect social developments associated with the migration. These developments include settlements, cultural exchanges, economic participation, political reactions by national and local agencies, and the emergence of institutions of an evolving culture of migration. While transcending formal international boundaries, the migration region still interacts with official political structures, thus throughout the region, migration-related developments push against and wear national borders.

Social Differentiation in Migration

The characterizations given in this section of the social, temporal, and social relational differentiation that exists in Guatemalan migration across the migration region defy simple generalizations. Overall, the Guatemalan migration experience has involved, and been composed of, a multitude of sociospatial and spatiotemporal "locations" in the migration region.

Guatemalan migration to North America since the late 1970s has not been a monolithic stream. Close examination of the migration reveals that it is a fused multitude of parallel flows, which coalesce at some moments of the migration and disaggregate at other moments, especially after the migrants' arrival in the United States. Most of the separate flows are spatial extensions of household and community social organization connecting migrants to sending communities, and in many cases to other migrants in U.S. receiving communities, as well (Hagan 2008). The parallel flows emerge as migrants individually or collectively follow sociospatial contours previously molded by migrating individuals, family households, and whole communities in some cases. Because conditions continually shift in the migration region (partly owing to enforcement activities and the arrival of new actors, e.g., criminal cartels) and because migrants have changing levels of resources, the migration process undergoes constant reorganization at macro and micro levels.

Differences in social and economic backgrounds, gender, and Mayan/ladino identities are among the factors that differentiate the Guatemalan migration northward. Moreover, the significant presence of unaccompanied minors (children under the age of 18) in the migrant streams also makes age a differentiating variable, not only in the composition of the migrant streams but also in the level of vulnerability during the journey (Urrutia-Rojas and Rodriguez 1997). Another differentiating factor is the status of migrants concerning whether they have been previously deported from the United States. Migrants who have been formally deported from the United States and re-migrate while still in barred status face a greater possibility of being sentenced to federal prison if they are apprehended for undocumented reentry into the United States.

The considerable differentiation in the Guatemalan and other Central American migrant populations interacts with sociospatial conditions in the migration region, producing an intricate probability matrix of risk, success, or failure (including death) in the migration process (Singer and Massey 1998; Eschbach et al. 1999; Durand and Massey 2006). Well-connected migrants, for example, can arrive in the United States without having experienced any threatening incident in the journey, whereas hundreds of others die annually in attempting to cross dangerous border terrain in the U.S. Southwest.

Another level of differentiation in the Guatemalan and larger Central American migration northward consists of the different temporal phases through which the migration has transpired. As we explain in Chapter 2, we mark temporal phases in the Guatemalan migration according to changes of 10 percent or more in the Guatemalan migrant streams of legally admitted migrants in the United States and of the estimated number who arrive as undocumented migrants. Various developments, e.g., the passage of new immigration laws, demark temporal phases, but we select significant changes in migration volume because we view these as reflecting structural changes that migrants respond to or that they themselves initiate.

Migrant generational groupings constitute another source of social and temporal differentiation in the migrant population. A generation is defined as having a common experience of opportunities or limitations on a large social and historical scale that lead to common potential for action. For Karl Mannheim, belonging to the same generation and belonging to the same class were analogous because both gave individuals "a common location in the social and historical process," which limited individuals to "a specific range of potential experience, predisposing them for a certain characteristic mode of thought and experience, and a characteristic type of historically relevant action" (1952, 366). We add to Mannheim's conceptualization the commonality of shared sociospatial experiences and possibilities for generations.

In the patterns of Guatemalan migration since the 1970s, it is possible to discern migrant generations that differentiate the migration experience across temporal phases. For example, there is the original migrant generation that immigrated in the late 1970s and early 1980s and established the first large-scale Guatemalan migrant ties to U.S. society, reaching significant levels of residential and economic security through the amnesty and legalization measures of the Immigration Reform and Control Act (IRCA) of 1986. Another example concerns the generation of Guatemalan migrants who were brought to the United States as small children and reached adulthood in the 1990s. From the conventional research concept of migrant generations, the waves of Guatemalan migration now includes three generations, that is, the first generation of immigrants, the second generation composed of the U.S-born children of immigrants, and the third generation composed of the U.S.-born children of the second generation.

Among undocumented migrants, one source of change in the sociotemporal dimension is the frequent social detachments and reattachments they undergo in the initial stages of the settlement process (Rodriguez 1987). With limited residential security and few economic resources, these migrants strive for social stability through a combination of social support (social capital) and labor market incorporation. This survival strategy involves a continual organizing and reorganizing of social relations by undocumented migrants in the areas where they settle.

It is in the later phases of settlement that undocumented migrants may decrease their social organizing and reorganizing of survival strategies as they settle into a stable routine or acquire legal status. But just as migrant cohorts enter into advanced settlement stages, new cohorts enter the migration region and begin the initial stages of forming social network strategies for survival. In the holistic interconnections of the migration region, migrant social dynamics in destination points reverberate and affect social dynamics in the communities of origin.[9] Migrant household stability gained in settlement areas in the United States becomes a resource for household development and status mobility in Guatemalan communities back home. Households in Guatemala that receive remittances from migrant members in the United States may undergo material and status mobility; by contrast, households that experience a loss of remittances, or the loss of a migrant member, e.g., from deportation, may experience downward mobility.

The need to develop social relations for survival does not completely explain why these relations emerge and endure among undocumented migrants. Cultural values and norms, as well as religious attitudes, family loyalties, and shared hometown identity, also lend support to the relational strategies of the migrants.

Transregional Migrant Rights Advocacy

Amidst the multiple structural factors throughout the migration region, the exercise of agency by Central American migrants has been crucial in shaping their own experiences.[10] In addition to the processes and constant reorganization of immigrants' strategies for survival and upward mobility, there is another layer of transregional activities and social actors: organizations, coalitions, and networks of migrant rights advocates, operating both in the United States and throughout the region. In contrast to the generally informal networks organized by migrants for their survival and well-being ("in-itself" goals), these networks of organizations—nongovernmental advocacy organizations (NGOs), community-based organizations (CBOs), and research centers with migrant advocacy agendas—are more formal. They have come together with deliberate political goals of engaging with and having impact (*incidencia*) on state policies, and of influencing (or countering) the strategies of other social actors.

Their rationale and goals at various intersection points and on many levels can be described as "for-itself" political organizing activity throughout the region.[11] In a region where the dominant forces have had a thoroughly neoconservative/neoliberal agenda for spatial restructuring, as Soja points out (1989, 173), "spatially conscious counter-strategies" developed by all progressive forces—for our purposes, including migrant rights advocates—must be "explicitly spatial movements" for social change. With their agenda being explicitly about migrant rights, the goals of these advocacy organizations and networks have been to change the quality of spaces and places throughout the migration region, including the highly contested borders and borderlands (border areas) between countries of origin, transit, and destination. In working to make these spaces less dangerous and to counter the ever more exploitative, punitive, and predatory practices directed against undocumented migrants throughout the region, rights advocates have become players in the social production of space for migration.[12]

"For-itself" advocacy has commonly accompanied migration streams since the late twentieth century, but it has had a higher profile in this particular migration region for two reasons. First, this region is characterized by geographical/physical contiguity (Central America/Mexico/United States), which is not the case for all migrations. Second, this migration region was shaped by an unusually high politicization during the 1980s, with ideological/Cold War conflicts between the U.S. government and strong leftist insurgencies in Central America.

As individuals, some of the organizers in the United States came from the ranks of the Guatemalan migrant/refugee stream of the late 1970s and early 1980s, but they rose to become the "middle" strata of that migration stream in at least two respects. First, from a vertical perspective, many were from middle-class origins, hence arriving with or subsequently gaining higher (university) education. Second, viewed horizontally, many had their origins in a middle stratum between the state and grassroots communities, the stratum of the "organized sectors" of Guatemalan civil society; in this regard, they were participants in highly "networked" social structures and organizations, to use the formulation by Castells (2004). Like their Salvadoran counterparts, they included a significant number of students, professionals, and others who had to leave Guatemala because their social justice and human rights activities made them "enemies of the state."

Once in the United States—or even while living in Mexico, where some remained—a number of them were able to reconstitute themselves as "organized sector" advocates. Among those in the United States, some were able to function publicly as activists by virtue of being among the less than two percent of Guatemalans (and less than three percent of Salvadorans) granted asylum during the 1980s, or having migrated early enough (by 1982) to benefit from the amnesty given by IRCA in 1986. As Legal Permanent Residents and eventually as citizens, they had more time and freedom to become public advocates, with less fear of deportation. Their campaigns for legalization of their fellow refugees during the late 1980s, with crucial support from U.S. lawyers, resulted in the landmark *ABC v. Thornburgh* settlement of 1990–1991 allowing previously denied Guatemalans and Salvadorans a chance to have their asylum cases reheard on a case-by-case basis. This assertion of agency, with Salvadorans being particularly proactive, gave those two groups of immigrants/refugees a unique history throughout the 1990s and beyond, establishing the bases for some to gain access to subsequent legalization options.

Sharing the historical experiences of Central America's civil war years, these Salvadoran and Guatemalan immigrant rights advocates have been part of parallel "political generations." The concept of "political generations," as opposed to temporal/chronological intrafamily or family-based generations, has been central since the seminal essay by Mannheim (1952). As applied to immigrants, particularly refugees, political generations can be distinguished from family-based generations, whether in the country of origin or destination. Mannheim (p. 282) identified a "qualitative" concept of generations, "centered about the notion of something which is not quantifiable, but capable only of being experienced"; "contemporaneity becomes a subjective condition of having been submitted to the same determining influences." Not every temporal generation has such a collective identity; a political generation is defined by sharing a particular common historical experience, leading to the shared consciousness of being a generation, which sometimes enables them to become a cohesive force.

In the Guatemalan and Salvadoran cases, as long as the civil wars continued, the organizing activities of this political generation in Central America, Mexico, and the United States were primarily oriented toward human rights and social justice struggles *in* the country of origin, although a secondary theme for those in the United States, with strong support from their allies in the sanctuary movement, was the campaign for asylum. Particularly after the signing of the Peace Accords that ended the war (for Salvadorans in 1992 and for Guatemalans beginning in 1997), many activists from this political generation in both cases turned their attention toward broader immigrant rights throughout the region encompassing the United States, Mexico, and Central America.

An examination of the complex interactions and dynamics of organizing in these multiple venues suggests the evolution of transregional political advocacy networks in which migrant rights organizers participate from different sites, with organizing initiatives undertaken in one location inspiring and impacting other locales. Rather than reify migrant advocacy networks, i.e., view the foundational organizations as remaining intact or as making progress in a linear fashion, we adopt Castells' characterization (2004) of such networks as constantly evolving and "self-reconfiguring." Hence, specific organizations, coalitions, and networks have developed, fractured, and emerged in restructured form as the immediate and long-range goals have shifted—or as divisions over strategy or tactics have emerged. Furthermore, state policies for immigration control or enforcement initiated by the U.S. government (and by Mexico, toward Central Americans) have continued to impact advocates as well as migrants themselves in diverse locations, in effect limiting their real options. For this reason, among many others, the process of migrant rights organizing described in Chapter 3 has not been linear, but has had energizing advances, periods of relative stagnation, dampening setbacks, and eventual restructuring—all of which constitute self-reconfiguration. These dynamics have added to the spatial dynamism of the migration region as various actors have accommodated to changing circumstances or initiated new strategies because of changing circumstances.

The ongoing struggle by Guatemalan and other Central American migrants for legalization and other rights in the United States has been increasingly matched by coalitions formed to promote migrant rights in their countries of origin and transit, and at the Mexico-Guatemala border as a specific focus of attention. The connections have not been simply bilocal, as between migrant communities in the United States and the sending communities (including urban centers) back home, but have also involved a variety of region-wide contacts and sometimes coordinated activities. To capture this multiplicity of social interactions, we use the formulation "transregional," in contrast to the more familiar "transnational," which focuses on durable cross-border linkages between the migrant communities in the country of reception and the country/communities of origin, and which has been most common in the migration literature. To put it another way: transnational processes span across nation-state boundaries; transregional processes span throughout an entire region, in addition to across borders. This regional stage is becoming increasingly interconnected and interactive, and the contacts among the different actors are multiple, overlapping, and at times quite dense.

It is also important to highlight the diverse worldviews, specifically the perspectives, agendas, and goals of actors (disproportionately women) based in Mexico and Central America (Jonas 2007, drawing largely on interviews in those countries). In addition to the legalization agendas defined by U.S.-based players, their counterparts based in the sending countries throughout Latin America have developed a critical analysis of migration as the outcome of neoliberal governments refusing to provide decent jobs or social services, leaving workers few options in the country of origin. From the perspective of those advocates, migration itself should be an option and a choice, not a necessity for survival; and they have been pressuring the home governments to develop sustainable and viable (vs. neoliberal) development strategies.

Social Reproduction: Women, Class, and Ethnicity

At its most visible level, the large-scale Guatemalan migration to North America appears as a dynamic flow, a continual movement of thousands of people arriving in settings that are distant and different from their places of origin. Yet, as is true of many migrant streams, the visible migration flow is a representation of a fundamental social process—the resupplying of human resources for *social reproduction* in the communities where the Guatemalan migrants settle. All social units that endure through time, e.g., families, neighborhoods, workplaces, cities, and societies, undergo social reproduction. That is to say, they undergo continual renewal over time of the cultures, social relations, and populations through which they are constituted. The family household is a basic unit of social reproduction in which women play a central role and which ultimately supports the reproduction of institutions in the larger society.

The reproduction of the population of a social unit (workplace, community, etc.) is a crucial part of social reproduction since new members are needed to take on new roles in expanding institutions or to replace departing members. Fertility normally accounts for much of a population's reproduction, but migration also can play a role in this process. This became especially true for the U.S. population in the late twentieth and early twenty-first centuries when large numbers of Latin American and other international migrants settled in the society, filling new jobs in the expanding economy or replacing U.S. workers who moved to better jobs or retired.

We argue that migration can also lead to *social recomposition* in the process of social reproduction. Social recomposition involves social and cultural changes brought about in a social unit, e.g., a workplace, community, or city, through the introduction of a new ethnic or racial population.[13] Invariably this produces changes in the way a community, workplace, or other social unit operates. In the economic arena, social recomposition is associated with the process of economic restructuring when business owners or managers use migrant workers from different ethnic or racial backgrounds to rearrange production (or consumption) in order to gain economic advantages.[14] Migration can produce different dimensions of social recomposition. In this section, we comment on the dimensions concerning gender, class, and ethnicity.

Through household work (cooking, cleaning, etc.) and through work in businesses that cater to migrants, migrant women play central roles in the daily reproduction of migrant labor. Daily reproduction of a worker's capacity to work through nourishment and other sustenance activities is carried out in Latin American working-class families mainly through the household work of women. Many Guatemalan and other Latin American migrant women from working-class backgrounds also have experiences in managing households with meager resources. This background knowledge becomes crucial for survival for many Latin American migrants who have low income and are barred from public assistance programs because of their undocumented status. Although not considered in analyses of economic restructuring, women's work thus usually plays an important role in the daily reproduction of migrant labor that enables employers to reorganize processes of production by using immigrant workers to replace U.S. workers.

Guatemalan and other Latin American migrant women also play other roles in sustaining social recomposition. These roles include producing and raising new cohorts of future Latina and Latino workers whose ethnic or racial distinctions are used by employers to recompose their workforces by switching to lower-paid or more malleable labor. In addition, migrant housewives and mothers often join the new workforces themselves when they take jobs outside the home, including for part-time work.

Some children of migrant women grow up to become workers for ethnic enterprises catering to migrant customers. Having been raised by immigrant parents, children of immigrants are usually prepared for this work because they often share cultural similarities (language, customs, etc.) with migrant customers. In the first decade of the twenty-first century, children of first-generation Guatemalan immigrant families could be found working in restaurants and other businesses that catered primarily to Latin American migrant customers. The production of the second immigrant generation thus reinforces commercial infrastructures that support the processes of social reproduction and recomposition through immigration.

Similar to other migrant women from Latin America, Guatemalan migrant women have taken on a variety of jobs outside their households. Some of the jobs have resulted from economic restructuring undertaken by employers who stopped hiring U.S. workers to take advantage of low-wage labor markets recomposed by immigration. These jobs include janitorial work in cleaning companies contracted by office-building owners and managers that previously hired U.S. janitorial work forces (Cranford 2004), garment production in assembly plants or at home contracted by apparel manufacturers that outsource their work (Bonacich 1998), and work in households that previously hired U.S. domestics (Hagan 1994).

Social recomposition, i.e., the remaking of a population with different ethnic or racial groups, creates working-class segments in local communities. In labor markets, social recomposition involves the introduction of a new worker category, which can enable new social relations of production, often to the advantage of employers. The mere growth of labor markets through immigration enables employers to expand their work forces or to gain greater control of wages (because of an increase of the labor supply), but the presence of new categories of immigrant workers such as undocumented Latino migrants creates opportunities for employers to restructure their industries. Reported weekly wages of Latin American immigrant labor as being only 63 percent of what U.S.-born workers earned in 2011 illustrates an advantage of this foreign-born class segment for employers (U.S. BLS 2012a, Table 5).

Compared with U.S.-born workers, a major difference of the class segment composed of Guatemalan and other Latin American migrant workers is the undocumented status of many migrants in this class segment. Undocumented workers are restricted to the lower echelons of the labor market because of their undocumented status, creating a tenuous base of existence for the workers. But it is precisely this tenuous quality that creates advantages for employers, as they find a work force in which many workers are forced to accept poor working conditions in order to obtain some level of economic survival or to derive as much income as possible amid uncertainty (Rodriguez 1986). Guatemalan and other Latin American migrant workers become a preferred source of ethnic labor in the informal sector of the labor market because of their greater labor force commitment given that many of these workers face very restricted job opportunities. For employers in the informal sector of the labor market, Latin American ethnic identity becomes a symbol of this greater labor force attachment.

Native labor groups or groups with a long-term presence in U.S. society have challenged the development of social recomposition that results from immigration. Historically, organized labor opposed labor immigration, and only since the 1990s have labor unions supported immigrant labor rights, as new migrant workers, including undocumented migrants, became a significant source of membership growth in unions. Challenges against social recomposition created by immigration, however, also developed in sectors outside the economy. Many groups that opposed Latin American immigration feared that Latin American ethnicities would supplant the dominant, European-origin, white culture (Huntington 2004). This fear grew partly from the projection that the non-Hispanic white population would become a numerical minority by the mid-twenty-first century.[15] Moreover, opposition to social recomposition in the society due to Latin American immigration did not emanate solely from non-Hispanic white members of society; other established residents, including some with Latino immigrant backgrounds, also developed apprehensions about the effects of immigration (Bach 1993). In 1996, owing partly to the fear that Latino immigration was recomposing the U.S. population, Congress passed the Illegal Immigration Reform and Immigrant Responsibility Act (IIRIRA) to facilitate the removal of immigrants who violated immigration regulations and to construct physical barriers at the U.S.-Mexico border to deter unauthorized entry. Moreover, in the first decade of the twenty-first century, a growing number of state and local governments reacted to growing social recomposition by enacting state laws and city ordinances to restrict the participation of undocumented migrants and other immigrants in their states and local communities.[16]

Indigenous Migration

Migrating in large numbers, the Maya from Guatemala add to social recomposition in the migration region that stretches from Central America northward to the United States. Mayan migration from Guatemala is part of a larger indigenous migration northward that gained considerable strength in the 1980s.[17] The migration originated in Mayan and other indigenous settlements in Mexico and Central America (Loucky and Moors 2000; Fox and Rivera-Salgado 2004), in Garifuna and other African-origin areas on the Caribbean coast of Central America (Gonzalez 1988; England 2006), and in areas as far south as Quechua- and Aymara-speaking communities in the Andes (Altamirano 1990; Kyle 2000). Mayan migration transpires along a sociotemporal dimension that is much older than the *mestizo/ladino* northward migration experience.

The present northward migration of Maya from Guatemala, which commenced in the late twentieth century, is but one additional phase in the 2,000 years of Mayan history (e.g., see Carmack 1981). By comparison, the ladino history of northward migration from Guatemala has transpired almost entirely during the same period of modernity.[18] In the sociotemporal dimension, the Maya are emigrating from historical settings of their racial subjugation and subordination, in which they were relegated to the lower stratum of Guatemala. Moreover, the indigenous racial identity accompanies Mayan undocumented migrants in the northern trek as they pass through nonindigenous environments. For some Maya, this identity creates a greater degree than normal of vulnerability to exploitation and abuse in the migration trail, especially when crossing the large Mexican land mass.

Similar to other migrants, Maya contribute to the sociospatialization of the migration region through which they cross and settle. In the 1970s, Maya began to spread out in Guatemala, including into Guatemala City and the southern coast (Jonas 1991), from their home communities located mainly in the highland provinces of the country. The army scorched-earth counterinsurgency campaigns in areas of the highlands in the early 1980s drove many thousands of Mayan families to seek refuge in adjacent Mexican areas (Manz 1988; Falla 1994, to mention only two of the many accounts). It is estimated that up to 200,000 Guatemalans fled to Mexico as political violence surged in Guatemala, with 46,000 Guatemalans (almost all Maya) being assisted by the United Nations High Commissioner on Refugees (UNHCR) to settle initially in U.N. refugee camps on the Mexican side of the Mexico-Guatemala border (Worby 1999).

In their new localities in Guatemala, in U.N. refugee sites and elsewhere in Mexico, and in their U.S. settlement areas, the Maya from Guatemala contribute to sociospatialization through cultural exchanges with the surrounding social environment. These exchanges occur because most groups have permeable cultural boundaries through which they trade cultural elements through markets or interpersonal exchanges with other groups. Normally, the first and second migrant generations are likely to experience the highest levels of cultural exchanges with other groups in their environment, but by the third and later generations, intercultural exchanges become mostly a unidirectional process of acculturation into the national cultures of the host society.

The social and cultural power to reproduce Mayan cultural institutions is greatest among settlements with large Mayan concentrations. In the refugee camps in southern Mexico, for example, Maya recreated their communities with considerable facility, not just because they were assisted by the UNHCR but also because they arrived in the thousands, mostly as family units from the same villages in Guatemala. As Manz (1988) explains, spatial contiguity also played a role in the recreation of Mayan refugee communities, since for indigenous populations in the region, the Mexico-Guatemala border is a political boundary and not a cultural divide, given that Mayan populations live on both sides of the border. The Mayan refugees from Guatemala, especially those who settled outside the U.N. camps, spread their ethnic cultures in Mexico through their settlements and by intermarrying with Mexicans. Moreover, some Mayan refugees and their children Mexico-born became citizens of the Mexican state.

The settlement in Mexico by Maya from Guatemala was not a temporary process. By 1999, almost twenty years after their initial arrival and a few years after peace accords ended the Guatemalan civil war, about 22,000 Mayan refugees remained in Mexican resettlement sites, with a majority of these Maya having been born in the refugee sites (Worby 1999). A larger number of

Maya remained scattered throughout Mexico, and some eventually migrated farther north, to the United States.

Because of their relatively smaller numbers, Mayan migrants do not usually dominate the surrounding social environments where they settle in the United States, in comparison, for example, to the dominance of cultural institutions by the larger groups of Mexican and Salvadorans. Yet, Guatemalan migrants contribute to social recomposition in settlement areas in a manner that is becoming a major source of social reproduction—by contributing to mosaics of immigrant-origin ethnicities that sustain migrant social environments in urban and rural centers across the country. This is particularly evident in places where Mayan migrants settle in sizeable numbers, such as in Los Angeles and Houston, and in rural areas of Florida and North Carolina (Loucky and Moors 2000). The mosaics achieve longevity as some migrant groups survive temporarily but others for a longer time, and as they accommodate the settlement of different migrant groups by concentrating a variety of resources (e.g., places of worship and ethnic markets) for ethnic reproduction.

Through the interconnections of the migration region that extends from Central America northward, new cultural experiences in Mayan settlement areas eventually reverberate in communities of origin in Guatemala. Initially, material objects may be the most conspicuously remitted cultural elements to Guatemalan home communities, but eventually, newly acquired social styles, ideas, and mannerisms can be remitted as well. Financial remittances, however, likely make the greatest impacts, as they transform social relations in the communities of origin of migrants by creating new distributions of property relations and ownership when families use remittances to construct new homes or buy land. In some cases, financial remittances can convert Mayan customs into an extravagant form. For example, families that years earlier could accommodate only a few dozen persons in family celebrations could, years later, use migrant remittances to invite several hundred guests to lavish social events costing thousands of dollars.

Similar to other indigenous migrants, the Maya from Guatemala experience the greatest contrast among Latin American newcomers between their communities of origin and the places they settle in the United States. Emigrating from social environments that are still substantially steeped in traditional customs and practices, many Mayan migrants from rural origins, nonetheless, have incorporated with relative ease into the modern and technologically advanced urban environments of some of their settlement areas, as has occurred in the Houston area (e.g., see Rodriguez 1987; Hagan 1994). They accomplish this by bringing social resources from their indigenous origins to fashion strategies of survival and upward mobility in their U.S. settlement areas. Yet, in other cases, Mayan migrants face major challenges to survive in their settlement areas, as the research by Loucky (2000) found in the city of Los Angeles.

Space and Place

Migration has been a major driving force in the social production of space, and Guatemalan migration has added to this process. As noted by social analysts (Soja 1989; Lefebvre 1991; Gottdiener 1994), the concept of the social production of space runs counter to the common assumption that space exists as an object that predates the social. As Lefebvre explains (1991), space in isolation, separated from social practice, is an abstraction. Similar to other social actors, migrants "produce" space when they establish, or reestablish, areas into arenas of social practices. The spaces migrants produce include domiciles, places of worships, recreational areas, neighborhoods, and urban districts (Gans 1962; Handlin 1974; Hagan 1994). Migrants and other social actors infuse ideologies and other normative properties into the spaces they produce, leading to a duality of space in which space has the role of medium and outcome. That is to say, space shapes social behavior, and social behavior shapes space (Soja 1989; Wolch and Dear 1989; Hayden 1995). As stated earlier, the similarity of this to Gidden's (1986) concept of the "duality of structure" is not coincidental, as the spatial is inseparable from the social.

With few exceptions, Guatemalan migrants reproduce space in U.S. settlement areas primarily by co-settling with other migrant groups, e.g., Mexicans and Salvadorans, or in some cases by appropriating spaces previously produced by other groups (Burns 1993; Loucky 2000). Because of their usual smaller numbers, compared with other migrant groups, the appropriation involves taking only partial social control of community and other public spaces that other groups previously dominated by virtue of their earlier arrival or their larger numbers. In Houston, for example, Mayan migrants undertook social appropriation of sections of large apartment complexes where they settled adjacent to Mexican and Salvadoran migrants in the west side of the city and the partial appropriation of public park areas to play soccer and carry out other social activities (Hagan 1994). Often the Guatemalan appropriation of space occurs as part of a larger Central American presence, especially of Salvadorans and Hondurans, that competes with other groups, e.g., Mexican migrants and U.S. long-term residents for public spaces. Frequent intermingling between Guatemalan and other migrant groups occurs in public spaces, but sociospatial boundaries can be drawn quickly in moments of social tension, as research in Houston found.[19]

The conversion of spaces into places involves the assigning of social significance to particular settings. It is the conversion of a spatial setting into a "significant symbol" (see Mead [1934] 1974) shared in a group.[20] With its particular symbolic significance, a place ceases to be like any other space. The social structure of the significant symbol consists of the spatial setting, the social interaction that transpires across it and characterizes it, and the images and emotional predisposition held by the group regarding the symbol (Mead [1934] 1974). Converting a space into a place, therefore, is at once a concrete and abstract process.

Conversion of spaces into places forms a basis for the development of institutions, as patterns of common responses become linked with particular spatial symbols (workplaces, places of worship, etc.). Moreover, the emergence of institutions helps to foster consciousness within a group about its sense of purpose and identity. This in turn helps social actors form a broader meaning of themselves as a people and a social order (see Mead [1934] 1974).

For Guatemalan migrants, as for other migrants with a high rate of undocumented entry, the conversion of spaces into places frequently occurs on contested settings (Bach 1993). This situation illustrates what some analysts have described as a flux of appropriation, resistance, and accommodation that result from local and larger processes that have influenced cultures historically (Marcus and Fischer 1986). The large numbers of undocumented Guatemalan and other migrants operate their everyday lives with a spatial consciousness of risks and restrictions. A number of ascribed and achieved social statuses (class, race, gender, etc.) condition the daily spatial practices of ordinary social actors, but undocumented status places additional restrictions on the spatial behavior of many migrants, ultimately including the risk of removal from society.[21]

Legislation enacted by the U.S. government in 1996 significantly increased the spatial restrictions of Guatemalan and other undocumented migrants in the United States. The legislation concerned the enactment of IIRIRA, which intensified attempts to barricade the most popular (safest) border crossing points for clandestine entry, and which initiated the program known as "Section 287(g)" to enlist the cooperation of state and local police agencies in immigration enforcement. By 2012, more than 1,300 state and local police agents from 19 states had been trained by the U.S. Immigration and Customs Enforcement (ICE) in immigration enforcement, resulting in more than 309,283 identifications of "potentially removable" migrants since 2006 (U.S.

ICE 2012a). The promotion of local immigration control by IIRIRA was followed by a growing number of ordinances passed by local governments to restrict the presence of undocumented migrants in their localities, as mentioned above. Facing severe restrictions of their movements, some migrants began to "self deport," according to some reports (Gaynor 2007). By late 2008, survey research found that 72 percent of foreign-born Latinos and 35 percent of U.S.-born Latinos worried "some" or "a lot" about deportations (Lopez and Minushkin 2008).

Other political and social conditions have affected the spatial resources of Guatemalan migrants in the United States. First, many Guatemalan migrants were restricted from qualifying for residency through amnesty and legalization provided by IRCA in 1986 because the U.S. Congress set an entry requirement of earlier than 1982. This requirement favored Mexicans, who had a long history of migration to the United States, but it disfavored Guatemalans, since Guatemalan immigration picked up in 1982 and later. Second, along with other Central Americans, Guatemalan migrants sometimes compete unsuccessfully with the much larger Mexican migrant population for spatial resources, including spaces for businesses and other ethnic enterprises that create spatial symbolic environments for migrants. Moreover, the relative proximity of Mexico facilitates the ability of Mexican migrants to have social exchanges with family and communities back home (e.g., see Hernández-León 2008), which Guatemalan migrants cannot enjoy with the same facility given their much longer distance from the homeland.

Plan of the Book

This book attempts to describe and explain Guatemalan migration to the United States since the late 1970s. In this chapter, we highlighted concepts that we view as particularly relevant for explaining Guatemalan migration to the United States. We used concepts that convey migration as principally a social process, and best understood as such. Moreover, we argued in this chapter that Guatemalan and other Central American migrant flows and the actions of various social actors that interact with the migrants have produced and shaped a migration region extending from Central America to North America. As we described, the spatial practices of migrants, the reactions of state agencies, the actions of other, nonmigrant actors, and everyday-life behaviors and symbols associated with the dramatic qualities of large-scale human movement keep the migration region in a dynamic condition.

Given the regional and transregional framework and dimensions of this book, we also rely on the scholarship by scholars in Mexico and Guatemala/ Central America, to be cited specifically as relevant throughout the book. Most of this scholarship has not been translated into English and is seldom incorporated in U.S.-based studies of Guatemalan/Central American migration. These scholars have done pioneering research on Mexico's "other" (southern) border, between Mexico and Guatemala—a spatial connection and demarcation that looms very large in the migration experiences of migrants from Central America to the United States. Their research fills in the gap concerning what is known about the transit-country experiences of Guatemalans, which is central to their entire migration process and its role in reshaping and resocializing various places and spaces within the migration region. These researchers have also carried out studies regarding the impact of migration upon the Guatemalan communities of origin, with particular implications for changing interethnic, gender, and household relations—as well as the reception experiences of Guatemalan returnees and deportees from the United States and Mexico.

Chapter 2 presents an analysis of Guatemalan migration to the United States based on phases derived from flow data. The analysis is conducted by dividing the migration flow since the late 1970s into phases distinguished by different estimated volumes of migration and contextualized by changing Guatemalan and U.S. societal conditions. As the chapter demonstrates, substantial changes differentiate the phases of the migration.

Chapter 3 focuses on organizing activities carried out by Guatemalan migrant rights advocates to improve the conditions of Guatemalan migration and for Guatemalan immigrant communities in the United States. The first part of the chapter highlights organizing by U.S.-based Guatemalan migrant rights advocates, primarily since the 1990s. The second part of the chapter focuses on transregional migrant rights organizations and networks in Guatemala, elsewhere in Central America, and in Mexico. The chapter demonstrates that, within this context, Guatemalan organizational actors and leaders have worked to address a host of state policy issues throughout the region, even as they have faced major challenges.

Chapters 4 and 5 describe the settlement experiences and conditions of Guatemalan migrants in Houston and San Francisco, respectively. The two urban settings contrast geographically and differ greatly in their industrial development. Houston developed into a major technological and production center in the world oil and petrochemical economy, and San Francisco became a postindustrial area of financial service and high-tech development.

Chapter 4 focuses on the immigration and settlement experiences in Houston of Guatemalans, especially of Maya, in the context of economic restructuring that occurred in the area in the early 1980s. The economic change created major settlement advantages for Guatemalan and other migrants. Moreover, internal social ties of the Guatemalan migrants facilitated their entrance into the work sector and their development of social institutions to support their settlement.

Chapter 5 presents survey and targeted interview research on Guatemalans in the San Francisco area. It also analyzes the contradictory settlement conditions during the ups and downs of the postindustrial, high-tech service economy, which restricted upward mobility for low-wage Guatemalan and other Latino immigrants. In the early 2000s, gentrification and general unaffordability disrupted their communities and community building, especially in San Francisco's Mission District, displacing many to other neighborhoods and outside San Francisco itself. Politically, the area's progressive, multicultural climate gave undocumented immigrants, especially Central American asylum-seekers, a favorable reception during the 1980s and 1990s and into the early 2000s ("sanctuary city"). But after 2008, there were visible signs that "sanctuary" for the undocumented was becoming a contested issue.

Chapter 6 highlights concepts we view as useful for analyzing Guatemalan migration to the United States. These include the social production of space, migration phases, transnational advocacy, and gendered migration. In addition, the chapter discusses the implications for migrants of changing subregions and weak states in the Mexico-Central America region. Finally, the chapter highlights the interdynamic basis of agency and structure in the development of migration patterns and regions.

CHAPTER 2

Phases of Migration

Introduction

Guatemalan migration to the United States has been more than a transfer of people from points of origin to points of destination. The very journey of Guatemalan migrants and the interactions they have had with the places they passed along their northward passage have produced a migration region where people, cultures, and institutions have become affected by, and in turn have affected, the migration. Along with other Latin American migrants, Guatemalan migrants have impacted national, regional, and local affairs across Mexico, and in many specific places in the United States, as they have organized their migration and settlement, and as a host of actors have attempted to assist or to restrict, or exploit, their flow. Therefore, across the different phases of their migration, Guatemalans have contributed to changing national and local priorities and agendas in the migration region that extends from Guatemala to the communities where the migrants have settled in the United States.

Guatemalan migration to the United States underwent a sharp upswing in the late 1970s from a previous trickle. The numbers of Guatemalans who were admitted as legal permanent residents, as well as those who were apprehended by the U.S. Border Patrol at the U.S.-Mexico border for unauthorized entry, noticeably increased in the late 1970s from previous years. Moreover, the 1980 census found that the population of foreign-born Guatemalans in the country had reached 63,073, which was a 263 percent increase from the 17,356 Guatemalan immigrants counted in the 1970 census (Gibson and Jung 2006, Table 3). It was the beginning of large-scale Guatemalan migration to the United States, bringing social change in Mexican and U.S. areas where Central Americans migrated and settled.

In 2011, the American Community Survey (ACS) of the U.S. Census Bureau counted the number of Guatemalans in the country to be 1,214,176, of which 850,882 were immigrants (U.S. Census Bureau 2011a).[1] By contrast, using survey data collected in Guatemala, the Organización Internacional para las Migraciones estimated the number of Guatemalan immigrants in the United States in 2010 to be 1.6 million (OIM 2011).

Undocumented and legal immigration have fueled the growth of the Guatemalan immigrant population in the United States. With a few exceptions, undocumented immigration has been a greater annual source of this growth. Moreover, some legal admissions of Guatemalan immigrants are status adjustments of previously undocumented migrants. A major instance of these adjustments was the amnesty and legalization of tens of thousands of undocumented Guatemalan migrants that occurred after the enactment of the Immigration Reform and Control Act (IRCA) of 1986. With the exception of the Guatemalans who legalized through IRCA and the relative few who have obtained asylum since then, most of the legal admissions of Guatemalan immigrants have occurred through applications made by family members in the United States to sponsor the immigration of family members.[2] As described later in the chapter, the U.S. government maintained an almost complete denial of asylum for Guatemalan applicants until the 1990s, even as these applicants mounted into the thousands, with political violence and massive human rights violations scourging many areas of Guatemala in the 1980s.

In this chapter, we describe phases of Guatemalan immigration in the United States since the 1970s (see Table 2.1). Our description is concerned with developments among the Guatemalan immigrant population and in the larger Guatemalan and U.S. contexts. The developments in the Guatemalan context concern mainly social, economic, and political conditions, while developments in the U.S. context include economic restructuring, new evolving intergroup relations, and societal and state responses to immigration. In each phase, we describe case studies of Guatemalan immigrant developments in U.S. settings. In addition, we address developments in the migration region that extends through Mexico affecting Guatemalan migrants.

Phases of Migration to the United States

This chapter distinguishes phases of Guatemalan immigration since 1970 by using the time serial data presented in Table 2.1, which we use to estimate fluctuations in the number of migrants entering the United States. U.S. governmental agencies responsible for handling official immigration and border enforcement functions provide the figures of "Guatemalans Admitted" and "Deportable Guatemalans Located" listed in Table 2.1. Until the formation of the Department of Homeland Security (DHS) in March 2003, these governmental agencies were primarily the Immigration and Naturalization Service (INS) and its subagency, the Border Patrol. After the formation of DHS, these governmental agencies consisted primarily of U.S. Immigration and Customs Enforcement (ICE), U.S. Customs and Border Protection (CBP), and U.S. Citizenship and Immigration Services (USCIS), all of which are located within DHS.

In Table 2.1, the column titled "Guatemalans Admitted" represents the numbers of Guatemalans who legally immigrated into the United States. These persons include mainly family-sponsored immigrants and small numbers of employer-sponsored immigrants, and recipients of asylum granted by the U.S. government beginning mainly in phase 4. In the next column, "Deportable Guatemalans Located" refers to Guatemalans apprehended mainly by the Border Patrol at the southwestern border. After 2003, DHS combined the data of ICE apprehensions in the interior with Border Patrol data for their annual reports. To correct for the ICE apprehension data, which does not represent undocumented entry data at the southwestern border, we interpolated the apprehension data after 2003 to estimate the number of "deportable Guatemalans located" at the southwestern border.[3]

The column titled "Estimated Total Guatemalan Migrants" represents the sum of legally admitted Guatemalans and the number of undocumented migrants who we estimate entered the United States without being apprehended. We estimate the number of nonapprehended undocumented Guatemalan migrants to be twice the number of apprehended migrants.

We assume in Table 2.1 that for every three undocumented Guatemalan migrants who attempt to cross the border into the United States, one is apprehended and two successfully cross the border. We consider this estimation to be a conservative count, and likely undercount, of the true figure for phases 1 through 4 when border control was less stringent than the heightened border enforcement that characterizes phase 5. Estimates of the probability of apprehension of undocumented migrants by the Border Patrol at the U.S.-Mexico border range from .20 to .40 (Espenshade and Acevedo 1995; Singer and Massey 1998; Massey, Durand, and Malone 2002). Using the long-established survey data of the Mexican Migration Project, Donato, Wagner, and Patterson (2008) found that for men and women the apprehension probabilities were .27 and .20, respectively, for the 1987–2004 period. As explained later in the chapter, however, increased border enforcement after 2005 may have raised the apprehension rate.

Compared with the smaller apprehension probabilities derived from em-

Table 2.1. Estimated Guatemalan Immigration in the United States, 1970–2011

Year	Guatemalans Admitted	Deportable[a] Guatemalans Located	Estimated Total Guatemalan Migrants	Y2-Y1	% Change	Approximated Phases
1970	2,130	1,504	5,138			Prelude
1971	2,194	1,321	4,836	-302	-5.9	
1972	1,640	869	3,378	-1,458	-30.1	
1973	1,759	1,331	4,421	1,043	30.9	
1974	1,638	1,686	5,010	589	13.3	
1975	1,859	1,589	5,037	27	0.5	
1976	1,970	1,271	4,512	-525	-10.4	
1977	3,599	5,093	13,785	9,273	205.5	Phase 1
1978	3,996	4,089	12,174	-1,611	-11.7	
1979	2,583	4,421	11,425	-749	-6.2	
1980	3,751	3,785	11,321	-104	-0.9	
1981	3,928	4,182	12,292	971	8.6	
1982	3,633	3,994	11,621	-671	-5.5	
1983	4,090	4,949	13,988	2,367	20.4	
1984	3,937	4,956	13,849	-139	-1.0	
1985	4,389	6,624	17,637	3,788	27.4	
1986	5,158	9,927	25,012	7,375	41.8	Phase 2
1987	5,729	6,722	19,173	-5,839	-23.3	
1988	5,723	9,246	24,215	5,042	26.3	
1989	19,049	13,434	45,917	21,702	89.6	Phase 3
1990	32,303	9,707	51,717	5,800	12.6	
1991	25,527	6,676	38,879	-12,838	-24.8	
1992	10,521	5,614	21,749	-17,130	-44.1	Phase 4
1993	11,870	6,696	25,262	3,513	16.2	
1994	7,389	6,422	20,233	-5,029	-19.9	
1995	6,213	6,450	19,113	-1,120	-5.5	
1996	8,763	6,659	22,081	2,968	15.5	
1997	7,785	7,437	22,659	578	2.6	
1998	7,759	8,455	24,669	2,010	8.9	
1999	7,308	7,688	22,684	-1,985	-8.0	
2000	9,970	7,748	25,466	2,782	12.3	
2001	13,567	7,474	28,515	3,049	12.0	
2002	16,229	8,344	32,917	4,402	15.4	
2003	14,415	10,355	35,125	2,208	6.7	
2004	17,999	14,288	46,575	11,450	32.6	Phase 5
2005	16,825	23,506	63,837	17,262	37.1	

Table 2.1. Continued

Year	Guatemalans Admitted	Deportable[a] Guatemalans Located	Estimated Total Guatemalan Migrants	Y2-Y1	% Change	Approximated Phases
2006	23,687	22,334	68,355	4,518	7.1	
2007	17,198	21,368	59,934	-8,421	-12.3	
2008	15,791	20,191	56,173	-3,761	-6.3	
2009	12,187	21,075	54,337	-1,836	-3.3	
2010	10,467	21,557	53,581	-756	-1.4	
2011	11,092	20,007	51,106	-2,475	-4.6	

[a]For 1970–1976, the frequency of deportable Guatemalans located are approximations based on counts of "aliens required to depart" to Guatemala.
Sources: Immigration and Naturalization Service, Annual Reports, 1970–2002; U.S. Department of Homeland Security, *Yearbook of Immigration Statistics*, 2003–2011.

pirical research, therefore, our assumed apprehension rate of .33 for undocumented Guatemalan migrants produces conservative estimates of the annual numbers of undocumented Guatemalan immigration.[4] Although reported apprehension probabilities have been determined based on surveys of Mexican migrants (Espenshade and Acevedo 1995; Donato, Wagner and Patterson 2008), we assume that these data are useful to approximate the probability of apprehension of undocumented Guatemalan migrants as well, since undocumented Mexican and Central Americans often have common crossing experiences at the U.S.-Mexico border. Indeed, undocumented Mexican and Central American migrants often attempt to cross the U.S.-Mexico border into the United States together in groups organized by smugglers (Spener 2009).

Guatemalan immigration phases are delimited in Table 2.1 by fiscal-year intervals that differ in mean immigration volume per year by about 10,000 or more, and for which the volume difference for the beginning years of successive intervals is also about 10,000 or more from the previous year. Moreover, the first year of each interval differs from the last year of the preceding interval by 33 percent or more. Admittedly, the 10,000-difference mark is arbitrary, but we think that this is a significant difference for an immigration flow in which the highest estimated annual volume is less than 100,000. Our assumption is that variations of 10,000 in an annual immigration flow of less than 100,000 can have significant qualitative impacts, whereas the impacts of such variations may be insignificant in an annual flow that is much larger than 100,000. Moreover, the impacts of immigration volumes are relative to the population size at the specific point of reception. An immigration flow of only a few thousand can settle practically unnoticed in a large city of millions of people, such as New York City or Los Angeles, but can draw much attention in a small urban area of fewer than fifty thousand residents, such as Dalton, Georgia (see Hernández-León and Zúñiga 2002).

Our concern with statistical data is to discern trends and approximate phases rather than to arrive at precise counts, which is impossible to do when a large proportion of a migrant population remains undocumented. Moreover, concerning the category of Guatemalans Admitted, the statistics reflect the years when the migrants received their permanent residential status (green cards), as opposed to the years when their sponsors in the United States actually applied for their visas. Given the time lag between the years decisions are made to migrate and the years visas are actually issued, we refer to the delineated intervals as "approximated phases." Although we use specific years to mark the beginnings of new phases, the years are approximate markers for changes in migration trends, which may have begun gradually in the previous phase. The phases thus represent temporal approximations rather than precise time periods.

Using the criteria we indicate above, we see the Guatemalan time-series data of total immigration in Table 2.1 as having a prelude (1970-1976) and five phases between 1977 and 2011.[5] The intervals and the estimated mean Guatemalan immigration volume per year of admitted and undocumented migrants in each interval are as follows: prelude (1970-1976) = 4,619 migrants per year; phase 1 (1977-1985) = 13,121 migrants per year; phase 2 (1986-1988) = 22,800 migrant per year; phase 3 (1989-1991) = 45,504 migrants per year; phase 4 (1992-2003) = 25,039 migrants per year; and phase 5 (2004-2011) = 56,737 migrants per year. The differences between the mean immigration volume per year and between the endpoint volumes for phases 1 and 2 fall slightly below our 10,000-difference criterion, nonetheless, there is a large percentage difference (41.8 percent) between the estimated total immigration volume of the last year of phase 1 and the beginning of phase 2.

Early 1970s Prelude

The early 1970s represented a continuation of the low level of Guatemalan immigration that occurred in the 1960s. With only about two thousand legal immigrants, and a few thousand undocumented migrants, per year, the total number of Guatemalans entering the United States in the early 1970s was relatively small—less than half the number of legal immigrants entering from several countries in southern Europe (e.g., Greece, Italy, and Portugal) and Asia (e.g., China, India, Korea, and the Philippines) (U.S. INS 1972, Table 9). Yet, the social forces that would affect the large-scale Guatemalan immigration beginning in the late 1970s were already in effect. We can describe these social forces for the national venues of Guatemala and the United States. Both venues can be seen as having structural influences for the Guatemalan mass migration to the United States that began in the late 1970s.

In the early 1970s, Guatemalan economic and political conditions did not progress in a manner that promoted population stability. Given conditions of rigid social inequality, while the large export sector of the national economy experienced growth or stability in the early 1970s, the living conditions of the majority of Guatemalans worsened, and this was especially true of the large Mayan peasantry. Modernization and diversification of agricultural exports helped keep economic growth rates at 5–6 percent annually, as the land area (hectares) used for export agriculture production increased by 28 percent between 1964 and 1979 (Jonas 1991; Villacorta Escobar 1984), but the benefits of this growth did not reach the impoverished peasants.[6] Whereas the land area for subsistence farming increased by only 6 percent in the same time period, the population of mainly poor small farmers grew by 54 percent (Villacorta Escobar 1984). In the small urban industrial sector, the already economically stressed working class faced more economic deterioration as the oil crisis in 1973 increased the costs of energy and industrial inputs, and as opportunities for industrial exports failed to improve (Jonas 1991).

Concerning health conditions, the infant mortality rate for Guatemala in the 1970–1973 period averaged 82.0, which was about 40 percent higher than in the adjacent country of El Salvador, which at the time had the second-highest infant mortality rate in Central America (Villacorta Escobar 1984). The mortality rate of infants, that is, the number of infants who die within the first year of life per 1,000 live births in a given year, has been viewed as a "good indicator of the health status of a population" (Haupt and Kane 1998, 28).

The political picture of Guatemala in the 1970s prelude was one of continuing domination of state power by a ruling coalition of the business elite and the top army officials, allied also with U.S. business and governmental (political and military) interests. This coalition had solidified during the late 1960s, during the counterinsurgency campaign of 1966–1968, directly supervised by the U.S. government. Although it was ostensibly directed against leftist insurgents in the Fuerzas Armadas Rebeldes (FAR), in reality the counterinsurgency war consolidated the apparatus of state violence directed against civilian organizations and populations, killing or "disappearing" 8,000 to 10,000 civilians during 1966–1968. It also included death squads financed by the ruling class and constituted by U.S.-trained off-duty or retired members of the state security forces, carrying out extralegal killings.[7]

The counterinsurgency state was institutionalized with the 1970 election of Colonel Carlos Arana as president, with primarily the Guatemalan elites voting. Because Arana had directed the 1966–1968 counterinsurgency operation, this election brought directly into the state apparatus the violent means of social control used in the 1960s phase of the civil war. Among the political targets of the counterinsurgency state were the social movements that emerged during the 1970s in response to worsening economic and political conditions (Jonas 1991). Participants in the new popular movements came from a wide spectrum of society, including peasants, urban workers, teachers, university professors and students, miners, and shantytown dwellers, as well as priests and congregations oriented toward Liberation Theology. The Arana regime (1970–1974) responded to the popular movements swiftly and brutally: government-directed death squads targeted reformist politicians and labor leaders; soldiers invaded the main public university, killing or forcing into exile prominent student leaders, professors, and intellectuals. More than 700 political killings were carried out in the five months after Arana declared a state of siege in November 1970 (Handy 1984). The military also moved more aggressively against organizers in the countryside, foreshadowing a second and far more brutal counterinsurgency campaign in the late 1970s and 1980s.

The United States also experienced dramatic, structural change in the 1970s prelude. Reacting to increasing global competition, which lowered corporate profit rates from nearly 10 percent in 1965 to lower than 5 percent in the mid-1970s, U.S. corporate managers initiated a series of organizational changes and cost-cutting measures that significantly restructured the economy. Economists Bennett Harrison and Barry Bluestone (1988) refer to this restructuring as "the Great U-Turn." The major characteristics of this economic change included corporate mergers, corporate warfare against organized labor, deindustrialization through the use of off-shore production, a shifting of investment patterns from manufacturing to financial markets, and federal policies to support the corporate sector, especially in the 1980s period of Reaganomics. For labor, the consequences of the Great U-Turn included job losses, wage and benefits cutbacks, a shift from more full-time to more part-time and temporary employment, and less support, if not outright assault, from the federal government.

In 1975, the growth of U.S. private investment abroad increased to $124.1 billion from $49.5 billion in 1965, as U.S. corporations sought to establish more of their labor-intensive production abroad (Harrison and Bluestone

1988). In addition, many corporations with labor-intensive production in the United States increasingly hired immigrants to work for scaled-down wages. Since it was not against the law to hire undocumented immigrant workers prior to 1986, some corporations turned to these workers to restructure their production activities (e.g., see Morales 1983).[8]

In 1975, as the early 1970s prelude drew to an end, 20,352 Guatemalan immigrants submitted their residential registration cards, as was then required annually of resident aliens by the U.S. government (U.S. INS 1975, Table 34). Of the 1,859 Guatemalans who immigrated legally that year, 996 were females, of whom 709 were ages 10–39 (U.S. INS 1975, Table 9). The largest three occupations listed among the new Guatemalan immigrants were housewives, operatives, and skilled blue-collar workers (U.S. INS 1975, Table 8). The year 1975 also saw 308 Guatemalan immigrants become U.S. citizens (U.S. INS 1975, Table 38). This number represented a steady increase from the 1960s, when fewer than 200 Guatemalan immigrants naturalized annually (U.S. INS 1975, Table 39). The Guatemalans who naturalized in 1975 had immigrated into the United States mainly in the mid-1960s (U.S. INS 1975, Table 44). Among the 3,208 Guatemalan visitors to the United States in 1975, which was the largest number of visitors from any Central American country, the most popular borderland ports of entry used were Nogales in Arizona, San Ysidro in California, and Brownsville, Hidalgo, and Laredo in Texas.[9] Several years later, these border ports of entry became among the most popular crossing points for the large streams of undocumented Guatemalan migrants.

Phase 1: Fleeing Social Turmoil, 1977–1985

The trickle of Guatemalan immigrants in the prelude interval turned into a current in phase 1, averaging more than 13,000 legal and undocumented migrants per year. This was a fundamental phase because along with the influx of other Central American migrants, especially Salvadorans, it established a pattern of dynamic Central American immigration in the United States.[10] Moreover, it was during this phase that the social forces of migration that led to the development of a migration region from Central America to North America via Mexico initially appeared. This initial phase led to the development of new relations between communities in the United States and in Central America as Central American migrants developed transnational linkages to their home communities. Central Americans had migrated into the United States for more than a century, but the total number of Central American immigrants counted by U.S. censuses never exceeded 50,000 until the 1970 census (Gibson and Jung 2006, Table 3). The 113,913 Central American immigrants counted by the 1970 census included 17,356 Guatemalans, which was a sharp increase of the 5,381 Guatemalan immigrants counted in the 1960 census (Gibson and Jung 2006, Table 3).

Neither the heightened political violence associated with the CIA-orchestrated overthrow of Guatemalan President Arbenz in 1954 nor the harsh counterinsurgency actions undertaken by the Guatemalan army against incipient leftist movements in 1966–1968 (Jonas 1991) had generated large-scale migration from Guatemala to the United States. Instead, Mexico was the destination for political exile during those years.

In addition to initiating a sustained pattern of large-scale immigration and settlement, the major developments of Guatemalan immigration in phase 1 included the establishment of Guatemalan immigrant settlements across different U.S. regions and the social responses to this influx. Major social change in Guatemala and the United States served as the context for phase 1 of Guatemalan immigration.

Guatemalan Context

In Guatemala, the social context of phase 1 involved a dramatic increase of political violence and a sharp decline of economic conditions, leaving the country in a state of generalized crisis. Political violence surged as government military forces and paramilitary groups responded to the leftist revolutionary insurgency, this time based in the western *altiplano*, or highlands, primarily a Mayan area. In reality, the ruling coalition was responding to the rising level of consciousness among those Mayan highlands populations (Falla 1978), which had greatly increased their level of organizing within and between communities in response to a massive earthquake in 1976.

In the late 1970s, coinciding roughly with the beginning of phase 1 of the migration, the civil war that had begun in 1960 escalated into its second full-blown surge. Beginning in 1978, security forces of the military government decimated unions, as well as urban-based social and political opposition movements, through targeted extrajudicial assassinations and "disappearances" of leaders and members. Many survivors fled, seeking refuge abroad. In 1981, and even more systematically after the March 1982 military coup led by General Efraín Ríos Montt, state violence and repression in the Mayan altiplano became a scorched-earth counterinsurgency campaign, carrying out massacres and destroying hundreds of entire villages—more than 440 between 1981 and 1983, by the army's own count. These army massacres left up to 150,000 dead and "disappeared" during those years alone, 200,000 refugees who fled to Mexico, and a million internally displaced.[11]

The army's campaign of terror was justified as being directed against the revolutionary movement, which united in 1982 as the Unidad Revolucionaria Nacional Guatemalteca (URNG–Guatemalan National Revolutionary Unity), other leftists, and suspected supporters. In effect, however, it targeted the civilian population in the highlands, on the premise that the entire Mayan population was inherently "subversive." Indeed, some communities had turned to the URNG to defend themselves, but under this premise, all Maya, even Mayan children below the age of reason, were considered to be enemies of the state, hence targets for execution, and the Mayas' guilt was viewed as biologically transmitted (Falla 1984). The army's implementation of this premise became the basis for the charge that the government and its security forces carried out a war involving acts of genocide (Comisión para el Esclarecimiento Histórico or Truth Commission 1999, REHMI/ODHA 1998).

With increasing turmoil, the Guatemalan economy fell into shambles during phase 1 of Guatemalan migration to the United States. Many indicators reflected the Guatemalan economic crisis: the real wage index (using 1973 = 100) fell below the 1973 level in 1974 and remained below through the mid-1980s; unemployment and underemployment rose from more than 25 percent in the mid-1970s to more than 40 percent in the mid-1980s; and rural poverty reached 84 percent, and urban poverty 47 percent, in 1980 (Gallardo and López 1986, Tables 1.10 and 1.12; Booth and Walker 1993, Tables 5 and 7; Booth, Wade, and Walker 2006). Moreover, a Latin American economic crisis in the 1980s ("the Lost Decade") affected the Guatemalan economy, which slowed down to a growth rate of about only 1 percent in the 1980s (World Bank 1990, Table 2; Portes and Hoffman 2003). As it grew at below-average rates, the agricultural economy, which employed the largest number of poor workers, could not provide enough jobs to maintain stable work opportunities in the countryside.

Political violence severely restricted the Mayan highland economies of peasant and artisan production. These economies depend greatly on the ability of the highland populations to travel frequently to marketplaces in order to buy and sell what has been recently produced. When the political violence escalated, many peasants and artisans restricted travel beyond their local areas to avoid encounters with soldiers, guerrillas, or death squads. This restricted travel greatly stifled economic activity in the highlands, even in areas that were not conflict zones.

U.S. Context

The U.S. context for phase 1 of Guatemalan immigration included at least three major currents of social-economic change—all of which made immigrant labor more attractive to U.S. employers. One current was the continuing transformation of the national economy into a service economy (Fuchs 1968). Many modern, industrialized countries have undergone a long-term transformation from agricultural, manufacturing, and extractive industries to being primarily a service economy, in which workers produce services rather than tangible goods (Singelmann 1978). Measurements of service employment vary, but most economists agree that by the 1960s and 1970s, the majority of U.S. employees worked in service industries and that in the 1980s the percentage of service workers kept increasing.[12]

A second social-economic contextual current was the continuation of the Great U-Turn, which reduced the power of labor with the assistance of Reaganomic supply-side policies.[13] Emboldened by Reaganomic policies, employers cheapened labor by cutting wages, obtaining labor concessions, and replacing higher-paid workers with lower-paid labor (in some cases with low-wage immigrant workers; for example, see Morales 1983). These actions raised the low-wage share of total employment, increasing the polarization of the job market (Harrison and Bluestone 1988). The third major current of social-economic change involved an urban economic restructuring that created a new demand for high- and low-skilled labor. According to Sassen (1988), the restructuring of the U.S. economy in the 1970s and early 1980s produced agglomerations of professional service businesses (legal, financial, data analysis, etc.) that attracted high-skill workers. The professional labor forces, in turn, created a demand for low-wage workers in personal service industries. These workers took jobs in restaurants, coffee shops, home cleaning, yard work, dog walking, and so forth. Industrial work that was downgraded to low-wage jobs or informal home work also stimulated the demand for low-wage workers (Sassen Koob 1984).

The three currents of social-economic change increased the significance of service work and directly or indirectly increased the attraction of immigrant workers as a source of low-wage labor for the lower echelons of the service labor force. As some analysts have explained (e.g., Piore 1979), low-paying service jobs were well suited for foreign migrant workers who could survive on low wages and who, at least initially, did not derive their social status from their positions in the U.S. labor market. From the perspective of the increased demand for low-wage service workers, the growth of low-wage immigrant labor in the restructured urban economies of the United States in the 1970s and 1980s was not simply a function of immigrants fleeing social deterioration in their home countries. It was also a consequence of a new capitalist arrangement of U.S. business development spurring the expansion of the service sector (Sassen Koob 1984), which attracted immigrant labor.

Settlement in Los Angeles

In the late 1970s and early to mid-1980s, the Los Angeles area in southern California became the most popular destination point for Guatemalans and other Central Americans. More Guatemalans migrated to Los Angeles than to any other U.S. locality. But this characteristic was not peculiar to Central Americans. In the period we characterized as the first phase of Guatemalan immigration, the Los Angeles area also became a major destination point for immigrants from Asia and other world regions, in addition to Latin America. Indeed, with high levels of immigration and the growth of its native ethnic and racial minority populations, the Los Angeles area became an intense multicultural and multiracial center, representing, for some, a new sociospatial form of urban life (Davis 1990). Michael Peter Smith (2001), for example, referred to this new local/global urban sociospatial arrangement as "transnational urbanism." The transformation in the Los Angeles area during the late 1970s and early to mid-1980s went beyond demographic change and involved major economic restructuring of manufacturing and service industries. This economic change included the growth of high-tech industries, low-wage manufacturing, and construction, with an expansion of garment sweatshops and service industries at all skill levels. For arriving immigrant workers, the Los Angeles area was a boomtown undergoing simultaneous deindustrialization and reindustrialization (Davis 1990; Smith 2001).

By 1980, the number of Guatemalans in Los Angeles had increased to 38,000, from 5,600 in 1970 (Popkin 1999; Hamilton and Chinchilla 2001). Along with other Central Americans, Guatemalan newcomers settled in low-income Mexican American neighborhoods, as well as in other areas not too distant from the downtown area. Relations with the larger Mexican-origin population fluctuated between friendly and contentious, and in time the Guatemalans, like the Salvadorans, developed social institutions (Hamilton and Chinchilla 2001). In the large Central American settlement in the Pico Union section of Westlake, which is west of downtown, many Guatemalans settled in run-down, low-rent housing surrounded by crime and delinquency. In the nearby parks, Guatemalan immigrant families with small children attended family festivals and other social events as drug dealers openly conducted their illegal business. A flurry of activity and an ethnic ambience of

Mexican and Central American restaurants, shops, markets, and courier and travel agencies characterized the Pico Union district as a prototypical immigrant settlement zone in the new age of immigration in the late twentieth century (Loucky 2000). The characterization included a sizeable number of Maya who emigrated from Guatemala and established organizations to maintain their identity (Popkin 1999; Davis 2007).

Responses to Guatemalan Immigration

Central American immigration during phase 1 of Guatemalan immigration created a divided U.S. response, partly because the majority of Central American newcomers were undocumented. Some communities, activists, and religious groups acted to support this immigration, while other community leaders and the U.S. government acted to oppose it (García 2006). The viewpoint taken of Guatemalan and other Central American migrants seemed to vary according to the view taken of U.S. military intervention in Central America in the 1980s. Those who viewed the intervention as U.S. support for right-wing governments tended to see Guatemalans and other Central American immigrants as refugees displaced by political violence and deserving of asylum. In contrast, those who viewed the intervention as a means to prevent a Soviet-supported leftist takeover of Central America tended to see the Central American newcomers as economic migrants or as dangerous leftists.

In the early 1980s, a sanctuary movement of religious persons and organizations emerged to support the immigration of undocumented Salvadorans and Guatemalans. The sanctuary movement transported and housed these migrants and publicized their cause for asylum (Crittenden 1988; Davidson 1988). By the mid-1980s, hundreds of religious congregations and organizations and several university campuses and city governments openly endorsed the sanctuary movement (Davidson 1988; García 2006).

In the Texas Lower Rio Grande border area, some Mexican American political leaders opposed the immigration of Guatemalans and other Central Americans because of the contrast these newcomers supposedly created with Mexican immigrants. This issue divided the small Texas border town of San Benito in the mid-1980s. Located just 10 miles from the borderline, the town became the site of a sanctuary center (Casa Oscar Romero) established by Catholic nuns in a Mexican American neighborhood to help Central American migrants. When fights broke out between youth in the center and the neighborhood, Mexican American city government officials expressed opposition to the center.

Mexican American elected officials of the town did not view the Central Americans with the same acceptance that they had for Mexican migrants. The officials claimed that the cultural differences of the Central Americans attracted by the center were disrupting the community. Some local Mexican American residents supported the sanctuary center, but the local government officials voted to levy fines against the center in order to force it out of town. When the nuns relocated the sanctuary center to the outskirts of the nearby city of Brownsville, the county commissioners of the area passed a strongly worded resolution against undocumented Central American immigration and in support of the U.S. Border Patrol (which was an important employer in the poverty-stricken county). A group of persons who opposed the center built a watchtower near the relocated center to monitor what the group claimed were smuggling activities conducted at the sanctuary center.

The U.S. government opposed Guatemalan and other Central American immigration in the late 1970s and early 1980s in various ways. One way was to infiltrate the sanctuary movement and arrest its members (Davidson 1988). A second way was to almost completely deny asylum for Guatemalan and other Central American petitioners, with the exception of some Nicaraguan cases (Gzesh 2006).

Analysts have related the decision of the U.S. government to deny asylum for Central Americans during the Reagan administration to the support the administration was giving the governments fighting leftist movements in Central America (Schoultz 1992; Hamilton and Chinchilla 2001; Gzesh 2006). Granting asylum to large numbers of Salvadorans and Guatemalans fleeing political repression by their governments could have meant ending U.S. military support for these governments, since Congress had temporarily banned U.S. aid during the Reagan administration to governments that violated human rights.

The INS process of deciding asylum cases involved seeking an "advisory opinion" from the Bureau of Human Rights and Humanitarian Affairs (BHRHA) of the State Department, which was considered knowledgeable of human rights conditions in foreign countries. While INS asylum reviewers and immigration judges on their own rejected most Central American asylum petitions, they also routinely deferred to the usually unfavorable advisory opinions of BHRHA in the relatively few cases for which they had preliminarily ruled in favor of the applicants.[14] The extremely low approval rates for Guatemalan and Salvadoran asylum applicants eventually were addressed in the class-action suit *American Baptist Churches v. Thornburgh* that was filed by religious organizations against the INS in 1985 (see Chapter 3). It was not until after the *ABC* lawsuit (as it was called) was settled in late 1990 that the U.S. government began granting asylum to significant numbers of Guatemalans.

Phase 2: Legalization through Amnesty, 1986–1988

In phase 2 of Guatemalan immigration, the average annual volume of total Guatemalan immigration increased to an estimated 22,800 legal and undocumented migrants per year, which was a rise of 74 percent from the level in phase 1. Phase 2 stands out among the phases of Guatemalan immigration because of the enactment by the U.S. government of IRCA in 1986. This law offered amnesty and the possibility of legalization for undocumented migrants who met the residential and work criteria specified by the law. Guatemalan migrants submitted 70,953 applications for amnesty and legalization, and 49,942 of these applicants were granted legal permanent residential status (U.S. INS 1992a, Table 22; 1992b, Table 3).

As legal and undocumented Guatemalan immigration increased in phase 2, Guatemalan migrants developed patterns of interaction with their households back home. Given their inability to travel freely prior to gaining legalization through IRCA, many undocumented Guatemalan migrants carried out this transnational interaction intermittently through occasional phone calls and through informal couriers, relatives, and friends who transported monetary remittances, letters, and voice recordings on audio cassettes to families in Guatemala.[15]

Emergence of a Migration Region

Large-scale Central American migration through Mexico to reach the United States represented a new migratory phenomenon in Mexico. The continual movement of Guatemalans and other Central Americans trekking northward increasingly affected Mexican social-spatial environments, and institutions within them, molding the environments into a migration region. The arrival of tens of thousands of Guatemalans (mostly Maya) in refugee camps of the United Nations High Commissioner for Refugees (UNHCR) in the state of Chiapas by 1983 had raised social and political issues that drew the involvement of Mexican governmental, military, religious, and human-rights institutional actors (Aguayo 1985; Worby 1999).[16] But this refugee migration, and the total settlement in Mexico of an estimated 200,000 Guatemalans fleeing conflict and repression in Guatemala (Aguayo and Fagen 1988; Manz 1988), was only a part of larger Guatemalan migratory social forces that, joined with other Central American migration, affected Mexican social-spatial environments. Guatemalan *campesinos* (peasants) have had a history of crossing into southern Mexico to interact with local communities or perform seasonal work in agricultural lands (Castillo 1997; Cruz 2009), but never before had such a large flow of Guatemalans and other Central Americans migrated through the length of Mexican territory to reach the United States (Aguayo 1985; Aguayo and Fagen 1988; Jáuregui and Ávila Sánchez 2009).

The continual migration of Central American migrants into Mexico on the way to look for refuge and work in the United States affected many institutions of Mexican society: bus companies provided transportation for the migrants (sometimes through special routes to avoid police detection); local police developed routines to inspect or shake down the migrants who might be carrying money (or to abuse the migrant women); commercial establishments and safe houses offered special arrangements for fast-moving migrants who needed only hours of lodging; small employers provided temporary work for migrants who ran out of money in the passage; political leaders debated policy responses to the migrant stream; and religious and human-rights workers acted to lessen the misery and vulnerability of the human flow in places along the migrant trail all the way to the U.S.-Mexico border (García 2006; Casillas 2006; Rodriguez 2007; Hagan 2008). The material and symbolic presence that Guatemalan and other Central American migrants had historically developed in southern Mexico (Castillo 2006) now became visible all along the long trail to the northern border of the country.

In small but revealing ways, the Central American migrants distinguished themselves from local residents on their journey north. Their dressing traits, linguistic styles, vocabulary, food preferences, and in some areas, such as in northern Mexican border states, the physical characteristics of the Mayan migrants set them apart from local populations. Individual Central American migrants were not easily distinguishable in Mexican settings, but they stood out against the Mexican social background when they traveled in groups.

Changing Guatemalan Context

In phase 2, the political-military conflict in Guatemala subsided somewhat because the most extreme cases of violence, i.e., the massacres by the Guatemalan army, were over. The civil war continued until peace accords were signed at the end of 1996, but the intense political repression experienced in the late 1970s and early 1980s decreased by the mid-1980s. Having accomplished its immediate mission of pacifying insurgency in the Mayan highlands, the army faced a crisis of legitimacy and participated in a transition process of returning to civilian rule. This became the basis for a new Constitution and the election of a civilian President in 1985. Even after the civilian Vinicio Cerezo of the centrist Christian Democratic Party was freely elected president and took office in 1986, the armed forces retained significant power as yet a third wave of leftist insurgency developed in the late 1980s. While the hopes for a truly "democratic transition" were not actually fulfilled (see Trudeau 1993; Torres-Rivas 1989, 1996; Jonas 2000a), nonetheless, across many areas of the country people felt less fear to move about. One sign that the violence had subsided was the return of people traveling at night from one town to another in some areas of the highlands.

The return to relatively normal activity in rural areas, where a large portion of the population lived (even as there was a general trend of increasing migration to urban areas), varied according to the degree of involvement in the civil war. Some communities, such as villages in the departments of Huehuetenango and El Quiché, had been war zones and thus suffered major destruction from attacks by the Guatemalan army (Falla 1994).[17] But other communities, such as some *municipios* in the department of Totonicapán, were not directly involved in the military conflict and thus experienced mainly a rise in fear—when soldiers passed nearby or when death squads brought victims to execute at night on rural roads—and a decline in economic activity.[18] Most communities, however, were subjected by the military to the forced recruitment of youth into the army and of the general male population into civil defense patrols (Patrullas de Autodefensa Civil, called PACs).

For the communities that had been war zones, a quick return to normal life was impossible because large segments of their populations had been killed or had gone into exile, and many villages had been destroyed. Although relatively small numbers of individual Guatemalan refugees in Mexico had begun trickling back to Guatemala in the mid-1980s, it was not until the 1990s that a steady stream of returnees developed (Nolin Hanlon and Lovell 2000). Return migration did not mean a quick return to previous routines in the areas most affected by the political conflict. Moreover, the government vacillated in its support of the return agreement formally reached with representatives of refugee populations within Guatemala and in Mexico (Jonas 2000b; Nolin Hanlon and Lovell 2000). Rather than face an uncertain future in Guatemalan, thousands of Guatemalan refugees chose to remain in Mexico and other countries (Nolin Hanlon and Lovell 2000).

As Guatemalan migrants in the United States sent information about jobs and other opportunities to their home communities, the possibility of migrating to the United States became an alternative in Guatemalan communities attempting to return to a stable life. Initially this was true mainly in the urban areas of Guatemala City and Quetzaltenango and for a few cities and municipios, such as Huehuetenango and Santa Cruz del Quiché, but later the emigration option spread across the western highlands and to other regions of the country as well (e.g., see Camus 2007).

U.S. Context

The enactment of IRCA in 1986 was the result of years of debate in Congress over how to handle undocumented immigration. Since the early 1970s, governmental policymakers had debated proposals for how to deal with undocumented immigration, which was seen primarily as a Mexican problem since Mexicans made up the majority of undocumented migrants. The debate lasted through four presidential administrations and finally produced concrete results when President Reagan signed IRCA into law on November 6, 1986.

Concern with illegal immigration rose among U.S. government officials when undocumented Mexican immigration surged in the late 1960s and early 1970s after Congress shut down the Bracero Program. This bilateral program between the United States and Mexico lasted from 1942 to 1964 and had annually imported thousands of Mexican workers to work temporarily in the United States, primarily in agriculture. After Congress terminated the Bracero Program in 1964, increasing numbers of former braceros and other Mexican migrants crossed the border yearly without visas to work in agricultural fields and other worksites where U.S. employers awaited them.[19]

IRCA proposed to deal with undocumented immigration primarily through a combination of positive and negative sanctions. On the one hand, the law offered amnesty and the opportunity to acquire legal status for undocumented immigrants who met a set of criteria. On the other hand, it provided penalties against employers who continued to hire undocumented migrant workers after the passage of the law.[20] IRCA provided amnesty through two programs. The Section 245A program provided an opportunity for legalization for undocumented migrants who had lived continuously in the United States since before January 1, 1982, and the Special Agricultural Workers program provided legalization for undocumented migrants who had worked in seasonal agricultural jobs for a minimum of 90 days in the year preceding May 1986. IRCA sanctions against employers who hired undocumented migrant workers ranged from fines for initial violations to criminal penalties for repeat offenders, but the sanctions were not rigorously enforced until the late 1990s.

The 49,942 Guatemalans who legalized through IRCA represented only 2 percent of the total 2.7 million undocumented migrants who obtained legalization (Kerwin 2010). Nonetheless, this small percentage represented a major foothold in the country for Guatemalans since it dramatically increased the legal resources for future Guatemalan immigration. Every Guatemalan who legalized became a potential sponsor for the legal immigration of relatives from Guatemala. The legalized Guatemalan migrants also became key resources to strengthen the transregional reach to their communities of origin because these migrants could now travel freely between the United States and Guatemala, which consolidated endpoints of the migration region.

Amnesty and Legalization in Houston

As did other major U.S. cities, Houston experienced a major wave of undocumented immigration beginning in the mid-1970s and thus became a major center for the amnesty and legalization measures of IRCA. The Houston IRCA office received 113,870 applications for amnesty. Mexicans filed 66 percent of the IRCA applications in Houston, and Central Americans filed 25 percent (Hagan 1994).

Guatemalans in Houston first viewed IRCA with uncertainty and suspicion rather than as an opportunity to gain legal resident status. The Spanish-language sources of information tended to emphasize the employer sanctions of the law more than its amnesty measure. Some Guatemalans speculated that if employers could no longer hire undocumented workers, a massive roundup of undocumented migrants was sure to follow. Rumors became a major source of information, and they spread rapidly. A few Mayan households returned to Guatemala voluntarily rather than risk being apprehended and handed over to the Guatemalan government, which they viewed as unfriendly. Some Maya headed for Canada to seek asylum, trying to stay ahead of the massive roundup of undocumented migrants they thought was sure to come. Even if the new law brought an opportunity for amnesty, the requirement that applicants must have lived in the United States since before 1982 seemed to many Central Americans to favor Mexican immigrants, who had a longer history of migrating to the United States. Thus many Guatemalan and other Central American migrants viewed IRCA with fear that their stay in the United States would soon end.

Several factors eventually encouraged undocumented Guatemalan migrants in Houston to apply for amnesty under IRCA. One factor was that local Latino community organizations, lawyers, and notaries increasingly advertised in local Spanish-language media about the importance for undocumented immigrants to legalize. A second factor was that undocumented Guatemalan migrants learned, as did other migrants, that they could receive temporary work authorization by simply turning in an application for amnesty. This provided time to work and save money to take back home if the application for amnesty was not successful. A third factor was the INS ruling that IRCA applicants could submit notarized statements from employers and other acquaintances in place of other official records to document their five-year residence and employment in the United States to qualify for amnesty.

Relying on networks for information and affidavits, Guatemalan migrants in Houston made the application for amnesty into a social process. As Hagan (1994) describes, this social process had a gendered nature. Since migrant men were more involved than migrant women in social networks inside and outside the migrant population, the men usually sought affidavits of support for the amnesty application from a number of former employers, while the women were often limited to only one or two employers.[21] This was especially true of migrant women who worked as domestics, since they usually spent years working in the same family household. A major disadvantage for migrant women of having only a few employers from whom to ask for affidavits was that some employers were reluctant to provide them because they feared getting in trouble for not paying Social Security taxes for their workers, or for not having paid the minimum wage. Also, in migrant households with very limited income, the decision was sometimes made to pay for only the husband's application fee, leaving the wife and the children out of the amnesty and legalization program (Hagan 1994).[22] In spite of the disadvantages faced by the migrant women, females accounted for 42 percent of all IRCA applicants who had been legalized through the Section 245A program by 1991 (U.S. INS 1992b).

Social Mobility through Legalization

Legalization through IRCA gave former undocumented migrants new opportunities in the labor market. For example, in Los Angeles, some Guatemalan migrants who legalized left their jobs in garment sweatshops for better work in other industries (Loucky 2005). With their new legal status, and with the English training required by IRCA to advance from temporary to permanent legal residency, some Guatemalans also underwent job promotions in the firms where they worked. For example, a number of Mayan Guatemalans who had worked as floor cleaners, stockers, and sackers in a supermarket chain in Houston were promoted after their legalization and English training to cashiers, deli workers, customer service staff, and eventually to managers of different supermarket sections (see Chapter 4).

Migrants who legalized through IRCA, however, became unattractive to employers in the secondary sector of the labor market. This labor-market sector depends on informal labor arrangements in which workers are often paid in cash with no benefits, e.g., health insurance and retirement pensions (Gordon 1972). Often the labor demand of the secondary sector of the labor market is met with undocumented migrant workers (Piore 1979). The legalization of undocumented migrant workers created a problem for secondary-sector employers because it made the need to pay minimum wages and Social Security taxes for these workers more salient. In a short time, many employers in the secondary labor market replaced their legalized workforces with new supplies of undocumented migrant workers. In some cases, corporations that contracted out building maintenance work changed their contracts to cleaning companies that screened workers for legal status; but in other cases, corporations kept their maintenance contracts with cleaning companies that paid little concern to the status of their workers.[23]

Phase 3: Transnational Development, 1989–1991

Phase 3 stands out as an important time period in Guatemalan immigration because it was in this phase that about 50,000 Guatemalan migrants received legal permanent resident visas through IRCA. As a consequence, it was in this phase that the annual number of admitted Guatemalan immigrants peaked in Guatemalan immigration in the United States. It was also in this phase that the estimated average annual volume of total Guatemalan immigration (legal and undocumented) reached the highest point, at 45,504, prior to phase 5, which began sixteen years later (see Table 2.1).

As stated above, the Guatemalan migrants who legalized through IRCA gained a valuable legal resource to reconnect to their homeland. Prior to the legalization provided by IRCA, undocumented Guatemalan migrants rarely visited their families in Guatemala because of the difficulty and expense of re-migrating to the United States without a visa. Undocumented Guatemalan migrants usually returned to Guatemala only when a death or other crisis occurred in their families, or when they were deported. But the visas obtained through IRCA enabled thousands of legalized Guatemalan migrants to visit their families in Guatemala as often as their incomes and free time permitted.

Through periodic return visits, legalized Guatemalans dramatically increased their interaction with their home communities. The ability to plan specific dates for their visits enabled returning migrants to participate in a host of family and community celebrations in their communities of origin. Some migrants also used their return trips to Guatemala to meet with homebuilders to arrange for the construction of new homes on lots purchased in rural areas or nearby towns. As the volume of Guatemalan migrants who returned to visit their families grew, so did the volume of monetary and material remittances they transported for their families and for friends and relatives. Eventually, airline companies increased the number of flights between the United States and Guatemala to accommodate the increasing numbers of legalized migrants making periodic visits. Return visits by legalized Guatemalan migrants also sparked the interest of many young men and women in Guatemala to emigrate to the United States, as the visiting migrants were usually seen as images of success.

In contrast to the experience of legalized migrants, who could travel freely, the land journey to the United States remained dangerous for undocumented Guatemalan migrants. Beginning in the southernmost region of Mexico, the thousand-mile journey to the United States passed through dangerous Mexican areas where bandits, gangs, and corrupt police waited to prey on U.S.-bound migrants (Rodriguez 2007; Amnesty International 2010).[24] The trip was even more dangerous for women, who were sexually assaulted. In addition, transmigrants faced the increasing immigration enforcement of the Mexican government. Agencies of the Mexican National Institute of Migration dramatically increased the interception and deportation of transmigrants crossing Mexico in phase 3 of Guatemalan migration to the United States. In 1990 and 1991, Mexican government agents conducted 126,440 and 133,342 deportations, respectively, almost all to Central America (Casillas 2006). Deportations to Guatemala accounted for 47 percent and 52 percent for each of the two years, respectively.

Beginning in the early 1990s, the U.S. government increased its efforts to prevent Guatemalans and other Central Americans from reaching the U.S.-Mexico border by providing training and financing for Mexican interdiction and deportation campaigns, particularly along the southern border with Guatemala (see details in Chapter 3). After the Zapatista uprising in Chiapas in January 1994, Guatemalan migrants also encountered more Mexican government personnel in the southern border region (Gzesh 1995).

Reaching the U.S.-Mexico border presented another major obstacle for undocumented Guatemalan migrants, that is, arid deserts and dangerous waterways in the southwestern U.S. border area. In the late 1980s, the number of undocumented migrants who died trying to cross into the United States increased significantly, reaching several hundred per year (Eschbach et al. 1999).[25] By the mid-1990s, the patterns of migrant deaths in border areas shifted to remote desert areas as the U.S. Border Patrol intensified enforcement in popular crossing points near cities.

Continuing Problems and New Hope in Guatemala

Continuing political conflict and economic deterioration characterized the Guatemalan context during phase 3 of Guatemalan immigration in the United States. While the Guatemalan military had gotten the upper hand in its war with leftist insurgents in the mid-1980s, it was not able to deliver a final blow to destroy the insurgency. Consequently, the insurgent URNG became reinvigorated in the late 1980s, causing more casualties among the Guatemalan army and drawing closer to Guatemala City (Jonas 1991). Yet, the political struggle was not without hope. With the signing of the Central American Peace Accords in 1987, all three Central American countries (El Salvador, Guatemala, and Nicaragua) involved in internal armed conflict were pressured into exploring the possibility of peace. The pressure to explore the possibility for peace increased as more organizations of civil society became involved in the discussion and as the URNG increasingly saw its struggle in political rather than military terms, subordinating military action to pressure for negotiations. The Guatemalan army and ultra rightists as well as CACIF,[26] resisted ideas of negotiating with the guerrilla to achieve peace, but other sectors of society met openly with guerrilla leaders in Canada and Spain, and in early 1991 the newly-elected president, Jorge Serrano, began open direct negotiations with the URNG.

Although some saw opportunity for improvement in the political arena, the economic situation remained dismal. By 1990, the country reached a population of 9.2 million with a poverty level of about 65 percent, and with about 40 percent of the population living in extreme poverty (World Bank 1992, Table 1; ECLAC 2007). Infant mortality remained high (62 infant deaths per 1,000 live births) in 1990 in the context of a greatly skewed income distribution in favor of the small, wealthy, elite sector of the society (World Bank 1992, Tables 28 and 30). As the presidency of Cerezo drew to a close in late 1990, his neoliberal model brought prosperity only to the speculative capitalist class, while the burden of austerity and of an inflation rate of 83 percent fell on the vast majority of the population of workers, peasants, and urban middle-class people (Jonas 1991). In 1990, the country faced an external debt of $2.8 billion, with half of the population struggling to find enough income to buy food (World Bank 1992, Table 21).

Yet, some communities that had experienced emigration to the United States began to receive economic resources to cope with the dismal domestic economy in the late 1980s and early 1990s. The economic resources came in the form of migrant monetary remittances and other material transfers from the United States, and also in the form of returning migrants who started new businesses with money earned in the United States. Regular remittances and visits by migrants who arrived with gifts created new lifelines that elevated households out of poverty. In poor villages and hamlets in the countryside, the financial income and material contributions arriving from the United States brought visible economic change, as demonstrated by growing numbers of newly built homes (Hagan 1994; Piedrasanta Herrera 2007).

Shifting U.S. Foreign and Domestic Concerns

In the United States, phase 3 (1989–1991) of Guatemalan immigration saw major changes in foreign and domestic policies. In the international arena, the U.S. overarching policy of containing Soviet influence shifted with the collapse of the Soviet Union. Coinciding with the end of the Cold War, U.S. support for its conservative allies in Central America became somewhat less monolithic, ideological, and militarized. Whereas the Reagan presidency had maintained an active anticommunist stance for U.S. involvement in Central America, seeking total victory over its leftist "enemies," the George H. W. Bush administration was more pragmatic and sought to lower the profile of Central America's 1980s civil wars in its overall foreign policy agenda (Jonas 1990). A key factor was the Central American presidents' own Peace Accords of 1987, which led to a remarkable process of prioritizing peace regionally and ending civil wars by negotiations. The United States did intervene once more in the region, invading Panama in December 1989 to overthrow an inconvenient president, but this was less driven by ideological factors. The Gulf War of 1991, beginning with the Iraqi invasion of Kuwait in August 1990 and the subsequent U.S.-led invasion of Iraq, signaled a new international struggle in U.S. foreign involvement that centered on the Middle East.

The beginning of the Bush presidency in 1989 also brought a lessening of the ideologically charged domestic policies of the Reagan administration. The labor policy of the federal government softened somewhat for the first time since before the Reagan presidency.[27] In the arena of immigration policy, the U.S. government raised the number of immigrants that could be admitted into the country. The Immigration Act of 1990 set the annual level at 700,000 immigrants for 1992–1994 and then at a permanent flexible annual cap of 675,000 beginning in 1995.

Among other changes, the 1990 Act also authorized the provision of Temporary Protected Status (TPS) for the safety of migrants who would otherwise be deported to countries where they would be persecuted or experience armed conflict, natural disasters, or other extraordinary and temporary dangerous conditions (U.S. DHS 2004).[28] But although TPS was granted to many Salvadorans in 1990 and provided relief for Hondurans and Nicaraguans in 1999, it was never used to help Guatemalan migrants. More important for Guatemalan migrants was the settlement of the *ABC v. Thornburgh* lawsuit in late 1990 because it gave Guatemalan and Salvadoran asylum seekers the chance to have their cases individually readjudicated.

In phase 3 of Guatemalan immigration, the U.S. service economy continued its long-term growth, creating more job opportunities for immigrant workers. With 40 million employees, the service industry accounted for 34 percent of the labor force in 1991, 5 percentage points higher than in 1980 (U.S. Census Bureau 1992, Table 632). The number of service workers was actually higher since many service employees worked in manufacturing and other industries. In personal service industries (households, hotels, etc.), the concentration of women reached 70 percent. In other words, the service industry growth included thousands of lower-status jobs through which poor immigrants could enter the labor force, especially if they lacked work authorization. The work opportunities that low-wage immigrants faced were undoubtedly more numerous than indicated by official statistics, given that many of these migrants found jobs that paid in cash and thus were not reported to official agencies. This was the condition in which many Guatemalans and other Latino migrant men and women found themselves in the third phase of Guatemalan immigration.

Settlement on the Southeast Coast

Much of the growth of the service industry occurred in large urban centers, attracting large numbers of immigrants to major metropolitan areas such as Los Angeles, Chicago, and Houston. Indeed, the early reports of large-scale Central American immigration focused primarily on these settings (for example, see Rodriguez 1987, Chavez 1992, Chinchilla, Hamilton and Loucky 1993). Yet, for Guatemalans and other Latino immigrants coming from rural origins, there was also a significant pull by agricultural and other rural-based industries located in southeastern areas of the country. Rural recruiters travelled from these areas to look for Latino migrant labor in other areas of the country.

The initial migration of Guatemalans to the southeast coast occurred substantially through step migration, such as from Guatemala to Mexico (to UNHCR refugee camps and other Mexican areas) and then to the United

States (Castañeda, Manz, and Davenport 2002; Kauffer 2005). But as more Guatemalans settled along the U.S. southeastern coast, the Guatemalan migration to the region increasingly came directly from Guatemala (Burns 1993).

An example of a Guatemalan settlement in the southeast coast during phase 3 of Guatemalan immigration occurred in the small agricultural setting of Indiantown in Florida. According to Burns (1993), a small group of nine Guatemalan refugees recruited in the early 1980s formed the basis of what was to become by the end of the 1980s a population of some four thousand Guatemalan migrants in Indiantown. The Guatemalans, who were mainly Maya, joined other groups of U.S.- and foreign-born migrant workers harvesting fruits and vegetables in the area of Indiantown. Some Guatemalans became labor subcontractors themselves. The Guatemalan women also labored in the fields, and some women who were too old or ill to work in the fields cooked and took care of children for others (Burns 1993).

In Indiantown, the Maya spoke several different Mayan languages, as well as Spanish, and were reinforced by the arrival of nonindigenous migrants (*ladinos*) from various areas of Guatemala. The annual fiesta of the patron saint of San Miguel Atacán in the Guatemalan department of Huehuetenango became the highpoint of the Q'anjob'al cultural celebration in Indiantown as numerous cultural and social activities were organized for the event. Attendees at the fiesta included Mayan migrants and others from distant areas of the United States as well as from Guatemala (Burns 1993). For the Mayan migrants, the fiesta represented an active, international connection to their Guatemalan homeland in Huehuetenango. According to Burns (1993, 130), "[t]he identity of Maya in exile is one in which refugee locales like Indiantown are infused with a sense of belonging to a natal community in Guatemala."

The statement by Burns is instructive for understanding the development of migrant transnational relations with home communities in Guatemala. Legal and economic factors affect the degree of interaction—for example, in the ability to travel back and forth freely with legal status or to remit larger sums of money—but the motivation for the interaction exists in preestablished sentiments and emotions that form a sense of identity and belonging with the community of origin. Yet, for some Mayan migrants, an increase of resources (legal status, higher income, etc.) did not lead to stronger linkages with families and communities in Guatemala. Some migrant men developed new social relations and families in the United States and consequently ended contact with their wives, children, and hometowns in Guatemala.

Phase 4: Developing into Guatemalan Americans, 1992–2003

In phase 4 of Guatemalan immigration in the United States, the estimated number of arriving legal and undocumented Guatemalan immigrants dropped to an annual mean of 25,039 from the estimated mean of 45,504 in phase 3. This 45 percent drop was due mainly to the thousands of IRCA applicants who had been processed into legal status and thus were counted as part of the number of "Guatemalans Admitted" in phase 3, which raised the total number of Guatemalan immigrants in that phase. In phase 4, the Guatemalan immigration ratio of undocumented migrants to legal immigrants returned to the previous pattern of phases 1 through 2, in which the number of estimated undocumented Guatemalan migrants was greater than the number of legal Guatemalan migrants.

Guatemalan immigrants and their U.S.-born children demonstrated a range of cultural characteristics in phase 4. Older members of the first immigrant generation maintained many of the Guatemalan cultural traits with which they had arrived in the country, but their children who grew up or were born in the United States demonstrated bicultural characteristics, such as conversing in Spanish and English (and in a Mayan language for some[29]). Moreover, in phase 4, many in the second immigrant generation of Guatemalans entered young adulthood with job aspirations higher than those held by their immigrant parents when they arrived in the country. Some Guatemalan American young men and women enrolled in universities and vocational institutes to pursue professional careers. In addition, in phase 4 the Guatemalan-origin population of foreign-born and U.S.-born individuals participated in more mainstream organizations (educational, religious, immigrant rights, etc.) than they had done previously. These developments represented a significant degree of social incorporation into U.S. society, especially for the second generation.

The spread of Guatemalan communities across the United States and the growing numbers of Guatemalan immigrants who became U.S. citizens demonstrated the increasing incorporation of these newcomers into U.S. society in phase 4. By the year 2000, the 50 largest population concentrations of Guatemalans were spread across 23 states, and the 100 largest concentrations were spread across 39 states (Spatial Structures in the Social Sciences 2005). The largest concentration consisted of the 181,419 Guatemalans in the Los Angeles–Long Beach area, and the 100th largest concentration consisted of 452 Guatemalans in the small town of Salem, Oregon (Spatial Structures in the Social Sciences 2005). Spurred by the number who legalized under IRCA, annual naturalizations into U.S. citizen status among Guatemalan immigrants rose from 1,086 in 1992 to 13,383 in 1996 and then dropped to 4,551 by the end of phase 4 in 2003 (U.S. INS 1997, Table 47; U.S. DHS 2006, Table 21). Among Central American migrants, only Salvadorans had a higher naturalization volume, with 8,719 naturalizing in 2003 (U.S. DHS 2006, Table 21).

Guatemala in Transition

Several social changes characterized the Guatemalan context in phase 4. These included the slow transition from a state of war to peace negotiations (1991-1996), the return of some communities in exile, and the growing dependence of some areas on remittances for household sustenance. These social processes and others combined to give Guatemala a different face—but no less dynamic or contradictory—from the one it had during the long period of widespread political conflict and violence.

Guatemalan social change in phase 4 transpired across conditions of very high levels of poverty. The poverty rate stayed above 60 percent of the total population during phase 4 and close to 70 percent among the large proportion of the population living in rural areas (ECLAC 2009, Table 1.6.1). Although the nonindigenous population had a poverty rate of 41 percent in 2000, the indigenous population had a poverty rate of 76 percent (World Bank 2004, Table 2.2). The open unemployment rate remained low to moderate during phase 4, with 3.9 percent of the labor force unemployed in 1995 and 5.2 percent in 2003 (ECLAC 2006, Table 1.2.17; 2010, Table 1.2.17). However, these official unemployment rates concealed much larger percentages of workers in greatly limited conditions of employment and subemployment, such as peasants and workers in the informal sector in the cities (World Bank 2004).

Income distribution in Guatemala remained highly skewed in phase 4, reflecting severe conditions of social inequality. In 1989, the top 10 percent of households received almost half (47 percent) of the national income distribution, and the top 20 percent of households received almost two-thirds (63 percent), while the bottom 60 percent of households received only 19 percent (World Bank 2011a). By 2002, as phase 4 was drawing to an end, income distribution increased only slightly: the share of income for the bottom 60 percent of the Guatemalan households increased to only 21 percent (World Bank 2011a). In a context in which a large proportion of the population lived on less than U.S. $2 per day (which was more than half of the population in 1997), the mortality rate of young children (a key indicator of inferior socioeconomic conditions) declined but still remained high during the span of phase 4. The mortality rate (deaths per 1,000 births) for children under 5 years went from 73 in 1992 to 34 in 2003 (U.S. Census Bureau 2011b).[30]

The exploration for negotiated avenues to end the thirty-six-year civil war resulted in the signing of peace accords between the Guatemalan government and the URNG at the end of 1996. At times the movement to peace was stalled and unpredictable, but when the Guatemalan parties accepted a central role for United Nations mediation in 1994, the avenue to peace acquired additional hope. The tenuous nature of the Peace Accords signed in December 1996 was revealed two years later when a May 1999 referendum to institutionalize certain measures of the Peace Accords in reforms to the Constitution was defeated—although only 18 percent of voters participated (Jonas 2000b).

Peace was also the logical development from the larger perspective of interglobal politics with the end of the Cold War. An apology made by U.S. President Bill Clinton in Guatemala in 1999 appeared to mark the end of this era. Clinton acknowledged that U.S. support for Guatemalan military and intelligence groups that conducted "violent and widespread repression . . . was wrong" (see quote in Jonas 2000b, 128).

The return to Guatemala of some rural communities that had fled to southern Mexico during the counterinsurgency operations and of other individuals who had fled abroad represented only a tiny fraction of the Guatemalan population (U.S. GAO 1984; Hagan 1987; Nolin Hanlon and Lovell 2000). But in the specific rural areas where they attempted to return, the returnees represented a significant presence. Their movement back to Guatemala had commenced with a trickle in the mid-1980s, but it was during phase 4 of U.S. Guatemalan immigration that the largest numbers of returnees entered in the country through a negotiated collective return. By 1999, the documented number of individual and collective returnees reached almost 43,000 (Nolin Hanlon and Lovell 2000). The collective return of communities was controversial and violent at times. Guatemalan military leaders and other groups viewed them with suspicion (as subversives or supporters of subversives), and violence sometimes erupted when the returnees attempted to resettle on lands they possessed but were taken over by other groups in their absence, or to settle in new areas in the countryside (Taylor 2000). The internal return to their areas of origin by "Communities of Population in Resistance," which had migrated far into mountain regions within Guatemala outside the reach of the army, added to the controversies of return and resettlement.[31]

Anti-Immigrant Sentiments in the United States

The U.S. context in phase 4 of Guatemalan immigration included a rising concern over what many perceived to be an uncontrolled wave of immigration, particularly of undocumented migrants. In the decade of the 1990s, more immigrants were admitted into the United States from throughout the world than in any previous decade in the history of the country. The 9.8 million legal immigrants admitted in the 1990s were 1.6 million greater in number than the previous all-time high of 8.2 million immigrants admitted in 1900–1909 (U.S. DHS 2011a, Table 1). With the estimated 4.6 million undocumented immigrants who also arrived in the 1990s, the total volume of immigration was much greater for the decade than the number of legally admitted immigrants (U.S. DHS 2011b, Table 1). Across the country, a host of organizations and special interests advocating immigration restrictions gained a greater voice in the context of continuing large-scale immigration. These were joined by other nativist organizations and movements with powerful media connections, such as English Only and English First, which acted to limit the cultural influences of immigrant populations in mainstream institutions (Perea 1997).

At the U.S.-Mexico border, the Border Patrol reacted to the undocumented influx with the implementation of high-profile enforcement campaigns not seen since the large-scale roundups of Operation Wetback in 1954.[32] In 1993, the Border Patrol in the El Paso area implemented Operation Blockade (diplomatically renamed Operation Hold the Line). Operation Gatekeeper followed in the San Diego area in 1994, Operation Rio Grande in the lower Texas border area in 1997, and Operation Safeguard in the Arizona border area in 1999.

Receiving the largest number of immigrants, California became the most intense setting of agitation for immigration restriction and border control. The reelection campaign in 1994 of Governor Pete Wilson in California brought the restrictionist movements into focus, as his reelection campaign concentrated on the issue of undocumented immigration. Wilson ran nightly television campaign advertisements showing migrants climbing over border fences to illegally enter the United States, as a voice overlay in the advertisement stated, "They keep coming." Wilson proposed to curtail immigrant impacts in the state, especially the impacts of undocumented immigrants, and his administration filed a legal claim against the federal government for the reimbursement of $10 billion, which Wilson claimed was the cost to California for the consequences of ineffective U.S. border control (Rodriguez 1997).

In November 1994, California voters also voted on a highly controversial state referendum, Proposition 187, which in many ways was designed to severely restrict the lives of undocumented migrants in the state. Fifty-nine percent of voters passed Proposition 187 (Chavez 1997), but federal judicial review later cancelled its measures as unconstitutional, ruling that it infringed on legislative powers that were reserved for the federal government. Proposition 187, however, sent a message to Washington, and only two years later its restrictive spirit was reflected in the enactment of a new immigration law, the Illegal Immigration Reform and Immigrant Responsibility Act (IIRIRA), which increased the resources for immigration enforcement and significantly curtailed immigrant rights.

Although many Guatemalan immigrants found more security by phase 4 in terms of having obtained secure employment, stable households, and especially legal immigrant status or citizenship, other Guatemalan migrants became more vulnerable to insecurity as the U.S. government toughened immigration enforcement through the enactment of IIRIRA in 1996.[33] IIRIRA facilitated the deportation of noncitizen immigrants and provided measures to ban deported migrants from reentering the country for several years or permanently.[34]

For Guatemalan immigrants who had not naturalized, being deported after the enactment of IIRIRA could mean permanent separation from their families and homes in the United States. Deportation also meant the termination of U.S. employment, which for many Guatemalan families in the United States and Guatemala was the means to have a relatively middle-income lifestyle. IIRIRA thus introduced a new dimension of risk and potential hardship for many Guatemalans and other immigrants who had not become U.S. citizens.

The number of Guatemalan migrants removed from the United States after the enactment of IIRIRA in 1996 rose sharply during phase 4 of Guatemalan immigration. In 1996, 2,106 Guatemalan migrants were formally deported, but by the end of phase 4 in 2003 the number more than tripled, reaching 6,848 (U.S. DHS 2003, Table 65; 2006, Table 41). Guatemalans had the second highest number of deportations among Central American migrants in 2003, with Hondurans in first place with 7,884 deportations (U.S. DHS 2006, Table 41).

Immigrating into the South

Many of the Guatemalan migrants who arrived in the United States during phase 4 settled in communities established by earlier Guatemalan migrants. This was especially true of the many migrants who migrated through social networks that connected their communities of origin in Guatemala to Guatemalan migrant settlements in the United States. But invariably, migrants eventually branched out to new settlement sites, and for Guatemalan migrants in phase 4, this brought a new settlement experience to the South.

Guatemalan and other Latino immigrants had trickled into the South in earlier years, but in phase 4 it became a sustained migration (e.g., see Zúñiga and Hernández-León 2005; Odem and Lacy 2009).

A case of this new settlement experience involved the settlement of Guatemalan migrants in Morganton, North Carolina, where Guatemalan migrants were recruited to work in a poultry plant. According to Leon Fink (2003), in the 1990s Guatemalan workers in the poultry plant swelled into the hundreds, alongside other Latino immigrant workers. The Guatemalans were primarily Maya who from 1989 to 1994 arrived in Morganton from other U.S. areas, but by 1995 they were more likely to arrive directly from Guatemala. Numbering 1,065 migrants by the 2000 census, the Guatemalan immigrants contributed to the Latinization of the Morganton area (Fink 2003). A local Catholic Church became a major agent of socialization for the Guatemalans and a means for their cultural participation, such as through the formation of Mayan choir groups and the arrival of a marimba at the church in 1998.

Some of the Guatemalan and other migrants protested against poor and unsafe working conditions in the poultry plant, indicating that the Latino migrant work forces in the region brought new labor struggles. Guatemalan and other migrant workers in the poultry plant reacted to poor and unsafe working conditions with a walkout in 1991, a work stoppage in 1993, and a strike and election of a union in 1995. The Guatemalans in Morganton, however, were not of one mind concerning the need to establish a union. According to Fink (2003), the support the Guatemalans gave to organizing a union generally varied according to hometown origins.

The Guatemalan settlement in Morganton demonstrates the relatively independent nature of new settlement experiences. New immigrants find familiar social and cultural resources when they migrate to established immigrant areas, but they have to create a settlement infrastructure (e.g., social networks and cultural institutions) almost from scratch when they migrate to areas with little or no previous immigration. The Guatemalans in Morganton faced many of the same challenges that their compatriots faced in the initial phases 1 and 2 of Guatemalan immigration. This was particularly true because of the undocumented status of many of the new Guatemalan immigrants. Newcomers who arrive with refugee visas from countries such as Vietnam, by comparison, can participate in national government programs for resettlement, which can homogenize the settlement experience across the country. In contrast, for undocumented new immigrants, each new settlement experience has to be negotiated with original social strategies to meet the challenges of the specific settings.

In other contexts, however, undocumented Guatemalan migrants derived an advantage from the consolidation of the migration region in phase 4. This provided some forms of support on the migration north. The support came from religious-based centers and human-rights workers that provided temporary food and shelter for migrants, smuggling networks that transported migrants for profit, and common people who offered water and meals to migrants who passed through their neighborhoods (García 2006; Menjívar 2000; Hagan 2008). Although often tenuous and limited, these forms of support provided temporary relief from the hardships of undocumented migration for thousands of migrants annually. The support was also important for migrants at the Mexico-Guatemala border who had been deported by Mexican authorities or attacked and injured by bandits, gangs, or other assailants (see Chapter 3).

Mexican immigration officials deported many Guatemalans during phase 4 as the Mexican government accelerated the number of deportations started at the end of phase 3 in the early 1990s. In 2001, Mexico implemented Plan Sur to continue its campaign to interdict and deport undocumented migrants (mainly Central Americans), with planning and financial assistance from the United States. Some observers viewed the intensified Mexican immigration enforcement at the Mexico-Guatemalan border as an attempt of the United States to move the U.S. border to southern Mexico (Flynn 2002).

By the end of phase 4 in 2003, Mexican officials conducted 178,519 deportations during the year, with Guatemalans representing 47 percent, Hondurans 34 percent, and Salvadorans 16 percent (Instituto Nacional de Migración 2003, Table 3.7). Moreover, deportations from Mexico in the latter part of phase 4 became more closely linked to regional programs of U.S.-related security and immigration control (Flynn 2002). Government officials in Mexico participated in Operation Disrupt, which the U.S. government coordinated in the Western Hemisphere to combat migrant smuggling as part of a larger U.S. enforcement program named Global Reach (Greene 2001).

Phase 5: Inclusion and Exclusion, 2004–Present

In the absence of available 2012 DHS data on deportable Guatemalans located, we project that phase 5 has continued into 2012.[35] We have confidence in this projection based on the facts that Guatemalan legal immigration changed only slightly from 2011 to 2012, dropping by 7 percent, and that the total count of migrants apprehended at the southwestern border for unauthorized entry in the same time period increased by only 9 percent (U.S. DHS 2012a, Table 3; 2013).

During 2004–2011 of phase 5, the estimated total Guatemalan undocumented and legal immigration in the United States reached a mean annual figure of 56,737, which represents a 127 percent increase from the annual mean of 25,039 in phase 4. The increase involved both men and women migrants, as well as unaccompanied children (Jonas 2013). Unaccompanied children had been part of the Guatemalan migrant stream since the 1980s (Urrutia-Rojas and Rodriguez 1997), but the numbers of these young migrants increased significantly in phase 5, partly because of rising economic hardships and insecurity in Guatemala (PNUD 2012).

Significant changes in border enforcement occurred in phase 5, however, that could affect the mean annual Guatemalan immigration estimate for 2004–2011. The changes included the construction of steel barriers at popular crossing points on the U.S.-Mexico border to block undocumented migration, and an increase in the size of the Border Patrol force. During phase 5, the construction of steel barriers at the border increased from 120 miles to about 650 miles, and the number of Border Patrol agents at the southwestern border increased from about 10,000 to about 18,500 by 2012 (U.S. GAO 2013; U.S. DHS 2013).

If the 85 percent increase in border enforcement personnel subsequently increased the proportion of undocumented migrants who were apprehended, then the 2:1 "got away" ratio we use to calculate the estimates of undocumented flow in Table 2.1 can produce overestimations of the annual immigration flow in phase 5. But even if the additional numbers of Border Patrol agents lowered the got-away ratio to 1:1, the estimated annual Guatemalan undocumented and legal immigration for phase 5 of 36,196 still would be 45 percent greater than the mean figure of phase 4.[36]

To be sure, worsening conditions in the U.S. economy that resulted in a major recession starting in late 2007 were seen as affecting immigration in the time period of phase 5, especially for undocumented migrants, who are the most vulnerable workers in the economy. Mexicans account for the large majority of "deportable" migrants apprehended at the southwestern border, and the apprehension of Mexicans declined by 77 percent, from 1,142,807 apprehensions in 2004 to 262,341 in 2012 (U.S. DHS 2013). For some analysts (e.g., Wilson and Singer 2009), the sharp drop in border apprehensions of Mexicans represented an actual decline in undocumented immigration, partly because of rising U.S. unemployment (Kochhar 2009). However, border apprehensions of Guatemalans have not followed a decline similar to the Mexican case. In contrast to the Mexican case, apprehensions of Guatemalans at the southwestern border actually rose by 40 percent from 2004 to 2011, according to the most recent DHS data (see Table 2.1).

Postwar Problems in Guatemala

Several contextual developments could be observed in the phase 5 period of Guatemalan immigration. In Guatemala, the national scene was greatly changed from the beginning of large-scale migration to the United States in the late 1970s and early 1980s. Even as the massive political violence that had largely motivated migration prior to the mid-1990s ended, economic problems and environmental disasters spurred emigration from Guatemala. Already in the postwar years of phase 4, beginning in 1997, and increasingly in phase 5, it became clear that the end of the war did not bring "peace" but rather a series of postwar problems to the country.

By no means the poorest country in Central America in macroeconomic terms, postwar Guatemala has remained among the countries with the highest levels of socioeconomic inequality in the world. Moreover, its level of human development is the lowest in the entire Latin American region. Worldwide, Guatemala ranks 131st of 187 countries, according to the United Nations' 2012 Human Development Index. Rural poverty and unemployment have been particularly rampant; additionally, some analysts (e.g. Reding 2002) have included "peasants involved in land disputes and those who assist them" as being among the politically "at-risk" groupings." Many key provisions of the Peace Accords were not implemented, particularly those that could have modernized the economy and improved the socioeconomic situation of the majority of Guatemalans. The economic elites continued to resist paying taxes that could have financed social programs or prioritized the creation of decent jobs. One scholar (Pérez Saínz 2001) has described the employment situation as "exclusion" from the labor market, combined with greater informalization of labor; 75 percent of the economically active population worked in the informal sector, according to the government's Instituto Nacional Estadística (cited in *Inforpress Centroamericana*, January 27, 2006).

These conditions were exacerbated rather than alleviated by the region-wide Central American Free Trade Agreement (CAFTA) that took effect for Guatemala in 2006, institutionalizing neoliberal economic policies. Additionally, Guatemala suffered a variety of environmental disasters in phase 5. Examples of these disasters include the destructive effects of the massive 2005 Hurricane Stan in western Guatemala and at the Guatemala-Mexico border, a calamitous drought in eastern Guatemala during some years of the first decade of the twenty-first century, and tropical storm Agatha and unprecedented mudslides in 2010, which caused a large number of deaths and widespread destruction in the country. The drought caused a major crisis of hunger and nutritional precariousness (especially among children)—a situation described by some as *hambruna* (famine) and by others as "starvation" (*Financial Times*, June 11, 2002).

Within the structural context of socioeconomic crisis, common crime (which correlates closely with inequality) increased significantly in Guatemala, and citizen security became a major concern. A significant rise in violence originated from organized crime, drug trafficking rings, and even with complicity from state institutions. Meanwhile, in the urban *barrios*, social violence became associated with the growth of gangs, some of which recruited deportees from the United States who did not find access to jobs in Guatemala. The crimes committed by gangs included attempts to extort money from business owners and families receiving remittances from migrant members in the United States.

Among the most dramatic indicators of social violence in Guatemala in phase 5 has been a wave of femicide, primarily in urban areas. These are cases in which women are targeted for torture and death, seemingly at random without any single logic or profile. Between 2000 and 2010, more than 5,000 women were assassinated, often after being raped, tortured, and their bodies mutilated, with the numbers of reported cases on the increase and not counting unreported cases (Torres and Carey 2010). An equally notable aspect of femicide has been the indifference of governmental officials and institutions, and a refusal or inability to investigate specific cases. The above structural features of the postwar Guatemalan landscape have persisted under all governments, whether their orientation was conservative, extreme right wing, or social democratic.

Other changes in the Guatemalan context have stemmed from the accumulated migration stream itself, that is, the development of sustained, large-scale migration to the United States. A change associated with the migration has been the large volume of remittances that the migrants sent to Guatemala. By 2008, Guatemalan migrants in the United States accounted for most of the $4.3 billion in remittances sent to Guatemala (about 11 percent of the Guatemalan GDP), but, as a recession affected the U.S. economy and many immigrants lost their jobs or suffered reduced work hours, this amount declined by 9 percent in 2009 (Inter-American Development Bank 2010). This decline produced a major disadvantage for many Guatemalan families for whom remittances had become a key resource for maintaining daily household consumption. By 2011, remittances had recovered to $4.4 billion (Inter-American Development Bank 2012).

Guatemalan workers also continued migrating to Mexico to look for work in phase 5, especially to the southern region of the country, for which some received special Mexican visas to work (Alba and Castillo 2012). Survey research found that about half of the Guatemalans deported from Mexico for not having visas in 2009 stated that they had planned to remain in Mexico, while only 2 percent of Hondurans and 18 percent of Salvadorans stated that Mexico was their final destination (Alba and Castillo 2012).

Two migration-related developments brought increased pressures to Guatemalan communities in phase 5. One development concerned the increasing numbers of deportations from the United States to Guatemala, and to Central America in general. Although deportations began rising rapidly after the enactment of IIRIRA in 1996, they increased even further after the formation of ICE in 2003, since this bureau focused much of its work in removing migrants from the country. The number of migrants deported to Guatemala increased by 212 percent during phase 5, going from 9,729 in 2004 to 30,313 in 2011 (U.S. DHS 2012a, Table 41). Most deported migrants arrived in Guatemala facing severe economic prospects.

The second migration-related development that brought pressures to Guatemalan communities concerned the actions of gangs that preyed on migrant families in Guatemala or on Guatemalan migrants during their journey north. In Guatemala, gangs began using threats and intimidation to extort money from families believed to be receiving remittances from the United States. In addition, in the migration routes through Mexico, criminal organizations and drug cartels kidnapped and held for ransom groups of Central American and other migrants journeying north, or killed them at transit points (Padgett 2011). Migrant women also remained vulnerable to rape or being kidnapped and forced into sexual work by gangs and criminal organizations. The risk of sexual assault remained so great throughout the phases of Guatemalan migration that a migrant shelter at the Mexico-Guatemala border town of Tapachula provided information on sexual attacks and contraception for women migrating northward.[37]

Changing Conditions in the United States

Developments in the United States in phase 5 included the continuing social incorporation of Guatemalans. Some Guatemalan families that had arrived in the early phases of Guatemalan immigration had third-generation members by the first decade of the twenty-first century. These were the U.S.-born grandchildren of Guatemalan migrants who arrived in the late 1970s or early 1980s. Although the Guatemalan-origin population had not achieved a critical mass to create a major visibility in the country, their numbers were large enough to mark a significant presence within the Central American migrant population, making them the second most prominent Central American migrant group after the more visible Salvadorans. Whereas Guatemalans were 2 percent of the foreign-born population in 2011, they were 5 percent of the estimated 11.5 million undocumented migrant population (U.S. Census Bureau 2012; U.S. DHS 2012b, table 3)

In some events, nonetheless, Guatemalans could create an impressive presence. One example was the presence of Guatemalan fans at a World Cup qualifier played by the U.S. and Guatemalan national teams in Birmingham, Alabama, in 2005. Some observers speculated that the U.S. team picked Birmingham for the qualifying site because it would produce a U.S. fan advantage ("How many Guatemalans can there be in Alabama?"); however, the media pointed out with surprise after the game that perhaps more than half of the 30,000 fans who attended were Guatemalans (*The Daily Utah Chronicle*, June 6, 2005).[38] Since the 2005 American Community Survey of the U.S. Census reported only 7,958 Guatemalan immigrants living in Alabama, the Guatemalan fans that attended the qualifier must have included thousands who traveled from other areas of the country and possibly some who arrived from Guatemala.

As Guatemalans and other new immigrants from Latin America continued to establish their lives and families in the United States in the first decade of the twenty-first century, the national policy focus began to return to immigration outright after being concerned primarily with immigration as a subcategory of national security and antiterrorist matters as a result of the terrorist attacks in New York City and Washington, D.C., on September 11, 2001. President George W. Bush's proposal in early 2004 for a temporary guest worker program and quasi "legalization"[39] of some of the undocumented migrants in the country sparked a heated national debate. The debate included proposals in Congress in 2005 to criminalize undocumented immigration and dramatically increase border enforcement. These proposals ignited an unprecedented series of massive demonstrations and marches by immigrants and their supporters across U.S. cities in the spring of 2006 to protest against the restrictive immigration bills being considered in Congress (see Chapter 3).

ICE also began increasing its enforcement in 2005 by working closer with state and local police forces in special operations.[40] These new initiatives included Operation Community Shield, implemented to apprehend and deport criminal immigrant gangs, and the Criminal Alien Program, through which federal and state prisons, and local jails, could share inmate information with ICE and permit ICE agents to interview inmates for possible deportation. Also, in late 2005, DHS launched the multibillion-dollar Secure Border Initiative (SBI) program to enhance protection at the U.S.-Mexico border and reduce undocumented immigration through new electronic detection technology and additional fencing, road, and lighting construction (U.S. GAO 2007).[41]

In 2008, ICE designed the Secure Communities initiative to create the most elaborate enforcement program ever devised to share information on immigrants that are arrested and booked (but not necessarily jailed) by federal, state, and local police departments. The purpose of Secure Communities technology has been to check the fingerprints of all arrested persons with the biometric databases of the FBI and DHS for information on previous violations and immigration status. Fingerprint matches with the DHS database automatically trigger an analysis request at an ICE support center for determination of the action to undertake. Initially implemented at the single site of Houston, Texas, in late 2008, by the summer of 2012 Secure Communities was operational in 97 percent of the 3,181 local jurisdictions in the United States (U.S. ICE 2012b).

The Great Postville Raid of 2008

On May 12, 2008, as helicopters circled overhead, ICE agents launched the largest single-site workplace raid until that time, rounding up and arresting 389 undocumented immigrant workers at the Agriprocessors kosher slaughterhouse and meat-packing plant in Postville, Iowa. Of the 389 arrested in this military-style dragnet, 293, or 75 percent, were Guatemalans (the rest Mexicans), giving the Guatemalans prolonged, high-profile, national exposure as a specific national-origin group. Many of the Guatemalans were Maya whose comprehension of Spanish (their second language) was faulty.

After their arrest, DHS buses took them in chains and shackles to the National Cattle Congress facility in nearby Waterloo, Iowa, which ICE had rented well ahead of time. This facility became a detention center, and its Electric Park Ballroom became a makeshift courtroom for expedited, "fast-track" processing of the hundreds of those arrested—in groups of ten, nine groups daily. Officials from ICE and other cooperating enforcement agencies pressured the arrested migrants to plead guilty to the felony of "aggravated identity theft" for their use of Social Security numbers not assigned to them. Pleading guilty would mean accepting a five-month detention (nearly the maximum sentence) in U.S. federal prisons, and subsequently being deported. If they refused to plead guilty, they would spend a minimum of two years in prison before being deported. Because they were being processed in groups, at an unprecedented speed and without adequate access to legal counsel (the lawyers for their "defense" were criminal rather than immigration lawyers), the immigrants had virtually no time to consider their options. Many did not even understand what a Social Security number was.

In the end, 270 of the original 389 arrestees were found to have used the Social Security numbers of real people, and these were primarily the un-lucky ones imprisoned. Most of the 270 convicted—232, or 86 percent, being Guatemalans—pleaded guilty in order to be deported as quickly as possible and reunited with family members back home. After being charged, more than 40 of the arrested migrants, mostly women, were released from prison for "humanitarian" reasons, mainly to care for their children. But the condi-tions of their release were far from humanitarian: they were not permitted to work, and they had to wear heavy ankle shackles with GPS devices that re-quired daily recharging while on their ankles. Ultimately, many were separated from family members.

There was another significant dimension of this case: Agriprocessors' mas-sive violation of U.S. labor laws, such as employing underage children and ex-posing workers to toxic chemicals and dangerous machinery. But when the time came (June 2010) for the trial of Agriprocessors' owner regarding more than 9,000 labor violations, he beat the charges because the jury simply did not believe the testimony of the Guatemalan immigrants, including the chil-dren who had worked there underage.

The Postville raid raised major debates about ICE workplace raid policies. The specific novelty of this raid was the en masse accusation of the several hundred arrestees with a *criminal* violation of the law, "aggravated identity theft," making their labor as undocumented workers using false Social Secu-rity numbers a felony in itself rather than an administrative or civil violation of the law. (Almost none of the arrestees had a prior criminal background.) From the perspective of ICE, the Postville operation was initially declared to be a major "success" (U.S. ICE Press Release, May 23, 2008). It also upped the company's compliance with quotas for deportation. Longer range, ICE intended to establish this raid as a precedent and model for future mass raids against immigrants using false Social Security numbers.

But it never became a precedent.[42] In subsequent 2008 workplace raids (e.g., Laurel, Mississippi), criminal charges were leveled only against workers who had actually committed crimes. And in May 2009, the Supreme Court ruled unanimously that the felony of "aggravated identity theft" cannot be applied to criminalize undocumented immigrants unless they "knowingly" use the Social Security number assigned to another actual person. Although it did not become a precedent, however, the Postville raid was emblematic of the excesses of U.S. "enforcement-only" immigration policies in phase 5, with its mass criminalization before deportation of undocumented workers.

From the viewpoint of the Guatemalan immigrants, Postville revealed migration's downsides in phase 5: the realities of family separations and cross-border family disruptions and damages. Many of the Postville migrants returned to their hometowns in Guatemala not as respected family members sending vital remittances, but humiliated and owing considerable sums of the money they had borrowed to get to the United States in the first place (Brosnan and Szymaszek, PBS *Frontline*, May 11, 2010).

Continuing Policy Stalemate and De Facto Enforcement-Only

By the end of 2008, the election of President Obama and of Democrats to majorities in both houses of Congress raised hopes among many migrants and supporters that the stalemate on a new immigration policy in Congress would finally be overcome in favor of new legislation that would support the growing immigrant population, which included an estimated 11.5 million undocumented migrants (Passel and Cohn 2008). But one year later, by the end of 2009, there was almost no sign from the Obama administration or Congress of preparations to move forward on new immigration legislation to alleviate the pressures and restrictions felt by the immigrant population, especially the millions of undocumented migrants, in the country.

An unrelenting economic recession, a widening military involvement in Afghanistan, and a major industrial oil spill in the Gulf of Mexico were among the problems that deterred the Obama administration and Congress from a sustained discussion regarding immigration policy. Also, the topic of immigration had become a hot button, and the Obama White House avoided addressing immigration issues directly. Nonetheless, within the executive bureaucracy of the federal government, the administration acted to replace large-scale workplace raids, as occurred in Postville, with "silent raids" in which ICE agents reviewed the personnel files of companies suspected of hiring undocumented workers, giving the companies the option to dismiss these workers and pay a fine in lieu of a raid (*New York Times*, July 9, 2010). Still, some immigrant advocates questioned why President Obama did not use his authority to stop deporting migrants who had not committed crimes.

At the state and local levels, however, pressures intensified for undocumented migrants and their families as state and local governments continued to enact measures to restrict undocumented immigrants and their employers. In spring 2010, the governor of Arizona signed into law a bill requiring immigrants to carry identification documents and giving police the power to question, arrest, and put in deportation proceedings immigrants considered to be in the country without authorization. Georgia and Alabama passed similar laws in 2011, and other states were expected to follow the restrictive actions of Arizona as well (*New York Times*, January 1, 2011).

The refusal of Congress to pass the Development, Relief, and Education for Alien Minors Act (the DREAM Act) in fall 2010 further demonstrated the hardening of U.S. government policy toward undocumented migrants, including many Guatemalans, during phase 5 of Guatemalan immigration. Supported by the Obama administration, the DREAM Act was a proposal to offer undocumented migrants who were brought to the United States on an unauthorized basis as minors a road to legal status if they graduated from a U.S. high school and met other residency and educational or military service requirements. The hardening of policies against immigrants, including noncitizen legal immigrants to some degree, represented a duality of U.S. immigration conditions during phase 5 of Guatemalan immigration. As the U.S. government granted a record number of permanent immigrant visas (more than 10 million green cards) in the period 2000–2009, it also deported record numbers of undocumented migrants and noncitizen legal immigrants, reaching 393,457 deportations in 2009, with a slight drop to 391,953 deportations by 2011 (U.S. DHS 2012a, Table 41).

In June 2012, President Obama signed an executive order instructing ICE to defer the deportation of migrants who had been undocumented since they were children. Titled the Deferred Action for Childhood Arrivals (DACA), the executive order deferred the deportation of undocumented migrants who met a set of requirements: had arrived before the age of 16 and lived in the United States for five years; had graduated from high school, had an equivalent degree, or had been honorably discharged from the U.S. military; and did not have a police record for significant offenses (U.S. DHS 2012c). From August to March 2013, 11,395 Guatemalan migrants received deferred status and work authorization under DACA (U.S. CIS 2013).

The reelection of President Obama in November 2012 with strong Latino voter support stimulated an interest in immigration reform legislation among some Republican members of Congress. Although some Republican leaders viewed legalization for the large undocumented immigrant population in the country as a means to gain Latino political support, the more conservative Republican congressional members felt that legalization would only add to the ranks of the Democrats. After negotiations during spring 2013, a bipartisan committee of senators arrived at a compromise bill that coupled legalization with a dramatic increase in border enforcement and visa tracking. If voted into law, the bill would provide legalization for undocumented immigrants who met stringent requirements, increase funding to complete a 700-mile fence at the U.S.-Mexico border, and double the Border Patrol force to 40,000 agents. Moreover, the bill would provide billions of additional dollars to place a large amount of high-tech equipment and drones to monitor illegal entrants at the U.S.-Mexico border (*New York Times*, June 21, 2013). Nonetheless, conservative Republicans in the House of Representatives stated that they would take to the end of 2013 or even longer to develop their own version of an immigration bill.

The Changing Pattern of Guatemalan Migration

This chapter has attempted to demonstrate that Guatemalan migration to the United States has not been a monolithic or linear process, but a movement of people characterized by changing phases of rising and falling numbers of authorized and undocumented migrants within a changing context of developments at the points of origin, transit, and destination that influence the migrant flow. We delineated five intervals of Guatemalan flows that developed after a prelude in the early 1970s, when no more than about 5,000 Guatemalan migrants were arriving annually in the United States. Guatemalan migrants, similarly to all migrants, have traversed across geographical terrain, but also across a temporal plane that has undergone changes across the migration region. For this reason, the phases of Guatemalan migration have represented new experiences for each new cohort of migrants. The Guatemala left behind by the migrants in phase 1 was different from the Guatemala that was left behind in phase 2, and very different from the Guatemala that was left behind in phase 5. The same principle applies to the United States encountered by the Guatemalan migrants who arrived in the different phases of their migration.

CHAPTER 3

Organizing for Migrant Rights

Introduction

In addition to the primary actors such as migrants and states in the migration region encompassing Guatemala, Mexico, and the United States, there is another layer of transregional social actors: organizations, coalitions, and networks of migrant rights advocates, operating both nationally and throughout the region. In contrast to the generally informal networks for migrant survival and individual mobility ("in-itself" goals), these networks composed of nongovernmental advocacy organizations (NGOs), community-based organizations (CBOs), and research centers with migrant rights advocacy agendas are more formal. They come together with the deliberate political goals of engaging with, making demands on, and having impact (*incidencia*) on state policies, as well as influencing or countering the strategies of other social actors throughout the region. Their rationale and goals at various intersection points and on many levels can be described as "for-itself" political organizing activity throughout the migration region (see Marx [1847] 1955)—strategies of resistance to state policies and struggles for the rights of the dispossessed and excluded, which could potentially contribute to long-range resocializations of the region (see concept in Harvey 2006).

An important point of reference for understanding advocacy networks as a middle stratum of transregional Guatemalan social actors is the internal armed conflict in Guatemala from the 1960s through the mid-1990s—and, for some purposes, the armed conflicts in El Salvador and Nicaragua during that era, all three of them ideologically polarized in Cold War terms. The entire migration region (Central America, Mexico, and the United States) was drawn into these conflicts and politicized by them, in part because the wars generated a large stream of political refugees. The middle stratum of

Guatemalan social actors identified as advocates for immigrant/refugee rights was marked by an unusually high level of politicization. It can also be seen as a political generation of Guatemalan activists/advocates, as they shared experiences and ideas from the most intense phase of Guatemala's civil war. During the war, their activities focused on the causes and consequences of the civil war in Guatemala. But in the postwar era of the late 1990s and subsequently, a number of activists from this political generation initiated advocacy activities for migrant rights in various sites of the region, including campaigns for legalization in the United States. They and their native-born allies in the United States and Mexico can be viewed as spatialized social actors or, in Soja's (1989, 173) conceptualization, "spatially conscious" actors, as their organizing in these multiple venues created transregional political advocacy networks for migrant rights.

Our research for this chapter and accompaniment of the organizing process began in 1994–1995. Given the paucity of in-depth published analyses of Guatemalan migrant rights networks and organizing, the experiences recounted and critically analyzed here are reconstructed primarily from many dozens of interviews and communications with key activists since the mid-1990s and with other players who interacted with them, from accompaniment/observation of meetings in multiple sites of the region, and from long-term collaboration with research institutions in Guatemala and Mexico. In addition to this field research, we draw on organizing documents, most of them unpublished, having been circulated by electronic mail, and sometimes on Internet sites. The analysis reflects the volatile, nonlinear process of Guatemalan advocates in the United States coming together and establishing ties with other U.S.-based migrant rights networks, with networks in Guatemala, and, less directly, elsewhere in the region. Hence, we locate their activities on a regional stage and argue that they have become significant social actors in both shaping and being shaped by the regional space.

This chapter is divided into two parts. Part I focuses on the evolution of Guatemalan immigrant rights organizing within the United States. Part II extends the focus to migrant rights organizing in Guatemala and at the regional level, and examines transregional organizing for migrant rights, primarily in Guatemala and Mexico. Conceptual sections will be interspersed throughout the chapter as relevant to frame the analysis of organizing activities.

PART I: MIGRANT RIGHTS ADVOCACY IN THE UNITED STATES

Conceptual Frameworks: Political Generations, Advocacy Networks

At the heart of this chapter is the political generation of late 1970s to early 1990s Guatemalans who became migrant advocates/activists. To simplify, we will refer to them as the "generation of the 1980s." The concept of "political generations," as opposed to intrafamily generations, has been discussed since the seminal essay by Karl Mannheim (1952) in reference to generations defined by sharing a particular common historical experience. This creates a shared consciousness of being a generation, and leads participants or members to become initially unified as political actors, although political differences can generate internal divisions. As applied to immigrants and refugees, political generations can be distinguished from family-based generations, which are analyzed in such works as Portes and Rumbaut (2001).[1]

Like their Salvadoran counterparts (Coutin 2000), Guatemalan activists who came to the United States beginning in the late 1970s brought experiences and ideas linked to the civil war in their home country.[2] This chapter examines their evolution primarily during the 1990s and early 2000s, as they turned from activities oriented toward solidarity with social justice/human rights movements in Guatemala to organizing for the rights of Guatemalans as immigrants in the United States, together with U.S. support organizations, and regionally. Hence, although we refer to a political generation whose shared experiences and consciousness came from an earlier period, the specific organizing activities of interest to us here began in the early 1990s and accelerated after the end of the war, in the late 1990s, and into the early 2000s.

Many Guatemalan migrants themselves during phases 1–3 (1977–1991) and the early years of phase 4, as described in Chapter 2, were refugees[3] from that same historical experience, as shown by the number of asylum petitions in the United States during the 1980s and 1990s. Most of the political activists came from a "middle stratum" of society in a dual sense: First, from a vertical perspective, many were from middle-class origins, hence arriving with or subsequently gaining a university education. Second, viewed horizontally, many came from a middle stratum between the state and (unorganized) grassroots communities; they constituted the stratum of the "organized sectors" of Guatemalan civil society. Like their Salvadoran counterparts, they included a significant number of students, professionals, and others who had to leave Guatemala because their social justice and human rights activities made them "enemies of the state"; some had ties to the leftist insurgent Unidad Revolucionaria Nacional Guatemalteca (URNG) or were accused by the army of having those ties. As an ironic result of this background, a number of them were among the relatively few Guatemalans who arrived as refugees or were granted asylum in the United States, which enabled them legally and financially to become activists.

In focusing on advocacy networks, we depart from the more common discussion of "networks" in the migration literature, which generally refers to informal contacts among migrants in the country of destination or between them and their sending communities for basic purposes of survival and individual/family upward mobility.[4] In advocacy networks, by contrast, the principal players are more self-consciously and formally organized to achieve specific goals, frequently by making demands on states. They are builders of "normative" political advocacy networks, broadly conceived as those that use general social/political principles or norms and accumulate/share knowledge (e.g., legal expertise), in order to impact state policies, to educate communities about their rights—in short, to transform broad social structures (Pisani et al. 2005; Keck and Sikkink 1998). As agents of social change, these activists are "carriers" of ideas of resisting political and socioeconomic exclusion.

U.S.-based Guatemalan activists from the 1980s political generation began building networks of local and national organizations for refugee and immigrant rights in the United States, somewhat tentatively during the early to mid-1990s, and more intensively during the late 1990s. Although it came together only toward the end of the 1990s, a principal network for our attention is the Coalición de Inmigrantes Guatemaltecos en EEUU (CONGUATE—Coalition of Guatemalan Immigrants Residing in the United States). CONGUATE was not the first network of Guatemalan immigrant rights activists in the United States, nor by any means the only or last such network; however, it was the main network consciously oriented toward immigrant rights advocacy during crucial early years, from 1999 through 2006. Since the late 1990s, the organizing efforts of CONGUATE—and by 2006, of new networks, organizations, and broader social movements to be mentioned below—focused largely on campaigns for legalization of thousands of Guatemalan immigrants who lived undocumented or in legal limbo in the United States, many for more than 20 years. These campaigns were crucial because, in addition to vastly improving the quality of migrants' lives in the United States, in the longer run, legalization would enable migrants to circulate freely to and from the home country, and to have a much greater impact on their communities of origin and on Guatemala nationally.

Sanctuary, ABC, and Atanasio Tzúl

Major Guatemalan migration to the United States accelerated in the mid-1980s—although, as seen in Chapter 2, internal and external migrations were increasing during the late 1970s and early 1980s. Along with Salvadorans, Guatemalans entering via the U.S.-Mexico border became more visible to the U.S. public largely because of the campaigns by the pro-asylum Sanctuary movement, which have been detailed elsewhere,[5] and simultaneously, the large political movement against U.S. intervention in Central America. Throughout the 1980s, Guatemalans and Salvadorans came to the United States fleeing the violence of the civil wars, or a combination of war and economic crisis in their home countries. Their applications for asylum in the United States were routinely turned down by the INS: from 1983 to 1990, only 2.6 percent of Salvadoran applications and 1.8 percent of Guatemalan applications were approved (U.S. Committee for Refugees [USCR] 1990, using INS data).

The bases for systematic U.S. government denial of the asylum petitions included several arguments. For one thing, U.S. officials argued, Mexico would be the country of first asylum or "safe haven" for bona fide Guatemalan refugees—although the evidence from Mexico was quite contradictory.[6] But the main argument was that the home governments in Guatemala and El Salvador were democratic U.S. allies, therefore incapable of "persecuting" anyone for political reasons. Hence, under the Reagan administration's anticommunist doctrine, these applicants were not political refugees but economic migrants, ineligible for political asylum. In fact, in addition to those seeking political asylum, others had come seeking jobs, or for a combination of both reasons (Hamilton and Chinchilla 1991). Many more than originally thought may have been economic migrants, because the entire phenomenon of labor migration by Salvadorans and Guatemalans was less visible until after the end of the wars, as pointed out by Mario Lungo, the insightful and prolific late Salvadoran scholar (e.g., Lungo 2004 and personal discussions). Nevertheless, the organizing efforts focused on the thousands of bona fide refugees fleeing death and human rights brutalities, and having a well-founded fear of persecution if deported back home.

The first major victory affecting both Guatemalan and Salvadoran asylum petitioners came in December 1990/January 1991 with the settlement of the *ABC v. Thornburgh* class action lawsuit (*American Baptist Churches v. Attorney General Richard Thornburgh*). This lawsuit had originally been filed in 1985 against then–Attorney General Edwin Meese on behalf of 150,000 Guatemalan and Salvadoran asylum applicants whose petitions had been arbitrarily denied by the Reagan administration. On December 19, 1990, the Justice Department under Thornburgh (for the G.W.H. Bush administration) agreed to settle the lawsuit (*New York Times*, December 20, 1990).[7] This was widely interpreted as an implicit acknowledgment that the INS had been systematically and unfairly discriminating against Salvadoran and Guatemalan asylum seekers, primarily for reasons related to the Reagan administration's foreign policies in Central America.

The ABC settlement entitled some 250,000 Guatemalan and Salvadoran asylum applications, both previous and new (Gzesh 2006), to be considered or reconsidered on a case-by-case basis. For the first time, flyers and posters could be seen throughout neighborhoods with concentrations of Central Americans, urging them—in the case of Guatemalans, those who had arrived by October 1, 1990—to register/apply for ABC status by the deadline of December 31, 1991, or in some cases, September 30, 1991. Given the limited resources in the INS for immigrant services, in contrast with enforcement, these cases only began to be heard in the very late 1990s and to be finally resolved mostly in the early 2000s. During the many years that the ABC applicants remained in limbo, they were not legalized, but in the meantime, they were not deportable unless they had committed a crime, and they were eligible for work permits until the final disposition of their case. In addition, during these 15-plus years, an undetermined number in the ABC category became legal permanent residents or citizens through marriage or employer actions on their behalf.

Guatemalans continued to seek asylum in large numbers into the mid-1990s. Even following the ABC decision, in fiscal year 1992, the number of asylum applications from Guatemalans was by far the highest for any country in the world—a striking 43,915 applications, 42 percent of the total, as compared with 6,781 from El Salvador, the second-highest on the list (U.S. INS 1993, Table 30). For at least the next two subsequent years, INS data showed that Guatemalans still constituted a very high percentage of asylum applications.

Unlike Salvadorans, who had additionally benefited from 1990 legislation granting Temporary Protected Status (TPS—a temporary stay of deportation and a work permit), Guatemalans never received TPS. Following the ABC settlement in the early 1990s, Guatemalan organizers, previously less proactive than Salvadorans, formed the Red Atanasio Tzúl (Atanasio Tzúl Network) and mounted their first major national campaign to gain TPS for Guatemalans. The main organizations that initially formed the base of the network were in Chicago and Houston, but it subsequently spread to California as well as Florida and northeastern cities. In the fall of 1993, Guatemala's Nobel Peace laureate, Rigoberta Menchú, met with Clinton administration

Attorney General Janet Reno to press for TPS for Guatemalans. Reno answered in a February 1994 letter, turning down the appeal on the grounds that conditions in Guatemala did not warrant TPS—even though the civil war was not over and human rights violations were still rampant at the time. Even after the end of the war in December 1996, some organizers carried on the campaign for TPS, but by this time the Atanasio Tzúl network had lost momentum in many U.S. sites.

Postwar governments in Guatemala proved unable or unwilling to fulfill the commitments made in the Peace Accords, to prevent a deterioration of socioeconomic conditions for the majority of the population, or even to generate decent jobs in Guatemala (see Jonas 2000b, Chapter 7). Hence, the era following the war is best characterized as "postwar" rather than the comprehensive "peace" envisioned in the Accords. Also for this reason, even after the political violence subsided, the Guatemalan migrant flow continued, indeed increased (see Chapter 2), in the postwar era during the 1990s and into the early 2000s.[8] To put it in other terms: many Guatemalans became migrants in order to achieve individually and for their families what had not been achieved through decades of collective political action and revolutionary insurgencies in Guatemala.

Specifics of Guatemalan Organizing

Although they had much in common, the Guatemalan and Salvadoran migrant flows should not be conflated. While recognizing the similarity of political/structural context in the Salvadoran and Guatemalan cases, which often leads to their being lumped together, we also note the particularities of Guatemalans. The most significant difference was the ethnic/cultural diversity (indigenous vs. ladino) among the Guatemalans, which did not exist for Salvadorans.[9] For a number of reasons, this made organizing more difficult among Guatemalans—not least because many Mayan Guatemalans did not speak or fully understand Spanish, and virtually all resources for Latin American refugees and immigrants have been in Spanish. As will be seen below, this also created challenges for coalitional organizing. There were also other particular characteristics of Guatemalan political culture and experience—most notably the very intense internalized culture of fear and habits of clandestinity among Guatemalans, who had suffered decades of civil war and brutal repression.

In addition to these significant differences of ethnic diversity and political culture, there were slightly different time-frames in the experiences of the two groups. The Salvadoran civil war was shorter (1979–1991) than the Guatemalan (1960–1996), and the Salvadoran Peace Accords ending that war were signed in January 1992, five years before Guatemala's Peace Accords (December 1996). In addition, some Guatemalans, especially Maya fleeing the army's scorched-earth counterinsurgency campaign of 1981–1983, came to the United States only after spending some years in southern Mexico during the 1980s, either in or outside of refugee camps run by the United Nations High Commissioner for Refugees (UNHCR).[10]

In each case, the end of the civil war became a kind of "marker" because it made the migrations more visible and because it opened up space for new forms of organization during the course of the 1990s, with an increasing focus on migrant rights. Hence, the level of organizing among Guatemalans on immigrant rights issues lagged several years behind the Salvadorans'. Furthermore, the Salvadoran organization/network of Central American Resource Centers, CARECEN, was founded in 1980, with offices in multiple cities, and worked with the Sanctuary movement during the 1980s, when Guatemalans were barely beginning to get organized for immigrant rights. Salvadorans were generally more visible organizers and could even be seen as having received more options for regularization from the U.S. government, for example, in gaining TPS (García 2006, 112).

1990s Turning Points

Fast-forwarding to the mid- and late 1990s and turn of the century, we begin with a brief summary of the overall changes in the region that impacted Guatemalan U.S.-based organizing. Prior to the 1990s, the only advocacy regarding their lives as Guatemalans in the United States was specifically oriented toward refugee/asylum rights and ABC/TPS. During the late 1990s, existing organizations of Guatemalans and some U.S. support organizations began a transformation, focusing increasingly on conditions affecting the daily lives of settled Guatemalan immigrants and their communities in the United States.

A major factor necessitating such a shift during the 1990s was the rise of anti-immigrant, sometimes nativist, sentiment in many sectors of U.S. society: undocumented Latino immigrants were coming to be viewed as a "national security threat" and were socially constructed as "illegal aliens." At the official level, the post–Cold War redefinition of "national security" incorporated domestic political concerns and perceived threats—in Keely's (1995, 223) terms, "soft security issues," which also included "culture, social stability, environmental degradation, population growth." In the conception of another analyst (Zimmerman 1995, 90–91), security meant freedom not only from danger but also "from fear or anxiety" on the part of U.S.-born citizens. This much broader definition of security expanded the reasons to exclude and punish immigrants, blaming them for real problems (e.g., job loss, declining wages, social service cutbacks) caused overwhelmingly by other factors (see Chavez 2007). The redefinition of U.S. national security doctrine, as laid out in various documents (see Teitelbaum and Weiner 1995) included immigrant/refugee flows as a top priority threat, along with drug trafficking and terrorism. In short, the politics of economic insecurity was dominated by the discourse of "national security" in the 1990s, a full decade before September 11, 2001 (see Jonas 1999).

Building anti-immigrant sentiment was reflected in the overwhelming voter approval of Proposition 187 in California (1994), as seen in Chapter 2. Almost all of Proposition 187 was subsequently found to be unconstitutional on the grounds that immigration policy is the responsibility of federal, not state, government. Nevertheless, immigrants' concerns became vastly more urgent after the political message from California reached Washington two years later, initiating a sea change in U.S. immigration policy. In 1996, the Republican-dominated Congress passed, and Democratic President Clinton signed, a trio of draconian laws, some of whose provisions affected both the undocumented and Legal Permanent Residents (LPRs).

The Illegal Immigration Reform and Immigrant Responsibility Act (IIRIRA) stripped undocumented immigrants of many basic legal rights, including due process rights. It facilitated and stepped up deportation proceedings (now called "removal") by eliminating the right of appeal and judicial review; in some cases, decisions could be made arbitrarily by one INS agent. The measure's "court-stripping" provisions overhauled the entire infrastructure of immigration procedures. In addition, IIRIRA greatly expanded the categories of "aggravated felonies" that could serve as the basis for removal and made their application retroactive without limit. It also promoted local police involvement in immigration enforcement and in other ways increased resources for immigration enforcement in the interior of the country and in border areas.

Finally, IIRIRA compounded harsh provisions for immigrants in two other laws passed previously in 1996: the Welfare Reform Act (formally, Personal Responsibility and Work Opportunity Reconciliation Act, PRWORA) and the Antiterrorism and Effective Death Penalty Act (AEDPA).[11] Taken together, the three laws stripped LPRs as well as undocumented immigrants of the very limited entitlements that previously existed, and of most due process rights, including appeals procedures.

In 1997, the U.S. Congress enacted the Nicaraguan Adjustment and Central American Relief Act (NACARA). Seizing what had originally been intended as an initiative to ameliorate the effects of IIRIRA for Central Americans (Giovagnoli 2011), congressional Republicans (including Cuban American Representatives) turned it into a Cold War redux, subtitling the Act as "Relief to Victims of Communism." NACARA automatically legalized all Nicaraguans and Cubans who were in the United States by December 1995 (outright "amnesty") but denied that prize to Guatemalans, Salvadorans, Hondurans, and Haitians.[12] For Guatemalans and Salvadorans who had received ABC status in the early 1990s, NACARA was, after a major struggle, interpreted to provide some relief from the harsh new laws of 1996: their cases for suspension of deportation (now "cancellation of removal") would be processed under the less punitive pre-IIRIRA guidelines, with a "rebuttable presumption of extreme hardship"—requiring in addition a continuous presence of at least seven years in the United States, "good moral character," and no criminal record. In these ABC cases, the burden of proof would fall on the INS to show why the migrants should be deported (Silverman and Joaquin 2005). By contrast, IIRIRA's new standard put the burden of proof on other immigrants to demonstrate "exceptional and extremely unusual hardship." NACARA provided a form of relief for some 240,000 Guatemalans and Salvadorans in the ABC class (Giovagnoli 2011), but this was still a far cry from automatic legalization, and post-1990 arrivals without ABC status or ABC nuclear family members gained nothing at all.

The vastly disparate treatment for migrants of different national origins gave rise to an organized campaign from 1997 through the early 2000s for "NACARA parity," equal treatment for all Central Americans and for Haitians as the counterpart of Cubans—or if not equal treatment, equivalent standards. We will refer to it as "NACARA parity," which was the language used by advocates. Pressure both from the Salvadoran and Guatemalan immigrant communities in the United States and from the home governments gained White House support for fairer treatment but never achieved parity.[13]

From the late 1990s into mid-2001, with a labor shortage in the United States, there were some signs of ameliorating the excesses of 1996 and of a "political opening" for immigrants.[14] Whether any of the proposed measures to "Fix '96" would have prevailed is an open question, but after September 11, 2001, it became a moot point, as did the proposal for NACARA parity. In March 2003, several Congressmen reintroduced the latter proposal in modified form under the name "Central American Security Act" (CASA), but even in this bipartisan, security-enhanced form, which excluded Haitians, there was virtually no chance that it would be passed.

Meanwhile, since the late 1980s and early 1990s, the U.S. government had been engaging in efforts to prevent transmigrants from ever reaching the U.S.-Mexico border by providing training and funding for Mexican interdiction and deportation campaigns, particularly along the southern border with Guatemala, and by pressuring Mexico to cooperate. Although the Mexican government denied this collaboration, the U.S. INS and subsequently Congress openly allocated funding for that purpose. In response to inquiries from one senator, U.S. officials maintained that the funds were used for repatriation of economic migrants (including Asians, Africans, etc.) rather than refugees, specifically Central Americans.[15]

But Mexico was elusive about defining who was a "refugee" (Gzesh 1995, 37–38; Frelick 1991b) and overall, this remained a contested issue. Because Mexico was not a party to the U.N. Refugee Convention, Central Americans had no recognized "right" to apply for refugee status in Mexico. Although there was a Mexican law that provided for political asylum applications, Gzesh (1995 and personal communication) argued that the law was not applied and that, in the mid-1990s, Mexico was not a "safe third country" of first asylum or a safe haven for Guatemalans and other Central Americans. More generally, as seen in Chapter 2, Mexican deportations of transmigrants increased dramatically beginning in the early 1990s. The routes through Mexico to the United States also became far more treacherous for transmigrants, including Central Americans, as various predatory forces attacked them throughout the region.

Central America itself in the postwar years was hit by a series of devastating environmental disasters, beginning with Hurricane Mitch in the fall of 1998. In response, Central American immigrant community campaigns for special treatment intensified, as did organizing against deportations — especially after Hondurans and Nicaraguans, but not Guatemalans[16] or Salvadorans, were granted TPS because of Mitch.[17] In 2001, Salvadorans were granted new TPS relief after strong earthquakes in El Salvador. But when Guatemala was hit by major natural disasters in 2005 and again in 2010 and 2011, repeated requests for TPS were not approved.

Initial Conformation of CONGUATE

In the wake of the punitive as well as restrictionist regime[18] imposed by the 1996 laws and the inequities of NACARA (1997), Guatemalan immigrant rights advocates shifted from the previous emphasis on TPS and, in tandem with Salvadorans, engaged in an extended campaign for permanent legalization through NACARA parity. In addition, the end of the civil war in Guatemala opened up for the first time the possibility for some collaboration in the United States between community immigrant/refugee organizations and the local Consulates of the Guatemalan government, such as joint "Know your Rights" workshops in a number of cities. In fact, it can be argued that the Consulates, having been the targets of community hostility until 1997 in some (not all) cities, and now representing a home government increasingly dependent on remittances from Guatemalan workers in the United States, needed the community organizations more than vice versa. The year 1997 was a time of transition and explorations at the local level of the potential for and limits on future collaboration.

In January 1998, Guatemalan activists—some from previous TPS campaigns, but many of them newcomers to immigrant rights issues—organized their first national march for immigrant rights, with as many as 3,000 participants from around the United States, according to organizers, converging on Washington to lobby both Congress and the White House. In the late spring of 1998, Guatemalan immigrant organizations convened their first formal meeting in Chicago, to discuss the creation of a national network; attendees included representatives from a broad range of organizations stretching across ideological and ethnic boundaries. Among these were some Mayan organizations, such as CORN-Maya of Indiantown, Florida (see below), *fraternidades* (hometown associations) from Massachusetts and Los Angeles, and the refugee organizations Atanasio Tzúl/Guatemala Support Network of Houston and Atanasio Tzúl/Casa Guatemala of Chicago. Also participating were the Guatemalan American Chamber of Commerce (Chicago), Comité Guatemalteco Americano of Long Island, NY, Asociación Guatemalteca Americana (AGA) of Miami, Asociación de Guatemaltecos Unidos (AGU) in the San Francisco Bay Area, and the Guatemalan Unity Information Agency (GUIA) offices in Los Angeles and Washington. Unlike the other organizations, which had characteristics of NGOs or CBOs, GUIA was a fee-for-service organization to help Guatemalans process immigration papers. It had been founded in 1997 at the initiative of the Guatemalan Consul General in Los Angeles, with a branch also in Washington, D.C., and was widely believed to be funded by the Guatemalan government. Hence, GUIA represented a stark contrast to organizations of refugees, especially Mayan, from the war zones in Guatemala, and to organizers in major U.S. cities, some of whom were leftist activists.

In September 1998, many of these groups convened the first formal National Assembly of the network that came to be known as "GUATENET" (Congreso Nacional de Organizaciones Guatemaltecas en EEUU, National Congress of Guatemalan Organizations in the United States). Such a broad coalition was bound to have a short life, given that GUIA leaders in Washington and Los Angeles were distrusted by many activists from other backgrounds. These activists charged that the GUIA offices had been organized by the Guatemalan government as a counterweight to Atanasio Tzúl and other "leftist" refugee organizations, and that key GUIA leaders had military backgrounds and conservative political ties—and that, in any case, they treated grassroots organizers disrespectfully. In addition, there were significant divisions over objectives and strategic approaches, including the issue of "amnesty" (legalization) for undocumented immigrants. These discrepancies were beginning to emerge by the second National Assembly of GUATENET, held in Miami in April 1999.

In the end, GUATENET proved to be a false start, plagued increasingly during the summer of 1999 by political/ideological and class tensions, and by ethnic divisions between GUIA and grassroots organizations from around the country. At the third meeting of the national network, held in New York in October 1999, other member organizations accused a GUIA/Washington leader of undemocratic decision making. GUATENET as previously constituted was dissolved, and a new Coalición de Inmigrantes Guatemaltecos en EEUU (CONGUATE—Coalition of Guatemalan Immigrants Residing in the United States) was formed. The organizations listed as founders of CONGUATE included: Comité Guatemalteco Americano de Long Island, NY; Guatemalan American Chamber of Commerce (Chicago); Asociación Guatemalteca Americana (Miami); Asociación de Guatemaltecos Unidos, AGU (Oakland); Grupo Maya Qusamej Junam (San Francisco/Oakland); Grupo Folklórico Rabinal Achí (Oakland); Centro Cultural Guatemalteco (San Francisco); Organización Maya Quetzal (West Palm Beach); Agrupación Cívica de Gente de Guatemala (Brooklyn); Agrupación Tecún Umán (Queens); Grupo Guatemalteco de Delaware; and Orden de Franciscanos de Manhattan.

A Miami dentist who had come to the United States in the late 1970s, after having been persecuted for university student activities, was elected as general coordinator. CONGUATE adopted, as its self-description in its founding document of October 1999, circulated by e-mail:

> a multicultural, multiethnic, and multilingual coalition, which brings
> together leaders of Guatemalan organizations in the United States, repre-
> sentatives of diverse cultural, political, economic, commercial, educational
> and occupational sectors, involved in the national campaign for *permanent
> residence* for Guatemalan, Central American and Haitian migrants in the
> United States. . . .

> Guatemalan migration to the United States has been principally the result of the civil war in our country . . . The diaspora in the United States increased at the end of the 1970s and increased geometrically in the 1980s, coinciding with the most brutal period of the war, 1978–1983. . . . Legally, it has adopted the status of refugees, not illegal immigrants. . . .
>
> We seek the participation of every Guatemalan leader who is disposed to work for permanent residence of Guatemalans, which for the moment is the #1 mission of CONGUATE. (our translation)

From late 1999 through mid-2001, CONGUATE participated in several marches and extensive Washington lobbying activities for immigrant rights, specifically against the 1996 laws and for NACARA parity, together with counterpart networks from other Central American immigrant communities—mainly Salvadoran and, in the aftermath of Hurricane Mitch, Honduran. In addition to coalitional efforts for NACARA parity, CONGUATE participated in broad-based pro-legalization activities organized by Mexican American organizations, and by the AFL-CIO after its February 2000 call for amnesty for all undocumented workers.

Between convergences on Washington and other national activities, the constituent organizations of CONGUATE engaged in community educational and lobby activities. On a day-to-day basis, given the financial and other obstacles to meetings, national communications were maintained through e-mail and conference calls. Although no longer working with GUIA, CONGUATE remained broad enough to include a representative of the Chicago-based Guatemalan American Chamber of Commerce, alongside veterans of the refugee movement in the San Francisco Bay Area and New York, a leader of the Bay Area's Grupo Maya, and members of other refugee grassroots organizations. Several member organizations led high-profile relief activities in response to Hurricane Mitch (late 1998–early 1999), while at the same time pressuring the Guatemalan government to advocate with the U.S. government for immigrant rights. In addition, during 1999–2000 initial contacts began with the immigrant rights coalition in Guatemala, Mesa Nacional para las Migraciones en Guatemala (MENAMIG—National Forum for Migration in Guatemala), when migration slowly emerged as a postwar issue there.

In 2000 and 2001, the San Francisco Bay Area–based AGU (see Chapter 5) organized and hosted national CONGUATE meetings in California. In late May 2000, AGU organized the second National Assembly of CONGUATE in Los Angeles, with a primary goal of structuring the network and planning for participation in the NACARA parity campaign. The meeting attracted representatives of the Los Angeles–based Asociación de Fraternidades

Guatemaltecas and MayaVisión (see below), as well as a number of individuals who had lived in Los Angeles for several decades—a poet, a bookstore owner, and the organizer of the Huelga de Dolores festivities in Los Angeles (see Chapter 5). Nevertheless, CONGUATE had no major local affiliate organization specifically focusing on immigrant political rights in Los Angeles since GUIA/Los Angeles was no longer part of the network—a serious gap, given that a significant number of all Guatemalans in the United States lived in the Los Angeles area. The meeting was held in the offices of the Salvadoran organization CARECEN/Los Angeles. In addition to lending its facilities, which were the product of an impressive campaign that had raised $3 million to provide community services, CARECEN led sessions on the strategy and tactics of lobbying Congress. The mood was upbeat; in many ways, this meeting served as a mirror, allowing CONGUATE to see its own potential.

The following year, in March 2001, AGU hosted the national CONGUATE meeting in the historic facilities of San Francisco's Presidio, with participants coming from various regions of the country—e.g., Los Angeles, Stockton, San Jose, Miami, Chicago, Long Island, each having a sizeable concentration of Guatemalans. (Houston and Washington were not represented even though they too had significant Guatemalan populations.) By this time, the CONGUATE network was deemed important enough to attract not only the Guatemalan Consul in San Francisco but also the Guatemalan ambassador to the United States at the time—who was notably proactive on migrant rights—a reporter from *Prensa Libre*, an activist priest from Guatemala, a representative of MENAMIG, and a staff member from the San Francisco office of Congresswoman Nancy Pelosi. The participation of important actors representing the Guatemalan state, press, and civil society was a significant advance. This meeting was featured in *Prensa Libre*, raising the profile of migrant rights issues and of CONGUATE in Guatemala.

Mayan Networks and Community Organizations

In addition to CONGUATE and other legalization/political rights advocacy networks and organizations discussed in this chapter, there have been a number of community-based networks with a Mayan identification. Several were formed in the 1980s and spoke for established Guatemalan Mayan communities in the United States. Among them were the binational Liga Maya Internacional/USA, based in Vermont, with its counterpart in Guatemala; Florida's Organización de los Pueblos Maya en el Exilio, which issued a 1999 *Declaración Maya* in Florida; the U.S.-wide Consejo de Mayas en EEUU, consisting of *catequistas* or spiritual leaders, and Consejo de Organizaciones Mayas; the U.S./Canadian Consejo del Pueblo Maya de Guatemaltecos en el Exterior; and the Los Angeles–based MayaVisión network (Maya Various Interpreting Services and Indigenous Organizing Network), which provided translation services for asylum and immigration hearings to Mayan petitioners who spoke neither Spanish nor English.

Moreover, as seen in the cases in Chapter 2, local community organizations have served Mayan immigrant/refugee populations for numerous day-to-day social and cultural purposes, including hometown associations, cultural and religious festivals, radio stations, liaisons with local hospitals and police, soccer leagues, job referrals, and even links with labor unions; some also trained women leaders and addressed the needs of U.S.-born children. One longstanding organization since the 1980s, the Comité de Refugiados Maya (CORN-Maya) in southern Florida, has provided a variety of community services, including asylum and immigrant legal referral services (Burns 1993; Loucky and Moors 2000). At the other end of the country, in Los Angeles, have been the Integración de Indígenas Mayas (IXIM), founded in 1986 primarily for cultural purposes but also addressing immigration-related matters, and indigenous *fraternidades*, or hometown associations (Hamilton and Chinchilla 2001; Loucky 2000). Hence, although these Mayan groups and networks were organized around social and cultural issues and rights more than political campaigns for legalization, several have provided community immigration services.

The Mayan networks and local organizations have been quite diverse, and not necessarily of one mind on all issues (research interviews). They have also evolved over time. For example, some of the older Mayan organizations such as CORN-Maya in Florida faced the challenges of adjusting to and incorporating the concerns of ladino and non-Guatemalan immigrants arriving in their communities beginning in the 1990s (Camposeco 2000; Burns 2000).

Post-9/11 National Security Context

Following September 11, 2001, the national security–based, anti-immigrant regime established in the 1996 laws was hardened and consolidated with a new rationale, the "war against terror." The U.S. government also imposed the national security mentality on other governments throughout the region, directly choosing some of the counter-terrorism coordinators. Although the stripping away of immigrant rights, including due process rights, dated back to the three laws of 1996, the post-9/11 conjuncture extended and consolidated these limitations for immigrants, both legal and undocumented. The USA PATRIOT Act of 2001[19] allowed arbitrary roundups and deportations, indefinite detentions (including preventive detentions) of noncitizens—legal permanent residents as well as undocumented immigrants—with no recourse to legal counsel or court appeals. Under regulations issued by the Justice Department, a function taken over in 2003 by the Department of Homeland Security (DHS), these detentions and deportations could include immigration violations completely unrelated to terrorism as a justification (*Washington Post*, March 20, 2003).[20] By December 2005, national security and nativist views about immigrants were so widespread that the Republican-dominated House of Representatives passed H.R. 4437, a bill designed to criminalize undocumented immigrants by converting their mere presence in the United States into an "aggravated felony."[21] The bill died in the Senate but sparked massive immigrant grassroots mobilizations in the spring of 2006.

Along with policies of excluding immigrants at the border, the major on-the-ground enforcement activities were carried out by the Immigration and Customs Enforcement (ICE) bureau of DHS. ICE was mandated to implement IIRIRA through raids at workplaces and in communities nationwide—in immigrants' homes, health-care facilities, schools, community gathering places such as shopping centers, restaurants, bars, and dance clubs, and transportation sites such as bus stops and on buses. Within ICE, the Office of Detention and Removal (DRO) developed a strategic plan called "Endgame" in August 2003 to accelerate the pace of deportations, with the goal of removing all deportable migrants by 2012 (U.S. ICE 2003). The steady intensification of this mission amounted to what had been previously feared but only now began to be implemented: a systematic drive for massive, forced repatriations of undocumented immigrants.

In addition, dozens of cities and communities throughout the country passed local ordinances designed to punish undocumented immigrants, as well as landlords and employers who rented to them or gave them work. Many of the immigrants deported were people who had lived in the United States since the 1980s. Meanwhile, in the "enforcement-only" environment, new legislation for regularization ("earned legalization") became much less feasible. Finally, new background check requirements greatly slowed down all immigrant status adjustment processing and raised the fees for all services by U.S. Citizenship and Immigrant Services (USCIS), also a bureau within DHS.

As a result of these programs, the years after 2005 saw increasing workplace raids, or *redadas*, by ICE throughout the United States; in some of these, as seen in the Postville case in Chapter 2, many of the workers were Guatemalans. Furthermore, unlike Central Americans from Honduras, Nicaragua, and El Salvador, undocumented Guatemalans were not covered by TPS, making them far more vulnerable than they would have been with TPS—the exception being those with access to ABC/NACARA protection from deportation.

In addition, Guatemalans, and Central American migrants in general, were affected by increased collaboration by the Mexican government with the United States in deterring, detaining, and deporting transmigrants. Although this collaboration predated 9/11 by more than a decade, the Mexican government increasingly militarized southern border operations to prevent entry and increase deportations of transmigrants (Ruíz 2006; Ogren 2007). During the three-year span of 2001–2003, Mexico carried out nearly 200,000 deportations (*devoluciones*, literally deportation events) involving Guatemalans, according to official figures from the Mexican government's Instituto Nacional de Migración (INM). For 2004, 2005, and 2006, Mexico carried out respectively 93,667, 99,315, and 84,657 deportations of Guatemalans; for all three years, Guatemalans represented close to 45 percent of all such deportations from Mexico (INM 2011, Table 3.7).

Despite all the above, during this same time period beginning in 1999 and into the early 2000s, the U.S. agency dealing with backlogged asylum cases (initially INS, subsequently USCIS of the DHS) gave high priority to processing the longstanding backlog of ABC/NACARA Guatemalans and Salvadorans. Furthermore, these cases were approved at a surprisingly high rate, well over 90 percent of those deemed eligible—at least for the relatively small number, around 66,000, in the ABC category who had actually registered for NACARA after 1997.[22] None of this helped the massive number of post-1990 arrivals who had no ABC family connections.

CONGUATE Responses

Subjectively, as a result of the above, immigrant communities experienced a heightened and more pervasive fear (see, for example, Rodríguez and Hagan 2004). This was especially the case in those communities and those strata of immigrants that were not organized. Given these conditions, the initial goals of virtually all Latino immigrant rights organizations became essentially defensive, i.e., to inform the affected communities of their rights and to work closely with those communities in designing strategies to mitigate the effects of the anti-immigrant regime. This was the context for CON-

GUATE's fourth National Assembly in Miami (March 2002), the first after 9/11. A major focus of this meeting was the Central American Security Act (CASA), the bipartisan, security-enhanced version of NACARA parity. This meeting also included participation by restructured chapters of GUIA, with new leadership, unconnected to ex-military officers, from both Los Angeles and Miami—as well as a representative from the Guatemala-based migrant rights coalition MENAMIG.

Also in March 2002, several CONGUATE representatives made a joint trip with their Salvadoran counterparts in the Salvadoran American National Network, to Guatemala, and subsequently to El Salvador, where President Bush was meeting with the Central American presidents regarding the Central American Free Trade Agreement (CAFTA). That meeting was punctuated by protests against free trade and for migrant rights. In Guatemala, the delegation met with several government officials, lobbying them to take a stronger position on the various U.S. laws that could benefit Guatemalans and to adopt a permanent, coherent "policy of state" to protect migrants in the United States. They were unable to get any real commitments from the government, at that time under the presidency of Alfonso Portillo (2000–2003) of the Frente Republicano Guatemalteco (FRG), the party of former military dictator Efraín Ríos Montt, who was head of the Guatemalan Congress during those years. Subsequently in 2002, CONGUATE delegations went to Washington several times, together with Salvadoran and eventually Honduran migrant advocacy networks, to lobby for CASA and to meet with their home-country Ambassadors about migrant issues.

CONGUATE's fifth general meeting was held in Los Angeles in November 2002, although security problems for community members, such as airport roundups and harassment, had prevented some members from traveling to the meeting. CONGUATE began serious discussions of new approaches, including the need to expand to new, "nontraditional" areas with sizeable Guatemalan populations, and to work with non-Guatemalan organizations, particularly Salvadoran. Additional attention was given to lobbying Guatemalan Consulates in the United States—in this case, with considerable success—on such issues as *matrícula consular*, an identity card issued by the Consulates to undocumented migrants from the home country, enabling them, among other things, to open a bank account to facilitate the sending of remittances. In fact, Guatemala was the second Latin American government after Mexico to do this, and the Consulates issued 33,000 ID cards just between August and the end of December 2002. The consular offices also initiated *cónsules móviles*, roving consulates to reach Guatemalans not concentrated in the major cities. Meanwhile, a dual citizenship law was passed by the Guatemalan Congress, assuring migrants that they would not lose their Guatemalan citizenship when becoming U.S. citizens, although they could not vote from abroad.

By 2003, CONGUATE was interacting in more diverse ways with the Guatemalan state, beyond the Embassy and Consulates. For the first time, leading up to the November 2003 election in Guatemala, some presidential candidates campaigned in several U.S. cities with sizeable Guatemalan populations. Anticipating that the Guatemalan government might finally take immigrants' problems seriously, CONGUATE sent a delegation to Guatemala in May 2003 to pressure the government (ultimately without success) to include migrant mobility and status issues in the CAFTA negotiations with the United States. While visiting Guatemala, as on previous occasions, CONGUATE members met and exchanged ideas with MENAMIG.

Short-Lived Central America Organizing Bloc

All these initiatives were predictable organizing goals for the anti-immigrant political climate both before and after 9/11. But in early 2003, CONGUATE was drawn into in a qualitatively new level of activity. Initiated and subsidized by EnlacesAmérica, a project of the Chicago-based NGO Heartland Alliance, which was led by a Salvadoran American by this time, a Central American Community Leadership meeting was convened for February 2003, in Ledbetter, Texas, between CONGUATE and the considerably stronger Salvadoran American National Network (SANN), in existence since 1992. CONGUATE had worked with Salvadoran organizations on previous occasions since 1998, primarily for joint lobbying; but this meeting represented a potentially crucial departure that could enable CONGUATE to emerge as part of a broader network of Central American migrant advocacy organizations. Also attending that *encuentro* (meeting) as observers were representatives from Honduran immigrant organizations and the Organización Negra Centroamericana (ONECA), representing Afro-Central American Garifunas in the United States and focusing largely on cultural ethnic issues.

Among the medium-range goals of the common agenda defined at the meeting were the following: to reverse the deterioration in immigrant rights; to increase the social base of the organizations/networks in their communities; to develop models of civic participation and visibility in the media; to influence free trade negotiations; to coordinate with organizations in their home countries; and to work on specific campaigns, such as increased immigrant access to higher education (report circulated by e-mail, *"Encuentro de Inmigrantes Centroamericanos, Ledbetter, 21–23 de febrero 2003"*). Also notable was the synergy of the meeting: as expressed in interviews, both Salvadoran and Guatemalan organizers emerged reenergized and with new approaches to organizing in this difficult conjuncture, when the possibilities for immigrant rights legislation in the U.S. Congress were virtually blocked.

A second joint meeting was held in Washington in October 2003. The meeting strongly emphasized the influence that Central American migrant organizations might collectively exert in upcoming congressional discussions of "guest worker" programs and in the CAFTA negotiations. The organizations began to gain a sense of the increased leverage they might be able to exercise as a Central American migrant bloc. At the same time, the *encuentro* was structured so as to educate participants about broader, pan-Latino immigrant rights concerns,[23] foreshadowing a future organizational reconfiguration (report circulated by e-mail, *"Segundo Encuentro de Líderes inmigrantes Centroamericanos, 16–18 de octubre 2003"*). From this point forward, CONGUATE became an actor on two levels: the specific needs of Guatemalan immigrant communities and the broader agendas of the pan-Latino immigrant rights networks. The idea of a formal immigrant organizing bloc limited to Central Americans was set aside.

The *encuentro* in Washington was also the occasion for a general meeting of CONGUATE to elect new leadership. Significantly, for the first time, both candidates for president were women. Contrary to the expectations of some veterans, the majority of delegates elected a high-profile, Chicago-based Guatemalan-American professional who had not participated in the early years of CONGUATE prior to Ledbetter, but who had a strong background in fundraising circles and in the immigrant rights community as Director of the nationally known Illinois Coalition for Immigrant Rights. While several veterans of CONGUATE decided to pull back, this infusion of new blood into the network opened up an opportunity to expand CONGUATE's horizons. The change in leadership signaled a different style of functioning and decision making, a focus on "capacity-building" that was key to NGO objectives generally, and an ongoing campaign to incorporate organizations from nontraditional sites around the United States[24]—although many smaller communities, especially rural or semirural, lacked such organizations and were never reached.

This change coincided with the November 2003 Guatemalan presidential election and January 2004 change of government in Guatemala. The incoming business-oriented president, Oscar Berger, and others in his cabinet, recognized the need to present at least an appearance of being more proactive on behalf of Guatemalan migrant rights, given the centrality of migrant remittances in the Guatemalan economy. The new vice president, Dr. Eduardo Stein, was an intellectual/professional with longstanding interests and connections in migration circles—leading to high expectations that were only minimally fulfilled (see Part II, below). At the same time, the Guatemalan news media were giving greater coverage to migrant communities living in the United States and to CONGUATE activities,[25] as CONGUATE leaders were making more regular visits to Guatemala.

During 2004–2005, as immigration issues rose to prominence on the U.S. national political agenda (crackdowns at the border and nationwide, juxtaposed with discussions about a new guest worker program), EnlacesAmerica, SANN, and CONGUATE leaders played an important role in broader meetings that included networks from other Latin American nationalities. These meetings evolved into the 2004 pan-Latino "Summit" meetings of the newly formed National Alliance of Latin American and Caribbean Communities (NALACC). These Latino Summits and SANN/CONGUATE individuals' relatively high-profile role in them became more pronounced in the 2004 U.S. electoral context and subsequently. In principle, this did not negate the need for a Central American immigrant rights bloc, but in practice, pan-Latino organizing became the prevailing tendency. In the words of a leading Salvadoran organizer, "we were overtaken by reality." Although it also included organizations representing such nationalities as Ecuadorans, Dominicans, and Brazilians, above all, NALACC brought the Central Americans together with the powerful Mexican immigrant advocacy organizations.

Nevertheless, CONGUATE and virtually all other Guatemalan migrant networks and organizations turned their attention to Guatemala-specific issues in the fall of 2005, after Hurricane Stan caused massive destruction in the country. In addition to raising funds for immediate relief to hurricane victims, CONGUATE and other Guatemalan migrant organizations launched a targeted campaign in late 2005 to gain TPS for Guatemalans—once again without success. This time the effort was doomed in part by unfortunate timing: it coincided with the hardline initiative in Congress, H.R. 4437. TPS would probably have been denied to Guatemalans in any case, but at that moment, it became unthinkable.

ICEberg Seen Too Late

After initially provoking increased fear in immigrant communities in the United States, H.R. 4437 sparked the opposite reaction. Its provisions were so extreme as to bring to life the unprecedented Immigrant Spring mobilizations of March through May 2006—this time bringing into the streets several million undocumented immigrants themselves, who had lived in fear for years or decades. During these mobilizations, the initiatives and the energy came from grassroots communities, hometown associations, Spanish-language talk radio, and individuals acting on their own behalf. Although the impetus came from the grassroots more than from NGO activists or other support organizations speaking on their behalf, networks such as SANN and CONGUATE participated actively. Subsequently, the mobilizations sparked a ferocious backlash from anti-immigrant, vigilante-style organizations such as the "Minutemen," and a spate of local city anti-immigrant ordinances. While raising the profile of the contentious debate about immigration, this conjuncture led to a complete paralysis on "comprehensive immigration reform" in the U.S. Congress, an impasse that lasted for years.

Rather than the extreme Right in Congress pushing for H.R. 4437 or even the Minutemen vigilante organizations, it was the ICE agency of DHS and its "Endgame" program and enforcement-only policies that most directly threatened immigrants and provoked their fear throughout the United States. The largest and highest-profile ICE workplace raid affecting particularly Guatemalan undocumented workers (although not the first or only such raid involving Guatemalans) occurred in May 2008 at the Postville, Iowa, kosher slaughterhouse and meat-packing plant Agriprocessors, as described in Chapter 2.

Even as collective deportations symbolized by this workplace raid provoked widespread criticism, ICE continued to carry out equally massive but less prominent individual arrests, detentions, and deportations. At workplaces, employers were required to submit information to ICE on workers through the "E-Verify" program. In communities, by 2011, ICE's "Secure Communities" (S-Comm) program described in Chapter 2 imposed mandatory cooperation from all local police forces, including some states and cities that objected, in sharing fingerprint information on immigrants booked or charged with, but not necessarily convicted of, any infraction, however minor (e.g., driving infractions). In practice, hundreds of thousands of undocumented immigrants or those not carrying their papers were summarily detained and deported without due process rights. The deportation offensives were stimulated by numerical quotas of deporting around 400,000 a year, and that goal was nearly reached in fiscal years 2009, 2010, and 2011, according to various sources.[26] Although the program was supposedly refined in 2011 to prioritize the deportation of serious criminals through the exercise of "prosecutorial discretion" by ICE, many caught up in the dragnet were innocent of any serious crime, and some were even U.S. citizens (Kohli et al. 2011). Notably, the category of serious crimes included the immigration violation of further unauthorized entries into the United States after having been deported. (For San Francisco area examples, see Chapter 5.)

Advocacy Network Reconfigurations

Diversifications and Transitions

With the particular conditions beginning in 2006, Guatemalan advocacy organizing underwent several significant reconfigurations. A new migrant advocacy network was founded in 2006, Movimiento de Inmigrantes Guatemaltecos en los Estados Unidos (MIGUA—Movement of Guatemalan Immigrants in the United States). The founders of MIGUA came from the same political generation as those of CONGUATE. Some had been part of the political network, Red por la Paz y el Desarrollo de Guatemala (RPDG—Network for Peace and Development in Guatemala), which had a broad political and human rights agenda, including the *voto en el exterior*, voting in Guatemalan elections by migrants living in the United States—see Molina 2005; subsequently, RPDG became active in immigration issues, particularly TPS for Guatemalans. Those who formed MIGUA in 2006 described it as a movement of pro-migrant organizations in a number of cities, including some nontraditional sites (e.g., Cincinnati, Ohio, and Atlanta, Georgia) that had not been represented in a national network, as well as individuals who had not participated in CONGUATE.

In other sites, there was overlap, as some local organizations participated in both networks. MIGUA and RPDG were also part of the broader NALACC coalition, along with CONGUATE and Guatemalan migrant community organizations that had not been part of CONGUATE. In short, CONGUATE was no longer the only network representing the immigrant rights goals of Guatemalans in the United States. By 2007, the various networks (CONGUATE, MIGUA, RPDG) worked together—or sometimes separately—and with organizations in Guatemala to raise migrant rights issues in the Guatemalan presidential election. A major emphasis for the networks after 2005 and after several environmental disasters later in the decade was the campaign for TPS for Guatemalans. Nevertheless, there were numerous new sites of Guatemalan immigrant settlement during the 1990s and the first decade of the 2000s where these networks were altogether absent.

Meanwhile, at its own 2006 meeting, CONGUATE (by this time, its first three initials standing for Coalición Nacional [National Coalition]) elected a new president, from GUIA/Miami. This marked the beginning of a transition from the political generation of the 1980s, as some of the new leaders were not rooted in the Guatemalan civil war and its ideologies, and did not come from the world of NGOs. Many of the priorities for organizing in the United States persisted, as well as active participation in the pan-Latino NALACC and ties to MENAMIG in Guatemala (see below). CONGUATE also continued its tradition of delegations to Guatemala, by itself or as part of NALACC delegations, for example, in April 2006 and mid-2007. In addition, some new approaches and areas of emphasis were opened up, including a focus on economic policy issues — e.g., development in Guatemala to minimize migration, microcredit as a development strategy, and the uses of remittances. A few years later, under a different leadership, CONGUATE developed ties to a different set of local organizations.

Challenges and Fault Lines

Viewed over the course of its growth, CONGUATE had faced major challenges, both external and internal. A major external, indeed structural, constraint was the absence of significant external funding and 501(c)(3) tax status, which in turn resulted in the lack of paid staff or a permanent office — a sharp contrast to the CARECEN network and other Salvadoran organizations. As another consequence, only activists able to pay their own way or find funding could attend the national meetings, and even they had problems taking time away from their daytime jobs.

A significant internal challenge, to a greater or lesser degree at different moments, was inconsistent "bridge building" to other Guatemalan networks and organizations, particularly Mayan networks in the United States. As seen above, most Mayan national networks and local organizations focused largely on cultural and social issues. In addition, some Mayan leaders viewed CONGUATE as dominated by ladinos. Several of the Mayan organizations had participated in the initial meetings for a migrant rights network. But the damage done during the GUATENET period was never fully repaired, and most of the Mayan organizations withdrew. Subsequently, CONGUATE did not always incorporate the Mayan agenda: for example, it did not sign the 1999 "*Declaración Maya*" put forth by Atanasio Tzúl and CORN-Maya, and did not link the immigrant rights agenda globally to priority issues for many Mayan organizations. As a result, CONGUATE was not strong in some key venues, e.g., Houston and smaller cities/semirural areas in Florida. At different moments, CONGUATE invited participation by Mayan organizations/networks but did not present the legalization agenda in a way that united them organically with Mayan organizations — exceptions being Grupo Maya in the San Francisco Bay Area, MayaQuetzal in West Palm Beach, Florida, and some fraternidades in Los Angeles.

Aside from the ethnic challenges, which often had class dimensions as well, other internal fault lines in CONGUATE stemmed from top-down, sometimes sectarian practices associated with political organizations — some that mirrored organizing practices in Guatemala itself. There was also a tendency common among networks of NGOs, as pointed out by Pisani and Arquilla (2004), of not having "organized accountability" to communities they claimed to serve. These issues made it more difficult to build lasting bridges and organic ties between small cores of activist leaders and grassroots community members, even in cities that had CONGUATE-affiliated organizations. While some have been critical of CONGUATE, from another perspective, this gap could be seen as almost unavoidable, since most immigrants experienced survival as their immediate goal. Despite its continuing objective importance, legalization was not widely perceived at the grassroots as the overriding goal and generally did not mobilize entire communities on a day-to-day basis.

In addition, there were gender disparities, given the general predominance of males in the CONGUATE leadership. Even after a professional woman was elected president of CONGUATE and served from late 2003 through early 2006, consistently gendering the organizational work and minimizing *machista* practices remained a challenge, making it a difficult environment for the incorporation of grassroots female community organizers (see examples in Chapter 5). Meanwhile, as always, female immigrants and activists had overwhelming household and family responsibilities, restricting their participation in political organizations and networks. These dynamics were not specific to CONGUATE, but rather typical of such networks.

But none of these internal fault lines challenged CONGUATE and other U.S.-based networks as much as structural changes in the U.S. immigration political context. Under the accumulation of policies and attitudes hostile to Latino immigrants, it was logical that Guatemalan organizations in the United States began working not only on their own but also in the national space provided by the pan-Latino NALACC. Although theoretically pan-Latino, on the ground, NALACC had more ties and specific weight in Mexican and Central American immigrant communities than among the considerably smaller South American immigrant groups and communities. Structurally, NALACC represented a respatialization for migrant advocacy campaigns, since it was not only a broader, more comprehensive, more diverse space, with many more specific sites, but also a somewhat "looser" space— meaning, for Guatemalan organizations and networks, that they would not have to compete with each other but could coexist and work together on common goals under the larger umbrella.

Generational Shifts

Finally, also showing shifts over time, immigrant rights campaigns began to be carried out by new generations of advocates. Although generational lines are never drawn neatly or across the board, by 2006–2007, there were signs of uneven generational transitions in leadership of several advocacy organizations and networks in the United States and, as will be seen, throughout the region. The political generation of the 1980s remained active, but it was joined by a new generation of Guatemalan migrants and organizers that was less directly motivated by insurgent "revolutionary" politics and more impacted by Guatemalan postwar structural neoliberal policies and post-1996 U.S. immigration polities. As seen in Chapter 2, Central American migrants were, like Mexicans, now coming primarily for economic reasons, or after environmental disasters. The generation of early twenty-first–century advocates was by no means apolitical, but framed issues differently and developed new styles of politics.

This next generation of Salvadoran Americans and Guatemalan Americans in the United States also had expanded priorities. The U.S.-born Central Americans were citizens, hence potentially part of the "Latino vote," and organized themselves in different ways. In addition to legalization campaigns (and, for Guatemalans, ongoing TPS campaigns), they expanded their agendas to include labor rights and working conditions, medical care, broad Latino rights (against discrimination or racialization and against second-class citizenship), explicitly feminist approaches to women's rights, including domestic violence prevention (research interviews; Coll 2010), and gay/lesbian rights (research interviews; Roque Ramírez 2005). Additionally, the Salvadoran Americans organized around community/*barrio* issues directly impacting the lives of immigrants' children and immigrant youth in the twenty-first century, such as alternatives to drugs and gangs—for example, CARECEN's tattoo removal program and gun buy-back programs. Other focuses included youth health care and educational rights/opportunities, including the right to a university education for undocumented students, i.e., various versions of the DREAM Act.

PART II: GUATEMALAN AND TRANSREGIONAL ADVOCACY NETWORKS

Thus far, we have focused on Guatemalan advocacy networks in the United States, even as we have noted above the beginnings of their ongoing collaboration with MENAMIG in the early 2000s. At this point, we turn to organizing by the latter network and other institutions in Guatemala, and we then present a broader transregional perspective and panorama, in order to highlight immigrant rights advocacy in several venues of the region constituted, for our purposes, primarily by Guatemala, Mexico, and the United States.

Prior to 1997, the entire issue of migration had been absent from public discussion in Guatemala, eclipsed by the civil war and peace negotiations and by conjunctural issues. In the summer of 1997, for the first time, a major television news program, *Notisiete*, ran a high-profile series about Guatemalans in Los Angeles. In September 2000, the principal daily newspaper, *Prensa Libre*, carried a special series spanning two weeks on Guatemalan migrants in the United States (Rodríguez 2000), leading in 2001 to more systematic coverage of CONGUATE activities. With the war over and deportations from Mexico increasing, during the late 1990s, Guatemala was at the same time becoming a country of transit for other Central American migrants, especially after Hurricane Mitch in late 1998, and for some migrants from the Andean countries (Smith 2006). In short, Guatemala emerged more visibly as a country with multiple borders, raising a plethora of migration-related issues.

Even before the end of the war in Guatemala, the Misioneros Scalabrinianos—a multisite Congregation of Catholic priests, nuns, and lay workers whose mission was care of journeying migrants, denunciation of abuses, and defense of migrant rights (Hagan 2006; Brown 2001)—had begun to set up a network of Casas del Migrante to attend to the needs of migrants, transmigrants, and returning deportees. Together with the Centro de Atención al Migrante (CAM), three Brazilian priests working in Guatemala established these Casas in Guatemala City and, for the first time, at crossing points at the Guatemala-Mexico border, particularly the one at Tecún Umán–Tapachula. They also operated Casas for the same purposes of protecting and assisting migrants in Mexico City and other points in Mexico, as well as at crossing points along the Mexico-U.S. border, such as Tijuana–San Diego. In Guatemala, the Scalabrinians worked with other institutions of the Catholic Church, primarily the Pastoral de Movilidad Humana (PMH—Pastoral Commission on Human Mobility) of the centralized Guatemalan Bishops' Conference. Catholic Relief Services (CRS) actively helped to pull together a migrant rights NGO network in Guatemala, and funded expansion of the Casas.

In the late 1990s, these pioneers were joined by a small but growing number of civil society NGOs and research institutions, which in 1999 coalesced into the formal network MENAMIG. This network, whose main organizers outside the institutions related to the Catholic Church were from the same political generation as the U.S.-based network leaders, was a product of Guatemala in the immediate postwar era. Its emergence reflected postponed but urgent concerns about the human rights of both Guatemalan migrants abroad and non-Guatemalan transmigrants in Guatemala—and the lack of government policies to address either situation.

After its formation in 1999, MENAMIG as a coalition began a series of high-profile activities, and relatively quickly became well structured and proactive. Aside from obtaining funding for an office and coordinator, MENAMIG was composed of longstanding, stable member institutions. Some of these were CAM/Casas del Migrante/PMH, all institutions of the Catholic Church, the Scalabrinians in particular, and CRS. In addition, MENAMIG included the Procuraduría de Derechos Humanos (PDH—Human Rights Ombudsman's Office), Comisión de Derechos Humanos (CDHG—Guatemalan Human Rights Commission), several urban and rural labor unions, several health organizations, Movimiento Tzuk Kim Pop (a Quetzaltenango-based NGO network/coordinating committee), and Coordinación de ONG y Cooperativas de Guatemala (CONGCOOP—Coordinating Committee of Guatemalan NGOs and Cooperatives). Also participating were representatives from two governmental institutions, the Ministerio Público (MP—Public Prosecutor's Office) and the union of workers in the government's Dirección General de Migración (DGM—General Directorate for Migration). Mayan rights organizations were not prominent in the coalition.

MENAMIG also included key research centers at the national Universidad de San Carlos and the Jesuit Universidad Rafaél Landívar, as well as intellectual institutions that were developing research and educational programs on migration, such as Facultad Latinoamericana de Ciencias Sociales/Guatemala (FLACSO/Guatemala—the Guatemalan academic center (*sede*) of the Latin American Social Sciences Faculty) and Asociación para el Avance de las Ciencias Sociales (AVANCSO—Association for the Advancement of Social Sciences in Guatemala). As throughout Latin America, there was generally no sharp dividing line between research/intellectual institutions and advocacy organizations in Guatemala. As one of MENAMIG's ongoing intellectual contributions, a researcher from AVANCSO wrote a monthly electronic bulletin of information and analysis from 2003 through early 2011 (Caballeros 2003-2011, *Voz Itinerante*, #1-#101). Other researchers and scholars produced analyses enriched by the discussions and interchanges with nonacademic activists at MENAMIG meetings.

Several of the member institutions also had offices and worked together in the department of Huehuetenango, in the highlands near the border with Mexico, where migrants were at great risk and in great need of services; the cooperation included NGOs and immigrant rights organizations at various moments working with representatives of governmental and semigovernmental agencies. Such collaboration supported the humanitarian *atención al migrante* (attention to migrants) maintained by the Scalabrinians in the Casas del Migrante at Tecún Umán–Tapachula and later, at other crossing points.

As part of its ongoing activities, MENAMIG participated in an annual "Migrant's Week" during the first week of each September, to give a higher public profile to the issue through a series of public educational, cultural, and religious events. MENAMIG was also among the major forces in successfully pressuring the Guatemalan government, historically one of the least sensitive to migrant rights issues, to be the twentieth government to sign the U.N. International Convention for the Protection of Rights for All Migrant Workers and Members of Their Families—the twentieth government being the one that brought the Convention into effect on July 1, 2003, hence, an important symbolic action worldwide. MENAMIG also actively lobbied the Guatemalan government to respect the rights of deportees and of transmigrants from other countries, as well as to develop a comprehensive migration "política de estado," or "state policy," i.e., one that would not change every four years with a new government, and to establish a Ministry for migrant affairs.

Complementing the emphasis on migrant rights protection, and like Mexican and other Central American organizations, MENAMIG strongly criticized the neoliberal policies that stimulated migration, arguing that migration should be "a choice, not a necessity"—meaning that the Guatemalan government had the responsibility of adopting policies to guarantee decent jobs and social services so that its citizens would not feel compelled to leave the country in search of adequately compensated work. This perspective has been encapsulated in discussions of "migration and development," which strongly critique neoliberal development policies. Another central concept was the redefinition of "security" in regard to migration, contrasting the U.S.-imposed national security approach with "human security," and eventually "migrant security."

As early as 2001, MENAMIG began coordination with CONGUATE, sending an observer to the yearly CONGUATE General Assemblies and inviting CONGUATE to its own activities. Throughout the early 2000s, this collaboration evolved significantly, with initiatives from both sides, leading to joint campaigns for more comprehensive, proactive, and humane Guatemalan government policies and practices to protect migrants and for TPS in the United States. As new migrant rights networks, both Guatemala-specific (MIGUA, RPDG) and broader (NALACC) arose in the United States, MENAMIG worked with them as well.

Despite its visibility and migrant advocacy achievements, over the years, MENAMIG both gained and lost organizational and individual members, as is typical of advocacy networks in general. MENAMIG also underwent other ups and downs common in self-reconfiguring NGO-based networks, including leadership changes and crises. In addition, MENAMIG exhibited specific dynamics typical of the highly politicized 1980s Guatemalan political generation. Given these elements of flux, it is not surprising that MENA-MIG did not consistently include or speak for all migrant rights institutions in Guatemala. Seen more structurally, during the early 2000s, the space for migrant rights advocacy came to be occupied by several layers of organizations and networks in Guatemala and regionally.

Another key social actor was the Instituto Centroamericano de Estudios Sociales y Desarrollo (INCEDES—Central American Institute for Social Studies and Development), founded in 2005 by researchers/public intellectuals previously based at FLACSO/Guatemala. They had been instrumental in the initial creation of MENAMIG but became somewhat distanced for a few years during the early 2000s. INCEDES defined itself first and foremost as a migration research institution, with close ties to prominent international scholars in Europe and North America, in Mexico and throughout Central America. But in the Latin American tradition, INCEDES was not separated from advocacy activities; in addition to social and participatory research, it formulated policy proposals to the Guatemalan government and sponsored other national and regional initiatives. From 2005 through late 2007, IN-CEDES also housed the Secretaría Técnica of the regional migrant rights advocacy network RROCM (see below).

In addition, INCEDES served as the Guatemalan base of the binational Grupo Guatemala-México Migración y Desarrollo (see GGMMD 2005)—the Mexican base being the Centro de Estudios Demográficos, Urbanos y Ambientales (CEDUA) of the Colegio de México.[27] Founded in mid-2003, the GGMMD reflected the reality of Guatemala's specific location in the region—its long border with Mexico and its role as a country of transit for non-Guatemalan migrants, as well as a migrant-sending country. The Grupo was a citizen/professional binational response by nonstate actors to the state-level bilateral policy collaborations by the Mexican and Guatemalan governments in a high-level group on "border security." Beginning in 2004, the GGMMD mounted an Observatorio Ciudadano (Citizen Observation/Monitoring) at the border, calling upon both the Guatemalan and Mexican governments to develop comprehensive and humane migration policies, and proposing specific policy elements to be included.

Other organizational actors took initiatives to impact the migration policies of the governments of Guatemala, Mexico, and/or the United States. In February 2006, for example, Quetzaltenango-based Tzuk Kim Pop, itself a coalition of grassroots community organizations in the Guatemalan highlands region, sent a trilingual letter (English, Spanish, K'iche') to the U.S. Senate, "*Por la vida, contra el muro y la Ley Migratoria H.R. 4437*"—"For life, against the [border] wall and the [proposed] law HR 4437." In the spring of 2006, the streets of Guatemala City were filled with marchers, expressing solidarity with the immigrant mobilizations in the United States; in this and other cases, institutions affiliated with or close to the Catholic Church and the PMH often took the lead.

For the Guatemalan presidential election of 2007, virtually all the major advocacy organizations in Guatemala publicly presented to the candidates a discussion document of principles and elements that should be included in the migration program of a new government, regardless of which candidate or political party won the election. This was followed in the presidential run-off election by a Forum in October 2007, to pressure the candidates for a comprehensive migration policy; the Forum was co-sponsored by MENAMIG, the three U.S.-based networks—and the government's Foreign Relations Ministry, which hosted the event. Subsequently, the nongovernmental networks and individual organizations often worked collaboratively.

Pressured by nongovernmental migrant rights organizations and networks in both Guatemala and the United States, and by increasing media coverage of Guatemalan migrants and their advocacy organizations, the Guatemalan state under successive regimes began, in the early 2000s, very unevenly and belatedly to pay attention to migrants' concerns. Above all, the government was motivated by recognition that remittances from Guatemalans in the United States had become an essential pillar of the economy, easing the pressure to provide governmental social service and equitable development programs. Following Hurricane Stan in 2005 and environmental disasters in 2010 and 2011, the Guatemalan government made some efforts in Washington to gain TPS for Guatemalans. But the Guatemalan government apparently had very little political capital or leverage in Washington and consistently failed in attempts to gain TPS for Guatemalans—although critics charged that its efforts were half-hearted.[28] The Guatemalan government became somewhat more vocal in protesting ICE raids and mass deportations of undocumented Guatemalan workers,[29] as these raids became more systematic and especially after the great raid in Postville, Iowa (May 2008)—but to no avail.

As seen in Part I of this chapter, during the early 2000s, Guatemalan Consulates in various U.S. cities became more proactive in attempting to protect Guatemalan migrants at the local level in the United States, and new Consulates were opened up as Guatemalan immigrants settled in more diverse sites (e.g., in Georgia, Rhode Island, and Arizona). But in Guatemala, it took a major struggle in 2006 to get the president to create and maintain a Vice-Ministry for Migrant Affairs within the Foreign Relations Ministry. At other levels of government, and largely as a result of the same pressures and education from nonstate actors, in 2004 the Guatemalan Congress created a formal Migration Committee, Comisión de Migrantes. In October 2007, Congress also approved creation of an official Consejo Nacional de Atención al Migrante Guatemalteco en el Exterior (CONAMIGUA — National Council for Attention to Guatemalan Migrants Abroad) to coordinate governmental social programs and policies for migrants, with emphasis on the needs of migrants in the United States.[30] Implementation was left for the new government taking office in 2008. Despite initially high hopes, as of four years later, CONAMIGUA did not live up to expectations and became largely a site of competition for political influence, both in Guatemala and in various U.S. cities that were represented.

Even as it was belatedly taking up issues affecting Guatemalan migrants, the Guatemalan state under successive governments was complicit in the regional anti-immigrant crackdown that was perceived as pushing the "U.S." border ever farther south, this time to Guatemala's Central American borders. In the late 1990s and early 2000s — with some U.S. assistance in paying the deportation costs, according to the Guatemalan correspondent for *Excelsior* in Mexico (October 10, 2000) and García (2006, 161, 230n19) — the Guatemalan state stepped up its programs directed against undocumented transmigrants, i.e., other Central Americans, South Americans, Chinese, and others using Guatemala to get to Mexico and eventually to the United States.[31]

Conceptual Framework: Transregional Advocacy Practices

Our conceptual point of departure is that the "social field" of Guatemalan migration is also a region defined by geographical contiguity and by highly uneven development (Harvey 2006). However, it is also a region that is being constructed and recreated by evolving collective social experiences and actions. Viewing this region as re-created by social experience avoids reifying it as solely geographical and static, and illuminates its shifts and evolutions. This is also a "flexible" region in that, for some purposes — e.g., the Conferencia Regional sobre Migración discussed below, and CAFTA-DR — it has been politically expanded to include Canada and/or the Dominican Republic.[32] At another level, the specific history of the Mexico-Guatemala border is a prime example of the shifting social/historical dynamics of borders within regions, with the "borderlands" sometimes constituting micro- or subregions.

Within this region, the ongoing campaigns by Guatemalan/Central American migrant advocacy organizations for legalization and other rights in the United States have been complemented by and sometimes coordinated with coalitions to promote migrant rights, not only in their countries of origin but also in Mexico, as the major country of transit. These connections are not simply bilocal, between Guatemalan migrant communities in the United States and the sending communities in Guatemala, but involve a variety of region-wide contacts and activities. In order to capture this multiplicity of social actors and interactions, we use the formulation "transregional," in contrast to the more familiar "transnational," which focuses on stable, long-range linkages between the migrant communities in the country of reception and the communities/countries of origin, and which has been most common in the migration literature. Our reframing (Jonas 2007) complements the extensive literature on transnational practices.[33] "Transnational" processes *span* nation-state boundaries, while "transregional" is used here to include multiple sites *throughout* an entire region.

Given the multidimensionality of "transregional," although the primary subjects/actors in this book are Guatemalan, some of their activities require reference to other actors throughout the region—most commonly, Central American, Mexican, and U.S.-based. The Mexican and Central American advocates can be described as "spatially conscious" (Soja 1989) insofar as their collective actions are designed to transform the quality of the regional space through which migrants pass, making it less hostile and dangerous, and introducing rights and protections for migrants. In addition, these advocacy networks, which include research institutions, contribute different perspectives or worldviews, as seen above with networks and organizations in Guatemala. We have argued (Jonas 2005) that the focus on collective social action for legalization and immigrant rights in the United States should be complemented by the perspectives, agendas, and goals from Mexico and the Central American sending countries.

On the multilayered, multidimensional regional stage described here, various actors in different geographical locations and from diverse levels or strata—state actors, corporate capital, nongovernmental migrant advocacy NGOs and CBOs, research institutions, and grassroots migrant communities themselves—are negotiating new relationships. Migrant rights organizing initiatives originate from different sectors/locales at different moments in the process, and initiatives undertaken in one location can affect players in other sites. This regional stage is interconnected and interactive, and the contacts among the different actors are multiple and overlapping; but these contacts and collaborations are not evenly dense or synchronized. And conditioning all activity by nonstate actors, state policies initiated by the United States (and by Mexico, toward Central Americans) continue to impact other players, in effect limiting their real options. For this reason, among many others mentioned above, the processes of migrant rights organizing described here are not linear but have had energizing advances, periods (and areas) of relative stagnation, and dampening setbacks.

Proceso Puebla and RROCM

The clearest and highest-profile example of transregional dynamics has been the intergovernmental Conferencia Regional sobre Migración (CRM— Regional Conference on Migration), undertaken in 1996, also known as the "Puebla Process." The CRM was a Mexican initiative at the regional level, which supplemented bilateral interactions with the U.S. government. Participating countries were the United States, Canada, Mexico, all seven Central American countries, and the Dominican Republic—and in the early 2000s, observers from South America, the Caribbean, and U.N. agencies (see Castillo 2003b; Ogren 2007). With governments being represented at the level of Vice-Ministers of Foreign Relations, the CRM was designed to serve as a forum for interchange and debate, from the perspectives of the sending, transit, and destination countries. It was not empowered to make binding agreements that would have to be approved by the legislatures of each nation; rather, it was intended to take a long-range view of the causes and consequences of migration and to develop standards for the protection of migrants' human rights. At least in the early years, the CRM was undertaken in the spirit of transcending traditional narrow viewpoints about migration, based solely on "national" interests, and even included discussions of the positive contributions of migrants to receiving countries (Castillo 2003b, 2005). The difficulties of actually putting these ideas into practice led to analyses of CRM as "a process in search of its own identity" (Castillo 2003b, 81).

With the beginning of the CRM in 1996, nonstate actors convened a parallel transregional network, subsequently known as the Red Regional de Organizaciones Civiles para las Migraciones (RROCM—Regional Network of Civil Society Organizations for Migration) to monitor and "accompany" the CRM. RROCM was designed to bring together nonstate organizations and networks from all eleven countries, although the level of development of the national networks was quite uneven. In action, RROCM at times made significant inroads as a network parallel to the CRM, reframing migration issues, closely monitoring and pressuring governmental actions in the Puebla Process, educating legislators in the country Congresses, and presenting its own written proposals to the CRM. In 2000, the CRM acknowledged RROCM's proposal, *"Lineamientos Regionales para la Protección de los Derechos Humanos de los Migrantes en Situaciones de Intercepción, Detención, Deportación, y Recepción"* ("Regional Guidelines for the Protection of the Human Rights of Migrants in Situations of Interception, Detention, Deportation, and Reception") (cited in Castillo 2003b). Given opposition from various CRM governments, it was never formally adopted, but it served the nongovernmental organizations as a useful tool for monitoring official practices.

RROCM focused on the human rights of the most vulnerable migrants: refugees (forced migrants), women and unaccompanied child migrants, those with HIV/AIDS, detainees, deportees, "disappeared" migrants, and those victimized by trafficking rings. It lobbied the sending governments to provide consular protection in countries of transit and destination. RROCM also pressured the governments at a time of great tension (post-9/11) to focus on migrant rights and "human security," and to resist U.S. government pressures to make "national security" the dominant issue (Castillo 2003b; 2005, 10). Equally important, the existence of RROCM became an impetus, to varying degrees, for organizing activities within most of the member countries.

RROCM came to be recognized as a player in regional policy debates and was making progress in pressuring the Mexican and Central American governments to address migrant rights issues, at least prior to September 11, 2001. After 9/11, in working papers and presentations to the CRM, RROCM became a source of alternatives to the U.S.-imposed national security framework that penetrated governmental immigration policies. Ironically, a key element in RROCM's counter-hegemonic mission was precisely to sustain CRM as a multilateral forum or space, at a time when Washington increasingly worked through bilateral contacts or unilaterally. RROCM also engaged in autonomous activities, separate from the intergovernmental CRM—for example, launching a campaign for implementation of the U.N. Convention for the Protection of Rights of All Migrant Workers and Members of Their Families.

Within RROCM, the Mexican migrant advocacy organization Sin Fronteras (Without Borders) played a central leadership role, both on its own and as coordinator of Foro Migraciones, a major Mexican network of 40 organizations and several leading public intellectuals. Sin Fronteras was led for many years by the former representative of the UNHCR, a European by birth, to oversee Guatemalan refugee camps in southern Mexico; by virtue of this in-

volvement, she was at least indirectly related to the 1980s political generation of Guatemalans. Sin Fronteras was an essential link in the chain, given
Mexico's triple role in the region, as a major sending nation, a major nation
of transit, and a nation of reception in the southern states. In these southern
states of Mexico, Guatemalan day-laborers and female service workers, including sex workers, have been a sector of the Mexican workforce that moves
back and forth across the border (Sin Fronteras 2005, citing Guatemalan
research on women by an academic researcher and participant in MENA-
MIG—see Ortíz 2005).

Since the 1990s, Sin Fronteras had been calling attention to human rights
violations against transmigrants through Mexico, and proposing standards
for their protection, especially the most vulnerable, women and children. A
central goal of Sin Fronteras, of the Foro Migraciones, and of other Mexican
advocacy/research institutions outside the Foro[34] was to make public and to
increase leverage against the Mexican government's coordinated efforts with
the U.S. government to prevent transit migration by militarizing Mexico's
southern border with Guatemala. In their efforts to counter abuses against
transmigrants in Mexico, these coalitions supplemented reports by the more
established Mexican Comisión Nacional de Derechos Humanos (CNDH—
National Human Rights Commission), which had become independent of
the government in 1995 and periodically published critical reports on the
worsening conditions for migrants in transit (Alba and Castillo 2012).

Taken together, the Central American and Mexican-based and regional
advocacy networks[35] generated new practices and paradigms. They saw themselves as working with migrants comprehensively, from preparation for their
journeys at points of departure and transit, to arrival, to reception of deportees
at the point of forced return. Largely under the leadership of women, they
paid particular attention to migration hazards facing women and unaccompanied children (Sin Fronteras 2005; see also Díaz and Kuhner 2007, 2008;
Escobar Sarti 2008), and in general could be seen as having a gendered approach to migration. In addition, they pressured the governments to take responsibility for the consequences of their actions—a very different concept of
"policy" than the linear view of governments unilaterally dictating measures.

Furthermore, within the context of free trade agreements, i.e., CAFTA-
DR, and Mexico's Plan Puebla Panamá (PPP) for investment in Central
America, these organizations attempted, without success, to insert migrant
labor issues such as mobility across borders and minimum standards for
labor, as part of an overall critique of neoliberal development in the twenty-
first century. In the sending countries, this meant pressuring their govern-

ments to undertake socioeconomically sustainable, equitable, and inclusive development.

Uneven Network Dynamics

The concept of transregional networks should not be read to imply synchronization or even coordination among nonstate collective actors throughout the region. U.S.-based networks maintained binational ties with their home-country counterparts, i.e., CONGUATE with MENAMIG and SANN with CARECEN Internacional in San Salvador. Despite occasional transregional interactions involving U.S.-based organizations, this did not become a regular practice. In fact, RROCM did not have a networked counterpart within the United States. Nevertheless, in 2007, as an initiative originating from the United States, NALACC held its *Cumbre* or major "Summit" meeting in Morelia, Mexico, inviting some participants from Sin Fronteras and other Mexican organizations, as well as other Latin American organizations and networks. NALACC also made site visits in 2007 to El Salvador, Honduras, and Guatemala, including meetings with in-country organizations and networks as well as government officials. Leaders of the U.S.-based Guatemalan immigrant networks participated in these NALACC initiatives but had little direct organizational articulation with Sin Fronteras or Foro Migraciones in Mexico or with RROCM.

Even among advocacy networks within Mexico and Central America, there were uneven dynamics and fault lines. In an open letter of July 7, 2005, MENAMIG, until then arguably the strongest of the home-country Central American networks, announced its decision to withdraw from RROCM, maintaining that its energies could be better invested in lobbying the Guatemalan government directly than in the regional intergovernmental arena of the CRM. In addition, MENAMIG's letter of withdrawal criticized RROCM for overly centralized functioning. Despite this decision by MENAMIG as a network—objectively a step backward from the regional stage—a number of member organizations and individuals within MENAMIG continued working within the RROCM framework. By 2003, RROCM had officially altered its original definition as a "network of networks," leaving room for such flexibility. Subsequently, by 2007, with new leadership, MENAMIG was petitioning to return as a network member of RROCM, also under new leadership, with its Secretariat being coordinated by the Honduran network Foro Nacional para las Migraciones en Honduras (FONAMIH—National Forum for Migration in Honduras).

This example suggests that MENAMIG and RROCM each exhibited some characteristics and fault lines common among NGO-based networks, although not necessarily in equal measure. First, as is typical of networks, member organizations were unevenly developed. Second, both developed unevenly over time, with ups and downs.[36] Third, as observed by a key player in Guatemala who participated in both entities, the focus on institutions (organizations, networks) too easily took precedence over the core mission of defending migrant rights. In his words when we interviewed him, "We need to start from what were the initial objectives and have the debate all over again, to reinvent ourselves, prioritizing *la causa* with migrants." Fourth, "tensions and competitions" were common, especially in a context of scarce financial and human resources (Castillo 2005, 11). Fifth, as with Guatemalan advocacy networks in the United States, individuals on all sides were at times caught up in relationships and dynamics of the particular Guatemalan political generation of the 1980s—a reminder that networks are made up of real people, and do not move forward on automatic pilot. Many of the above factors were implicitly or explicitly acknowledged in our interviews with participants in both networks and could be seen in extensive self-assessments that took place in 2007 within both MENAMIG and RROCM.

More structurally, as Castells (2004) has observed and as suggested earlier in this chapter, such networks at the national, transnational, and transregional levels are self-reconfiguring—meaning that when circumstances change, these networks adjust or are transformed. From this perspective, recompositions, restructurings, or transformations of existing organizations and networks into new network formations can be considered a natural part of their life cycle and culture within the "network society." Other dynamics common among the NGO-based networks in general have been manifested in the cases studied here, to different degrees. These national and regional networks were composed of organizations whose purpose was to represent migrant interests but which were not always solidly rooted in grassroots sending or receiving migrant communities. As with the "organized sectors of civil society" in many other arenas, and as seen above for the U.S.-based networks, insufficiently deep roots in the community can structurally limit the success and accountability of middle-stratum ("third sector") NGO-based networks. This can be the case even when their stated goals and principles objectively represent real interests and objectives that need to be articulated (Howell and Pearce 2001, Pearce 2005, Pisani and Arquilla 2004).

Despite these characteristics, the migrant advocacy networks discussed throughout this chapter achieved defined objectives and made some limited advances for their constituencies vis-à-vis state policies—in a sense, mitigating the deterioration of the regional space for migrants. Each of the networks and organizations in the region had moments of great visibility—e.g., in community "Know Your Rights" meetings after *ABC v. Thornburgh* (CARE-CEN, Atanasio Tzúl, and their U.S. lawyers and organizational allies); in the campaign for NACARA parity during the late 1990s (CONGUATE and SANN); in lobbying the Guatemalan government and educating legislators (MENAMIG, INCEDES); in the campaign for "minimum standards" and for U.N. monitoring at the Mexico-Guatemala border (Sin Fronteras, Foro Migraciones, RROCM, GGMMD); and in the multiple campaigns for TPS for Guatemalans after Hurricane Stan. But because they were up against neoliberal states acting in concert, and protecting migrant interests only when serving their own interests or those of their business sectors, nonstate advocacy networks could not have the systematic influence over state actions that remain, as they have always been, in the hands of the networked business sector of civil society—the situation that Castells (2004, 25) refers to as "relations of domination between networks."

Unequal Interstate Relations

Even as states in the region remained dominant actors vis-à-vis migrants and advocates, there have also been relations of unequal power/domination and uneven interactions among the state players in this region, since they range from a core superpower to semiperipheral to peripheral. Increasingly after 2001, the more powerful states appeared to prioritize bilateral coordination at the U.S.-Mexico and Mexico-Guatemala borders over the CRM multilateral regional forum. Within Central America, bilateral and regional meetings among government officials and congressional delegations involved both coordination and frictions, e.g. over Guatemalan deportations of other Central Americans. Overall, the U.S. government's national security and antiterrorism view of borders and migrations influenced its counterparts in Mexico and Central America, turning the entire region into a kind of national security zone. Washington also used immigration policy to achieve other U.S. foreign policy goals,[37] thereby further distorting the migration agenda and reinforcing the unequal power relations with its "partners."

For its part, the Mexican state, under the governments both of the Partido Revolucionario Institucional (PRI) during the 1990s and the Partido de Acción Nacional (PAN) from 2000 to 2012, cooperated with the U.S. government to keep Central Americans from ever reaching the United States, through increasingly active southern border operations to prevent entry, and increasing deportations of transit migrants. Compounding its official anti-migrant operations, the Mexican government was uninterested in regulating or unable to regulate the often-overlapping, predatory, nonstate actors that made the journey through Mexico a nightmare for migrants: organized crime rings, traffickers of all kinds—drugs being the most visible and powerful, but also sex and children—and gangs, as well as police and other government forces. The entire experience for migrants was characterized as creating a "grim calculus of risk" (Gorney 2008). These conditions were an especially bitter irony for Guatemalans: during the worst period of the civil war, the army's scorched-earth counterinsurgency campaign of 1981-1983 in the Mayan highlands, some 200,000 Maya had fled from army repression to southern Mexico as their "safe haven," and Mexico had played a leading role in facilitating the 1991-1996 Guatemalan peace negotiations. In this new era, however, Mexico became a major deporter of Guatemalans, as seen from the statistics cited throughout this chapter.

But Mexico has always been complex and contradictory. Even as the essence of Mexico's deportation operations was maintained, some limited shifts occurred as a result of internal and international monitoring. Following Hurricane Stan in 2005, which also impacted the Guatemala-Mexico border area at Tecún Umán-Tapachula, Mexico briefly halted deportation of Guatemalans, giving them *permiso temporal*, the right to be in Mexico if they had a consular ID card—but only for six months (*Prensa Libre*, November 2, 2005). Mexico's CNDH monitored some of the most abusive practices of migration agents in Mexico. The Central American Consulates in Mexico formed a network to jointly address issues of treatment of their nationals, and to raise these with the Mexican government. In April 2008, the Mexican Congress approved a reform of Mexico's Ley General de Población (LGP—General Population Law) decriminalizing the presence of undocumented migrants, i.e., changing it from a major crime to a minor offense, not punishable by detention in jail. The reform was approved in principle in July 2008, but in the absence of further migration legislation at that time, it changed very little on the ground.

At the level of international monitoring, the UNHCR maintained an Oficial de Protección (Protection Officer) in Tapachula, on the Mexico side of the border with Guatemala, to report on the conditions at that border crossing. The U.N. Children's Fund (UNICEF) visited the border to monitor the situations of unaccompanied child migrants and child trafficking. In the spring of 2008, the U.N. Special Rapporteur for the Human Rights of Migrants, within the U.N. High Commissioner's Office for Human Rights, Dr. Jorge Bustamante,[38] delivered blistering reports on the situations of migrants throughout the region—in the United States, in Mexico, at the U.S.-Mexico and Mexico-Guatemala borders, and in Guatemala. He concluded that migrant rights violations against undocumented Central American migrants in Mexico were as bad as or worse than those against Mexican migrants in the United States (*La Jornada*, May 20, 2008). He also criticized the Guatemalan government for not being in compliance with international agreements it had signed regarding the rights of transmigrants, nor even maintaining reliable migration statistics (*Reforma* [Mexico], April 2, 2008). Bolstered by U.N. monitors, migrant advocates called public attention to these situations, and the borders in the region came to be internationally recognized areas of serious human rights violations.

Mexico and Northern Triangle Organizing Challenges

A shift in the Central American regional context for immigrant rights advocacy emerged more clearly late in the first decade of the twenty-first century. One element of this most recent shift, with profound effects for migrants, was the emergence of the "Northern Triangle" (NT) sub-region (Guatemala, El Salvador, and Honduras) as a zone of Mexican influence, becoming more visible after 2008. Migrants to the United States via Mexican land routes—both the traditional western route via Tecún Umán–Tapachula and new routes, notably through Guatemala's Petén region and eastern Mexico, the extremely dangerous *ruta del Golfo* (Gulf route)—were drawn into the violent dynamics of narco-traffic, organized crime, and human smuggling operations, both in the home countries and in Mexico. In the NT countries, these dynamics both built on and aggravated previously existing social violence. They also built on continuing poverty and unemployment, which remained constitutive elements of postwar Central America and fed ongoing migration.

In Mexico, nonstate actors such as drug traffickers and organized crime rings became more powerful and preyed upon transit migrants, mainly NT Central Americans. These migrants were left defenseless, insecure, and with no rights or recourse to protection, given the complicity of corrupt government "security" forces—by no means a new situation, but more pervasive and pronounced. The vulnerability of transmigrants in Mexico exploded into worldwide public view with the August 2010 massacre of 72 migrants, mostly Central Americans and a few South Americans, in San Fernando, Tamaulipas, relatively close to the U.S.-Mexico border. Allegedly, the Zeta drug cartel had attempted to forcibly recruit this group of transmigrants; when they resisted the demands, they were slaughtered in cold blood, their cadavers left in the open air.

This was by no means the first or the only such incident of a mass crime against transmigrants, extortion of money from migrants or their families, kidnappings, and "disappearances," followed by the discovery of mass graves in various states of Mexico. However, the scale and brutality of the Tamaulipas massacre were unprecedented at the time and brought to public attention, even in the United States, the harsh realities of migrant transit experiences. Other incidents of collective migrant kidnappings were carried out by groups involved in *trata* (human trafficking—a human rights violation, involving abuse and exploitation of victims) and *tráfico ilícito* (illegal smuggling—a cross-border violation of the law). Both categories of crimes, which were the subjects of a 2000 U.N. Convention against Transnational Organized Crime and subsequent Protocols on each, became major issues in Mexico and throughout the region, especially as they affected women and unaccompanied children. Trata had already been the focus of attention for advocacy organizations and networks throughout the region for many years.

In addition, the NT societies themselves suffered increasing social violence, largely because their governments, regardless of ideological orientation, chronically lacked fiscal resources to create jobs and economic opportunities in a strong formal economy. This was notable in Guatemala, where the postwar state has operated with a long-range, structural deficit of decent jobs, social programs, and resources to alleviate the factors stimulating migration.[39] In addition to resources, the Guatemalan state has lacked the authority, capacity, and political will to attend to the needs or human security of the population; it also chronically lacks functional political and judicial institutions. In short, it is a classic "weak state."

The multiple deficiencies described here have left a large opening in Guatemala for uncontrolled criminal activities by drug cartels, other criminal organizations, and gangs, with some collaboration from Guatemalan paramilitary forces.[40] In many areas of the country, entire communities were coerced into participating in the drug trade. These practices compounded other forms of coercion by criminal organizations and gangs, e.g., directed against migrants' families believed to be receiving remittances, as seen in Chapter 2. Variations of these conditions existed in El Salvador and Honduras.[41] Overall, the NT subregion was considered by a U.N. unit on Armed Violence and Development to be the world's most violent peacetime region, i.e., not in a state of civil war (García 2012; Schwartz 2012).[42]

For many families in Guatemala and other NT countries, a further source of insecurity and instability that reverberated throughout the region came from accelerating U.S. deportation policies, with a variety of ICE programs such as Secure Communities. In 2011 alone, Guatemala experienced an influx of some 30,300 deportees from the United States (U.S. DHS 2012a, Table 6), in addition to more than 31,000 deportation events from Mexico (INM 2011, Table 3_3.2.1). Many deportees arrived in a country where they would find no employment, no governmental services or resources for reintegration, and sometimes no family.[43] One Guatemalan study of deportees from the United States noted that those who did find work in Guatemala earned a scant 5.2 percent of what they had earned in the United States, even as their families were suddenly cut off from the flow of remittances previously sent by their U.S.-based immigrant relatives (Dardón 2009).

But migration from the NT countries continued, even without home-government protection against increased risks. An undetermined number of deportees made subsequent attempts to re-migrate to the United States. The ineffectiveness of the NT states in protecting their migrants in the United States became chronic.[44] In Guatemala, one government after another during the early 2000s, whether conservative or social-democratic, was lethargic rather than proactive in regard to protecting its migrants. Guatemalan, transregional, and U.S.-based migrant advocacy organizations waged repeated campaigns urging the Guatemalan government to adopt a comprehensive migration state policy and to prioritize migrant protection, but as of 2012, without success.

Given these convoluted situations and other conditions described above, migrant rights advocates in Guatemala and elsewhere in the region found that some of their previous activities were less effective—for example, the leverage that RROCM had exercised within CRM in the late 1990s and especially before 9/11. These groups were now challenged to develop new forms of action. Veteran advocacy organizations and networks, together with emerging civil society actors, generated transregional responses and remained active, with varying degrees of success. Scalabrinian missionaries remained among the most vocal defenders of migrant rights, and the regional network of Scalabrinian *albergues* (shelters) such as "La 72" in Tenosique, Tabasco, Mexico, remained central to protecting migrants at some level from kidnapping, extortion, and worse forms of violence along all corridors and routes through Mexico—although by 2011–2012, some of these shelters themselves were targeted for attack, and their staff and leaders subjected to threats on their lives or safety.

In addition, some organizations became more visible. The Mexico-based Movimiento Migrante Mesoamericano (M3), founded by activists from Mexico's center-left Partido de la Revolución Democrática (PRD), undertook a series of initiatives.[45] After the Tamaulipas massacre, in 2010–2011, M3 supported and helped organize high-profile transregional caravans of Central American mothers looking for "disappeared" migrants, marching from various points in Central America to Mexico City. This culminated in an August 2011 dialogue with Mexican senators and peace conference *"Paso a paso hacia la paz"* ("Step by Step toward Peace"). As the Mexican Congress unanimously passed the 2011 *Ley de Migración* (Migration Law), an addition to the earlier

LGP, specifically designed to eliminate the abuses against migrants and transmigrants, a range of Mexico-based organizations and networks pressured the Mexican government to implement its reforms. The regulations operationalizing the law were finally issued in November 2012, but experts (e.g., Alba and Castillo 2012) and civil society organizations remained skeptical as to how much these would change on-the-ground realities.

In Guatemala, where the executive branch of government was chronically ineffective or disinterested in migrant protection, new initiatives were launched by elected legislators of the congressional migration committee, Comisión de Migrantes, and at the regional level by the Parlamento Centroamericano (PARLACEN—Central American Parliament) and its migration subcommittee, Consejo Parlamentario Regional sobre Migraciones (COPAREM—Regional Parliamentary Council on Migration). In the 2012 hearings held by the Comisión, for example, experts and migrant advocates called upon the executive branch of the Guatemalan government to initiate reforms of the 1998 Migration Law and institutions such as CONAMIGUA,[46] as well as its policies on the treatment of other Central American migrants and effective measures against trata, tráfico ilícito, and other abuses. Meanwhile, COPAREM pressured the regional governments to adopt migrant-protective measures. In Guatemala, the nongovernmental institutions and networks PMH, INCEDES, and MENAMIG worked with both of these legislative bodies.

Additionally at the binational nongovernmental level, MENAMIG coordinated participation with the M3 caravans. In another example of binational collaboration, the Mexico-based research/advocacy Instituto de Estudios y Divulgación sobre Migración (INEDIM—Institute of Migration Studies and Public Education) partnered with INCEDES in Guatemala to hold a mid-2011 conference and publish a report on "Migrant Security." The report was deliberately designed to counter the national security paradigm emanating from the United States and adopted by governments in the region, and to propose an alternative paradigm (INEDIM and INCEDES 2011).

Even after 15 years of advocacy experience, the long-range impact of these and other civil society advocacy initiatives, including the most creative and effective, remained to be seen. The objective challenges posed by violent non-state forces in the region, as well as by the growing accumulation of deportees from the United States and Mexico, became ever more daunting in Central America's Northern Triangle. Once again by 2012–2013, as many times since the late 1990s, civil society immigrant rights advocacy networks and organizations throughout the region were undergoing a period of self-reconfiguration, in search of strategies that could address these challenges and effectively impact state policies.

El Mezquital, like some other shantytowns in Guatemala City, was largely the product of rural migration to the city in the 1980s (see Chapter 2).

Many of Guatemala City's shantytowns like El Mezquital are situated on steep ravines and with unpaved streets, residents suffer serious mudslides during the long rainy season (see Chapter 2).

In shantytowns like Betania, residents who have accumulated sufficient resources move out, and some eventually migrate north from Guatemala (see Chapter 2).

In Betania, some homes are protected from the elements only by newspapers or corrugated cardboard (see Chapter 2).

Betania's homes are also built on steep ravine slopes, subject to rivers of mud and lacking in basic public services (see Chapter 2).

In Guatemala City's Ciudad Peronia shantytown, newspapers serve as walls for many homes (see Chapter 2).

The sign on Ciudad Peronia's Pentecostal "Church of God" reads "Doorway to Heaven" (see Chapter 2).

A man crossing without authorization over bridge between Tecún Umán, Guatemala, and Tapachula, Mexico (see Chapter 2). By permission of Jacobo Dardón, INCEDES.

Street in Tecún Umán leading to Suchiate River dividing Guatemala from Mexico (see Chapter 2). By permission of Jacobo Dardón, INCEDES.

In Guatemala, destruction by natural disasters such as this causes migration (see Chapter 2).

A roadside memorial near Victoria, Texas, where 19 Central American and other migrants died in 2003 from dehydration and suffocation in a trailer truck; passersby leave water jugs at the site as well as toys in memory of a child victim (see Chapter 2).

Guatemalan informal couriers crossing a tropical region in Mexico on the way to Guatemala (see Chapter 2).

RESIDENCIA
Guatemaltecos y Salvadoreños
SOLICITEN SU RESIDENCIA PERMANENTE
GUATEMALA
EL SALVADOR
por medio del programa NACARA
Si usted se encuentra bajo el Programa del ABC o ha sido parte del TPS,
ASISTA A UN TALLER INFORMATIVO
IGLESIA PRESBITERIANA DE OAKLAND
(Esquina de High St. y Foothill)
SABADO 12 DE JUNIO - 9 DE LA MAÑANA
Patrocinado por la Asociacion de Guatemaltecos Unidos (AGU) · LB-CREEI · y Proyecto de Inmigración de Caridades Católicas del Este de la Bahia

Poster urging Guatemalans and Salvadorans with ABC status or TPS to take advantage of the provisions of NACARA to gain permanent residency (see Chapter 3).

Businesses on San Francisco's 24th Street, heart of the Latino community, were totally shut down on May 1, 2006, to honor the historic mobilization for undocumented immigrant rights (see Chapter 3).

Banner at Guatemala City's 2006 Migrants' Day celebration: "I am a migrant on the path of life; don't single me out" (see Chapter 3).

Banner at Guatemala City's 2006 Migrants' Day celebration: "To migrate is not a crime; the crime is in the causes of migration: lack of work and land, injustice, violence."—CAM (Centro de Atención al Migrante) (see Chapter 3).

Juan and Florinda Chanax migrated to Houston from San Cristóbal Totonicapán as a young couple to find work to pay for medical treatment for their son, Marco Antonio (see Chapter 4).

Overview of the town in the municipio of San Cristóbal Totonicapán (see Chapter 4).

Materials used for housing construction in San Cristóbal Totonicapán changed from adobe bricks to cinder blocks after the arrival of migrant remittances (see Chapter 4).

Inside Houston's Guatemalan bakery El Quetzal (see Chapter 4).

Guatemalan highland delivery service for sending letters, VHS cassettes, and packages to immigrants in the United States (see Chapter 4).

At San Francisco celebration of Guatemalan Independence Day (September 2009), from left to right: Félix Fuentes (Guatemalan American), Senior Outreach/Education Manager, San Francisco Office of Civic Engagement and Immigrant Affairs; coauthor Susanne Jonas; and Supervisor David Campos (Guatemalan American), elected to represent District 9 on San Francisco's Board of Supervisors (see Chapter 5). By permission of Félix Fuentes and David Campos.

La Victoria, long-standing, well-known traditional Mexican bakery on lower 24th Street, Mission District (see Chapter 5).

By 2011, the bakery was renamed "La Victoria/Wholesome Bakery" to appeal to newer, non-Latino professionals in the gentrifying lower 24th Street area, as well as the traditional Latino clientele (see Chapter 5).

La Victoria/Wholesome Bakery's upscale English-language menu of beignets and cupcakes also lists connections to social media sites (see Chapter 5).

La Victoria/Wholesome Bakery also sells expensive Fair Trade organic coffee (see Chapter 5).

Palacio Latino restaurant on Mission Street. Owned by a Guatemalan American, it serves as a social gathering place for Guatemalans; the owner also sponsors Guatemalan cultural events and has connections to a business providing transnational services (see Chapter 5).

Gracias Madre, an upscale Mexican-vegan restaurant owned by non-Latinos, recently opened up on Mission Street, with an English-language menu (see Chapter 5).

Wise Sons Jewish delicatessen is now in the lower 24th Street space formerly occupied by a traditional Mexican restaurant (see Chapter 5).

Enrique's Journey: On Balmy Alley, the core Mission District's famous site for murals painted on houses and garage doors, this mural (partial view) depicts a Central American migrant theme (see Chapter 5). By permission of muralist Josué Rojas.

Those we love we remember: Also on Balmy Alley, this mural is a memorial to children who died of AIDS (see Chapter 5). By permission of muralist Edythe Boone.

CHAPTER 4

Settlement and Transformations in Houston

Introduction: The Guatemala Left Behind

In the early 1980s, Guatemalan immigrants started arriving in Houston in sizeable numbers as part of a large Central American influx mainly from El Salvador, Guatemala, and Honduras. The best-organized immigration stream of Guatemalans arriving in the city consisted of Maya from the western highlands of Guatemala. In this chapter, we primarily focus on one group of Mayan migrants, the *sancristobalenses*, who migrated from the *municipio* of San Cristóbal Totonicapán in the western highlands of Guatemala.[1]

Situated at an elevation of 7,664 feet (2,336 meters) in the Sierra Madre mountains, San Cristóbal Totonicapán had a population of 20,000 living mainly in artisan and peasant families in the early 1980s, when growing numbers of migrants began leaving for the United States (Dirección General de Estadística 1984). About 3,400 residents lived in the town of San Cristóbal, with the reminder in seven surrounding *cantones* (villages) and a few *aldeas* (hamlets). Ninety-three percent of the population in the municipio was Mayan.

The sancristobalenses were not representative of the larger Guatemalan immigration experience in Houston in the initial immigration stages in the early 1980s. As we describe below, because they found a labor market niche, the sancristobalense migrants achieved faster economic mobility than most other Central American or Latino migrants in Houston. It was only after the beginning of stringent immigration enforcement in the 1990s that the newer sancristobalense migrants began to take on the general characteristics of Latino migrants living under the weight of restrictive immigration conditions (Lopez and Minushkin 2008).

Similarly to other Maya who arrived in Houston in the 1980s from the western Guatemalan highlands (e.g., from the municipios of Santa Cruz del Quiché, Huehuetenango, and Chimaltenango), the sancristobalenses came from a background greatly affected by the social turmoil of civil war in Guatemala (Jonas 1991). San Cristóbal Totonicapán was never a battle zone in the civil war, but the conflict in surrounding areas and accompanying economic decline pressured many sancristobalenses to emigrate. During the early years of the civil war, death squads would bring victims to the municipio at night to execute on the village roads, leaving the corpses to be discovered in the morning by villagers. Army patrols and military checkpoints near the municipio were also constant reminders of the surrounding presence of war as well as constant menaces to the stable life the sancristobalenses had known. When army roadblocks in the municipio failed to provide enough male youth to force into military service for the war, army soldiers entered the towns and villages of the municipio to forcefully draft male youth into the army, creating enormous distress among Mayan mothers, who would huddle crying at the gates of the municipal government building to beg military commanders for their sons' release, usually to no avail.

Although San Cristóbal Totonicapán escaped direct military conflict during the civil war, the fighting was never far away. In the surrounding departments of Huehuetenango, Quiché, and Sololá, the Guatemalan army laid waste to numerous Mayan villages through massacres, intimidation, and forced relocations (Carmack 1988). At the height of the army's scorched-earth policy of counterinsurgency in the early 1980s, a human wave of Mayan refugees crossed the Guatemalan border into the Mexican state of Chiapas to escape the violence brought by the army to their towns and villages. The refugees were escaping some of the worst atrocities committed against human communities recorded in modern history. In some of the villages in the departments surrounding Totonicapán, the army had declared war on the Maya, who had no means to defend themselves other than to try to hide or outrun the soldiers. In some areas near San Cristóbal Totonicapán, the intimidation and coercion came from Mayan men who were organized by the military into civil defense patrols.

Sancristobalenses responded to the surrounding violence by becoming politically invisible in order to avoid becoming a target for either the army or the guerrillas. To prevent arousing any suspicion of political activity, the sancristobalenses disbanded social organizations (recreational, religious, etc.) that were not critical to the life of the municipio. All terms and names associated with political groups or activities were stricken from everyday vocabulary, and in a conscious act of self-censorship, the very word *politics* was stricken from everyday use as well—the word *problems* was substituted in its place as a sort of code word.[2] So fearful were the sancristobalenses of political violence that by sunset they would go into their homes and shut themselves in for the night to protect against even the slightest possibility that some *oreja*, literally "ear" or secret informer, would accuse them of being involved in nocturnal political activity.

Political survival, however, did not mean economic survival. In the artisan and peasant economy of the Mayan highlands of western Guatemala, travel and transportation to and from the marketplaces of handicraft and agricultural products are essential. The marketplaces of the municipios rotate daily, guaranteeing municipios a large flow of buyers and sellers for at least one day a week. A large volume of taxis, buses, vans, trucks, and private cars transport people to and from the town squares and plazas where the marketplaces are held. The transportation businesses in turn stimulate local economies by creating a demand for fuel and vehicle maintenance services.

When artisans and farmers cannot travel to the marketplaces to sell their products or to buy other products, the regional economy falters and unemployment and poverty increase. This is what happened when the political violence escalated in the western highlands in the early to mid-1980s, inflicting heavy damage on the artisanal, agricultural, and marketplace activities of the region. A survey conducted by anthropologist Carol A. Smith in the community of Chipol in the department of Totonicapán, for example, found that nearly half of the artisans had gone out of business by 1984 (Smith 1988). In San Cristóbal Totonicapán, bakers, weavers, and other artisans, as well as farmers, became increasingly reluctant to travel to surrounding marketplaces when bodies of the victims of political violence began appearing on the sides of roads. The sancristobalenses greatly feared encountering army soldiers or guerrilla fighters on the roads to the marketplaces. They feared that such encounters could easily expose them to violence.

This is the background of, and the Guatemala left behind by, the sancristobalenses who traveled, mostly as undocumented migrants, about 1,500 miles to reach the metropolis of Houston in the foreign land of the United States. For the pioneers of this migration in the early 1980s, the travel was more than geographical—it was also a journey through time into an urban, modern culture where the norms and values of Mayan municipio society did not exist. Although some of the migrant pioneers had previously traveled to Guatemala City on business or to visit friends or relatives, a few had not ventured far from their villages in San Cristóbal Totonicapán before migrating to the United States. Some in the first groups of migrants to leave the municipio spoke mainly their indigenous language of K'iche' and only a little Spanish.

If the Mayan migration from Guatemala to the United States appeared as an historic feat in the 1980s, as pointed out in Chapter 1, it is true only within the scope of recent history. Within a longer historical scope, travelers from Mayan populations in the Central American isthmus traveled to regions far from their homes in pursuit of trade (Carmack 1981). Even in more recent times, the grandfathers of the sancristobalenses who migrated to Houston traveled in the early 1900s for months at a time in mule and horse caravans to sell handicraft products (rope, saddle blankets, etc.) made in the municipio to buyers in El Salvador, Nicaragua, and Honduras. Long-distance travel for extended periods of time for economic reasons thus was not a novelty in the Mayan municipio when the sancristobalenses left for Houston.

In the sections that follow in this chapter, we look at the aspects of settlement, work incorporation, community building, binational linkages with community back home, different migrant experiences in the Houston area, impacts of immigration enforcement, and interconnected transformations of migrants and the Houston area.

Transformative Change

The early phases of Guatemalan immigration in Houston transpired during a social-economic change that the city experienced in the 1980s and early 1990s. The story of Latino immigration and the transformation of Houston during this period are interconnected. New immigration helped change the city, but the city and settlement experiences also changed the migrants.

As pointed out in Chapter 1, the social change evident in many U.S. urban areas during the second half of the twentieth century and, indeed, across other world regions, is an outcome of the intersection of global processes with the dynamics of local "places." In the post–World War II era, and especially beginning in the 1970s, in large U.S. cities local economies underwent restructuring as foreign workers, especially from non-European regions, immigrated in large numbers. According to Saskia Sassen (1988), the Manhattan area of New York City, for example, experienced major economic and social reorganization as the populations of both high-income and low-income residents expanded in the city, with the latter population expanding mainly through the immigration of non-European groups. Through new sociospatial configurations, the high-income commercial and residential lives of affluent residents in Manhattan became intertwined with the presence of low-income immigrant communities and their trends of economic informalization. Michael Peter Smith (2001) has used the phrase "transnational urbanism" to capture the cultural ramification of the intersections of global processes with local places, and uses this metaphor to refer to changes at the places of destinations as well as the places of origin of international migrants.

Regardless of what terms or metaphors are used, it is clear that, perhaps at a scale not witnessed before, or not witnessed since the early 1900s, the intersection of international migration and local development in the last few decades has created new sociospatial conditions in which places and immigrants mutually transform each other. Similar macro transformative changes occur across U.S. urban areas, but a challenge is to study the unique features of particular settings, that is, to focus on the importance of place. Ultimately, the impacts of macro-level transformative forces are grounded in sociophysical environments, that is, cities, communities, and neighborhoods. We come to understand the specific effects of transformative developments by understanding how they play out in particular places.

Settlement

The arrival of Guatemalan immigrants in Houston in the early 1980s, as part of a larger Central American influx, coincided with a dramatic economic downturn of the metropolitan area. When the price of oil in the world economy fell by 32 percent between 1981 and 1985, the Houston economy entered a steep recession since its growth was strongly related to the development of the world petrochemical industry (Feagin 1988).[3] Economic decline precipitated a major opportunity for low-income people of color in Houston, including immigrants, to locate housing in the western half of the city, which was historically dominated by white middle-class residents.

The dramatic growth of the oil-related economic sector had stimulated an equally dramatic growth in the real-estate industry of housing construction. By the late 1970s, real estate investment in Houston had produced 3,067 apartment complexes, comprising 400,725 units, and several hundred suburban subdivisions (Feagin 1988). By 1986, however, when the Houston economy had 200,000 fewer jobs than in 1981 (Feagin 1988; Rodriguez and Hagan 1992), large numbers of apartment complexes and suburban subdivisions quickly became ghost towns as thousands of unemployed blue- and white-collar workers left Houston in search of jobs elsewhere.

The scene of abandoned apartment complexes became especially concentrated in the city's northwest and southwest sectors where real estate investors and developers had been most active in constructing apartment complexes of several hundred or more units. Throughout the city, unemployed workers abandoned housing units, which accounted for the largest number of the

25,602 properties foreclosed in 1986 (Feagin 1988). In the apartment housing sector, the number of vacant units rose from 86,961 in 1981 to 220,709 in 1985 (Smith 1986; Rodriguez and Hagan 1992).

The Houston area thus was undergoing a major economic crisis when Guatemalan and other Central American migrants were in the initial stage of their arrival in sizeable numbers in the early 1980s. For the Guatemalan and other Central American newcomers, most of whom entered the country without visas and with little knowledge of the area, the challenge was how to survive in the early stages of settlement, that is, how to find work and affordable housing.[4] The economic crisis of the area provided a major part of the solution for this challenge.

One response of apartment owners to the severe downturn in the Houston real estate industry was to destroy empty apartment complexes in order to avoid paying property taxes and maintenance costs. Apartment owners razed thousands of apartment units in the city between 1987 and 1989 (*Houston Business Journal*, October 1, 1990). Another response was to cut losses, that is, to file bankruptcy and let the lending institutions take possession of apartment properties, which in turn were taken over by federal agencies that managed mortgaged properties when the lending institutions themselves failed. But destroying apartment units and filing bankruptcies were not the best solutions to protect the billions of dollars invested in the Houston apartment housing market. The principal solution that the owners and managers of the apartment complexes adopted was one that dramatically altered the course of social development in many neighborhoods in the western half of the city. That solution was to turn to the arriving Latino immigrants to reconstruct tenant populations. This created a housing windfall for the Guatemalans and other Central American immigrants arriving in the city.

The tactics used by apartment owners and managers to attract the new Latino immigrants included changing apartment names from English to Spanish, replacing front office staff with bilingual rental agents, and providing special amenities to the Latino renters on the apartment grounds, such as Latino night clubs and even free English classes. The most dramatic tactic was to cut rental prices by as much as two-thirds in some cases, from $600 a month to $200 or even less a month. It was a massively ironic scene: thousands of apartment complexes that had been built with tennis courts and large swimming pools for the lifestyles of young, single, white, middle-income people were now being converted into living spaces for low-income, undocumented immigrant workers and their families. In contrast to manufacturing capitalists in other cities of the country who had used Latino immigrants to restructure production (e.g., see Morales 1983), real estate capitalists in Houston used Latino immigrants to restructure apartment housing consumption.

**Table 4.1. Guatemalan Immigrants in Houston:
Metropolitan Area and Central City, 1980–2010**

Census	Metropolitan Area	Central City	Percent in Central City
1980	826	n/a	n/a
1990	5,306	4,070	76.7
2000	14,126	10,509	74.4
2010	32,866	23,599	71.8

Sources: U.S. Census Bureau (1983a, Table 195; 1993; 2000; 2010b)

In general, the Guatemalans who arrived in the city in the 1980s settled in dispersed areas without any particular concentrations other than usually settling in the large areas of apartment complex concentrations in the northwest and southwest sectors of the city about 10 miles from downtown. This was generally true of the ladinos, who arrived from such places as Guatemala City, Quetzaltenango, San Marcos, and Chiquimula, but it was not true of all Mayan immigrants, who immigrated from such western highland areas, such as the municipios of Momostenango, San Francisco El Alto, Sololá, San Pedro la Laguna, San Miguel Totonicapán, San Cristóbal Totonicapán, and Santa Cruz del Quiché.

Table 4.1 shows the dynamic thrust of Guatemalan immigration into the Houston area in the 1980s and continuing to the 2010 census. The Guatemalan immigrant population grew by 542 percent in the Houston metropolitan area in the 1980s, concentrating by 77 percent in the city of Houston. Even as the Houston metropolitan area expanded from three to ten counties between the 1980 and 2010 censuses, 91 percent of Guatemalan immigrants resided in Harris County in 2010, where most of the city of Houston is located.

Being the largest Mayan immigrant groups in the city, the Maya from San Cristóbal Totonicapán and Santa Cruz del Quiché stood out in the residential concentrations they formed in the northwest, west, and southwest areas of the city. Sancristobalenses settled mainly along Westheimer Avenue, a major commercial avenue lined intermittently on both sides by large apartment complexes, in an area about 10 miles west of downtown and in the southwest corridor of the city, which had the largest concentration of apartment complexes in the city. The Maya from Santa Cruz del Quiché, on the other hand, settled mainly in apartment complexes in the northwest sector of the city, in a suburb named Spring Branch. In these apartment settlements, the Maya and other Guatemalan and Latino immigrants resided more than a dozen miles away from the old Mexican-origin neighborhoods on the east side of the city, where Mexican migrants had settled since the early 1900s.

In the western half of the city, the Maya developed "urban villages" with strong social bonds and frequent interaction among their apartment households. Even the physical appearances in some of the apartment complexes symbolized a village theme, as apartment sections were often separated by grassy and wooded spaces. Mayan tenants sometimes created trails between apartment complexes through these spaces as they constantly traveled to and from apartments to visit brothers, sisters, cousins, and other family members or friends from the same communities back home. The trails between apartment complexes usually ended at apartment back fences that had been bent or cut to allow visitors to pass. It was not until the late 1980s that the social interaction among Mayan apartment households lessened a bit when apartment managers started to control entry into apartment areas through the installation of new fences and electronically gated entrances.

The sancristobalenses were the largest Mayan group and thus their village-like existence was more visible. Initially, in 1979 and 1980, the group consisted of only a few households of men from the same families and villages back home, but by 1981 wives and other young women started arriving from the municipio. What was a trickle of sancristobalense immigration in the very early 1980s became a strong current by the mid-1980s as hundreds of sancristobalenses from the municipio arrived and settled, usually in the apartment clusters of relatives and friends alongside immigrant neighbors from other Central American countries, Mexico, and the Caribbean. About 300 sancristobalenses resided in 80 households by late 1985. Practically all the sancristobalense households consisted of different family generations or of nuclear families and close relatives or friends. Doubling up in apartments in the initial settlement stages helped to locate temporary housing quickly and at the same time helped pool incomes to afford rent payments with low wages. Yet, the development of mixed households did not serve solely an economic function. In the family system in the municipio, sancristobalenses sometimes developed extended and mixed households to provide social support during special circumstances, such as when a young couple was starting out in their marriage and needed support from family members.

Measured from the perspective of household turnover in the initial stage of settlement, the apartment clustering of the sancristobalenses was an effective strategy for providing social support. Interview data from a survey of undocumented Central Americans in Houston in 1985–1986 showed that the sancristobalenses had the lowest rate (.98) of household turnover per year of all the Central American migrants in the sample, while Salvadorans and Hondurans had the highest turnover rates (1.43 and 1.47, respectively).[5]

The initial stage of settlement can be stressful for immigrants because it brings major concern for locating housing and work. Some migrant families who have trouble finding housing and work sometimes migrate to other cities to look for better opportunities. For the sancristobalenses, this was never a major issue, given their strong bonds. Yet housing among the more cohesive Mayan migrants was never an absolute guarantee. In one household of Maya from Santa Cruz del Quiché, family members threatened to send a brother back to Guatemala if he did not show more interest in looking for work.

In the apartment complexes, the sancristobalenses attempted, as much as possible, to continue living as they had back home. Gendered social relations inside the family households remained fairly the same as back home, with the women doing all the cooking, washing, and cleaning. The men tended to be more concerned with the maintenance of vehicles, work issues, and social interaction outside family networks. On weekends, several families occasionally came together for special celebrations (birthdays, baptisms, etc.). The family gatherings were joyous occasions in which the women, dressed in traditional Mayan garments, prepared favorite dishes of the municipio and different tamales of the western Guatemalan highlands. Although a majority of the sancristobalenses was Catholic, the sancristobalenses who were evangelical Protestants would usually invite a pastor or other religious leader to give an invocation at the events. The host of the event would line up chairs against the walls of the living room for the guests to sit and chat, just as they did on similar occasions in the municipio. Almost all conversations were conducted in Spanish, with K'iche' used mainly with elders visiting from Guatemala or in jest among the young migrants.

Reestablishing the gendered relations of the municipio was part of the sancristobalense settlement process. In contrast to other Central American immigrants, who formed groups of men renting apartments or houses to live in dorm-like conditions, the sancristobalense men formed all-male households only briefly in 1980 and 1981 after the arrival of the first group of migrants from the municipio, since women did not arrive from the municipio until late 1981. The first women to arrive were the wives and sisters of the first male migrants.[6] They were women in their twenties who, like their young husbands, came from a village background in peasant and artisan households. Also like their husbands, they were mainly Spanish speakers but also understood K'iche'. Some of the women had several years of schooling but had not gone beyond the sixth grade.

By 1982 the formation of almost every sancristobalense migrant household in Houston included one or more female members. Women played critical roles in the formation of the migrant households in part because they prepared the traditional foods of the municipio to which the men remained attached. This was one reason that single men or men who had left their wives behind in the municipio usually attached themselves to households with women present.

In the late 1980s and early 1990s, the housing conditions of the Guatemalans and other Central American migrants in Houston began to change. As the area's economy improved, some apartment complexes with Central American and Latino immigrant tenants converted to higher priced rental properties, and thus many Latino immigrant families relocated to affordable housing elsewhere. Some sancristobalense families, however, moved into homes they bought a few miles west of the apartment complexes, and a few other families begun to construct homes in the municipio. A handful of sancristobalense families started constructing homes in the municipio at the same time that they bought homes in Houston.

Several significant changes affected the sancristobalense families, motivating them to buy homes in Houston or construct new ones in the municipio, or both. One major change involved the new opportunities brought by the passage of the Immigration Reform and Control Act (IRCA) of 1986, which provided amnesty and legalization for undocumented migrants who had resided in the United States since before 1982. The majority of sancristobalenses applied and received amnesty and legal status (Hagan, 1994), which enabled them to apply for mortgage loans. Another major change was the selling by real estate firms and government financial agencies of the glut of thousands of repossessed, vacant, single-family homes through dramatically reduced prices, special low-interest mortgage programs, and subsidies to pay closing costs for first-time buyers. Some sancristobalense families, for example, bought three-bedroom suburban brick homes with two-car garages and manicured lawns for as little as $40,000 at mortgage rates of 4.5 percent, with little money down. The economic downturn of the area brought a windfall of housing opportunities for the sancristobalenses, as well as for other Latino migrants, and, coming mainly from an artisan and peasant background, in which financial calculations are second nature, many of the sancristobalenses quickly realized the financial advantages of the times.

Yet it was more than economic factors that motivated the Guatemalan migrants to consider buying homes in Houston. Another major change affecting the first generation of Guatemalan migrant families was that they had entered a third settlement stage in which they enjoyed greater economic security and in which their children had more prominence in family decisions. In the initial settlement stage, the migrants had located temporary housing, found jobs, and begun sending remittances home, and in the second settlement stage, they had established residential and substantial employment stability. In the third stage, however, the migrants accumulated economic resources beyond what was necessary for survival and remittances, and furthermore their children, many of whom were U.S.-born, were approaching their teen years and advancing in their education. By the early to mid-1990s, when the children of the first Guatemalan migrant generation started entering middle school, the parents began to see a longer future in the United States, at least until their children finished school.

The first sancristobalenses to buy homes in Houston started a trend followed by other families as information about how to find realtors and get mortgages was shared through social networks. By the late 1990s, perhaps a third of the sancristobalense families had bought homes or were planning to buy homes in the near future, and by the early 2000s a few families had sold their first homes in Houston to buy newly constructed, large, two-story brick houses in fashionable subdivisions of homes selling for $140,000 or more, farther out in the western and southwestern reaches of the city.

By the early 2000s, Guatemalan migrants who had arrived with their families as small children in the early 1980s had become young adults, and some had married. Although technically these young migrants constituted part of the first generation of immigrants, their socialization occurred almost entirely in the United States. When they reached their twenties in the late 1990s and early 2000s, their social, cultural, and economic characteristics indicated how the settlement experience of the younger generation of Guatemalan migrants would continue to unfold. Insight into this development can be gained through the details of the social scene of a housewarming that occurred in the summer of 2002, when a sancristobalense couple in their mid-twenties bought a home in a suburb about twenty miles southwest from the downtown area of Houston after two years of marriage.

In several ways, the housewarming resembled the celebrations that the older generation of sancristobalenses had held in Houston since their arrival in the 1980s. Friends and relatives were invited, mainly through the networks of an evangelical church to which the couple and many of the sancristobalense group belonged. Several of the sancristobalense women over the age of thirty arrived wearing the traditional Mayan garments worn by women in the municipio. As in the celebrations of the older generation of sancristobalense migrants who belonged to the church, the event commenced with an invocation by religious leaders and a lengthy session of praying and religious singing. This was followed by an invitation to family and friends to give encouraging comments to the young couple as they faced the future together in their new home. After this session ended, the guests were treated to plates of food and dessert with punch drinks. For the remainder of the event, the guests conversed in similar age groups of older and younger adults, while the small children ran throughout the house playing hide-and-seek in the bedrooms and closets of the large house. It was a joyous occasion, and in some respects similar to the many events that the older members of the sancristobalense group had organized before in Houston.

But although the housewarming had similarities with past celebrations, it had significant differences as well, and these show how some among the younger generation of sancristobalenses were extending the settlement experience in Houston beyond what the older generation had established. For example, the main food served to the guests consisted of barbecued beef and sausages, not the traditional *estufado* dish served by the older generation in their celebrations. Moreover, the encouraging comments given to the couple by the younger generation tended to lapse into English after starting out in Spanish, demonstrating that the younger group members had sufficient ease with English to address a public gathering using it. None of the women younger than thirty wore traditional garments. And most of the youth and all of the small children interacted in English. Almost all of the persons in their twenties and younger dressed like youth anywhere in mainstream America, with the young men wearing the latest fashions of starched baggy pants and sporting shaven heads or spiked, colored hair. The social and cultural characteristics of the younger generation members at the event demonstrated that they continued to follow the community gathering practices of the older generation, but did so while displaying U.S. cultural themes of self-presentation in their dress and using English rather than Guatemalan languages.

The significance of place for the settlement of the sancristobalenses and other Guatemalans in Houston was clear in their ability to locate abundant housing in the western sectors of the city. Unlike other U.S. urban settings, where Guatemalan newcomers settled in inferior housing conditions, such as the Pico-Union district of downtown Los Angeles (Hamilton and Chinchilla 2001) or the Mission District in San Francisco, in Houston many Guatemalans were able to locate better quality housing. As we described above, the Houston economic recession in the early to mid-1980s opened a huge apartment housing market for low-income Guatemalan migrants and other Latinos entering the city, as thousands of unemployed, middle-income renters left to look for jobs elsewhere. Moreover, the lingering glut of repossessed residential properties created an affordable market for Guatemalan homebuyers. This experience would be partly repeated to some extent during the national economic recession that began at the end of 2007, as some sancristobalense families and other Latino migrants in Houston bought homes whose prices had fallen substantially by 2010.

Work Incorporation

The successful settlement accomplished by many of the sancristobalenses was a function of exceptional labor incorporation by many of the men and women in the group since their arrival in Houston in the 1980s. Whereas many Central American immigrants in the United States in the 1980s located jobs in the secondary labor market of unskilled, low-paying jobs, most of the sancristobalense men and a few of the women in Houston located jobs in the primary labor market of higher paying and stable employment, namely, in the workforce of a prosperous Houston supermarket chain, which catered mainly to middle-class and more affluent customers. With husbands or other family members working in the supermarket chain, many women and a few men also found employment as maids and servants in middle- and upper-middle-class households, usually of white families in the western sector of the city. Some of the maids found live-in jobs in high-income households where they enjoyed considerable privilege, but others complained of missing their families during weekdays, when they stayed in the households of their employers.

Work in a Supermarket Chain

The story of the labor incorporation in the supermarket chain begins with the story of Juan Chanax, who as a young husband and father migrated without papers to Houston in 1978 from the village of Xesuc in the municipio of San Cristóbal Totonicapán. The declining highland economy and a need to obtain medical treatment for his small son's illness motivated Juan, in his mid-twenties, to leave his wife and their two small children behind in the municipio and seek work in the United States. Having heard about Houston from another Guatemalan in the municipio who had traveled to the United States, he headed north through Mexico to cross the U.S.-Mexico border into Texas. When he finally reached Houston after several unsuccessful attempts to cross the U.S.-Mexico border, he soon found work as a handyman in a middle-class white household. He left his handyman job to work in a supermarket chain after running into an old acquaintance from Guatemala City who worked at one of the chain stores. The Guatemalan acquaintance also recruited Mayan migrants who were emigrating from the war-torn, highland department (regional province) of Quiché. Juan and the other Mayan workers were placed in floor maintenance crews to sweep, mop, and wax the floors of the supermarket stores where they were assigned.

The Guatemalan acquaintance also helped find jobs in the supermarket for Juan's brothers-in-law and a few friends. A competition for jobs developed between the workers from San Cristóbal Totonicapán and towns in Quiché. The sancristobalenses got the upper hand, however, when a supermarket manager asked Juan to recruit more workers from his group to work in the maintenance crews of the supermarket chain. Soon sancristobalenses were entering the workforces of the supermarket chain in sizeable numbers, replacing Mexican American and African American workers, who were reassigned to other tasks or who left the supermarket chain after the arrival of the Guatemalan migrants.

Sancristobalense migrants were greatly attracted to the supermarket jobs, turning their entry into the supermarket chain into a sort of gold rush for jobs in which some migrants could earn in a day what for many took almost a month to make back home. Wages for the sancristobalenses in the stores of the supermarket chain started above the minimum wage, and the workers were given health and pension benefits as well as the option to buy stock in the supermarket company. After several years, with periodic wage increases, the first sancristobalense to enter the supermarket workforce reached the top pay of $13 per hour in the floor maintenance crews, and even the lower paid workers who worked as sackers made significant amounts of extra income from tips earned for carrying grocery bags to the cars of affluent customers. Some sancristobalenses left the floor cleaning crews and went into the bakery section of the stores, where they were able to make more money than the top pay of the floor cleaning crews.

A small number of sancristobalense women also found jobs in the supermarket stores. Some were hired to work in the deli departments, customer service booths, and bakeries, and to work as cashiers as well. But the number of sancristobalense women working in the supermarket chain always remained much smaller than the number of sancristobalense men, who occupied the jobs in the numerous floor maintenance crews.

The Social Organization of Work

The hiring of the sancristobalenses into the work forces of the supermarket chain added a new personal and cultural dimension to the supermarket's social organization of work. First, only workers personally recruited or recommended by Juan, or by other sancristobalense crew leaders in other stores of the supermarket chain, were hired in the floor cleaning crews. In contrast to the normal hiring procedures of the supermarket, in which persons looking for work were asked to fill out job applications in the stores' offices, the sancristobalenses were hired through letters written back home or through personal contacts in the migrants' apartment homes, places of worship, or in Houston neighborhood soccer fields. Technically, a sancristobalense was not officially hired until an Anglo supermarket manager gave his approval, but managers rarely turned down the recommendations made by Juan or any other *encargado* (the Spanish term given by the sancristobalense workers in the supermarket stores to their informal crew leader).

Second, it was the sancristobalense customs and practices of family and interpersonal relations that made sancristobalenses migrant workers attractive to the supermarket managers. The Guatemalan workers that Juan and other encargados were recruiting were mostly their relatives, friends, and other acquaintances from the municipio, and occasionally from surrounding Mayan localities in the highlands as well. Only rarely were workers recruited into the floor maintenance crews who were not from the municipio or other Guatemalan communities. To be sure, family or national ties were not always the principal criteria for recruiting new workers. Some encargados occasionally recruited good soccer players from the municipio to work in the supermarket chain and play on their soccer teams in Houston as well.

The work relations that evolved from previous social relations or common backgrounds among the sancristobalense workers thus were partly extensions of Mayan cultural bonds that created strong social cohesion in their Guatemalan communities of origin. In other words, the work relations between the encargados and their crews were mediated by their Mayan culture regarding respect for social status and proper role behavior. For example, a sancristobalense worker who showed up late for work was breaking a supermarket rule and at the same time violating the group's cultural norms of social responsibility towards elders. The sancristobalense who came late to work, therefore, had to explain his tardiness to an encargado who might be his uncle or other family elder. This was a powerful cultural reinforcement of the social organization of work in the supermarket stores.

The use of sancristobalense social and cultural capital became stronger when, after a few years, supermarket store managers simply gave encargados a budget of work hours for doing the floor maintenance work and turned over the organization of the work to these informal crew leaders. Encargados divided the work hours among the workers in their crews, usually attempting to be as fair as possible. To maximize their incomes, the workers wanted to work at least 40 hours per week, but the work hour budget given in each store varied according to the volume of business in the store.

Developing a Company Identity

In the municipio, Mayan sancristobalenses did not generally develop a strong sense of identity with particular workplaces. Social identities were attached mainly to one's municipio, village, school, family, and church. Moreover, the Mayan sancristobalenses also did not seem to have a strong national identity as Guatemalans. The world outside their municipio, and especially beyond the highlands, seemed remote and foreign for many residents of the municipio. Employment in the supermarket, however, brought a major contrast with this previous experience of social identity.

The sancristobalenses developed a strong sense of identity with the supermarket. Sancristobalense workers wore the supermarket uniform of dark slacks, a white, long-sleeve shirt and a dark tie eagerly and proudly. The workers prominently displayed items with the supermarket logo in their apartments and sent such items as gifts to their families back home. When asked where they worked, the workers responded quickly with the supermarket's name in a way that indicated pride. To be sure, it was a choice employment place for undocumented workers, since the supermarket chain paid more than the minimum wage and offered worker benefits, in contrast to the usual inferior workplaces of undocumented labor. Employment in the supermarket chain remained a prized possession among the sancristobalenses even after they legalized their immigrant status under IRCA and thus could look for work in a larger range of the Houston labor market.[7]

The sancristobalense workers were well aware that most stores of the supermarket chain catered mainly to middle-class and affluent customers, and many of the workers felt it was a privilege to interact in the store with members of this social level. Interacting with rich and socially privileged people, especially whites, had not been a common experience for the sancristobalenses in Guatemala. Sancristobalense workers interacted with affluent customers in the supermarket stores when they worked as sackers and carried grocery bags to the cars of the customers, and when affluent customers approached them looking for Guatemalan women to work in their households as servants. The daily interaction with affluent customers, who were usually friendly to the workers, made the supermarket stores a special place for many sancristobalense workers who, in Guatemala, had lived with a low social status because of their indigenous and class backgrounds.

The development of a strong identity with the supermarket chain was also demonstrated in the workers' organizing of soccer teams of supermarket workers. The work networks became principal sources of players for the soccer teams, and encargados often became the soccer team captains. As mentioned above, occasionally encargados would recruit new workers from Guatemala because they were known to be good soccer players. These workers were literally recruited from "farm" teams in the municipio to make the sancristobalense teams more competitive in the immigrant soccer leagues in Houston. For the sake of forming a strong team, in a couple of cases an encargado recruited non-Mayan workers (a Middle Eastern immigrant, for example) into his floor maintenance crew who were known to be especially talented soccer players.

The sancristobalenses' identity with the supermarket company was also related, no doubt, to social issues in the larger society. In the pre-IRCA days, the sancristobalenses in the supermarket stores formed a higher status labor group through their relatively higher pay and job benefits, while many other undocumented workers attempted to survive in the inferior jobs of the secondary labor market. For the men, the supermarket was also the basis for the sancristobalense soccer teams, which enjoyed considerable success and status in the Latino immigrant soccer leagues in the city. Finally, the supermarket stores provided a space where some of the sancristobalense workers could ascend socially, if only momentarily, and interact with white persons of a higher social status, although at first this produced nervous moments for some sancristobalense workers.

A New Work Culture

Wage labor in the supermarkets was not a new experience for most of the sancristobalenses. Many of them had been paid daily wages as agricultural workers or had been paid piecemeal for artisan work. What *was* new was the regimentation of time and the formal hierarchical supervision of work—the basic features of the U.S. capitalist workplace. In contrast to work in the open agricultural spaces and lightly supervised artisan workshops in the municipio back home, in the supermarket, work tasks had to be completed on schedule, and store managers were quick to point out faults and demand that work be done over when it was not done properly.

Most workers assimilated extremely well into the new work culture since the supermarket work usually required less physical effort and paid much higher than work done back in the municipio. Eventually, however, some problems surfaced among the sancristobalense workers in their new work environments. Community social relations that functioned very well in organizing the floor maintenance crews sometimes became disadvantages for the encargados when their work authority was challenged because they had lower social statuses in community circles. Also, some encargados who were less socially related by kinship to their crewmembers sometimes faced problems in the sancristobalense migrant community when they disciplined workers in the supermarket stores.

Major Changes in the 1990s

In the 1990s, the experience of the sancristobalense migrant work force in the supermarket underwent several significant changes. One change was that a number of the sancristobalense had been promoted to higher status and higher-paying jobs. A major catalyst for this development was the migrants' participation in the amnesty and legalization programs of IRCA. This law required that undocumented immigrants attend English and civics classes to qualify for legalization. Almost all of the sancristobalense workers in the supermarket applied for amnesty and legalization, and when their English abilities improved, some were subsequently promoted from floor cleaning crews to higher-paying jobs in the supermarket stores. This was especially true for the workers with higher levels of education. Some of the workers were promoted to managers in different sections (deli, bakery, and so forth) of the supermarket stores, and a few were even promoted to assistant store managers. Of the few women who worked in the supermarket chain, one young woman who graduated from a Houston high school in 1988 started as a salad bar worker and moved to cashier and then to video rentals and finally to the courtesy booth, becoming the first Latino worker to hold such a job in the store, and making $11 an hour. She then moved to the bakery section to gain baking experience in order to open a bakery in the future.

A second change was the growing pattern of worker resistance in the supermarket workforce. The sancristobalense workers remained an impressive labor force in the supermarket in the 1990s, but some worker dissatisfaction emerged that was not visible in the 1980s. Having legal immigrant status and greater knowledge of the labor market in the Houston area, some sancristobalense workers became less hesitant to express their dissatisfaction with working conditions that they viewed as unfair. In one store, sancristobalense workers staged a temporary walkout when they felt they were being treated unfairly. As a second example, in a large warehouse of the supermarket, many of the sancristobalense workers voted in favor of having a labor union after the supermarket lowered the "top pay," and the pro-union vote almost won.[8] In individual stores, some Maya workers left their jobs when they felt they could find better working conditions in other supermarket chains or when they decided to open their own businesses (e.g., bakeries and landscaping). No doubt what affected the change in some of the workers' attitude in the 1990s was that their economic reference point was less and less their municipio of origin and more and more the Houston setting. The supermarket jobs appeared golden in the 1980s when the sancristobalense workers were emigrating from the extremely low-paying wage structure of indigenous settings in Guatemala, but after residing in Houston for more than a decade, the sancristobalense workers increasingly saw the supermarket jobs as common and not always superior to other jobs in the Houston area. The supermarket jobs maintained their special attraction mainly among the new undocumented workers who faced employment restrictions under IRCA, which made the hiring of undocumented workers illegal and provided for hefty fines against employers who broke this law.

A third major change in the supermarket's sancristobalense workforce in the 1990s was the appearance of a new generation of young workers who were new migrants from the municipio or who had grown up in Houston. According to some of the older workers, the new generation of workers lacked discipline and was accustomed to a material life that included color televisions, stereos, CD players, and other material goods acquired in the municipio through remittances or in Houston through steady incomes. Older workers also saw some of the young migrant workers as detached from the traditional work values that they had known in the municipio of their youth.

From the perspective of the new young workers, who came from either the municipio or from families in Houston, the supermarket jobs were not seen as a scarce good to be coveted, as sancristobalense migrants had done in the 1980s. Indeed, some young workers who were born in Houston made plans to leave the supermarket for office work elsewhere or to pursue college degrees. The second-generation workers were simply not a major resource for reproducing the culturally based sancristobalense work teams of years past in the supermarket.

Finally, a fourth major change in the work experiences of the sancristobalense migrant workers in the supermarket was that the supermarket chain was sold in the late 1990s to a national chain that restructured the labor-intensive work in the supermarket stores. The new owners of the supermarket chain contracted the floor maintenance work with a cleaning company and thus did away with the floor maintenance crews. The Mayan workers in the floor maintenance crews were sent to different sections in the supermarkets. In some stores of the supermarket chain, workers no longer wore a store uniform. Some of the older sancristobalense workers felt that the new management brought a reduced interest in the welfare of the workers. Experiencing a drop in morale and identity with the supermarket chain under the new management, some of the sancristobalense workers began to look for jobs in other supermarket chains.

Looking for other jobs became a necessity in the early 2000s for sancristobalense workers in the supermarket chain, as a drop in sales in some of the supermarket stores caused a reduction in the number of work hours allotted to workers or in the number of workers needed in the stores. Facing a reduction of work hours, some of the sancristobalense workers sought part-time work in other jobs to maintain a 40-hour week, or planned ahead to meet the 30-year employment requirement for retirement from the supermarket chain.

In the early 2000s, the supermarket chain ceased to be the lucrative entry point into the Houston job market that the sancristobalenses had known since the early 1980s. By 2010, it was almost impossible for a worker to get a job in the supermarket chain without being legally in the country. Many of the sancristobalense workers who continued to arrive in Houston now joined the rest of the Latino undocumented migrant workers in the city looking for jobs, sometimes finding small niches in restaurants and service jobs that usually paid below the minimum wage.

Domestic Work

Although a handful of sancristobalense women found employment in the supermarket chain, the central source of employment for these women became white, upper-middle- and upper-class households in the western sectors of the city. To be sure, household employment also became a source of work for a handful of sancristobalense men who lived with wives working as live-in maids, or who worked as handymen and chauffeurs. The women who arrived as wives and relatives of the first small group of sancristobalense men in the city initially found domestic jobs through contacts with the wives of their husbands' employers. This initial labor incorporation into domestic work soon led to a labor stream of women migrants from the municipio to work as domestics in affluent households in Houston.

For analytical purposes, we separate the labor incorporation of sancristobalense men and women, but in reality the labor incorporation of the two genders was often interdependent since their basic unit of social support in Houston was usually a co-gendered household. In the early 1980s, the sancristobalense women obtained their first domestic jobs through information provided by fellow sancristobalense women migrants, similar to the manner in which the male migrants found jobs in the supermarket. In the sancristobalense migrant households, husbands and wives and other male and female relatives discussed whom to inform back home about the availability of work in households or in the supermarket chain, and when new migrants arrived unexpectedly from the municipio, both male and females in the sancristobalense households provided for their support until they found work. Ultimately, it was the women who introduced the new female migrants to their household employers, as the men did with the new male migrants in the supermarket stores, but this was only the final stage of a labor incorporation process that was anchored in co-gendered family households.

The labor incorporation of sancristobalense migrant women into domestic work ran mainly along two networks of women, that is, the networks of sancristobalense women who recruited new workers and the networks of the mostly white women who provided domestic jobs. The sancristobalense women shared information concerning prospective employers concerning how much they paid and the conditions of work, and the women employers shared information regarding the reputations and skills of the available domestic workers. Whereas household employers often hired sancristobalense domestics by working through the network of sancristobalense women, some employers asked the sancristobalense workers in the supermarkets whether they knew of women looking for domestic work. This method of recruiting domestics increased in the early 1990s as the supermarket chain expanded its maintenance workforce of sancristobalense workers.

As reported by Hagan (1998), the job careers of the sancristobalense women started as live-in or day maids, which restricted their participation in the growing community of sancristobalenses in Houston since work schedules often ran from Monday through Saturday and included evenings. In the households, the sancristobalense women cleaned, took care of small children, washed, ironed, and cooked. The starting salary for the women was usually less than $100 per week in the 1980s, and even by the mid-1990s the salaries for live-in maids were about $125 per week. In the 2000s, the salaries increased, to about $250 per week by 2010, but only kept pace with the rise of the cost of living. In terms of real income, therefore, the salaries of the sancristobalense domestic workers remained close to what they were paid in the early 1980s.[9]

In some cases, the live-in maids were permitted to have visiting female relatives stay for periods of time, and some married live-in maids were permitted to have their husbands stay with them. For many sancristobalense women with family in Houston, however, the goal was to obtain cleaning contracts to clean homes during the day and return to their family households in the evenings. In the late 1990s and early 2000s, women who were doing contract cleaning work were earning $55 or more per household.

For many household employers, Mayan women stood out as superior workers for household labor in comparison with other immigrant or U.S-born women they had hired previously. Household employers viewed Mayan women as highly disciplined, reliable, and trustworthy. For example, according to one employer, her sancristobalense maid was heaven-sent compared to an earlier Mexican maid, who always had boyfriends calling, and a Salvadoran maid, who supposedly took silverware from the house. In another example, an employer in Houston's most fashionable upper-class neighborhood rated her sancristobalense maid as more spirited and assertive in her job performance than her previous U.S.-born maids.

Doubtless what the employers saw as superior virtues in their Mayan maids was related more to the women's indigenous Mayan background than their Guatemalan nationality. The indigenous women were coming from backgrounds in Guatemala in which relations between indigenous and nonindigenous peoples (ladinos) followed centuries-old, strict norms of hierarchical interaction, framed within the larger structure of colonial power relations (see Wolf 1959). Occupying a lower social stratum, indigenous groups enhanced their survival partly by consciously manifesting attitudes of deference and acquiescence in interactions with higher-status groups. This interactional strategy thus was a product of past colonial relations. Yet, the effects of an indigenous Guatemalan background were not everlasting. Like their male counterparts, the women began to plan and strategize about their live-in or day domestic work conditions more from a U.S. perspective when they gained more knowledge about work conditions in the local labor market.

As described in Chapter 2, the sancristobalense women doing domestic work faced more limited and restricted work conditions than their male counterparts in the supermarket chain. The men were able to cope with the rigors of work through internal social strategies in the encargado system of labor organization and to receive steady wage increments through the regulations of their primary labor market workplace. In contrast, working as individuals, the women faced work problems alone in the households where they were employed. As also described in Chapter 2, working in smaller workplaces and interacting in more limited social networks meant that the women never had access to the greater number of work opportunities the men did, nor were the women able to access networks external to the sancristobalense group to reach additional job markets, as some of the men did. While the men's networks expanded, the women's networks contracted, according to Hagan (1998).

By the late 1990s, the gendered advantages and disadvantages of the sancristobalense immigrant workers began to change, and reverse in some cases. Two factors affected this change. One factor was the enactment of the Illegal Immigration Reform and Immigrant Responsibility Act (IIRIRA) in 1996 (see Chapters 2 and 3), which made it harder for undocumented immigrant workers to find jobs in the primary labor market. The second factor was that after spending a long period doing domestic work, some sancristobalense women used the experience to create their own cleaning businesses, in contrast with most sancristobalense workers in the supermarket chain, as they could not easily leave their jobs and start businesses from their supermarket experiences.

IIRIRA brought a new get-tough-on-immigration policy. The act threatened employers of undocumented immigrant workers in the primary labor market sector of formal employment, especially in large workplaces where workers have public visibility. The Houston supermarket chain always required proper documentation from the workers, but the older sancristobalense workers had helped the newcomers maneuver through this requirement. The supermarket chain became more demanding of proper documents from its workers after the passage of IRCA in 1986, which introduced federal requirements for the inspection of employment eligibility. After the passage of IIRIRA in 1996, the supermarket chain made it much more difficult for workers to obtain jobs at its stores without authentic documents.

By comparison, the enactment of the two immigration laws did not have a similar impact in the secondary labor market sector of informal and casual employment. In private households, undocumented domestic workers and their employers were not publicly visible and not vulnerable to federal inspections. The federal measures to control undocumented immigrant labor thus placed greater pressure on the employment of men working or seeking to work in the supermarket chain than on the women working in private households.

After spending years working in private households, some of the sancristobalense domestics started small businesses. With the knowledge they gained about various household appliances and about the cleaning standards of middle-class homes, the women started informal businesses cleaning homes through verbal weekly contracts. The cleaning work usually took half a day per home, for which they were paid $40 to $55 per job in the late 1990s, and $65 or more in the 2000s. Contract household work became a natural step for the women who had worked in households in which children had grown up. In these households, the sancristobalense women had often looked after the children and in some cases took on the role of nannies. When the children grew up, however, some employers did not see a need to pay the women to work the whole day in the household.

Contract house cleaning work provided important advantages for the sancristobalense women. One advantage was the increase in income. Even the women who had the most years in household work and were paid more than $125 per week could make more money if they cleaned four or five homes per week. Another advantage for the women was that they could control their work schedule and spend more time working in their own homes, or on church projects or other activities with which they were involved. By contrast, doing contract work was not an option for the men working in the supermarket stores. They were firmly tied to wage work, and only in a few cases did supermarket workers leave to start their own businesses, as bakers and landscape contractors. For the men in the supermarket chain, the way to increase their income beyond pay raises was to work part-time or even full-time in other jobs, which meant spending more time at work.

As the men had experienced in the supermarket chain, the domestic labor market of the sancristobalense women underwent major changes in the early 2000s, and by 2010 had experienced major restrictions. Newly arriving sancristobalense women, whose numbers slowed after 2005, found it much harder to find domestic jobs than the earlier migrant women who arrived in the 1980s and 1990s. There were several reasons for this change. One reason was that older domestic workers hung on to their jobs, especially as new legal restrictions made it harder for undocumented workers to locate new jobs. A second reason was that the 2007 recession reduced the ability of some households to hire domestics, while other households became fearful of hiring undocumented workers in the face of mounting immigration enforcement. A third reason was that large-scale immigration swelled the labor force of domestics, which in the 2005–2010 period included numbers of Guatemalan women who were not indigenous. The sancristobalense women themselves began helping other women from Guatemala find domestic work in the 1990s.

The second generation of women in the sancristobalense group, that is, those who were brought from the municipio as small children or were born in the United States, did not follow the first generation of women into the labor market of domestic work. Instead, this generation of young women took jobs in a variety of occupations, mainly in the service sector, and some enrolled in universities or professional schools to train for careers, such as in nursing, accounting, pharmacy, and cosmetology.

Building Community

The arrival of Guatemalans in Houston added to the Latino community-building process in the area at various levels. This process included developing institutions and sets of social relations that promoted social identity among various groups. One level concerned the community building of the larger Latino population. A second level concerned the community building of the Central American population, and a third level concerned the community building of the Guatemalans.

Building the Larger Latino Community

Before the arrival of large numbers of Latino immigrants in the 1980s, U.S.-born Mexican Americans were the main source of Latino community building in Houston (De Leon 2001). Immigrants had remained a small percent of the city population until the 1980s. The 1970 census found that the foreign-born population was less than five percent of the city population, and the 1980 census found that the foreign born were still less than ten percent of the city population (U.S. Census Bureau 1983a). Among Latinos, the foreign-born population was a larger percentage than for the city population as a whole in 1980, but still less than a third of the total Latino population. Of the 424,903 Latinos counted by the 1980 census in the Houston metropolitan area, 116,084 were Latin American immigrants, including 93,718 Mexicans, 1,790 Salvadorans, and 826 Guatemalans (U.S. Census Bureau 1983a, Table 195; 1983b, Table 59). Being predominantly U.S.-born, the Latino population in the Houston area was very U.S.-focused, with its Mexican American leadership concentrating on social issues such as equal employment opportunity, political redistricting, bilingual education, affirmative action, and so forth.

Community building among Latinos in Houston exploded in the 1980s with the large-scale immigration from Latin America, especially from Mexico and Central America. Whereas the 1980 census had found 116,084 Latin American immigrants in the Houston metropolitan area, the 1990 census found 192,231 Latin American immigrants in the city of Houston alone (U.S. Census Bureau, 1993, Table 168). Mexicans accounted for 132,596 of the Latin American immigrants, and Central Americans accounted for 39,289, of which 27,660 were Salvadorans, 4,070 were Guatemalans, and 3,970 were Hondurans. The explosive Latin American immigration took the larger Latino community development in different directions from the community concerns of the Mexican Americans, who for decades had dominated the Latino scene of the city.

Geographically, Latin American immigrants, especially Mexicans and Central Americans, did much to expand the presence of the Latino population into the far reaches of the northern and western sectors of the city.

Whereas U.S.-born Mexican Americans and earlier Mexican immigrants had concentrated in the east side of the city and in nearby working-class suburbs, the immigrants of the 1980s extended Latino community life more than 10 miles away from downtown into northern and western sectors of the city. By the early 2000s, the Latino population expansion stretched as far as 20 miles from the downtown area in several directions.

In the 1980s and through the mid-1990s, the signs of Latino community life in these stretches included new Latino neighborhoods in apartment complexes, Latino churches, public schools with large numbers of Latino students, and shopping centers with a variety of Latino businesses, such as restaurants, international courier services, music stores, meat markets, night clubs, and so forth. By the late 1990s and through the first decade of the 2000s, the signs of Latino community life in these far reaches of the city also included Latino homes in new subdivisions.

Central American Community Building

The Latino settlements that emerged outside the old Mexican-origin neighborhoods near downtown included diverse Latin American nationalities, albeit dominated by Mexican immigrants. In the southwest sector of the city, Central American immigrants built their largest concentration in the Gulfton neighborhood area. Salvadorans predominated among the Central Americans in this neighborhood area, but Guatemalans and Hondurans also made their presence felt in places of worship, community-service agencies, and recreational places of the area.

The initial Central American community building in the early to mid-1980s included the formation of Christian community-based organizations (*comunidades de base*), organized mainly by Salvadorans, with the involvement of other Central American and U.S. supporters, including Catholic religious activists.[10] These organizations promoted community projects and provided information concerning political developments in Central America. The organizations became points of contact for U.S. supporters who wanted to assist the arriving Central American immigrants. By the early to mid-1990s, however, most of these organizations dissolved as their members became incorporated into U.S. organizations or took full-time jobs, leaving little time for organizational activities.

Two community organizations with strong Salvadoran leadership survived among the Central Americans in Houston into the 2000s. The organizations, the Gulfton Neighborhood Organization (GANO)/Central American Resource Center (CARECEN) and Centro de Recursos Centroamericanos

(CRECEN), are connected to organizational networks in the United States and include Latina and Latino leaders from other groups. In Houston, both organizations work to support Central American causes in the area, in addition to helping immigrants with legal paperwork concerning their immigration status.

Guatemalan immigrants have also organized community organizations in Houston as a part of their community building. The organizations include the Consejo Comunitario Guatemalteco, Comité Guatemalteco, and Red por la Paz y Desarrollo de Guatemala, which is the local office of a national organization with the same name (see Chapter 3). In the 2000s, these organizations and the community-oriented Unity Soccer League came together to form the Alianza De Organizaciones Guatemaltecas de Houston (ADO-GUAH) to address community and immigration issues affecting the Guatemalan population in Houston. The organizations of ADOGUAH have different patterns of leadership and community involvement, but they share the priority, along with other, less formal Guatemalan groupings in the city, of working with a national effort of Guatemalan immigrants to bring about Temporary Protected Status (TPS) for undocumented Guatemalan migrants (see Chapter 3).[11] In 2010 and 2011, the Guatemalan organizations in Houston became heavily involved in a national petition drive requesting TPS for undocumented Guatemalans.

Being the second-largest Latino group in the city, numbering 75,907 U.S.- and foreign-born residents in 2010 (U.S. Census Bureau 2010b), Salvadorans have the greatest potential among non-Mexican Latinos to develop an ethnic residential zone, especially in the southwestern Gulfton area where they have the largest concentration. Large numbers of other Latinos who also live in the Gulfton neighborhood, however, have kept the area from having a strong Salvadoran identity. The Guatemalans, who have become the fourth-largest Latino group in the city, after Mexicans, Salvadorans, and Hondurans, are even less able to build a separate ethnic community with their smaller numbers, and thus they mainly reside interspersed with other Latino immigrants.

Guatemalan Community Building

Although Guatemalans have not developed a strong community identity recognizable by other residents in Houston, many have developed a sense of community among themselves based on common origin, common concerns, and frequent interaction within their group. By the late 1990s and early 2000s, the most visible Guatemalans involved in community activities involved the

Maya from various Guatemalan departments (Quiché, Quetzaltenango, Sololá, Totonicapán, and others) as these migrants interacted among themselves or with other groups in neighborhoods and in institutional settings, such as places of worship, workplaces, retail areas, and recreational places. The Maya have the most visibility because many stand apart in gatherings, but their interaction does not exclude ladinos, who sometimes join in the interaction in these institutional settings through friendships or family connections with Mayan individuals.

Further research remains to be done on the topic, but preliminary observations indicate that the marked divisions between ladinos and indigenous groups in Guatemala have not been reproduced in the Houston area and definitely are not a concern manifested by the second generation of Guatemalans in the Houston area. At this point, we can only speculate that the social divisions between ladinos and Maya in Guatemala have not been recreated in Houston because the Maya have not pursued a strong indigenous identity and because the two groups have not developed in large enough numbers to confront each other competitively in institutional arenas across the city. Moreover, the rapid economic success of the sancristobalenses through their labor market niches propelled them into a higher social status in the new Central American immigrant labor force in the city, making them sources of potential support for other Guatemalans. In other words, it is likely that the common immigrant challenges that motivate compatriots to seek mutual support have prevailed over any potential concerns for social divisions among the two Guatemalan groups in Houston.[12]

It was the Maya from San Cristóbal Totonicapán and Santa Cruz del Quiché who reached the strongest community cohesion in the Houston area, although they sometimes lived interspersed among other Latino immigrants in the city. We have shown above how the sancristobalenses developed internal community relations in their settlement and labor incorporation. In addition to these sources of community development, the sancristobalenses participated in two types of formal organizations that became major resources for community building. The formal organizations consisted of evangelical Protestant churches and soccer teams.

Among the evangelical Protestant churches that the sancristobalenses organized in Houston, one church in particular had a major impact on community building in this migrant group because its membership included many of the first sancristobalense migrants to settle in Houston. Mexican migrants founded the church originally in an old Mexican neighborhood in the eastern side of the city, but the sancristobalenses became the dominant membership by the mid-1980s when the Mexican members left to start a new church elsewhere. Undoubtedly, cultural differences split the Mexican and sancristobalense members in the church, but the sancristobalenses were bound to gain control of the church because they had extensive experience participating in evangelical Protestant churches in the municipio.[13]

The sancristobalenses reorganized the operation of the church in ways that maximized its utility for their community development. Working with a young Mexican American pastor, the sancristobalenses developed an elaborate church program of religious and Bible-reading classes for the adults and youth in the church. The main church services were held on Sundays and Wednesdays, and Bible-study sessions led by women for the women and their daughters were held on Saturdays, with additional *cultos de hogar* (home worshiping) on Tuesday evenings, when church members met in each other's homes to discuss the ways in which Bible teachings could be used to improve life in the family and community (Hagan, 1994). At one point, the sancristobalenses also had a program in the church to teach K'iche' to the youth.

While the formal membership of the church never reached one hundred, the community influence of the church reached a relatively large population of sancristobalenses. Especially in the early settlement years, church members frequently used the church to organize family and community activities that attracted a large attendance of sancristobalense immigrants and their U.S.-born children. A core group of mainly women used the church to organize such family and community events as baptisms, weddings, funerals, quinceañeras for young women, ceremonies for school graduates, and housewarmings. Through the church networks, the core group divided the work that needed to be done to hold the events, which usually involved a large number of sancristobalenses.

Having the pastor present to lead prayer sessions at the events produced an atmosphere of moral authority and institutional order, enhancing the sense of community beyond a simple gathering of friends and acquaintances. The prayer sessions, which were led by men, involve explicit comments regarding the welfare of the church members as a community. The fact that several of the women in the core group wore traditional Mayan garments to the events undoubtedly served to promote ethnic identity, not as Mayan but as sancristobalenses, as the designs of the traditional garments symbolized specific municipios. At all the events, the church members enthusiastically welcomed the participation of other group members who arrived.

The evangelical Protestant church also performed community-building functions by serving as a means through which church members gained new social status and positions within the larger sancristobalense immigrant population. For example, the church social activities provide opportunities for different women to take on roles of leadership among the larger group of women. Some men trained as pastors or deacons through church affiliations and thus obtained more formal and elevated social positions within the church membership. In a situation in which the sancristobalenses initially faced a marginal status as undocumented immigrants with jobs low on the occupational prestige scale, the church helped many sancristobalenses to develop a sense of community membership and identity against the background of the larger society.

By contrast, Catholic churches did not fulfill a similar role for the many sancristobalenses and other Guatemalan migrants who were Catholics. With their hierarchical structure and mixed memberships of Anglo and Latino parishioners, many of whom spoke primarily English, Latino migrants found little space to take "ownership" of Catholic churches, as some migrants did in the smaller evangelical Protestant churches. Nonetheless, Catholic priests and nuns did as much as or more than any other religious leaders in the city to bring attention to the suffering in Central America as a source of immigration in the city. Some Catholic priests and nuns, as well as Lutheran workers, helped Central American migrants develop community-based organizations during the 1980s.

The sancristobalense men developed an additional organization to create community structure during the early settlement. They helped to develop a soccer league that included several soccer teams of sancristobalense immigrant men along with about three hundred other immigrant players mainly from Central America. In addition to bringing hundreds of young immigrant men together on a weekly basis to play and to exchange information about work or family concerns, the soccer league provided an organizational image and voice through which the men could relate to other social actors, especially in the search for public space to play soccer.

At the beginning of the larger waves of Central American influx in Houston in the early 1980s, Guatemalans and other Central American soccer players made do with makeshift playing arrangements throughout the parks and public school grounds of the city, particularly in areas near Latino neighborhoods. Some of these arrangements created opportunities for abuse and exploitation, however, as persons with more experience in the United States attempted to charge the immigrant soccer players for the use of public parks. For example, an immigrant who had been in the United States for several years could organize a league and request a periodic fee from each team supposedly to help pay the cost for using park fields. Being new in the country, migrant soccer players did not realize that it was not necessary to pay to play in a public park.

In one case, several Central American teams of Guatemalans and Salvadorans in a soccer league learned that it was not necessary to pay when they decided in the summer of 1997 to leave the league and form a new one after they felt the league director had become excessive in his fees. In a meeting with a local community organizer, the Guatemalan and Salvadoran team captains learned that to use the playing fields in a neighborhood county park, they simply had to ask permission from the county commissioners. The Guatemalan and Salvadoran team captains asked to be placed on the calendar of county commissioner meetings to request the use of the park playing fields.

Facing the county commissioners in their meeting chamber was a dramatic moment for the Guatemalan team captains because it was their first collective political activity in the United States. The Guatemalan team captains and their players had avoided any kind of political activity or gathering since arriving in the country for fear of reprisals. Some of the Mayan team captains were quick to point out that they would not have taken a similar action of making demands of political officials back in Guatemala.

The county commissioners advised the new league leaders to meet with a rugby team that had already received permission to use the park and work out an arrangement for sharing the playing fields. After the new league leaders met with the rugby team and agreed on a plan to share the playing fields, the new soccer league started its playing season. It was a crowning moment of a community victory in the summer of 1997 when the Guatemalan and Salvadoran team captains turned on the park lights as darkness approached in the first day of play of the new league. In previous years of playing in the park, the soccer games would stop at sunset or continue in the dark because no one in the soccer league had the authority, or the keys, to turn on the park lights. When the new league leaders turned on the field lights, the Central American soccer players and spectators cheered loudly, as if to express a sense of community ownership and belonging in the park.

A major function performed by the soccer leagues was to help structure community relations among the players. Living marginalized lives as undocumented immigrants or as minorities after legalization, Guatemalan and other Central American immigrants were little served initially by the community-building functions of the large social institutions (social, cultural, political, etc.) of the mainstream population. In this situation, then, the soccer league, like the evangelical church of the sancristobalenses, became a source of community social relations for the hundreds of players in the league. This effect also carried over into the lives of immigrant women who spent Sunday afternoons in the park, usually with their small children, eating and socializing as they watched their husbands or other male family members play soccer.

The soccer league also formed a source of social capital as the players drew social support, including information about job openings, from social networks in the league. Moreover, the league provided economic benefits for the large immigrant community in Gulfton when some of the teams raised funds for special needs. For example, when a death occurred unexpectedly in the sancristobalense group, the sancristobalense players organized a collection of donations to help pay for the transportation of the body back to Guatemala. Another collection was taken to help cover living expenses for a soccer player who broke his leg during a game. Some Guatemalan teams also raised funds to help support the annual, patron-saint fiestas in their municipios in Guatemala.

Whereas the Mayan immigrants usually developed community structures associated with the spatial settings of their residences, workplaces, places of worship, and playing fields mainly in the western half of the city, other Guatemalan migrants of ladino background lived in a more general Latino community structure. For this population of Guatemalan immigrants, the Guatemalan community was detached from specific spaces and grounded more in their imagination of fellow Guatemalan immigrants in the city.[14] That is to say, for these immigrants, the sense of a Guatemalan community consisted of the awareness of a compatriot population and the occasional opportunity to interact with fellow Guatemalan immigrants, rather than of specific spatial localities. In the 1990s, the opening of a few Guatemalan restaurants and bakeries, the reputation of strong Guatemalan soccer teams, and the organizing of a *reina indígena* (indigenous queen) contest all reinforced the imagined Guatemalan community in the city.[15] Moreover, the social and cultural elements for building and strengthening Guatemalan community structures expanded as the number of U.S.- and foreign-born Guatemalans in the city grew in the 2000s and reached 25,205 by 2010 (U.S. Census Bureau 2010b).

Transnational Community

Many Guatemalans maintained strong connections with their households and communities in Guatemala after arriving in Houston. Indeed, some Guatemalan households in Houston became extensions of households in Guatemala when Guatemalan men or women migrants working in Houston became major sources of economic support for their families back home. To the extent that family clusters of related individuals in both countries shared information and other resources back and forth between the two countries, the long-distance interaction took on the character of a binational community.

In the early 1980s, the first groups of Guatemalan migrants stayed in touch with friends and family back home through letters. The letters sent by migrants usually inquired about family matters and provided information about jobs in Houston. The first small group of sancristobalense migrants also started receiving several letters from friends back home wanting to know about jobs after their Houston addresses started circulating in the municipio. Initially, sancristobalenses sent letters through regular mail service, but after a year, informal couriers emerged and began hand-carrying the mail, which sometimes contained cash, between Houston and the municipio.[16]

Personal delivery of letters back in the Guatemalan highlands was not always a simple matter of dropping off a letter at a residency. Sometimes migrants who took letters for friends were asked to read them by the recipients in Guatemala. If a letter contained photos of a social event, the migrant would add her or his own description of the event, using intonations to recreate the mood of the event. Sometimes migrants who took letters to Guatemala for friends offered possible or soothing explanations to a wife who worried that her husband's letter was too brief or sent without remittance.

By the late 1980s and early 1990s, communication between the sancristobalense migrants and their families and friends in the municipio included long-distance telephone calls, audio- and videocassette recordings, and faxes. The availability of telephones remained limited in the municipio until the early 2000s, when a few families in the municipio started telephone businesses for international calls. Prior to the early 2000s, families in the municipio traveled regularly to the city of Quetzaltenango eight miles (13 kilometers) away to call their migrant family members in Houston from offices of the Guatemalan national telephone service, GUATEL.

The use of audio and video recordings significantly increased the quality of communication between the immigrants in Houston and the municipio. Audio recordings could include more voices than a letter, and some of the recordings included comments in K'iche', which was not used as a written language among the sancristobalenses. Video recordings conveyed graphic representations of family life and social events and were widely shared among the immigrants in Houston. Telephone calls and audio and video recordings had a stronger effect than letters, reinforcing ties in the Houston–San Cristobal transnational community because these means of communication were better able to convey more meanings through voice inflections and visual symbolism. Spouses and parents in the municipio, for example, could hear and see through audio and video recordings that their spouses and children in Houston were in good health.

Communication between Guatemalan migrants in Houston and their communities back in Guatemala greatly improved in the early 2000s as Internet offices arrived in Guatemalan communities, and as families in Guatemala also bought personal computers through which they could communicate with family members in the United States. Eventually, families also began visual communications between Guatemala and the United States through Skype Internet calls. Moreover, the use of cell phones for international calls greatly expanded in Guatemala in the 2005–2010 period, enabling many families to stay in close contact with family members in the United States.

In the late 1980s and the 1990s, Guatemalan immigrants in Houston also strengthened their ties to Guatemala by building new homes in their municipios of origin. The construction of new homes kept Guatemalan migrants focused on the municipios as they interacted by mail or phone with the homebuilders and sent money to pay them. In addition, some migrants made trips to Guatemala to check on designs for their new homes or to assess the progress of the home construction. Some of the first Mayan migrants to construct new homes in Guatemala used traditional adobe brick designs, but by the 1990s and into the 2000s, new homes built by the sancristobalense and other migrants in the western highland region of Guatemala used cinder blocks for construction and resembled U.S. homes.[17]

The new home construction designs demonstrated an impact that migration to the United States had for social change in the Guatemalan communities of the migrants. Even though the very first homes were constructed with adobe bricks and a customary large opening in the middle to focus family life inwardly within the housing structure, the new U.S.-style homes were built with large windows and doors (sometimes with burglar bars) facing outward toward the streets.

New homes built by migrants in Guatemala also symbolize a new way of life, a transnational existence in which life must be shared between two distant regions. Yet the sharing is not equally divided. "They belong more over there, than over here," said a mother in the town of San Cristóbal when she reflected on how the migrants return to the municipio for only a few weeks during the annual festivals of Christmas in December and the celebration of the patron saint in July. The signs of the effects of the emigration to the United States are present daily in the municipio in the construction of new homes and in the opening of new businesses that cater to families of immigrants; it is during the festival periods, however, that the effects of migration are greatly visible as the visiting migrants represent a mass of prosperity.

Against the social background of their highland municipio, the sancristobalense migrants have undergone dramatic economic mobility since the 1980s but in the larger Houston social context, their social status remains little changed. The migrants remain Latino minorities working in relatively low-status jobs. It is in the municipio where the migrants are recognized as having undergone dramatic social mobility, as they have become, even in their absence, the "new rich" of the municipio.[18] To be sure, the new U.S.-related social status of migrants transcends their former municipios and affects relations in a larger social context in Guatemala. Some migrants traveling to market places in the highlands find themselves having to haggle more than usual for lower prices as some merchants identify them as affluent buyers. Moreover, local police sometimes defer to migrants, such as in traffic accidents, when the migrants claim a U.S. identity. This a particularly striking change for indigenous migrants, who rarely if ever received social deference from authorities prior to their migration.

Different Guatemalan Experiences in Houston

The initial settlement experiences of the Guatemalan migrants in Houston varied among the different groups. Mayan groups had the most cohesive settlement experiences, but differences could still be detected among these groups. For example, the sancristobalenses maintained stable contact with their community back home almost from the beginning of their migration to Houston, whereas Mayan migrants from war-torn areas in the department of Quiché had more limited interaction with their fragmented communities of origin located in a war zone of the civil war. This difference affected the ability to develop transnational exchanges between the migrants in Houston and their families and communities in Guatemala.[19]

At another level, the experiences of Mayan migrants and other Guatemalan migrants who came from a ladino background also differed in Houston. Mayan migrants from Santa Cruz del Quiché and San Cristóbal Totonicapán, for example, settled in apartment clusters, which facilitated the reproduction of their ethnic culture, while the migrants with ladino backgrounds diffused into the larger Latino population. In contrast to Mayan migrants, therefore, non-Mayan Guatemalans survived socially and culturally in a broad Latino culture consisting of various national backgrounds. In this regard, the immigration experience represented a greater loss of national culture for the Guatemalans with a ladino background than for the Maya. Yet this comparison should not be overstated, as the Maya migrants were more conscious of their ethnic culture and identity than they were of a Guatemalan national culture. They became Guatemalan in Houston more as a reference to their place of origin than as a reference to a national culture of origin.

Moreover, for the Maya, migration to the United States was more a process of *moving out* of a minority group status, that is, being indigenous in Guatemala, while for the Guatemalans with a ladino background, migration to the United States was a process of *moving into* a minority group status, that is, becoming Latina or Latino in the United States. Mayan migrants were also classified as Latinos in the United States by public institutions such as schools and health agencies, but their bigger transformation was the lessening for many of an indigenous ethnic identity.

Conscious of their social status change, the sancristobalense immigrant men occasionally told stories about how indigenous migrants sometimes acted in ways that were contrary to the expectations of nonindigenous persons. One story, for example, told of a Mayan family in Houston who wanted to buy a vehicle. When the family approached a dealership lot to look at new cars, the sales personnel ignored the family. When the father in the family inquired about the cost of a new sports utility vehicle he liked, he was told it was "too expensive." When the father persisted in knowing the price of the vehicle, a salesperson responded "$30,000!" in an impatient tone. The father then pulled out $30,000 in cash from a bag the mother was carrying and proceeded to pay for the vehicle, to the amazement of the salesperson. Since the sancristobalenses rarely use the term "Maya" to identify themselves, they usually make self-references in these stories by saying "*nuestra gente*" ("our people") or "*gente natural*" ("natural people").[20]

While Mayan immigrants in Houston are identified in official records as Latinos or Hispanics, as the Guatemalans with ladino backgrounds also are identified, for some Maya the larger concern is not to be identified as "Indian" or indigenous, which denotes inferior status for many nonindigenous people in Guatemala. When the *Houston Chronicle* newspaper ran a front-page story in 1988 on the immigration of the sancristobalenses and included photographs of their municipio, several sancristobalense migrants called the sancristobalense migrant who was the informant for the story to complain that the newspaper publicity would only serve to identify them as "Indians" all over again in Houston. Concerns over indigenous identity seemed to have declined considerably by the 2000s as many Mayan migrants became securely incorporated in the city, and as the second-generation participated in the mainstream.

New Developments in the Early 2000s

The U.S. government measures to restrict undocumented immigration described in Chapter 2 concerning phases 4 and 5 of Guatemalan immigration in the United States had significant impacts for Guatemalan immigrants in Houston in the 2000s. One impact was the decline of new migrants arriving from Guatemala due partly to the increase of border control, which raised smuggling costs for Guatemalans to $5,000 and more per migrant in the 2000s.[21] The surge of Guatemalan immigration in Houston in the 1980s and 1990s slowed by the 2000-2010 period. Although the number of Guatemalan immigrants increased in the Houston area in the early 2000s, the rate of growth was lower than in the 1990s (Table 4.1). Undocumented Guatemalan migrants continued to arrive, but they did so in smaller groups or as individuals rather than in the sizeable numbers that arrived almost weekly in earlier decades. The number of Guatemalan migrants who immigrated into the Houston area as legal permanent residents also declined in the 2000-2010 period, from 523 in 2000 to 278 in 2010 (U.S. DHS 2006, Supplemental Table 2; U.S. DHS 2011, Supplemental Table 2).

The consequences of stricter immigration enforcement for Guatemalan migrants in the Houston area went beyond a drop in immigration numbers to a major decrease of job opportunities for undocumented migrants. Economic decline accounted for part of the reduction in jobs, but for undocumented migrants, an equally or more important reason was that federal enforcement activities had made employers more attentive to the regulation that potential employees needed to have work authorization, which could be checked through the federal Internet-based system E-Verify. This caused the previous pattern among many undocumented Guatemalan migrants of quick entry into the labor market through family or hometown networks to greatly diminish in the early 2000s, even among Mayan migrants, who previously had used ethnic networks to catapult into the job market.

In addition, in contrast with previous decades in which hundreds of undocumented sancristobalense men often found supermarket jobs that paid at least the minimum wage, by the 2005-2010 period, new, undocumented Mayan migrant men usually found jobs working for immigrant business owners, such as in restaurants, wholesale companies, and landscaping services, paying $5 an hour, which was far less than the minimum wage. Guatemalan men with ladino backgrounds also appeared in greater numbers in sites near large apartment complexes and busy street interactions where day laborers gathered to look for work that paid whatever casual employers offered.

Federal enforcement against undocumented migrant labor was also a factor in the tightening of the labor market of office-cleaning work, where thousands of immigrant women, including Guatemalan women, had found jobs in companies contracted to clean the thousands of business offices in the Houston area. In many cleaning companies, undocumented women workers who had secured jobs in earlier years were asked to present documents to show they were authorized to work; without the documents, they faced dismissal.

As described in Chapters 2 and 3, large-scale deportations introduced by the passage of IIRIRA in 1996 were another major development that brought new pressures into Guatemalan migrant populations in the country (Rodriguez and Hagan 2004). Deportations of undocumented migrants and other noncitizens who committed deportable offenses under IIRIRA intensified in the Houston area, keeping pace with rising national deportation trends. The number of pending deportation cases in the Houston immigration court rose from 1,835 in fiscal year 2000 to 5,198 in fiscal year 2005, and to 11,390 cases by fiscal year 2012 (TRAC Immigration Project 2012).[22] Guatemalans accounted for 714 of the pending deportation cases in the Houston immigration court in fiscal year 2012.

Moreover, the Houston area became a major detention site for migrants awaiting deportation, with a large, privately operated detention center located just a few miles away from the Houston international airport from which migrants were deported to Central America and other world regions.[23] The numbers of deportations from the Houston area grew as local police departments began to report suspected undocumented migrants to federal agents.[24]

Guatemalan immigrant families that for decades had known security and tranquility in their Houston settings began to describe feelings of fear and anxiety about losing family members to deportations in the 2000s, and especially after enforcement increased through collaboration between federal agents and local police. A husband-and-wife couple without papers in one Guatemalan immigrant family, for example, never traveled outside their apartment together so that one of the two could stay behind with their two small daughters in case the other was arrested and deported. In another undocumented migrant family, a Guatemalan husband grieved the loss of his wife, who was deported back to Guatemala, leaving their small children crying for their mother. Other Guatemalan immigrant families complained of the constant transfer of arrested migrant family members from one detention center to another, making it difficult to stay in contact with detained family members and get legal help for them.

Undocumented immigrants, who have been a major focus of deportation officials, constitute an integral part of larger immigrant populations as household members and participants of community institutions. Moreover, their U.S.-born children make up sizeable numbers of public school students in settings of immigrant concentrations (Olivas 2012). Consequently, many of the restrictions that undocumented migrants face reverberate across immigrant communities and into mainstream institutions such as public schools. New enforcement measures, such as deportations, have major impacts on Guatemalan immigrant communities because a large number of Guatemalan immigrants are undocumented migrants.[25]

The new enforcement developments of the 2000s, and especially of the post-2005 years, brought a new character to the Guatemalan immigrant population in the Houston area. Thousands of these immigrants had legal status or had even become citizens, but their journey into U.S. society was not completely secure as long as a large segment of their population, including legal immigrants, remained vulnerable to deportation (see Chapters 2 and 3).

Interconnected Transformations

As we stated in the beginning of this chapter, Guatemalan immigration in Houston, along with the immigration of other groups, helped transform the Houston area, and in return, the area transformed the new migrants coming from Guatemala and other countries. The large-scale Latino immigration in the 1980s that began in the metropolitan area, and especially in the city of Houston, created new labor supplies, new cultural spheres, and new linkages to Latin American regions. These new developments transformed the metropolitan area from an oil- and petrochemical-related industrial monoculture to a vibrant, diversified, urban metropolis that extended its reaches to markets and populations around the world.

The large-scale arrival of Guatemalan and other Latino immigrants in the early 1980s coincided with the dramatic economic downturn of the Houston area, which caused more than a hundred thousand workers to leave and look for work in other labor markets. As the Houston labor market faced a labor exodus and rising unemployment of skilled, higher-paid labor, the massive arrival of Latino immigrants, who were mainly undocumented migrants, led to a new labor force that would help propel the area economy into greater economic diversity, including the growth of new service industries.

It was a propitious development for Houston employers as the mainly undocumented new Latino workforce not only worked for low wages but also manifested a disciplined character, usually showing little resistance to work even in the harshest conditions. Moreover, employers were not prevented from hiring the arriving undocumented migrant workers since penalties against employers of undocumented labor were not enacted until late 1986.[26] This was a major opportunity for Houston area employers as well as for many new immigrants who themselves started a host of new repair, maintenance, and service businesses using undocumented labor. Through their lower wages, the new immigrants helped subsidize the economic revitalization of the area in the late 1980s and 1990s.

In the neighborhoods where they settled, and later in the mainstream, Guatemalan and other immigrants introduced new resources (languages, cuisine, music, arts, etc.) that expanded the cultural sophistication of the Houston area. By the 1990s, Houston took on a cultural character that began to match the cosmopolitan character of world cities, with great linguistic diversity and genre associated with different world regions; the city contrasted greatly with its former appearance as an East Texas oil town. Moreover, the cultural expansion had economic impacts when it reached mainstream markets and when it attracted foreign investors to the area, such as when a Hong Kong investor opened a large Latino/Chinese restaurant in the largest Latino migrant neighborhood in the city.

The Houston area also expanded its links to Latin American countries substantially with the growing Latino immigration from those countries. Although Latin American elites had established ties to the large medical center complex in Houston since at least the 1970s, Houston area connections to other social classes of Latin America remained very limited until the large-scale Latino immigration that started in the early 1980s. Immigrants channeled the new linkages connecting social, economic, and cultural institutions directly from Latino neighborhoods in Houston to neighborhoods in Mexico and Central America. For example, a church started by the sancristobalense migrants in Houston interacted closely with a church back in their municipio, and informal couriers transported enough used cars from Houston to Guatemala to establish used-car dealerships in various places of the country. These middle- and working-class international linkages brought advantages to the Houston area by creating informal services that could be transferred into profit-making businesses (such as delivering packages to Guatemala for a fee) and by providing alternative sources of economic support for migrant labor groups that lived remote from mainstream institutions.[27]

As the Guatemalan and other Latino immigration brought structural changes to the Houston area, formal and informal institutions of the area likewise affected the immigrants, bringing many of them significant social and cultural transformations. One transformation concerned the new role for many migrants of taking on a proletarian lifestyle. Previous wage labor experiences in Guatemala were not as regimented as what many Guatemalan migrants found in the U.S. workplaces. For many Guatemalan migrant workers, Houston brought a new lifestyle that rigidly divided time at work and time away from work. This included migrant women doing domestic work as live-in maids who did not see their families for several days at a time, even when their families lived just a few miles away from the households where they worked. The new labor experience involved socialization into a life pattern regulated by the clock, in which work was rigidly separated from nonwork activity much more than in highland municipios where artisan and agricultural work blended with the tempos of family and community life. "Here we do not work to live—we live to work," said a Guatemalan migrant of his new life routine in Houston.

Another transformation that the Houston area brought to the Guatemalan migrants was their change into the role of denizens of an advanced modern industrial city with a complex population. Some Guatemalan migrants came from Guatemala City and Quetzaltenango, the second-largest city in Guatemala, which are complex urban centers in themselves, but Houston presented an even more complex urban environment with its much more diversified racial and ethnic populations and institutions that operated in English. In Houston, the Guatemalans were also just one of many different Latino groups, and not among the first in rank, since in many Latino settings the Mexicans, followed by Salvadorans, had a greater cultural presence. The transformation into residents able to maneuver across complicated, multilayered cultural and institutional landscapes of the Houston area was a particular achievement for Guatemalans coming from small towns and rural areas with much less diversity and with traditions and other customs that provided guidelines for social life.

A final transformation involved the emergence of many of the Guatemalan migrants into transnational actors planning and carrying out the development of their families and themselves in two national spheres. To some extent, it becomes a balancing act in which many migrants and their families attempt to divide resources and responsibilities between the two countries that frame their lives. It is also a condition that brings contradictory outcomes, usually of upward mobility in the country left behind and a new minority group status in the adopted new country.

CHAPTER 5

Contradictions of the San Francisco Area

Introduction

This chapter focuses on the specific experiences of Guatemalan low-wage immigrants who settled in San Francisco and its immediate surroundings. Our purpose is to elucidate the complex dynamics of the San Francisco area as a postindustrial urban context for these low-wage immigrants and the challenges of immigrant incorporation in this setting. We argue that even as they have suffered relatively little political intolerance in this area, many low-wage Guatemalan immigrants have faced significant difficulties and have achieved limited socioeconomic upward mobility. Although some Guatemalan immigrants arrived as middle-class professionals and retained that status, or rose above low-wage jobs, that is not the case for the majority.

To delineate the specific spaces and places covered in this chapter, for some purposes we include, in addition to the City/County of San Francisco, its closest environs: Alameda County in the East Bay (e.g., Oakland, Hayward, Fremont) and San Mateo County on the peninsula just south of San Francisco (e.g., Daly City, San Bruno, South San Francisco, Redwood City). We refer to this somewhat larger urban unit as the "San Francisco area," which has been a socially and culturally linked urbanized core of the sprawling nine-county San Francisco Bay Area (SFBA) and is also connected by public transportation systems. The SFBA as a whole represents a much larger-scale "city-region,"[1] which is too diverse and heterogeneous for our specific focus on Guatemalan immigrants in the urban San Francisco area. For example, some of the northern and eastern counties are rural or semirural rather than urban, and the SFBA's other major city, San Jose, while larger and growing faster than San Francisco, does not have a sizeable Guatemalan-origin population.[2]

San Francisco was not included as a "global city" in early studies (e.g.,

Sassen 1991—although [p. 176] it was among the top 12 banking centers ranked by assets in 1985–1986), nor has it ever been a leader in size or population. However, it is still a "world-class" city in perspectives that theorize scale by a variety of criteria other than, or in addition to, size and population—for example, as a "centre of economic, political, or cultural capital" (Glick Schiller and Caglar 2009, 188) and by virtue of its positioning with regard to the Pacific Rim. San Francisco has developed important commercial and cultural ties with rising Asian powers, which have become increasingly important in the late twentieth and early twenty-first centuries. In addition, the specificity of the San Francisco area can be characterized by its "urban specialization" or niche (Rodríguez and Feagin 1986): in contrast with industrial Houston, the San Francisco area has been postindustrial for many decades, not counting construction-related industries, and has specialized in financial, technological, and tourist services.

Unlike case studies focusing on immigrant groups that "just happen" to live in a particular city or area, in Waldinger's (1989) words[3]—that city being a locus or "container" for immigrant settlement—we also view the San Francisco urban area itself in its evolution over three decades as a subject of analysis. Drawing upon urban as well as migration studies and conceptual framings, we include the specificity of place, the contestations over the uses of space, the resocializations of urban space and place by immigrants and other groups, and the interactions between the structural changes in the urban area and survival strategies/organizing activities by its low-wage immigrant populations. It is this *interaction* between the context of settlement and the arriving Guatemalan immigrants and their communities as social actors that has resocialized particular spaces and places in the San Francisco area, primarily San Francisco's Inner Mission District[4] and, more recently, East Oakland. Since this is an urban area in flux, in large part because of the high level of in-migrations during the late twentieth century, and some out-migrations in the early 2000s, there is also a temporal dimension. We identify two broad time periods: the 1980s–1990s and (more briefly, and only in regard to specific issues) the "Sequel," the first decade of the twenty-first century, with the latter bringing new socioeconomic dynamics and some new patterns of Guatemalan migration to, from, and within the San Francisco area.

The empirical analysis in this chapter emerges from published studies of the San Francisco area (e.g., the structural impact of the large-scale "development" dynamics/developer campaigns of San Francisco), from Census data about Guatemalan immigrants in this area, and from the results of a two-phase collaborative study, conducted at midpoint (mid- to late 1990s) of the 30-year period, with some elements subsequently updated. As will be seen below, the first phase of the study was a 1995 survey of 99 Guatemalan (and 175 Salvadoran) immigrants in the San Francisco area. The second phase of the study consisted of in-depth, targeted interviews beginning in the mid-1990s and continuing at different moments through 2012 with Guatemalan immigrant organizational and community leaders, and with a few knowledgeable non-Guatemalan observers. Finally, the analysis presented here has been shaped by the author's experience as a San Francisco resident for 25 years, most of that time (1985–2001) as a renter in the heart of the Mission District, which was also, during that time, the major center of the Guatemalan immigrant community. That personal experience has been updated through new interviews and observations as well as incorporation of newer studies in the early twenty-first century, discussed in the "Sequel" section of this chapter.

Given our purpose of demonstrating the specificity of place of the San Francisco area as a context of reception and settlement for Guatemalan immigrants, the chapter begins with a brief general description of that context. While it has one of the highest percentages of foreign-born residents—30 percent for the San Francisco-Oakland-Fremont Metropolitan Area by 2010[5]—the San Francisco area's overall population is smaller than several other urban destinations for Guatemalan immigrants, such as Los Angeles, Chicago, and Washington, D.C. The Guatemalan communities are also smaller, which affects the particular ways in which San Francisco–area Guatemalans have organized themselves.

Other key factors in defining the San Francisco area's place-specificity include, on the one hand, the area's ethnic diversity and pride in being multicultural, its widely recognized progressive political culture on many social issues, its openness to Latin American immigrant/refugee rights, and its political generosity specifically toward Salvadorans and Guatemalans during the 1980s–1990s and into the early 2000s. But on the other hand, structural transformations in the postindustrial political economy of the San Francisco area (and larger Bay Area) since the 1980s have made life more difficult and less secure for Guatemalan and virtually all Latin American low-wage immigrants. The effects of living in a postindustrial, "dot-com" technology-driven economy that has undergone spectacular booms and precipitous declines since the 1990s have been felt throughout the San Francisco area's labor and housing markets. In San Francisco, unlike Houston, both boom and bust periods have made life virtually unaffordable for low-income residents.

Against the San Francisco–area backdrop, this chapter will briefly trace the demographics of Guatemalan immigrant communities. The chapter then presents a survey-based and gendered profile of Guatemalan communities in the area, and details Guatemalan immigrant organizing efforts and inter-actions with other players in the San Francisco area. On the one hand, the very presence of the Guatemalans has diversified the culture and politics of the San Francisco area. In addition, through their participation in Guatemalan-specific and pan-Latino organizations and coalitions, some Guatemalan im-migrants became social actors who contributed to resocializations of this urban area and to a larger process of community building. On the other hand, San Francisco's power structure has made organizing efforts quite difficult, as immigrants have focused on economic survival and have found few ways of influencing the city's macro socioeconomic policies, e.g., regarding redevelop-ment and the uses of sociospatial environments. Apart from developer-driven policies, in the Guatemalan case, organizing efforts have been characterized by internal divisions based on ethnicity as well as class, gender, and ideology. To the extent that many of their organizations have not become more stable and institutionalized, we will suggest that Guatemalans in the San Francisco area constitute in many respects a "*comunidad fragmentada,*" a fragmented community.

City of Refuge, City of Survival Struggles

In following the general argument that global changes are mediated by the particularities of specific sites and should be analyzed in their local manifes-tations—with "local" meaning, in some situations, particular neighborhoods as well as particular cities—we draw on the frameworks developed by Smith (2001), Waldinger (1989 and 2001), Mollenkopf (1983), Dreier, Mollenkopf, and Swanstrom (2001), Brettell (2003), Arreola (2004), Ellis (2001), Ellis and Almgren (2009), and many others who have focused on the politics of urban place and space.[6] In these frameworks, specific immigrant groups are seen as differentially integrated in specific urban contexts, and differentially interact-ing with other social players.

Turning to the specificities of the San Francisco area, this chapter empha-sizes the 3.5-decade span from the late 1970s and 1980s through the early 2000s (for some purposes, through 2012-2013), which has been the most relevant period for arriving Guatemalan immigrants. The summary presented here regarding the area's particularities is based primarily on the more exhaus-tive urban studies mentioned throughout this chapter. What emerges from those studies is a unique combination of the niche occupied by San Francisco's postindustrial political economy and its political and cultural traditions—a combination that differentiates it considerably from the Los Angeles, Houston, Chicago, Washington, and New York areas, and other major cities as specific contexts of settlement for Guatemalan immigrants.

As mentioned above, metropolitan San Francisco (the San Francisco-Oakland-Fremont Metropolitan Area) has been one of the metropolitan areas with immigrants comprising well over 25 percent of the population; it is one of eight urban centers in the United States with more than 1 million foreign-born residents and is characterized by "hyperdiversity" in the composition of foreign-born (Price and Benton-Short 2007).[7] Within that context, Latinos ("Hispanic-origin population") remained more or less stable at 14 percent of the total population of San Francisco between 1970 and 2000 (Godfrey 2004, 79–80), while the Asian-origin population increased greatly and African Americans declined significantly.

The striking changes in San Francisco's political economy during the second half of the twentieth century—near-total deindustrialization and transformation into a service/financial economy controlled by developers' interests—greatly altered the city's neighborhood structure and polarized its class and racial structures. During these decades, from mid-century to 2000, increasing immigrant populations inhabited neighborhoods that became contested areas in struggles between developers and antidisplacement or neighborhood preservation coalitions. Hence, the developers' interests were in constant interaction with the low-wage immigrant labor forces that were essential to their functioning. Critical analyses focus on the role of the "urban growth machine" (as Molotch [1976] first developed the concept)[8] in remapping the Bay Area's political economy, including financial centers and the high-tech "dot-com" industries in Silicon Valley. Economic redevelopment polarized San Francisco into a "Gold Coast" lifestyle for the wealthy, to borrow the phrase from Castells (1983), and a life of constant struggle or economic exclusion/expulsion/exile for low-wage populations, particularly African Americans, U.S.-born Latinos, and Latin American immigrants.[9]

These struggles over redevelopment, affordable housing, displacement, and gentrification have been detailed in various case studies of San Francisco, including Wirt (1974), Castells (1983), Mollenkopf (1983), McGovern (1998), Brechin (1999), and several books by Hartman—(1974 and 2002—the latter a revised version of an initial book in 1984). Similar themes are central in Walker et al. (1990), Solnit and Schwartzenberg (2000), and Godfrey (1988, 2004, 2006). Miller (2009) details the resistance to redevelopment led by the Mission Coalition Organization (MCO) in the period 1968–1971. Although most of these studies do not focus on the implications of San Francisco's developer strategies specifically for Central American and Mexican low-wage immigrants, we shall draw such implications from their presentations of the developers' impact, especially in the Mission District. In addition, Mexican and Central American immigrants became players, as they were drawn into antigrowth coalitions at various moments since 1980 (Godfrey 2004).

There is another theme in the literature about San Francisco that focuses on the city's almost legendary political progressivism—as DeLeon (1992) called it, *Left Coast City*.[10] These studies present San Francisco as a supportive and tolerant place for groups (e.g., gay and ethnic immigrant) that were often rejected or received with hostility in other cities. Even as the fiercely anti-immigrant Proposition 187 had won overwhelmingly by a 59 percent majority state-wide in 1994, San Francisco voters decisively opposed the measure. However, it is important to note that some of the more outlying parts of the larger San Francisco Bay Area have not shared this identity as "tolerant," and cities such as Fremont (in Alameda County) have even witnessed anti-immigrant activities carried out by a chapter of the Minutemen organization.

San Francisco had already gained prominence as one of the most favorable destinations politically for Central American asylum seekers during the 1980s and 1990s. Additionally, San Francisco became a leader among "Sanctuary Cities," with new initiatives, to be detailed below, long after the Central American civil wars were over—but by the early 2000s, subject to major controversies. The combination of all these conflicting tendencies over the course of three decades constitutes the uniqueness of San Francisco as a context-in-flux for Guatemalan immigrants and refugees.

"Aquí no se vive; se sobrevive"

During several decades in the mid-twentieth century, San Francisco was restructured by the exodus of whatever manufacturing industries still remained to lower-wage areas, a decline of traditional blue-collar jobs except construction, and the consolidation of a postindustrial service and commercial economy with dual high-end-low-end labor markets—a process that has been analyzed more generally by Sassen (1988, 1991). In the San Francisco area, the postindustrial two-tier system was specifically configured by the city's proximity to the high-technology Silicon Valley, by San Francisco–based banks' financial empires, including commercial relations with the Pacific Rim, and by the city's attractiveness for professional conventions and general tourism. Since the new economy required expanding various categories of low-wage service workers, the arrival of new immigrant populations became a central part of the restructuring process itself. Within this context, many Central American and Mexican immigrants were employed in the low-wage jobs in services (e.g., janitorial, hotel, restaurant) or in the growing informal economy of non-unionized day laborers (men) and house cleaners/nannies (women).

Adding to an already polarized situation, the San Francisco region became the scene of one of the major boom/bust cycles of the late twentieth century, the "dot-com explosion." In very visible ways, both the high-tech industry's expansion in Silicon Valley that began in the mid-1990s, affecting the Mission District in the late 1990s, and its subsequent collapse (2000–2001) exacerbated all the tendencies toward socioeconomic polarization and inequality. During both boom and bust, the San Francisco area became an extremely difficult environment for low-wage working-class immigrants as well as native-born Latinos and African Americans. The cost of living, and particularly of housing, made it one of the least affordable urban centers in the United States. San Francisco was already heading in that direction during previous decades, but property values and rents increased geometrically during the dot-com years, as documented extensively in Hartman (2002) and other studies.

As in other cities with extremely polarized high-end/low-end service sectors (Sassen 1988, 1991), many Latino low-wage immigrants, most notably men working in San Francisco, had little upward mobility and tended to remain trapped as the "working poor" (Ellis 2001, 125–127, 148). Steadily during these decades, including the early 2000s, economic crisis alongside high-end development led to economic volatility, with small businesses closing and unemployment increasing in many sectors. Within this environment, only the more fortunate Latino immigrant workers had steady jobs in the unionized formal sector (e.g., for men in construction and for women as cleaners and janitors in hotels and skyscraper office buildings). Many others were kept in or pushed down into the informal sector, some forced to work at several jobs; men became day laborers while women worked as nannies or cleaned the homes of middle/upper-class professional families, including Latina women who had steady jobs. It was striking to observe how hard San Francisco–area low-wage immigrants worked just in order to live at a near-subsistence level, while at the same time sending remittances to their families back home. This was the context for the statement by a Guatemalan soccer-club organizer familiar with the situations of dozens of families when we interviewed him: *"Aquí no se vive, se sobrevive"* ("Here, we don't live, we survive").

These characteristics of the political economy could be seen in spatial arrangements. Overall, the San Francisco area has been characterized by micro-neighborhoods, with Latinos heavily concentrated in the Inner Mission District in San Francisco, along outer Mission Street and in the Excelsior District, and following farther along the Mission Street spatial corridor to Daly City in San Mateo County—and in the East Oakland/Fruitvale district in Oakland (Godfrey 1988; Rhomberg 2004). Whether viewed as economic "segregation" (exclusion from other neighborhoods) or, more positively, as "ethnic clustering" for mutual support (Pamuk 2004), the results were the same. An even more important characteristic was segmentation *within* neighborhoods. This could be seen clearly in the Mission District, whose central location just 10–15 minutes from downtown, convenient public transportation, and good weather (the sunniest part of San Francisco) greatly increased the value of land. In this area, high-priced condominiums came to dominate some blocks or sub-neighborhoods, while other areas, occupied by arriving Central American and Mexican immigrants, deteriorated even amidst the gentrification around them. Condominium and office construction continued unabated during the late 1990s and into the early 2000s, even as many residential and commercial spaces went unoccupied after the dot-com crash because they were overpriced—and eventually because San Francisco, along with the rest of California, headed into financial free fall.

Conversion of Space to Place around Lower 24th Street

On a day-to-day basis, the core or *micro-barrio* 24th Street area, between Mission and Potrero Streets, and immediate surroundings seemed in many respects to be a "little Central America," even amidst enterprises owned by Mexicans, Cubans, Asians, and non-Hispanic whites. Although some Central Americans ended up elsewhere, many arrived there initially during the 1980s–1990s and established a notable social presence in and around the lower 24th Street area. This marked the beginning of the process, introduced in Chapter 1, of converting a space into a place, investing it with significant symbolic meaning, and stamping it with a unique sociospatial identity within the San Francisco area and known widely throughout the United States. Arreola (2004, 6) refers to this process as establishing "place identity."

In the very heart of the 24th Street micro-barrio, was St. Peter's Church, one of the early sanctuary churches during the 1980s. Aside from providing humanitarian services and space for arriving Guatemalans and Salvadorans to stay while they got their bearings, the Church hosted cultural and political solidarity events and was for several decades the home of CARECEN/San Francisco (Central American Resource Center), which became the most active and prominent Salvadoran immigrant rights organization. During the 1980s and early 1990s, St. Peter's also gave office space to the Comité de Unidad Guatemalteca (Guatemalan Unity Committee) until it splintered into fragments, and to the Guatemalan Grupo Maya Qusamej Junam, among others. More broadly in the neighborhood, as Walker et al. (1990, 40) maintain, "Because of the politicization of Central Americans [arriving in the 1980s], the Mission District, where most live, has been the political and cultural center of the Bay Area left in the 1980s." This included such activities as Central American solidarity and anti-intervention movements, local ballot measures criticizing U.S. policy in Central America, provision of medical assistance, support for union actions, and Sister City/people-to-people programs.

The cultural impact of the Central American immigrants and asylum seekers was visible in murals throughout the Mission District and beyond, the most notable being the multipanel mural by Salvadoran artist-in-exile Isaías Mata on the outside walls of St. Peter's Church, on 24th Street between Florida and Alabama Streets. Nearby, the one-block Balmy Alley (between 24th and 25th Streets, and parallel to Harrison and Folsom Streets) provided striking and well-known cultural representations of the Central American social justice/human rights struggles and civil wars of the 1980s, with murals painted on house walls and garage doors. Throughout the district, other murals depicted these wars, virtually all carrying implicit or explicit messages protesting U.S. policy. Guatemala's Nobel laureate (1992) Rigoberta Menchú was the dominant figure of the nationally acclaimed mural on the Women's Building on 18th Street between Valencia and Guerrero Streets. Central American artists were among the pioneers of a movement for muralization and street art that spread to other areas of the city.

For many years and through the 1990s, the lower 24th Street corridor seemed to have too much cultural and commercial capital as a Latino barrio to be fully gentrified or de-Latinized in the linear, unstoppable way that had been long predicted; rather, as will be seen, gentrification would occur in stages. This area featured three major pan-Latino festivals each year—15/16 de Septiembre (Independence Day for Central America and Mexico, respectively), Cinco de Mayo (a historic date in Mexican history), and Carnaval (a Memorial Day version of the Brazilian festival, timed for good weather)—each attracting many participants and several hundred thousand spectators from around the San Francisco area. Smaller events included Día de Cesar Chávez and Día de los Muertos (Day of the Dead), each with parades and/or exhibits. The Mission Cultural Center and the Galería de la Raza, with their rotating exhibits and other cultural events, often focused on Central America.

The neighborhood Mexican restaurants such as La Posta were becoming Mexican/Salvadoran, serving *pupusas* alongside tacos. Guatemalan-owned enterprises included El Triúnfo market and Panadería Centroamericana bakery on 24th Street, as well as several restaurants nearby on Mission Street. These Central American enterprises blended in with Mexican-owned bakeries

(La Victoria and Domínguez), the Casa Sánchez restaurant, and Casa Lucas market, featuring Latin American produce and newspapers from Mexico and Central America. Nearby were Cuban- and Nicaraguan-owned restaurants, markets, and record stores (Discolandia and Discoteca Habana).

The core area of the Mission District around lower 24th Street was an ethnic enclave, albeit with multiple dynamics. While many residents were recent Central American arrivals living in cramped, overpopulated apartments, Central Americans owned fewer businesses than more established Mexican, Cuban, Asian or U.S.-born entrepreneurs, many of whom did not live in this neighborhood. During the 1990s, there were visible manifestations of social/economic restructuring, deterioration, and impoverishment, expressed in the larger numbers of tenants per apartment, increasing crime, drugs, and gangs. Yet despite the neighborhood's widespread security issues, 24th Street itself was not totally insecure. It was well-lit at night; there were generally enough stores open, enough people out on the street, and enough of a "family" culture to ease fears about walking on 24th Street at night to a store that stayed open late or home from the 24th and Mission Street BART (subway) station or bus stops.

As a veteran renter in the 24th Street core of the Mission District from 1985 through 2001, this author witnessed these contradictory realities firsthand. A few blocks away were gentrified spaces occupied by the dot-com population that made (and later lost) millions overnight—and their trendy cafes and bars. But in my own building on 24th Street, five out of seven apartments were Latino immigrant households (several undocumented), one Chicano, and one Anglo (myself and my daughter). The building itself was a microcosm of different currents. Several apartments were overcrowded, with the primary family subletting a room in order to pay the rent, even though it was still far below average San Francisco rental prices during the 1990s. There were tensions between Central American and Mexican tenants. Aside from different national, ethnic, and class origins of the tenants, there were disagreements about the building's "public" social spaces. One tenant ran a mini day-care center out of her apartment, which spilled into the hallways as a site for toddlers' games and children's indoor sports. There were also contestations about the use of both the garage and the roof for barbeques or celebrations (Christmas Eve, New Year's Eve, July 4 *cohetes*, or small fireworks), or for putting up friends who needed a place to sleep.

The Mission core area that was left mostly untouched by dot-com gentrification during the 1990s remained in essence a low-income area, surrounded by pockets of significant wealth. Even in these blocks on or around 24th Street where older buildings were not yet being torn down or converted to make way for high-priced condominiums, many small businesses began to be displaced by astronomically rising rents. This process could be seen in boarded-up store-fronts on 24th Street during the late 1990s, with longtime established shops closing down, such as White's Dry Cleaners, Jesse's Shoe Repair Shop—even, for some months, the nationally famous St. Francis Creamery. San Francisco's changing economy was taking its toll on the neighborhood, paving the way for major changes in the early twenty-first century, discussed in this chapter's "Sequel" section.

Paradox for Guatemalan Immigrants

Looking at the San Francisco area as a political and cultural context of settlement, Central Americans and specifically Guatemalans, as seen above, were received with great sympathy. In 1985, San Francisco–based lawyers initiated the class action lawsuit *ABC v. Thornburgh*, and in December 1990/January 1991, won a settlement with the Department of Justice, saving thousands of Guatemalans and Salvadorans throughout the United States from immediate deportation (see Chapter 3). The San Francisco area has been renowned for the number of pro-asylum lawyers working there, some working pro bono out of major corporate law firms, some in immigration law offices and NGOs, and some within the INS Asylum Office—since 2003, part of U.S. Citizenship and Immigration Services (USCIS), within the Department of Homeland Security (DHS). With the asylum office staffed partly by progressives, Central Americans felt that they had a better chance of gaining approval for their asylum applications.[11] During the 1990s, San Francisco's federal asylum office led all others nationally in approving cases of asylum seekers (U.S. INS 1997, Table 30), and this pattern continued almost uninterrupted into the first decade of the twenty-first century. Additionally, San Francisco and some other municipalities in the San Francisco area (although by no means consistently throughout the entire Bay Area) became "Sanctuary Cities" in the 1980s, meaning that they would protect and shield undocumented Central American asylum seekers from deportation and would not cooperate with the INS (see below).

   Nevertheless, the above scenario has been countered by a paradox first identified by Manuel Castells (1983) in his pioneering study of San Francisco's Mission District in the early 1980s, which in many respects has remained relevant into the early 2000s. On the one hand, the area's diverse Latino communities made visible cultural contributions to the San Francisco area, such as murals, restaurants, festivals, and cultural events, and accumulated considerable cultural capital. On the other hand, despite being highly mobilizable around particular issues, these same Latino communities did not increase their political or economic power vis-à-vis the area's ruling elites and developers. This is not totally surprising, since the Latino communities had a high proportion of noncitizens who could not vote. Furthermore, at least until the 1994 "wake-up call" (Proposition 187), many Latinos eligible to become citizens and vote did not do so. Castells (1983, 136) found that Latino community organizations were more oriented toward obtaining programs and services that could subsequently be taken away or phased out than toward changing the political system or social policies.

Hence, the paradox in the Mission District of "a highly mobilized community that achieved substantial changes at the urban, social, and cultural levels, while being totally unable to become politically influential in the local power system. . . . [T]he Latino community appears to be the most deprived of access to municipal power of all ethnic minorities," despite being 15 percent of the city's population (Castells 1983, 136). There were dense networks of community organizations to stop gentrification at key moments, such as 1968–1971, but the momentum was not sustained on a permanent basis (Miller 2009). Another striking manifestation of the "political marginality" of the Latino community (Castells 1983, 137) in municipal electoral politics was the absence, prior to 1999, of any Latinos elected to the Board of Supervisors (City Council). By 2003, there were two Latinos on the board, both of them progressive. Most of the Mission District itself, which shared a municipal voting district with Bernal Heights, a middle-class, primarily non-Latino neighborhood, was represented for a number of years by Tom Ammiano, a leading progressive, gay, white politician who was extremely sympathetic to and highly knowledgeable about the agendas of Latinos. As will be discussed, it was not until 2008 that the Mission District was represented on the Board of Supervisors by an elected Latino politician.

Nor did the antigrowth, progressive allies of the Latino community achieve strategic, lasting victories against developers (Walker et al. 1990; Miller 2009). For decades after San Francisco's restructuring began, the plethora of left/progressive organizations, some being Latino organizations, in the San Francisco area did not automatically bring significant socioeconomic gains to the Latino community and were still struggling to construct lasting electoral coalitions of benefit to that community.

A Brief Demographic History

Even taking into account that the San Francisco area has never had the sheer numbers of Central Americans found in the Los Angeles area, the relative weight of Central Americans in San Francisco was significant, constituting

35.3 percent of all foreign-born Latinos in the (coterminous) City/County of San Francisco in 1990 (U.S. Census Bureau 1993)—although some sources cite as high as 38 percent, only 2 percent less than Mexicans, and mention this as a likely undercount (e.g., Wells 2000, 114 and note 5).

Among those Central Americans, Salvadorans had shown a presence in the San Francisco area since early in the twentieth century (Córdova 2005). But only a limited number of Guatemalans came to the Bay Area as individuals during the mid-twentieth century, and there were no real "waves" of migration or Guatemalan communities prior to the late 1970s.[12] Even by 1980, although their first migration phase to the United States had begun (see Chapter 2), Guatemalans were not yet recognized as a significant group in San Francisco. In mentioning the presence of Central Americans as the "main" Latino population, Castells (1983, 100, 118, and note 14) was referring to Salvadorans and Nicaraguans (see also Wirt 1974). The 1980 Census reported the presence of 3,395 foreign-born Guatemalans in the San Francisco/Oakland "Standard Metropolitan Statistical Area," of whom 881 arrived between 1975 and 1980; numbers were not given for San Mateo County (U.S. Census Bureau 1983c, Table 195), although some Guatemalans lived there (Vlach 1992, research interviews).

The 1990 Census reported 6,498 foreign-born Guatemalans, a mere 13.27 percent of 48,969 foreign-born Central Americans in metropolitan San Francisco (formal Census category San Francisco "Primary Metropolitan Statistical Area," or PMSA). Of these foreign-born Guatemalans, 3,105 lived in San Francisco itself and 3,393 in nearby surrounding (suburban) areas, i.e., "Not in central city," a category that included San Mateo and Marin Counties, although there were no specific county breakdowns. For Alameda County, no specific figure was given, but 1,792 foreign-born Guatemalans were reported in Oakland PMSA as part of the San Francisco-Oakland-San Jose "Consolidated Metropolitan Statistical Area," which reported 10,248 foreign-born Guatemalans (U.S. Census Bureau 1993, Table 28).

By the time of the 2000 Census, the numbers of foreign-born Guatemalans had increased to 4,734 in San Francisco City/County—an increase of 52 percent over 1990; to 4,345 in Alameda County, which included Oakland and Hayward, among other cities; and to 4,345 in San Mateo County, which included cities such as San Mateo, Redwood City, Burlingame, and Daly City, just to the south of San Francisco—a total of 13,424 (U.S. Census Bureau, 2002). Eight years later, the American Community Survey (ACS) for 2008 gave the following one-year estimate of foreign-born Guatemalans: 5,120 in San Francisco City/County, 7,784 in Alameda County, and 5,060 in San Mateo County—a total of 17,964 (U.S. Census Bureau, 2009), an increase of 33 percent over 2000. Whereas the number of foreign-born Guatemalans in San Francisco grew by 8 percent and in San Mateo County by 16.5 percent, the growth in Alameda County was a striking 79 percent. By contrast, the 2009 ACS reflected a sharp decline (to 3,032) in the number of foreign-born Guatemalans in San Francisco, while decreasing to 5,470 in Alameda County; for San Mateo County, the ACS stated that it "cannot estimate with 90 percent confidence" because the numbers were too low (U.S. Census Bureau, 2010a).[13]

A 1995 Survey Profile of Guatemalan Immigrants

We provide here a profile of Guatemalan immigrants, based on a 1995 survey of 99 Guatemalans and 175 Salvadorans in the San Francisco area[14] in which this author participated as part of a four-person team in the Los Angeles and San Francisco areas. Similar numbers from both groups were interviewed in the Los Angeles area.[15] Initially, the survey was designed to determine whether Salvadoran and Guatemalan immigrants in the two major California urban centers planned to return home after the end of the civil wars in the home countries—and simultaneously, what kinds of transnational ties they maintained with their families and communities of origin. But the full survey consisted of in-depth, hour-long interviews touching upon many other aspects of their lives before and after their migration, and suggestive of their level of incorporation in these two California venues as of 1995.

Given the difficulty of carrying out a random survey among a population that included many undocumented immigrants, the method used was snowball sampling based on informal social networks. The San Francisco survey population of 99 Guatemalans was made up of 60 women and 39 men. We will point out some of the significant (more than 10 percent) gender differences. Since this was not a random survey, and in order to take account of missing values (m.v.), that is, participants who did not answer all questions, we present the responses in numbers of respondents (frequencies) rather than percentages.

Of the sample of 60 women and 39 men, all 99 were born in Guatemala; of the 93 who answered (6 m.v.), 80 came to the United States from urban centers—although this may not have been their place of birth—and 13 from the countryside. This represented a much higher proportion of urban origin than was the case with Guatemalan immigrants in many other U.S. settlement contexts. Among Guatemalans in the city of San Francisco, there were fewer Maya in proportion to non-Mayan ladinos than in some less urban surrounding areas (e.g., San Rafael in Marin County). At the time of being interviewed in 1995, the great majority were in their 20s, 30s, or 40s and had been considerably younger when they arrived, most during the 1980s. Their educational level was relatively high compared with Guatemalans in some other U.S. venues, with 36 respondents (more than one-third) having some post–high school education and slightly less than two-thirds having completed only high school or less.[16]

The great majority (69) arrived between 1980 and 1990, with 29 during 1982–1986 being the highest number, and only 8 between 1991 and 1994; 22 had arrived during or before the 1970s. In short, nearly all had been living in the United States for 10 years, some for much longer. They came for a variety of reasons (in each case, being allowed to answer Yes/No, and being allowed to answer Yes to more than one factor): 26 (more men than women) cited political conditions in Guatemala, 32 cited economic conditions in Guatemala, 17 cited economic opportunities in the United States, 24 to reunite with family, 12 for personal reasons, and 10 in order to undertake an "adventure" in the United States.

Of the sample, 53 (especially men) had arrived undocumented, while 43 came on tourist, student, or family visas, and 3 answered "other" (unspecified). By 1995, 47 (a higher proportion of women than men) were Legal Permanent Residents, 6 had received amnesty with a work permit (IRCA), 22 had received asylum with a work permit, 14 were U.S. citizens, and 8 of the original 53 were still undocumented. Of those eligible to naturalize as U.S. citizens, 58 (especially women) said they planned to do so.

Of the Guatemalans surveyed (identified by neighborhood they stated and zip codes, with 1 m.v.), 20 lived in the Mission District—for many years the main Central American/Latino barrio—24 in the nearby Outer Mission and Excelsior Districts, and 20 in other districts of San Francisco, for a total of 64 in the City/County of San Francisco. Of the other 34, 16 lived in northern San Mateo County (7 of whom were in Daly City) and 6 in Alameda County (4 of whom were in Oakland). In short, 86 lived in those three counties constituting what we have called the "San Francisco area." The other 12 respondents lived in more extended environs of the San Francisco Bay Area: 3 in Contra Costa County in the East Bay, 4 in Marin County (San Rafael), 4 in Solano County (Vallejo)—both in the North Bay—and 1 in San Jose, in the South Bay.

The survey measured their level of satisfaction with their neighborhood. Asked whether they felt that their neighborhood was a good one to live in, a very high number (71 out of 98—especially men) said yes. Of the 98 who answered, only 13 viewed their neighborhood as primarily Central American, while 46 saw it as mixed Latino (Central Americans with Mexicans). All the rest viewed their neighborhood as mixed with non-Latinos—Asians, African Americans, and non-Hispanic whites. Asked what was the largest ethnic group in their neighborhood, only 1 answered Central Americans, 5 stated Mexicans, 25 stated Central Americans and Mexicans, and the rest (67) stated a non-Latino ethnicity. By 1995, then, these pioneer Guatemalans were somewhat integrated spatially, as opposed to being segregated in purely Latino neighborhoods.

In specifying their 1995 jobs, 94 answered, broken down as follows: 37 were in service jobs (especially women), 5 in sales/office, 20 in professional jobs (including business or small business, management—especially men), 8 answered "laborer" (including basic or skilled manufacturing, day labor, domestics), 10 were students (including some half-time employed), 2 were unemployed, and 12 stated "other." As for benefits/social services received: of the 94 who answered, 62 had some benefits (workers' compensation, health, retirement, vacation) while 32 had no benefits. Outside of their jobs, 24 had received unemployment insurance and 36 had medical benefits (Medi-Cal), with only 9 having received Aid to Families with Dependent Children (AFDC) and 9 others having received welfare benefits. Of 80 who answered, 55 paid taxes through their job (Social Security deduction).

Regarding relations with their employer (only 74 answered): 60 characterized them as "good" (a higher proportion being women), the rest as "fair." Asked about discrimination at work on the basis of their nationality, race, color, or language: of the 88 who answered, the overwhelming majority (72) responded that they had not experienced such discrimination—although some may have been afraid to "complain." Describing their main challenges at the workplace, 71 identified a combination of problems related to English language proficiency, documentation status, training, and contacts needed to get ahead.

Asked about their social/recreational activities, both public and at home (music, film, television, radio, magazines/newspapers), most answered that they engaged with these media biculturally—not only those media that were specifically targeted for Latinos (Spanish language), but also in the broader U.S. culture (English language). Other measures of their integration/incorporation were language and contact with childrens' schools. At work, nearly half spoke English; the rest spoke Spanish only or both languages. At home, by contrast, most communicated in Spanish, even with their school-age children. Of the 54 respondents who said they had children in U.S. schools, 46 knew their children's teachers, 50 said they helped with school functions, and 50 said they were in contact with their children's school. In relations with children's schools, mothers had a notably higher connection than fathers.

Responding to a question about whether they thought that conditions for immigrants had gotten better or worse: of 97 who answered, an overwhelming 76 (especially women) felt that conditions had worsened—which was objectively the case in 1995, the year after the landslide passage of Proposition 187 in California. Asked whether, based on their own experience, they would advise others from Guatemala to migrate to the United States: of 95 who answered, fewer than half (40) said yes, and only 43 out of 98 were actually helping others to migrate. In short, while many from this sample, having been here for a number of years, expressed some degree of satisfaction with elements of their own lives (e.g., neighborhood, job, children's schools), they saw, at the same time, that new immigrants would face increasing obstacles and discrimination.

Return vs. Stay, and Transnational Ties to Home

Two sections in the middle of the questionnaire were at the heart of the survey's original intent: what the respondents' plans were to remain in the United States vs. return to Guatemala after the end of the 36-year civil war, and what kinds of ties they maintained with home. The survey was conducted in 1995, when Guatemala's civil war was not yet over; the final Peace Accords were signed on December 29, 1996. Nevertheless, by 1995, a number of partial accords had been signed and the peace process was moving forward (Jonas 2000b). Our central and perhaps most significant finding was that—although half had planned only a temporary stay in the United States when they arrived—*not one* of the 93 Guatemalans who answered this question planned a permanent return to Guatemala immediately, and only 6 planned to do so anytime soon (within a "*plazo determinado*"); 25 projected sometime in the more distant future, 12 said they might or might not ("it depends")—while 50, more than half, said they had no plan to return to Guatemala to live. Overall, only family reasons might influence most of them to change their plans (i.e., to return).

Yet at the same time—and in relation to the above, the other major finding of the survey—respondents were clear about maintaining very close transnational ties[17] with their relatives in Guatemala (family more than community ties). Most could not do so by traveling back and forth to Guatemala: only 14 answered yearly or more, while 85 answered less frequently: every 2-3 years (13), occasionally (31), or never (41). Asked how they kept in touch with news from home, the 96 who answered (more than one answer allowed) cited phone, radio/television, newspapers—by multiple means, and essentially by all means available to them—which, as of 1995, was not yet primarily through electronic communications.

Another important measure of ties with family back home was sending remittances: of the 92 who answered, most said they sent remittances monthly or occasionally. Of those who did send remittances, only 2 sent more than $400 a month, while 26 sent between $50 and $200 a month. A majority considered that the remittances were used by family members for basic necessities (rent, utilities, education) as opposed to investments. These remittances went to family members, not communities, as there were virtually no hometown associations in the San Francisco area.[18] The pattern of family relations was clear from other questions. Of the whole sample, nearly two-thirds had relatives in San Francisco before they came (and 68 had come directly to the San Francisco area); of the 83 who answered, 63 had received help from relatives—mainly economic and housing assistance, with a significant drop-off to 18 for assistance in getting employment. By contrast, only 16 had received assistance from nonfamily Guatemalan community networks.

To summarize: in spite of not having plans to return permanently to Guatemala anytime soon, at least during the rest of their work life, and in spite of not being able to travel to Guatemala regularly, the majority maintained close contact with family back home. Furthermore, at the same time that the majority were naturalized as U.S. citizens or planned to be, they also retained their self-identification as Guatemalan. When asked about their "ethnic (national) identity," 63 considered themselves Guatemalan, only 2 "American," 2 neither, 2 "other" (possibly Maya), and 30 mixed/both. In various ways, many lived as de facto binational citizens of two countries.

Given that most of the respondents had come to the San Francisco area during or before the 1980s, by 1995 they manifested varying degrees and means of settlement and incorporation. Even as they continued to struggle with affordable housing, financial, legal, and other major challenges, many were on their way to becoming part of the fabric of society in the San Francisco area. But most of the participants in this survey were being incorporated into the low-wage sector of the San Francisco–area's workforce, with only 20 having professional jobs. Even among those with basic education or more, most were not necessarily able to translate that education into upward mobility to better-paying or higher-status jobs, or to stable higher-income, higher-quality, middle-class lives all around.

Organizational Affiliations

The survey also addressed the ways in which these Guatemalans had been involved in organizations of various types both in Guatemala before migrating and in the United States after settlement. The first phase of the project reported results of the 1995 survey-based answers and indicated organizational affiliations at the grassroots. Some types of organizations were more Guatemalan-specific than others, i.e., were organizations only or primarily of Guatemalans. (Respondents were not directly asked to make this characterization.) In addition, many types of organizations—with the major exception of cultural associations, which were also divided between ladino and Mayan—had both Guatemalan and pan-Latino expressions, or evolved from one to the other, generally from Guatemalan-only to pan-Latino.

The phase 1 survey demonstrated how Guatemalan respondents were participating in organizations or less formal networks of various types as of 1995. Results are summarized in Table 5.1, which breaks down answers both by gender and respondents' membership/participation in Guatemala before migrating and in the San Francisco area. The table shows only "Yes" (participation) responses.

Since this was a nonrandom sample, it cannot be generalized to the larger Guatemalan community; however, it does suggest some observations. The level of organizational affiliation was quite low in the San Francisco area, and certainly lower than in Guatemala, with the exception of religious (presumably, going to church and participating in church-related activities), especially among women. As with most of the organizations other than cultural and political, religious affiliations involved pan-Latino institutions. Community organizations, i.e., neighborhood, were second in importance (more or less at the same level as in Guatemala), although these were more likely networks rather than formal organizations. Participation in both cultural and sports organizations declined significantly from Guatemala to the San Francisco area, especially among women. The smaller number of men in sports such as soccer teams in the San Francisco area was notable.

At the low end, social organizations declined significantly among women and remained very low for men. "Social" meant different things to different respondents: for some, it referred to organizations such as school PTAs or Alcoholics Anonymous; for others, it overlapped with community/neighborhood networks or cultural organizations. Both political and labor/professional (work-related) organizational affiliations were extremely low, in both Guatemala and the San Francisco area. In the end, survival/maintenance activities

Table 5.1. Organizational Affiliations: Frequencies Before and After Migration (1995 survey)

	Female (n = 60)		Male (n = 39)	
	Guatemala*	SF Area	Guatemala*	SF Area
church	32	38	20	15
sports	26	9	27	16
cultural	28	14	10	11
social	22	12	5	6
political	7	7	8	3
neighborhood	19	17	10	12
work	7	5	9	3
other	3	0	3	2

*Eighty-seven respondents answered regarding their participation in Guatemala, while 98 answered regarding participation in the San Francisco area (of whom 12 lived elsewhere in the larger San Francisco Bay Area).

and a culture of keeping a low profile appear to have made organizational affiliation or participation of any type more difficult. If these immigrants were being incorporated, it was not primarily through organizations.

Architecture of Organizations: Interviews with Leaders

Given the daily survival struggles for most Guatemalan immigrants, their limited level of participation in formal organizations was not surprising. Yet within the fabric of their San Francisco–area communities, such organizations sometimes played important roles, if only semi-visible. We examine here some of those organizations in their strengths and weaknesses, based on late 1990s in-depth targeted interviews with leaders of both Guatemalan-only organizations and Guatemalan community leaders participating in pan-Latino organizing (phase 2 of the study)[19] — as well as periodically updated interviews and firsthand observations through 2013. With a few exceptions, the emergence of most Guatemalan immigrant organizations during the 1980s and 1990s was not linear, but involved ups and downs, and evidenced the particularities of Guatemalan immigrant political culture in transformation.

We begin by highlighting the specifically Guatemalan immigrant organizations (e.g., cultural and political), without suggesting that pan-Latino institutions have been less important. Some of the San Francisco–area Guatemalan organizations also maintained links to organizations in their home communities or to Guatemala nationally; others participated in transregional networks and operated across region-wide social spaces, as seen in Chapter 3. Beginning in the late 1990s, Guatemalan state actors in the United States (Embassy, Consulates), as well as the government in Guatemala, also came to play a role.

Based on both the survey and the interviews, formal organizations often interacted with informal support networks. Whereas organizations are more formal and consciously constructed, social networks generally refer to informal ways in which people use contacts to get or give help—see, for example, Manz et al. (2000) and Castañeda, Manz, and Davenport (2002) on Guatemalan networks in some parts of the larger San Francisco Bay Area, and Menjívar (2000) on Salvadoran networks in San Francisco. But the distinction is not rigid: some of the "organizational" types listed in Table 5.1 were less formal organizations than associational contexts and practices (e.g., going to church—which doubtless played into the networks), and some emerged from networks. Additionally, networks could be intertwined with organizations and/or get people involved in organizations. Although there were no organizations to do for women what the soccer teams did for men, women's networks could be quite dense, even as they may have tracked women not upward but downward into informal sector jobs as housekeepers and nannies.[20]

From the two phases of the study, we could observe a significant gap between leaders and grassroots Guatemalan immigrants in regard to priorities and emphases. Furthermore, while there was an overall process of community building, it resulted in a *comunidad fragmentada*.

Cultural Organizations and Cross-Border Reproductions

The San Francisco area's Guatemalan communities involved both ladino and Mayan migrants. In this summary, "cultural" and "social" are being combined because the cultural activities of the Centro Cultural Guatemalteco (CCG) and the Grupo Maya have been social spaces for many Guatemalans. "Social" means different things to different people, and what is "cultural" to organizers is often "social" to community members (see also Hamilton and Chinchilla 2001). CCG was founded around 1970, but for many years, it was perceived as "exclusionary," according to subsequent organizers and community members, holding events in hotels and being inaccessible to many lower-income community members. Its orientation and outreach began to change under successive new leaderships during the 1990s and early 2000s. Its center of gravity and many of its activities remained in northern San Mateo County (e.g., Daly City, South San Francisco, San Mateo).

Even as it moved back and forth between different leaderships, CCG organized a series of traditional activities—e.g., a "Miss Guatemala" event (designed to involve younger women), on holidays such as Valentine's Day, Mother's Day, and Father's Day, as well as on Guatemalan national holidays such as Independence Day (September 15). The different generations of organizers and active members of CCG, who helped finance its activities, have generally been more professional and middle class in origin than working class or poor, but at times they reached out to other strata of the community. CCG was a 501(c)(3) nonprofit organization except during a period in the 1980s–1990s when that status was lost through negligence and had to be reestablished. CCG was stipulated to be "nonpolitical" and "nonpartisan" as an institution. The line was sometimes blurred in practice—e.g., during the late 1990s and early 2000s, when several successive leaderships collaborated with political immigrant rights organizations in new ways.[21] In 2001, CCG cosponsored a successful community event, bringing lawyers to inform Guatemalans about their legal rights as immigrants, and subsequently it gathered signatures for a measure that would grant drivers' licenses to undocumented immigrants in California and supported the campaign for TPS for Guatemalans.

In 1997, CCG sponsored a major public transnational event, bringing the Ballet Folklórico Nacional de Guatemala to San Francisco's Yerba Buena Gardens Center for the Arts. The event was staged in collaboration with the San Francisco Ethnic Dance Festival and with Global Exchange, a prominent San Francisco–based NGO, and informally with the Guatemalan Consulate, gaining financial support from some Guatemala-based businesses. It brought together a large number of Guatemalans in the Bay Area. Strikingly, considering the magnitude and expense of the event, there was little visible evidence of outreach or publicity beyond the Guatemalan community, i.e., to the broader San Francisco public or to the city's mainstream media that doubtless would have covered the event.

CCG developed other transnational ties to Guatemala—for example, financing scholarships for students in Guatemala and sending a representative to participate in Independence Day activities organized by the Casa de la Cultura de Occidente in Quetzaltenango. In some years, when it was financially possible, CCG's Reina (Queen, or "Miss Guatemala") in the San Francisco area, an event designed to attract youth participation in CCG activities, was sent to Quetzaltenango to participate in Independence Day festivities there. In addition to bridging physical borders between the United States and Guatemala, hence strengthening transnational ties, cultural/social events have sometimes been important in bridging ideological borders and in diminishing previously existing tensions within the Guatemalan community.[22]

Beginning in 2001, for several years, CCG celebrated the "Huelga de Dolores," a uniquely Guatemalan, century-old tradition, held even under military governments, in which university students and other sectors of the population parade/dance throughout the capital on the Friday before Good Friday, satirically protesting anything and everything. The Los Angeles community had been celebrating the Huelga for more than 15 years, and in 2001 its organizers were invited to come up to San Francisco to initiate the tradition for San Francisco–area Guatemalans.[23]

Another transnational/binational cultural space developed during the late 1990s was *La Hora Chapina* (The Guatemalan Hour), an hour-long Saturday morning radio program on a Mexican-owned radio station that reached Bay Area counties from San José to Marin and Napa. Mixed in with the (primarily) cultural content of the program were interviews with immigrant rights organizers, visiting Guatemalan activists and officials, sports personalities, and others. In December 2002, the organizers established a radio hookup with station TGQ, based in Quetzaltenango, Guatemala's second-largest city, enabling Guatemalans in the greater Bay Area to send messages and greetings to their family and friends back home. At its most active, CCG provided various spaces for cultural reproductions, including those with explicitly transnational/binational content, in this way enabling some Guatemalan migrants to negotiate their dual identities—their roots in Guatemala and their new lives in the United States.[24] Subsequently, San Francisco–area Guatemalans initiated other community-based radio programs.

Separate from these ladino-run institutions, the most visible cultural organization within the San Francisco area was Grupo Maya Qusamej Junam ("Working Together"). Formed in 1991 primarily by a small group of refugees from Guatemala's civil war, Grupo Maya developed a high profile, organizing a series of solidarity cultural events that attracted a broad constituency of supporters beyond the Guatemalan community. For a number of years, the Grupo was given office space in St. Peter's Church in the heart of the Mission District, but it subsequently moved to Oakland.

Some of the group's main initiatives were cultural/spiritual ceremonies, particularly an annual event to honor the Mayan New Year—a dawn ceremony in San Francisco's Dolores Park led by Mayan priestesses/priests brought to San Francisco from Guatemala. This event was widely advertised and drew people, including many non-Guatemalans, who were not religious in any formal way. Grupo Maya sponsored a number of events featuring indigenous arts and music[25] and offered classes in indigenous Mayan languages. It also worked with a national (U.S.-wide) Consejo del Pueblo Maya de Guatemala en el Exilio (Council of the Mayan People in Exile). During the 1990s, Grupo Maya collaborated directly, transnationally, with Mayan organizations based in Guatemala, sometimes bringing their representatives to the San Francisco area. It also became an affiliate of COPMAGUA, a coalition of Mayan organizations in Guatemala, formed to pressure the government on issues related to the signing and implementation of the 1996 Peace Accords on indigenous rights. Hence, some of these ties were political as well as cultural.

In the early 2000s, Grupo Maya became "pan-Mayan," including Mexican Maya who had migrated to the Bay Area from the Yucatán, Oaxaca, and other areas of Mexico (Burke 2002). Going even beyond pan-Mayan, in some years, the dawn ceremony featured Aztec dancers, suggesting a nascent pan-indigenous, multinational/transregional orientation in this new environment. But during the first decade of the twenty-first century, even as more Mayan immigrants arrived from Mexico, the Guatemalan Grupo Maya had a lower profile and moved to Oakland, with no organizational office.

Political Organizing for Immigrant Rights

The factors that assured an ongoing presence of Guatemalan immigrants in the United States, as well as their need for protection as immigrants, served as the backdrop to the creation of formal immigrant rights political organizations at the local level. As seen in Chapter 3, after the end of Guatemala's civil war, many activists who had previously focused on human rights and solidarity turned to issues affecting the lives of Guatemalan immigrants. Yet as we found in our survey (see Table 5.1) and in interviews, very few grassroots Guatemalan immigrants participated in political organizations, suggesting that such groups were primarily made up of activists. Even as some of these activists and their organizations engaged in transregional advocacy networking, many of their local affiliates did not have broad grassroots membership on a sustained basis.

Prior to the late 1990s, at the local level, much of the organizing around immigrant status and rights was carried out by Guatemalans in conjunction with San Francisco–based legal support organizations such as the Lawyers' Committee for Civil Rights, Immigrant Legal Resource Center, National Lawyers' Guild, Catholic Charities, as well as the immigrant rights organizations CARECEN (Salvadoran) and La Raza Centro Legal (pan-Latino).

In both San Francisco and Oakland, prominent law firms were eager to do *pro bono* work on Central American asylum cases, and the San Francisco INS Asylum Office was notably favorable in granting asylum. Also crucial since the mid-1980s were longstanding Oakland-based institutions such as the National Network for Immigrant and Refugee Rights as well as the faith-based organizations East Bay Sanctuary Covenant, Catholic Charities of the East Bay (an office of the Catholic Archdiocese), Casa Oakland, and the Oakland Catholic Worker (research interviews; Manz et al. 2000). Like St. Peter's Church and Catholic Charities in San Francisco, these religious institutions provided a "sanctuary" space for Central American refugees to stay and to receive legal aid for asylum petitions and other forms of assistance.

The San Francisco Archdiocese, furthermore, worked with sanctuary activists to advise city officials about procedures for becoming a Sanctuary City (Mancina 2012). Although San Francisco's Sanctuary (nonbinding) resolution originated in 1985 with a specific orientation toward these Central Americans, in 1989 the city passed a full-fledged, enforceable ordinance forbidding police cooperation with the INS, thus extending protection to undocumented immigrants in general. In addition to San Francisco, Oakland, Berkeley, and other Bay Area cities passed Sanctuary City measures.

Significantly greater activity by Guatemalans began in 1991, with the *ABC v. Thornburgh* class action settlement: Guatemalan along with Salvadoran organizations and their allies undertook a widespread campaign to get eligible individuals to register as part of the ABC class, with posters throughout the community reading *"Guatemalteco: Viva Sin Miedo y Reciba un Permiso de Trabajo Temporal"* ("Live without Fear and Receive a Temporary Work Permit"). Also during the early 1990s, local Guatemalan political activists combined efforts with Atanasio Tzúl, a national network whose goal was to gain TPS for Guatemalans, as it had been granted to Salvadorans as part of the 1990 Immigration Act (see Chapter 3).

In 1997, the Asociación de Guatemaltecos Unidos (AGU—Association of United Guatemalans) emerged in the San Francisco area with a specific focus on lobbying for immigrant rights. AGU was founded primarily by refugees who had been progressive/leftist activists in Guatemala. The leadership was overwhelmingly male; of the few women activists initially involved, some eventually shifted their attention to work in pan-Latino women's organizations such as Mujeres Unidas y Activas (MUA) (research interviews, Coll 2004)[26] or in human rights campaigns. In 1997–1998, AGU began coordinating with a variety of organizations and with the Guatemalan Consulate. This was a notable change, given the long-standing hostility between the Guatemalan refugee/Mayan communities and any representation of the Guatemalan government during the long civil war. Despite minor criticism of AGU for working with the Consulate, and even as many in the grassroots community remained hesitant to come forward publicly, the general tendency was toward greater openness to such collaboration, most visibly among activists.

One of AGU's first public activities, together with Grupo Maya and CARECEN, was a fall 1997 community workshop on immigrant/refugee rights and protection from INS persecution. This event, also formally sponsored by the Guatemalan and Salvadoran Embassies and their local Consulates, drew upon the expertise of veteran legal support institutions and community organizations mentioned above. In 1998, AGU played a major role in coordinating San Francisco–area fundraising for Hurricane Mitch relief. Beyond its purely local activities, AGU participated in the national network of Guatemalans working on immigrant rights organizing (marches in Washington, lobbying—see Chapter 3). Subsequently, AGU took on the major task of organizing two meetings of the national Guatemalan immigrant rights network, CONGUATE: in May 2000 (Los Angeles) and March 2001 (San Francisco).[27]

Even without a sustained mass base, and despite political divisions among leaders, at some points AGU served both directly and indirectly as a public face of the Guatemalan community, articulating its needs to broader non-immigrant organizations and U.S. society. But between its bursts of energy, AGU's level of activity varied, largely because of a lack of permanent staff and financial resources. Nor did AGU have the capacity to provide legal and community services such as the Salvadoran CARECEN/San Francisco had. By the early 2000s, as AGU activists became involved with national-level organizations (NALACC), AGU ceased to function as an organization in itself and was replaced by networks rather than a new organization. In addition, as in other cities, immigrant rights activists from a new generation were more at ease working in coalitions that crossed specific organizational lines.

Guatemalan Consulate's Role

At another level, the Embassy and Consulates representing the Guatemalan state expressed interest in working with Guatemalan communities in San Francisco and elsewhere. In fact, it was the Consulate in San Francisco that needed the community contacts, once the Guatemalan government finally decided, in the late 1990s, to become involved in issues affecting the treatment of Guatemalan immigrants. A major motivation was the state's interest in remittances sent by migrants in the United States, which by the early 2000s surpassed coffee as a source of foreign exchange. In the aftermath of Hurricane Mitch (October/November 1998), the Guatemalan Consulate in San Francisco and AGU worked out a division of labor for sending relief resources. By 2002–2003, the Consulate followed the Mexican government's example of issuing consular identification cards enabling Guatemalan nationals, for example, to open bank accounts. It also became more active in holding *"cónsul móvil"* (roving consul) events for Guatemalans living in more outlying areas of the very large region it covered, reaching up to Oregon, Washington, and other states—although new consulates subsequently reduced the reach of the San Francisco Consulate.

Other Guatemalan and Pan-Latino Organizations

POLITICAL SOLIDARITY ORGANIZATIONS

During the decades of Guatemala's civil war and as late as the mid-1990s, human rights and "solidarity with the Guatemalan people" were the most visible organizing focuses, encompassing the major activities of the Grupo Maya and a number of organizations that eventually disappeared. After 1997, solidarity work for human rights and social justice in Guatemala continued among some activists, although less prominently than during the war years.[28] The broadest human rights campaigns were carried out—very prominently after the 1998 assassination of Auxiliary Bishop Juan Gerardi in Guatemala, a peacetime assassination—by the coalition Nunca Más (Never Again), which organized an annual anniversary commemoration on April 26. In these activities, the Guatemalan immigrants and refugees worked with U.S.-based solidarity and support organizations, particularly the Guatemala News and Information Bureau.[29]

SPORTS (SOCCER TEAMS)

An important associational activity—for male Guatemalan migrants only—revolved around sports, primarily soccer. For several decades, the Club Deportivo de Guatemala had organized several soccer teams in San Francisco. One team was for former workers in the Ministerio de Comunicaciones in Guatemala. Some were organized by communities or departments of origin, each with its own sponsor. For example, the group from San Miguel Ixtahuacán (located in the western department of San Marcos) was sponsored by a Guatemalan restaurant owner; others represented Retalhuleu, Mazatenango, and Suchitepéquez. A local Guatemalan paint store owner sponsored yet another network. In addition to facilitating the weekly soccer games, some of these groups also functioned as a network to help newly arriving male immigrants to obtain work, shelter, and assistance with specific problems. Women were involved with these teams only in relation to their children's activities.

RELIGIOUS INSTITUTIONS

As mentioned above, during the war years, several churches and faith-based organizations played explicitly political as well as religious roles in establishing the basic institutions of asylum and sanctuary throughout the San Francisco area (e.g., Catholic Charities, St. Peter's Church, the Oakland-based Catholic Worker, and East Bay Sanctuary Covenant). At the same time, churches and religious institutions were a crucial and central source of spiritual, moral, and social support in the daily lives of many Guatemalan immigrants, especially women (see Table 5.1). Non-Catholic churches, including both traditional and Pentecostal Christian churches, became prominent, and some immigrants belonged to more than one church.

During the late 1990s, one Catholic church in San Bruno, in northern San Mateo County, sponsored the specifically Guatemalan congregation, Fraternidad del Señor de Esquipulas, a center for a variety of religious and nonreligious activities (e.g., Mayan cultural events and immigrant rights education).[30] In the early 2000s, the fraternidad worked actively out of a Catholic church in Oakland. However, this was an exceptional case; most Guatemalans in the San Francisco area belonged to churches with pan-Latino congregations.

BUSINESSES, RESTAURANTS, BAKERIES, AND
FINANCIAL AND SERVICE AGENCIES

Beginning in the 1980s and 1990s, Guatemalan restaurants and bakeries became increasingly popular as gathering places for Guatemalans in the Mission District, with some clustered around the strip of Mission Street between 18th and 20th Streets. For example, on Mission Street between 18th and 19th, the Palacio Latino restaurant was not only a social space but also a space for Guatemalan cultural events sponsored by its owner. On the same block was the Acaxutla Restaurante y Panadería, specializing in Guatemalan and Salvadoran food. The Guatemalan Restaurante San Miguel on 20th Street near Mission Street (subsequently on Mission Street near 29th Street) was a meeting place, in part because its owner helped sponsor the San Miguel soccer league. The Universal Bakery/Panadería Centroamericana on 24th Street was Guatemalan owned and at one point during the 1990s carried the Guatemalan daily newspaper *Prensa Libre* once a week. Also on 24th Street was El Triúnfo market, run by a family from the Petén. Both of the latter closed down in 1999–2000, for the economic reasons affecting dozens of 24th Street small businesses, primarily higher rent, although Universal Bakery later re-opened on Mission Street near 30th Street.

Of the various banks and other financial agencies (e.g., courier and travel agencies) used by Guatemalans and other Central Americans to send packages, letters, and remittances or to arrange travel back and forth to the home country—in short, to maintain transnational links to home communities—most were not Guatemala-specific but transregional in scope. Similar to other Central American-owned enterprises, they had outlets throughout Central America and served all Central American immigrant populations. One courier agency, King Express, was Guatemalan owned, with affiliates in many parts of the Bay Area. Overall, however, there were relatively few Guatemalan-owned businesses, and during the 1990s there was no Guatemalan Chamber of Commerce in the San Francisco area, such as existed in Chicago and Los Angeles. A Chamber was subsequently formed in the early 2000s.

LABOR UNIONS AND DAY LABOR CENTERS/STREET SITES

In the workplace, Guatemalans were organized or networked not as Guatemalans per se but as low-wage (mainly Latino) immigrant workers, primarily in service sectors. Hence, those engaged in union and other labor activities (e.g., day labor centers) were part of pan-Latino efforts and beyond—generally including Salvadorans, Mexicans, other low-wage Latino and non-Latino (Asian) immigrants, and U.S.-born workers. Some male Guatemalans worked in construction, in building maintenance/cleaning, in hotels and restaurants, and as gardeners throughout the San Francisco area; there was also a network of mechanics and a group of stereo installers. Some women, meanwhile, also became janitors in office buildings and hotels and formed part of key labor struggles—in contrast to domestic housecleaners and nannies, who were not unionized, mainly because there was no central workplace. According to Wells (2000), Central Americans outnumbered Mexicans in hotel work. Some of the main labor organizing campaigns in the mid- to late 1990s and early 2000s were directed by service worker unions, such as Unite-HERE (Hotel Employees and Restaurant Employees) Local 2 and SEIU (Service Employees International Union).[31] But even among formal-sector unionized workers in the San Francisco area, Guatemalan and other Latino immigrant workers were subject to severe wage disparities in comparison with U.S.-born workers (Ellis 2001; Waldinger 2001).

For day laborers (informal workers) in San Francisco, the issue was not so much to establish the existence of a day labor center (i.e., for workers to move from street corners to a center) but the more partisan issue of who would run it. In San Francisco, this became the subject of a drawn-out struggle between the Mayor and the community-based pan-Latino organization La Raza Centro Legal (LRCL). This struggle was finally won by LRCL in 2004, which was viewed as a victory for the day laborers.[32] Beginning in 2001, LRCL organized a "Women's Collective," with particular emphasis on helping domestic workers and nannies lacking a common workplace to fight for minimum work standards. The Collective also provided other services and training to these domestic workers, and engaged in advocacy lobbying at the state level.

During the early 2000s, day labor centers were also established in various communities throughout Alameda and San Mateo Counties—some of them functioning very successfully, others less so (Bowman and Marmor 2007). In the East Bay, these included the city-funded center in Hayward and the West Berkeley–based Multicultural Institute (which had well-functioning employer/worker job-matching services both in West Berkeley and in Redwood City, San Mateo County). There was a successful, publicly funded center in the city of San Mateo, also providing some social services.[33] By contrast, there was no city-run center in Berkeley, and the Oakland center ended up being shut down after six years, in 2009 (*Contra Costa Times*, July 30, 2009)—both of these cities having high percentages of Guatemalans at street sites. In Oakland, day laborers were being pushed into ever more dangerous neighborhoods (Bowman and Marmor 2007). Particularly at informal day laborer gathering places, there were multiple divisions among the low-wage immigrant workers—e.g., between Mexicans and Central Americans at day laborer sites (Quesada 1999). Furthermore, at some sites where Guatemalans were mixed together with other Latino immigrant workers, observers noted a hierarchy in which Mexicans, Salvadorans, and Guatemalan ladinos fared better and were paid more than Guatemalan Mayan workers; in some cases, they discriminated against the Maya, who were also the most vulnerable to employer abuse (Bowman and Marmor 2007).

Comunidad Fragmentada

We return to the specificities of place and of Guatemalans as themes that shaped the dynamics of their organizing and community building in the San Francisco area. There has been a slow, uneven strengthening in the case of some networks and organizations, linking Guatemalans together in the San Francisco area, with some of them maintaining transnational or transregional ties to Guatemala. Meanwhile, other networks and organizations became weaker over time. Interactions among organizations of different types, e.g., overlap between the cultural and the political, at least at the level of leaderships, were part of the community-building experiences described here—although such collaboration was not linear, but had ups and downs.

Even as they were limited by their survival struggles, Guatemalan migrants helped transform the San Francisco area in some ways, giving these migrants a degree of agency and empowerment (Wells 2004). Most visible were the cultural contributions of the Guatemalan immigrant communities, giving the San Francisco area transnational and transregional cultural links to Guatemala that would not otherwise exist. Guatemalans became central to international solidarity movements in the late 1970s through the 1990s and, particularly when they worked together with Salvadorans, to immigrant rights movements subsequently. As they became incorporated and integrated, however tenuously, into the daily life of urban areas in and around San Francisco and central to their economies, the early cohorts of Guatemalan immigrants and refugees laid the groundwork for their successors.

The growing links to the outside environment, beyond the strictly *chapín* (Guatemalan), allowed some of their communities to become somewhat more established in the San Francisco area and, in this new context, to slowly diminish the cautious, sometimes insular attitudes initially observed among many Guatemalans (see Vlach 1992, 148–149). During "regular" time periods, that is, most of the time, the accumulation of cultural/social/political capital was largely symbolic or representational, even latent. At key moments, however, it took concrete, visible forms—as in the high-profile cultural events, the collection of relief funds and materials for natural disasters in Guatemala and the Central American region, and the participation in various local and national immigrant and labor rights organizing campaigns, as in May 2006.

Perhaps the specificity of Guatemalan "community building" in the San Francisco area can best be understood by focusing on the process as a whole, since specific organizations arose and then either evolved or declined. That process, which moved forward and backward unevenly, included persistent ethnic, gender, class, and ideological fault lines. One Guatemalan we interviewed, who has lived in the San Francisco area for several decades and knows the community well, aptly characterized this process as the building of a *comunidad fragmentada*.

The Sequel: Twenty-First Century Contestations

By 2012–2013, the changes that had accumulated throughout the first decade of the twenty-first century became more visible, both in the San Francisco area itself and among the Guatemalan migrants living and working there. We shall emphasize two of the most important changes in the interaction between San Francisco's dominant economic and political elites, on the one hand, and low-wage Guatemalan and other Latino immigrant actors on the other. The two contestations are emblematic of structural shifts in the San Francisco area affecting Guatemalan immigrants. They concern, first, the uses of urban space and place in a new era, and second, the specific meanings of Sanctuary City policies and the political will and ability to resist hardline national DHS immigration policies. Both sides of these contestations became more complex because they were constituted by multiple players and forces that operated at different levels, with local actors at times gaining influence, and at other times and over the long range losing some of their relative autonomy to national-level players, institutions, and laws. California state politicians and political entities were also important actors on many immigration-related issues,[34] although their role was not always highly visible at the local level.

Many factors changed with the onset of new economic conditions. The San Francisco area's boom in high-technology sectors (1995–2000) ended in a recession in 2001, with widespread effects throughout the area. Far more serious were the Great Recession and chronic budget deficits at all levels of government, beginning in late 2007 and still rampant in 2011–2012—although even during this recession, economic recovery was being sought in some parts of the San Francisco area through the development of new high-tech and biomedical projects. One consequence of the severe contraction was rising unemployment in sectors that had employed largely immigrant labor, ranging from construction to female domestic work, the latter as middle-class spending patterns reflected less disposable income to pay household workers, leading to a "Nanny glut" (*San Francisco Chronicle*, September 15, 2010). Politically, although the San Francisco area and California generally did not pass extreme anti-immigrant measures, as happened in states such as Arizona and Alabama, federal Immigration and Customs Enforcement (ICE) crackdowns increased dramatically at workplaces and on the streets throughout the San Francisco area.

Dominant Gentrification and Latino Displacement

Rapid-fire boom and bust cycles in the high-technology sectors after the mid-1990s took a great toll on Latino neighborhoods and spaces of the San Francisco area (e.g., the Inner Mission District and the Fruitvale area in Oakland). Increasing poverty resulted from scarce access to decent jobs and simultaneously the extraordinarily high cost of living, including unaffordable housing. The political progressivism of San Francisco had never brought upward socioeconomic mobility for most low-wage immigrants such as the Guatemalans, even during the 1980s and 1990s. But by the early 2000s, this was combined with gentrification-driven evictions and Latino displacement. Subsequently, the Great Recession beginning in 2007 cut into the availability of even low-wage jobs for Latino immigrants in San Francisco.

As of 2000, Latino ("Hispanic-origin") residents had resisted demographic decline, remaining more or less stable at 14 percent of San Francisco's population, concentrated mainly in the Mission District and along the Mission Street corridor to Daly City (Godfrey 2004). During the 1980s and 1990s, outright gentrification and eviction/displacement of Latin American immigrants in the Mission District had advanced, but only partially and in stages, more slowly than had been predicted. Unlike other neighborhoods of San Francisco, which had been completely transformed by these dynamics during several decades of the twentieth century (Hartman 2002; Solnit and Schwartzenberg 2000), gentrification began on the edge of the Inner Mission District (e.g., Valencia Street [Mirabal 2009]) but did not yet occur wholesale in the core (lower 24th Street). In addition to the neighborhood's long-standing Latino cultural and commercial capital, activist organizations such as the Mission Anti-Displacement Coalition, San Francisco Tenants' Union, St. Peter's Housing Coalition, and a variety of Latino organizations "fought [the growth coalition] to a standstill" in the Mission District, at least temporarily, and staved off a wholesale rollback of rent control (Domhoff 2005; for related articles, see also www.beyondchron.org). Longer range, however, the Mission District—entire, Inner, and core (see note 4)—became a target for gentrification.

As of 2000, Latinos still made up 60.9 percent of the Inner Mission District population, compared to 62.3 percent in 1990. For the entire Mission District, including the northern and western areas, Latinos were 50.1 percent in 2000, a slight decline from 51.9 percent in 1990 (Godfrey 2004, 2006). During the 1980s and 1990s, the Inner Mission District could be characterized as an area of "ethnic immigrant clustering" (Pamuk 2004) by Mexican and Central American immigrants, along with U.S.-born Latinos. Dominant characteristics/processes included "neighborhood disinvestment, housing deterioration, linguistic barriers, and poverty" (Godfrey 2006, 345—confirming this author's observations during the 1980s–1990s). Together with these dynamics came a wave of street crime, much of it drug related, and increasing activity by Salvadoran/Central American as well as Mexican youth gangs, which eventually undermined residents' sense of living in a "safe" neighborhood. Despite the many problems in this barrio of the working poor, Inner and core Mission District Latinos regarded it as *their* space/place.

But between 2000 and 2010, Latinos declined sharply from 60.9 percent to 50 percent of the Inner Mission District population, and from 50.1 percent to 41 percent in the entire Mission District (U.S. Census Bureau 2010b, Table QT-P4; City and County of San Francisco Planning Department 2012, using ACS 2006–2010 data). Meanwhile, the non-Hispanic white population (counted as a race rather than as a multiracial ethnicity, as in the case of Latinos) increased notably in the Inner Mission District to 53 percent in 2010 (U.S. Census Bureau 2010b, Table QT-P4), up from 46.6 percent in 1990 and 47.3 percent in 2000 (Godfrey 2006 and personal discussion), and the Asian presence increased slightly.

Where Latinos saw their barrio, developers saw a prime property location. Beginning in the late 1990s, gentrification and skyrocketing rents as well as outright evictions of all kinds, some being wrongful evictions, accelerated significantly, now reaching the Inner Mission District (Godfrey 2004, 99; *San Francisco Examiner*, January 21, 1999 and November 5, 2000). Increasingly during the next decade, the Mission District was no longer one of the least expensive neighborhoods; rentals and home prices were much higher there than in the nearby Outer Mission and Excelsior Districts, and median home prices were virtually as high as the mostly upscale Bernal Heights, according to the Real Estate section of the *San Francisco Chronicle*, September 4, 2011, and October 9, 2011.[35] New condo developments were being built, with even more being planned throughout the Mission District.

No longer was the lower 24th Street core simply a Latino ethnic enclave, although Latinos maintained a significant presence amidst overall changing demographics. Spatially interspersed with the remaining Latino businesses, Internet cafes such as L's, exotic ice-cream parlors, trendy Oriental and organic restaurants (e.g., Sushi Bistro), and businesses such as Metro/PCS took over some spaces near to or previously occupied by traditional Latino restaurants such as La Posta and Margarita's Pupusería. In addition, some of the surviving Latino businesses began catering to new clienteles, mainly recently arrived professional residents. For example, the longstanding Mexican restaurant and bakery La Victoria survived but became La Victoria/Wholesome Bakery, offering pricey cupcakes and expensive fair-trade coffee alongside traditional *pan dulce*—in order to "keep up with the changing neighborhood," as the second-generation owner told us. Another neighborhood favorite, the Roosevelt Tamale Parlor, remodeled and offered a menu in English.

The space occupied for decades by the Cuban-owned record store Discolandia was taken over, when the owner retired, by a very un-Latino restaurant named Pig and Pie. The space formerly occupied by Discoteca Habana, the other record store that had closed down, was now shared by the Humphry

Slocombe ice cream parlor and Bello Coffee and Tea. El Tonayense, a long-time Mexican restaurant, became a food truck, with the restaurant space replaced by a Jewish delicatessen, Wise Sons. San Francisco's premiere progressive bookstore, Modern Times, downsized and relocated to lower 24th Street after being financially forced to leave its Valencia Street location. Other new businesses in the 24th Street microspace included Center Nails Pedicure Spa and an upscale law firm in the middle of Balmy Alley, Oliver & Sobec, which described itself as a "boutique law firm" with a progressive orientation. Meanwhile, some of the original, Central America–oriented murals of Balmy Alley were replaced by multi-themed murals addressing broader issues such as AIDS, the environment, and various international crises.[36]

On Mission Street between 18th and 19th Streets, new restaurants such as Hog and Rocks and the vegan Gracias Madre were juxtaposed with traditional Latino businesses that survived as of 2011. Some Latino restaurants and bakeries formerly on 24th Street relocated to Mission Street (around less expensive areas at 20th Street or 29th–30th) when 24th Street rents shot up. Meanwhile, Mission Street's longstanding "Giant Value" large discount retail store was razed to the ground in 2013 and was slated to be replaced by an "85-foot, eight-story structure [that] will combine 114 one- and two-bedroom market-rate condominiums with 14,750 square feet of retail space and 89 parking spaces on the ground floor . . ." (*Mission Loc@l*, July 17, 2013). This would be the second-tallest building in the Mission District.

But perhaps the quintessential symbols of the Mission's transformation were the very wide buses with tinted windows, making designated stops in the Mission District, to transport 7,500 high-tech workers on weekday mornings to their Silicon Valley jobs. As veteran columnist Carl Nolte observed (*San Francisco Chronicle*, June 16, 2013), the buses' destinations were marked in code ("GBUS TO MTV"), conjuring up images of "the kind [of bus] Darth Vader might ride"—or, quoting Rebecca Solnit, "spaceships [for] alien overlords."

In the 24th Street apartment building where this author had lived during the late 1980s and the 1990s through 2001, instead of six Latino tenants and one Anglo, as in 2001, Latinos become a small minority of tenants, judging by the names listed at the secure entry door. Gone were the graffiti that had frequently defaced the building's exterior during the 1990s; other upgrades by 2011 included a good security system at the building's entrance, substituting names for apartment numbers. More broadly, throughout the Mission District, issues of "live-work" loft spaces and zoning regulations remained highly contested (Godfrey 2004, 92). This time, the antidisplacement organizations put up a fight, but ultimately were unable to stop the gentrification/expulsion process, as 10 percent of San Francisco's Latino community left the city between 2000 and 2005 (Mirabal 2009, using data from 2005 ACS).

From a top-down analytical perspective, this resocialization of space would be seen as a triumph for developers and new middle-class residents. Viewed from the bottom up, it is best captured by Godfrey's (2004) formulation of a "barrio under siege" in regard to "Latino sense of place" in the Inner Mission District. He subsequently refined the analysis of the Inner Mission District as a "defensive urban landscape of ethnic contention" (2006, 345)— i.e., defensive responses to the threat of displacement—in contrast with the "consolidated" Chinatown neighborhood across town. Murals and poster art as well as community organizing had always been cultural weapons of resistance against neoliberal spatial restructuring. In the early twenty-first century, however, community organizations were not strong enough to stop the developers' condominium steamroller and professionals' preferences for the Mission District.

A different bottom-up and critical perspective on this resocialization of space is that of Mirabal (2009), based on oral histories with the Latina/o residents who had been or were about to be displaced. From this perspective, gentrification was not simply a blind economic, race- or gender-neutral profit-making process by developers and their middle-class beneficiaries and should not be represented as such in public discourse. Rather, in a narrative constructed from the neighborhood's historical Latina/o and immigrant residents, key spaces in the Inner Mission District were taken over in a racialized and gendered process of "communal exclusion."

One response to intensified displacement of low-wage Guatemalans and other Latinos, both immigrant and U.S. born, during the early 2000s was out-migration from the Mission District to less expensive neighborhoods in San Francisco such as Excelsior and Bayview-Hunters' Point, the latter traditionally African American; in addition, the latter neighborhoods were becoming destination sites for new Latino immigrants (*Mission Loc@l*, June 23, 2011). Furthermore, both trends (out-migration and changing destination points for newly arriving immigrants) were increasing Latino immigrant populations in Oakland and other cities in the East Bay. A major side effect of this displacement from San Francisco that emerged by 2011–2012 was the partial exclusion of Latino workers from city-funded construction jobs in the central city: a 2011 local hire ordinance required that a growing percentage of such jobs (from 20 percent in 2011 to 50 percent by 2017) be filled by residents of San Francisco. Latinos, previously two-thirds of the workers on these projects, were projected to suffer the greatest negative impact of this new law (*Bay Citizen*, April 6, 2012).

Another tendency noted by demographers comparing 2000 and 2010 Census figures (Wilson and Singer 2011) was the shift of immigrant populations from central San Francisco to suburban areas—as was the case for primary cities and suburbs of metropolitan areas throughout the United States. In the case of the San Francisco-Oakland-Fremont Metropolitan Area, the "suburban" areas included all of San Mateo, Marin, and Contra Costa counties, as well as the Alameda County areas outside of Oakland and Fremont. And whereas many immigrants were forced to move for financial reasons, others chose to do so, out of such considerations as safety and better schools (Wilson and Singer 2011, 7).

In the East Bay, Oakland had been a gateway city for Guatemalans, both Maya and ladinos, since the 1980s, with larger contingents during the mid-1990s (Bohn 2009). Hayward had been a destination for Guatemalans since the mid-1990s (O'Brien 2007). In the early 2000s, new low-wage Guatemalan migrants to the area, a large number of them highlands Maya, completely bypassed San Francisco, going directly to Alameda County and even farther east—e.g., Contra Costa County to the north, Stockton and Fresno to the east—outside the Bay Area altogether (*Contra Costa Times*, July 22, 2009). After 2000, Alameda County was the fastest-growing county in California in terms of new immigrant arrivals (Bohn 2009, 24 and Table 6). By mid-decade after 2000, there was a sizeable and prominent migrant community of several thousand Mam Maya in Oakland, notably (but not only) from Huehuetenango towns such as Todos Santos; a high-profile grassroots Comunidad Maya Mam emerged in the Fruitvale area of Oakland. This community maintained close transnational ties to hometowns in Guatemala.[37]

Alameda County and the East Bay more generally have been experienced as several different worlds, spatially divided by freeways, with their own particularities for Guatemalan immigrants. In the early 2000s, as some areas in Oakland underwent relative gentrification combined with scarcer jobs and higher unemployment, many Guatemalan immigrants were increasingly relegated to more dangerous eastern neighborhoods (Bowman and Marmor 2007), and new migrants went directly to communities farther east (*Contra Costa Times*, July 22, 2009). But at the same time, some East Bay Guatemalans had access to resources for assistance as workers and immigrants. Oakland and Berkeley were Sanctuary Cities; in addition, these immigrants were served by health clinics as well as day labor centers and the Centro Legal de la Raza. The East Bay Sanctuary Covenant continued to work with law students at the University of California, Berkeley's Boalt Law School, to win asylum cases.[38]

By contrast with Alameda County, San Mateo County on "the Peninsula" south of San Francisco is part of the "suburban" component of the San Francisco-Oakland-Fremont Metropolitan Area. Although San Mateo County was a space for some older Guatemalan settlements, it did not generally become a destination for most Guatemalan workers displaced from San Francisco or for newly arriving Guatemalan immigrants.[39] Many of the long-time Guatemalans in Daly City, San Mateo, Burlingame, and other nearby communities were more middle class and professional, and less likely to have come as refugees during the 1980s (research interviews, Vlach 1992). Daly City and South San Francisco in northern San Mateo County remained the center of gravity for the Centro Cultural Guatemalteco into the early 2000s. But even in this urbanized area of San Mateo County, Guatemalans and Latinos generally were not represented in elected political positions, nor were they strongly networked or mobilized by social or religious immigrant rights organizations that could challenge traditional power holders (*New York Times*, May 15, 2011).

Other areas, farther south in San Mateo County (e.g., Redwood City/ North Fair Oaks, San Mateo, Mountain View), had Guatemalan immigrant working-class populations (mostly ladino) whose jobs serviced the needs of wealthy households in surrounding high-end Peninsula communities. Southern San Mateo County was spread out along the Peninsula to the south of San Francisco and included some unincorporated areas of the county. This spatial dispersion made political organization somewhat more challenging, but some immigrant and day laborer services became available in the county, and by 2012 the San Mateo County Coalition for Immigrant Rights began more proactive campaigns to protect immigrants from ICE raids and detentions.

The most dramatic form of displacement of Guatemalan immigrants in the San Francisco area became manifest late in the decade: involuntary return migration to Guatemala, either through deportations or because of job loss when the recession impacted such sectors as construction in most places. Whatever their intentions, neither day labor centers nor unions in the formal economy were able to remedy the major structural challenge of job scarcity during a deep and ongoing recession. Even for those low-wage immigrants who had jobs, the fact that spaces and places previously occupied by low-wage Latino immigrants in San Francisco and Oakland were being steadily resettled and resocialized by nonimmigrant, middle-class non-Hispanic whites signified major structural demographic changes beyond any effective resistance by activist organizations. This process of displacement of low-wage workers was characterized by Richard DeLeon (personal communication) as a form of "economic cleansing" in the context of globalized circuits of capital.

Contrapuntal Politics: Sanctuary Contested

During the early 2000s, the City and County of San Francisco faced growing pressures from various players to redefine its Sanctuary City policies. The original Sanctuary ("City of Refuge") policy was adopted in 1985 to protect specifically Salvadoran and Guatemalan refugees and asylum seekers who had entered the United States without authorization. Confronting the Reagan administration's denial of 98–99 percent of their asylum petitions, the San Francisco Board of Supervisors 1985 Sanctuary City resolution urged city officials to protect them, i.e., not to "jeopardize their safety and welfare" or contribute to their deportation (Mancina 2012).

As mentioned above, in 1989, following increased and more aggressive INS raids in the Mission District and new federal legislation (employer sanctions), city authorities adopted an ordinance, which the Board of Supervisors unanimously passed, extending Sanctuary City protection to undocumented immigrants in general, and strengthening the ordinance administratively to mandate "binding limited cooperation" with the INS, i.e., only what was required by federal or state law or a court decision. A further memorandum stipulated that information about immigrant status would not be shared with federal authorities in the case of undocumented arrestees until their conviction for a criminal act (Ridgley 2008; Wells 2004)—a provision that survived intermittent challenges during the 1990s. Taken together, these measures gave San Francisco the political-spatial designation of a sanctuary or safe social space, "where people are protected from the exercise of [national state] sovereign power" (McBride 2009).

Following the federal Congressional anti-immigrant laws of 1996 and their hardening after 9/11, national immigrant enforcement policies and structures underwent massive changes, all of which reverberated at the local level.[40] In 2003, furthermore, the INS as part of the Justice Department was replaced by new agencies—ICE, CBP (Customs and Border Protection), and USCIS, all within the DHS. In the national security environment, ICE attempted to establish the primacy of national over local authorities, and to carry out anti-immigrant raids and deportations without following local norms, practices, or public opinion.

During the first decade of the 2000s, this tug of war among national and local authorities and community organizations in the San Francisco area became more intense and complex. ICE stepped up its raids, undertook new programs, and used new technologies to find undocumented immigrants at their workplaces and in their communities. In addition to the E-Verify workplace-based program, in 2008, ICE initiated "Secure Communities"

(S-Comm), designed to identify deportable immigrants through local police sharing fingerprints with ICE; this program was intended to be mandatory rather than voluntary, but local resistance to it was initially met with mixed messages from ICE. Although it was supposed to focus on immigrants who had committed serious violent criminal acts, S-Comm caught up and deported many noncriminal immigrants, as seen in Chapters 2 and 3. And in the San Francisco area, it presented a structural challenge to longstanding Sanctuary City policies of not sharing information with deportation authorities.

Beginning in 2008, other local events set the stage for a showdown over the specific meaning of Sanctuary City in San Francisco. The issue created increasing tensions largely because of a few high-profile cases in which juvenile undocumented immigrants committed serious felonies after having been freed from jail for previous crimes under Sanctuary policies. Additionally, some Mexican and Central American youth were involved with gangs and drug dealers. These cases led to a backlash, raising questions among politicians, including the mayor, as well as among the mainstream media (particularly the *San Francisco Chronicle*) and broader public as to whether Sanctuary City amounted to systematically "protecting" undocumented juvenile criminals from being turned over to ICE for deportation.

This struggle came to a head in 2008–2009. On July 2, 2008, the mayor responded to the pressures and criticisms by suddenly reinterpreting Sanctuary policy so that police would share fingerprint information with ICE about juvenile undocumented immigrants at the time when they were first arrested and *charged* with committing a crime. After a year of struggle over this issue and with strong community pressures against the mayor's action, in the fall of 2009, the Board of Supervisors passed a veto-proof (8–3) ordinance, technically an amendment to the Sanctuary City ordinance of 1989, mandating that information about these juveniles should be shared with ICE not at the time of arrest for a crime but at the time of their actual *conviction*, hence protecting their due process rights. This measure was spearheaded by Guatemalan-American Supervisor David Campos,[41] the first Latino ever elected to represent voting District 9, which included most of the Mission District as well as neighboring Bernal Heights, with its base of progressive professional middle-class voters. The battle between the mayor, who refused to implement the law, and the Board of Supervisors continued into 2010 but was somewhat defused in 2011, when a new interim mayor interpreted it in a way that would preserve due process for many (although not all) undocumented juvenile arrestees.

Meanwhile, progressive politicians, strongly supported by community organizations, in early 2009 finally achieved implementation of a measure that had been passed by the Board of Supervisors in 2007 to protect undocumented immigrants and other vulnerable constituencies such as the homeless by offering "Municipal ID" cards. These cards allowed recipients to apply for jobs, open bank accounts, and report crimes without fear of being detained or deported. San Francisco sent another signal in late 2009 by deciding not to impound the cars of unlicensed undocumented immigrants. Additionally, since 1997, the San Francisco government had established an Immigrant Rights Commission—stipulating that 8 of the 15 members be immigrants—to hold public hearings and to advise the mayor and Board of Supervisors.[42] In 2010 the Commission sent an official letter to the Obama administration urging that Guatemalans be granted TPS.[43]

But by 2010, unconditionally pro-immigrant policies could not be taken for granted. As one reflection of public opinion, both in 2004 and in 2010, San Francisco voters soundly defeated initiatives that would have permitted immigrants, regardless of status, to vote in elections for the Board of Education—a measure that some major cities had adopted.[44] The mainstream media polarized public opinion and fed an anti-immigrant backlash (San Francisco style—minor compared with other venues). Self-interest became one dominant tendency among voters, with greater constituent support for developers' projects, and even some NIMBY undercurrents in regard to the uses of urban space and gentrification, including the Inner Mission District. In addition, low-wage Latino immigrants could not rely on San Francisco voters outside District 9, which remained one of the city's most progressive, to consistently defend immigrant rights laws. The electoral demographics of San Francisco were changing as new jobs and preferences brought in new residents/voters, both old and young, many of them financially well off, and generally non-Hispanic white and Asian. The 2010 Supervisors' election shifted the board from a "progressive" to a "moderate" majority, and an Asian centrist (the previous interim mayor) was elected mayor in 2011, although the most progressive Latino candidate took second place (*Bay Citizen*, November 10, 2011; *San Francisco Chronicle*, November 13, 2011).

Complicating the panorama, even as ICE raids and arrests/deportations increased after 2008, there were mixed messages from other San Francisco-based federal authorities. Throughout the 1990s and even as late as 2010, the San Francisco Asylum office (under the USCIS branch of DHS) continued to receive significant numbers of asylum applications from Guatemalans living in Northern California and the Northwest.[45] According to lawyers and legal organizations representing them, a surprising number of these cases were won on the grounds that the applicants would suffer persecution or "other serious harm" because of past political activities or discrimination for being indigenous, as well as current conditions of very widespread social violence and violence against women.

On the enforcement side, the struggle shifted from a confrontation among local politicians (e.g., between the mayor and the supervisors) to the more structural level, specifically in regard to the ICE S-Comm program. Mandated by a strong Board of Supervisors' resolution that passed 9–2 in June 2010, the San Francisco sheriff, a progressive, formally petitioned to "opt out" of S-Comm as it pertained to undocumented residents who had committed minor offenses. For many months, ICE did not give a clear response as to whether it would permit this or punish local jurisdictions that opted out.[46] The DHS moved toward a hard-line interpretation and in mid-2011 took a definitive stance against allowing state or local jurisdictions to opt out. In perhaps the bitterest irony for the San Francisco area, San Francisco and Alameda Counties had among the highest rates of deportation of noncriminals or minor offenders under S-Comm: 77.6 percent (of 241 cases) and 67.2 percent (of 625 cases), respectively, between October 2008 and February 2011, with similar percentages for other San Francisco Bay Area counties (*The Bay Citizen*, March 31, 2011, based on ICE information obtained through a Freedom of Information Act initiative by several institutions).

During 2012–2013, the resistance to S-Comm and the tug of war with ICE continued at both the San Francisco and the California state levels. Although they could not opt out of S-Comm overall, in the fall of 2013, both the San Francisco and California governments enacted laws stipulating that, with limited exceptions, local law enforcement agencies should not comply with ICE requests for "holds" or "detainers" of undocumented immigrant arrestees (requests that those immigrants be held in custody for extra time so that ICE could pick them up, presumably to detain and process them for deportation). These measures—"Due Process for All" in San Francisco and the "TRUST Act" (Transparency and Responsibility Using State Tools) for California—represented an advance for immigrant due process rights.[47] The underlying premise at both local and state levels was that, although S-Comm was mandatory, the detainers were only requests from ICE and should be denied. In short, these were mechanisms for reasserting local and state discretion in some respects, although it remained to be seen how they would be implemented on the ground and what effect they would have for S-Comm.

In the various San Francisco–area struggles traced above, there were significant grassroots mobilizations, with CARECEN/SF generally playing a prominent role in broad coalitions and sometimes involving Guatemalan activists. The coalitions included many pan-Latino, Asian, Asian-Pacific Islander, African, Arab, and overall legal immigrant support organizations.[48] The proactive role of these coalitions suggests an accumulation of political capital over the years by organizations based in immigrant communities in the San Francisco area, even though they could not prevail in stopping ICE arrests and deportations.

The mixed record described above revealed some fault lines of twenty-first century San Francisco–area immigration politics. Although San Francisco remained overall a politically pro-immigrant jurisdiction, there was still an underlying issue of how much autonomy it actually had. Using San Francisco as one example, Wells (2004) made a nuanced and visionary argument that "the state" is multilayered and should not be viewed monolithically as the U.S. "nation-state"; interventions by "local actors, deploying normative arguments as to the issues at stake, [can] reshape the outcomes of U.S. immigration policy on the ground" (p. 1308). From the perspective of the very early 2000s, before the consolidation of ICE and programs such as S-Comm, it may have been possible, or appeared possible, to "reshape immigration policies from the grassroots." But by 2012–2013, even as they moved to reassert discretional power whenever possible, San Francisco and other local jurisdictions had lost some of their relative autonomy on immigration issues. The advances for immigrant rights were not won easily; they required complex negotiations and compromises by legislative advocates with other elected officials who had different views about undocumented immigrants. Within this complex scenario, furthermore, as seen above, the dense field of players at the local level included some local players representing state or federal authorities.

We refer to this complex scenario of players as "contrapuntal" politics, reflective of the musical figures of counterpoint and fugues, because of the multiple voices/players all focusing on the same themes but involving inversions of the voices, dissonances, transpositions, embellishments, and melodic and rhythmic variations on the major themes. This musical metaphor signifies our emphasis on not reducing these complexities to a simple binary of national versus local players, but rather on illuminating the alliances and divisions among many players at various levels.

Guatemalan Voices in the Counterpoint

Among the multiple players and voices in this counterpoint have been those of Guatemalan low-wage immigrants, who initially appropriated and resocialized whatever spaces they could and for as long as they could within the context of a changing San Francisco area. Their sizeable migration since the late 1970s and early 1980s contributed to making the San Francisco area part of the larger migration region and impacted the quality of the region, often in ways that the migrants did not necessarily plan. Their presence became part of the movement to make San Francisco a more secure social space or "sanctuary." At some points, they participated in organizations, broad alliances, or grassroots rights movements (e.g., the May 2006 demonstrations) and they engaged in constant campaigns to gain TPS. In so doing, Guatemalan immigrants *as a collective social actor* found their voice to interact with powerful San Francisco area politicians and interest groups with a surprising degree of agency.

But by 2012, various places in the San Francisco area were being resocialized once again, with specific neighborhoods no longer "saved" for Guatemalan or other low-wage Latino immigrants. At the same time, the area was becoming less secure as a "sanctuary" space. In the words of one prominent Latino leader we interviewed, "the quality of sanctuary has deteriorated." Among Central Americans, many Guatemalans, with the exception of those who had found channels for legalization, were especially vulnerable and insecure because they lacked whatever protection from deportation they might have gained from TPS. The fact that this deterioration could happen in the San Francisco area was certain to reverberate throughout the migration region, especially when combined with the fact that San Francisco was no longer an affordable destination for low-wage Guatemalan migrants. In short, Guatemalan immigrants *as individual social actors* faced an uncertain future, as they were caught up in exclusionary macroprocesses that have characterized the San Francisco area's contradictory dynamics.

CHAPTER 6

Transregional Passage

We conclude our book by highlighting and reflecting upon concepts that we view as particularly useful to summarize our analysis of Guatemalan migration to the United States.

Social Space and Place

As we described in Chapter 1, the process of migration contains within its many facets the social production of space. The large-scale migration of Guatemalans and other Central Americans to the United States beginning in the late 1970s produced a migration region in the social environments through which they migrated, in which social activity became connected to the migrants' passage. This developed as the migrants interacted with local residents for support, or as social actors (religious and human rights workers, merchants, criminal organizations, authorities, etc.) reacted to their passage. In many cities and towns, the passage of the migrants became a source of social change as local institutions were increasingly oriented toward the migration. This was especially the case when Guatemalan and other Central American migrants settled temporarily or permanently in transit locations across the migration region.

Throughout the region from Central America to the United States, national governments developed various policies and border control strategies in response to the migrant flow. This politicized the migration region, as social actors and institutions took different positions to support or restrict the migrants. In some cases, as the chapters above describe, the transregional migration of the Guatemalan and other Central American migrants drew transregional policy responses, with the U.S., Mexican, and some Central American governments collaborating on migration control strategies. As seen in our case studies in Chapters 4 and 5, however, urban governments in the United States did not always follow U.S. national policy, creating different levels of policies shaping migrants' lives.

Over time, the migration region became more than a social artifact left behind by migrants passing through local settings. It became an integral sphere affecting the amount and quality of resources needed to migrate in the different migrant phases. For example, rising migrant vulnerability to arrest by authorities or assaults by criminal groups in the migration region raised the amount of social and financial capital necessary for undocumented migrants to succeed in the migration. That is, the evolving region that resulted from large-scale Central American movement northward reflected back on new migrants, affecting the cost and likelihood of success or failure in their journey.

Changing Sub-Regions

Migration processes have impacted an important sub-region at the Guatemala-Mexico border, which we highlight because it is a major crossroads, as emphasized by Mexican and Central American migration scholars and rights advocates. This borderlands sub-region has a unique binational history, as Mayan people and cultures spanned, and today still span, across the administrative Guatemala-Mexico nation-state border.[1] This sub-region has also felt the effects of variations at the state level: there have been periods when the differences between the Mexican state and the Guatemalan state were more sharply defined, as during Guatemala's 36-year civil war, in contrast to periods when these differences have been less sharply defined, as during the late 1990s and early twenty-first century (Nash 2008 and personal discussions). Spatially, in recent times, the Mexico-Guatemala border has been simultaneously a delimitation against migrants and a cultural and commercial link to Guatemala and Central America, part of an investment/free-trade "corridor," and increasingly a corridor of narco-traffic and other illicit activities.

Looking farther south, "Central America" as a source of migrants has experienced varying degrees of unity in different sub-regions and during different eras. In recent times, from the 1960s through the mid-1990s, for example, there was a political sub-region of the three countries (Guatemala, El Salvador, and Nicaragua) that were enveloped in the violent dynamics of leftist insurgencies and civil wars and that by the 1980s were generating large streams of forced migrants/asylum seekers. But at the same time, most of the region was exporting labor migrants as a result of the economic disasters of the 1980s "Lost Decade."

During the 1990s, the region was reshaped politically to include Panama and Belize. In the early twenty-first century postwar era, neoliberal free-trade schemes, most notably CAFTA-DR and Mexico's Plan Puebla Panamá, impacted the region, as economically motivated emigration continued from most countries. The most recent shift in the Central American region, late in the first decade of the twenty-first century, has been the higher profile of the Northern Triangle (NT) sub-region (Guatemala, El Salvador, and Honduras) as a zone of Mexican influence, and also one where endogenous factors have led to rampant social violence and insecurity. As explored in the book, this shift has had profound effects for migrants in the region.

Finally, in the sociospatial approach of this book, in which migrant actors turn spaces into places, we have highlighted Guatemalan migrants' experiences in particular urban places of settlement in the United States. Our case studies of industrial Houston and the postindustrial San Francisco area demonstrated the variance in opportunities and incorporation for these Guatemalan migrants (primarily low-wage, at least initially) as they have arrived and settled since the late 1970s through the first decade of the twenty-first century. We also traced how these migrants have interacted with other social forces (e.g., developers, local officials, changing workforces) in forging and transforming urban landscapes, neighborhoods, and sociospatial class and ethnic communities.

Time Dimensions: Migration Phases

Chapter 2 described in detail a prelude and five phases of Guatemalan migration into the United States to illustrate changes in the flow that occurred due to changing conditions in Guatemala and in the United States. The analysis of the migration by phases provides two advantages for interpreting the flow across time intervals. First, it presents an understanding of how contextual changes at one moment (phase) of the migration affect later phases, differentially for different categories of migrants. For example, the undocumented Guatemalan migrants who underwent legalization in phase 2 through the amnesty provided by the Immigration Reform and Control Act of 1986 increased the number of legal Guatemalan immigrants admitted in later phases (see Table 2.1)—in addition to themselves, the family members they were able to sponsor later. Similarly, the settlement of the *ABC v. Thornburgh* lawsuit in phase 3 enabled many Guatemalans to obtain legal status, eventually even citizenship, in phases 4 and 5, and to sponsor family members.

Second, analyzing Guatemalan migration by phases illuminates the links of migration flows to contextual structural changes at points of origin and destination. At a basic level, human migration results from the interaction between structure and agency. Thousands of Guatemalans were forced to leave their country beginning in the late 1970s as worsening structural relations in the political-military system made daily life dangerously insecure; others chose to emigrate because of worsening social-economic situations. Changing conditions in the U.S. economy also attracted immigrant labor, when employers restructured firms with foreign-born, low-wage labor (Harrison and Bluestone 1988), and when growing professional workforces increased the demand for low-wage service labor (Sassen 1988). Disaggregating a pattern of migration into its multiple phases thus enables an examination of how contextual structural conditions affect migration volumes at specific moments, beyond the effects of individual or family socioeconomic factors that sustain the flow internally.

Weak States

A key structural change in the migration region has been the weakening of states vis-à-vis other actors, partly as a consequence of region-wide neoliberal policies. In Mexico, this can be traced back to the late 1980s and early 1990s: a precondition for the 1994 North American Free Trade Agreement with the United States and Canada was the dismantling of the strong national-development-oriented welfare state created by the Mexican Revolution during the 1930s. As we have seen, in addition to changing Mexican migration policies, diminished state control and authority has left space for powerful criminal nonstate actors and corrupt official forces to prey upon Central American transit migrants in Mexico. These factors also created a need and a space for humanitarian organizations to build institutions of shelter, challenging Mexican policies and practices. Furthermore, the Mexican state has lost some of its relative autonomy vis-à-vis the United States that had allowed it to serve as an intermediary in ending Central America's civil wars in the late 1980s and 1990s—and that, in the Guatemalan case, had provided a U.N.-supervised refuge for Mayan war survivors during the early 1980s.

Next to a weakened Mexican state, the majority of Central American countries are characterized by chronically weak states, lacking both fiscal resources to create decent jobs and opportunities at home and comprehensive *políticas de estado* (state policies continuing from one government to the next) to protect migrants. Weak states in the NT have failed to prevent greatly increased social violence in the postwar period, from the mid-1990s to the present.

As suggested in Chapter 3, postwar Guatemala is a striking example of a weak state, lacking the authority, capacity, and political will as well as the financial resources to attend to the needs of the population and guarantee citizen security. The 1996 Peace Accords had initiated significant steps intended to demilitarize and democratize, hence strengthen, the Guatemalan state politically;[2] on paper, they also included measures to establish stable political parties, an effective Congress, and a functional judicial system. But in practice, progress has been very slow and incomplete; on some issues there has been no progress at all.

Other reforms were envisioned to strengthen the state in regard to socioeconomic policy—above all, a tax reform that would generate resources to address Guatemala's massive problems of inequality and poverty, to create decent formal sector jobs at home, and to pay for a stable peace.[3] But more than a decade and a half later, the necessary reforms still faced stiff resistance from the economic elites and other sectors, and have not been implemented by any of the postwar governments. These and many other deficiencies of the postwar state have become chronic, as comprehensively analyzed by the Guatemalan office of the U.N. Development Program in its Human Development Report for 2009–2010 (PNUD 2010). These structural weaknesses contributed to ongoing migration, regardless of the increased risks or the increasing severity of anti-immigrant measures by the U.S. and Mexican governments. They have also impacted virtually all aspects of Guatemalan migrants' lives: initial migration, transit through Mexico, life and work in the United States, and, in some cases, involuntary return through deportation. Additionally, successive postwar Guatemalan governments have been very lethargic about protecting Guatemalan migrants and reintegrating deportees.

Variations of this situation have prevailed elsewhere in Central America, although perhaps only in Honduras to the same degree.[4] In the face of unprecedented inequality and poverty, and the severe shortage of adequate jobs at home, these weak Central American states cannot control new migration, protect migrants at any stage of their journeys, or do much to incorporate those who are involuntarily deported to their home countries.

In the early twenty-first century, the weak NT states have faced recurrent environmental disasters as well as chronic, uncontrolled social violence, as detailed in the above chapters. Particularly in Guatemala, the social violence has included femicide, the targeted killing of women, with no governmental attempt to investigate or prosecute the perpetrators in the overwhelming majority of cases.[5] These developments have made the profile of the Guatemalan and NT migrant streams more diverse. In addition to postwar labor migrants, many emigrate to escape from intolerable conditions at home. Some analysts and advocates even refer to a new generation of "forced migrants" or the "forcibly displaced" as part of the migration stream.

Transregional Advocacy Networks

Against this backdrop as well as the intensification of U.S. deportation policies, Guatemalan and Salvadoran migrant advocacy organizations and networks in the United States and transregional advocacy networks in Mexico and Central America have continued to challenge state policies. However, they have not necessarily gained more leverage vis-à-vis the various governments involved. Aside from their own internal instabilities and reconfigurations, these nonstate advocacy actors have generally not had strong and willing negotiating partners: even more in the early twenty-first century than during the 1990s, the states are either unwilling or unable to engage with them to develop a new normative framework for the treatment of migrants throughout the region.

Despite these obstacles, the nonstate transregional advocacy networks have played a crucial role by giving the discussion of migration a normative dimension that it would not have had without their persistent efforts and participation in regional forums. The advocacy forces have also at times been strengthened in their campaigns by the transregional ties forged during the last two decades, albeit with notable ups and downs. Furthermore, the political generation that first initiated advocacy activities for Central American migrants is being joined by new generations of leaders and activists throughout the region — in many cases women and young activists, who pay increasing attention to issues of migration by women and unaccompanied children. Standing on the shoulders of their dedicated predecessors, these new players contribute new energy, ideas, abilities, and political styles.

Gendered Migration

Thousands of Guatemalan migrants continue to undertake the perilous passage to the north, even as they are aware of the obstacles and risks that await them. Nonetheless, the human agency exercised in planning, organizing, and actually undertaking the migration northward is not a constant. Human agency varies by degree, e.g., with economic migrants usually exercising more degrees of freedom than refugees, and by circumstances that may limit the ability of migrants to carry out their journey in particular moments and places of their travel. For many, migration involves continual processes of negotiation with different actors that can facilitate or impede their migration. This has become a much more arduous process for female migrants, who are more vulnerable in many respects during migration than their male counterparts, including the strong possibility of being raped.

Guatemalan large-scale migration to the United States has been gendered from its inception, since Guatemalan women have maintained a major presence in the migrant stream to the United States, if not at all times equal to men. Moreover, Guatemalan women have played central roles in the social reproduction of the migrant streams and of the Guatemalan migrant communities in the United States. Since the initial processes of settlement in new environments, they have experienced incorporation (or lack thereof) in ways that are often quite different from men, as seen in our case studies of Houston and the San Francisco area. As mothers with the primary responsibility for child-rearing, they have generally interacted intensively with their children, hence providing for some continuity with the next generation and contact with the broader community. These bonds are being seriously disrupted by deportations of mothers, who are thereby forcibly separated from their children.

Nevertheless, the experiences of many Guatemalan migrant women as heads of households in the United States is likely to have given them an independent self-image and identity. In short, along several dimensions, the social lives and experiences through which male and female migrants are differentially incorporated into U.S. society are affected by their gender as well as their ethnicity and class.

Conclusion: Structure and Agency

From the larger perspective of the modern world system (Wallerstein 1974), the migration to the United States undertaken by thousands of Guatemalan men and women represents a transfer of labor power from peripheral to core regions of the capitalist world economy. As noted earlier, migratory behavior may appear to be individualistic and autonomous, because individuals and families use free will to carry out their migration. However, the migration of individuals and families merges across time and regions into structural patterns effecting moments of change and transformation throughout the migration region. Some of these patterns may have been established decades earlier, in linkages which, as Sassen (1992, 1998) noted, subsequently served as "bridges" created by longstanding relations, such as foreign investment or interventions, between the country of migrant origin and the country of destination.

To varying degrees, human agency has been the origin of the structural forces of labor transfers from the periphery and semiperiphery to the core of the world system (Rodriguez and Feagin 1986), with the important exceptions of slave and other completely forced transfers. The development of these structural forces does not depend on any unique or specific individual migration but rather on the net aggregate outcome of migration. Moreover, the net migration outcome, and the very existence of the migration region, is dependent on a multitude of journeys that migrants undertake (initial, secondary, periodic visits to the home country, returns, re-migration), seeking the best conditions of social and economic accommodation—or that they are forced to make, in the case of the large numbers of deportees.

The relationship between agency and structure is not unidirectional. Social forces create structures and conditions that influence the decisions to migrate. That is to say, migrants, especially undocumented migrants, may make their own decisions in planning and implementing their journeys, but they direct their migration mainly to places of opportunity, or away from dire situations. Migration regions evolve, therefore, as a consequence of the interactions between willful intent and structure, as well as the responses of local communities and other actors to the human passage. Such is the case in the transregional passage from Guatemala.

Notes

Chapter One

1. In this regard, the book reflects the observation by David Harvey (2006, 115–116) that "case study work should internalize theorizing practices," and particular experiences can lead to greater conceptual illumination of the processes under study.

2. It was not until the mid- to late 1980s that U.S. researchers began to write on the Central American influx; see e.g., Loucky (1987), Rodriguez (1987), Aguayo and Fagan (1988), and Chavez, Flores and Lopez-Garza (1989).

3. See Rodriguez (2007) for some comparisons between Central American and Mexican migration.

4. Penalties against employers for hiring undocumented workers started with the enactment of the Immigration Reform and Control Act of 1986.

5. Some analysts, e.g., Wilson and Portes (1980), see this entrepreneurial stratum as helping to produce immigrant "enclave economies" as alternative forms of social integration outside the mainstream. For a discussion of the enclave economy thesis and refinements of the concept, see Li and Dong (2007).

6. We see the continual passing down of spatial symbols and practices across generations as part of social reproduction.

7. For illustrations of these social-spatial contexts of social interaction, see Rodriguez (2007), Nazario (2006), and Hagan (2008).

8. María Cristina García (2006) traces Central Americans seeking refuge in Mexico, the United States, and Canada.

9. See Rodriguez and Hagan (2004) for an example of how new immigration enforcement activity in the United States affects communities in El Salvador.

10. Several theoretical sources inform our views regarding human agency (including its autonomous form)—the praxis that produces space; among them are such writings as Marx ([1887] 1967), Mead ([1934] 1974), Cleaver (1979), and Smith (2001). As Giddens (1986: 2) adds, in regard to the notion of praxis, "Human social activities, like some self-reproducing items in nature, are recursive. That is to say, they are not brought into being by social actors but continually recreated by them via the very means whereby they express themselves *as* actors. In and through their activities, agents reproduce the conditions that make these activities possible." (italics in the original)

11. We adapt the concept of "for-itself" as developed by Marx ([1847] 1955) in differentiating "class in-itself" and "class for-itself."

12. On agency in the production of space, see also Gottdiener (1985: Chapter 6).

13. This is one of the focuses in the field of diaspora studies, which includes in its research the impacts of, and reactions to, new populations in settlements abroad.

14. Rebecca Morales's (1983) study of the use of undocumented migrant labor to restructure the manufacturing industry of automobile parts in the Los Angeles area remains an insightful analysis of this process.

15. This development has already occurred in the five largest U.S. cities, which contain large numbers of new immigrants.

16. IIRIRA also motivated local involvement in immigration enforcement by providing a measure in Section 287(g) of the law to train state and local police forces in immigration enforcement.

17. This book is concerned with the migration northward to the United States; nonetheless, in the 1980s Mayan refugees were part of the 25,000-refugee population reported to be in Belize (Stone 2000).

18. The age of modernity is seen as following the Middle Ages and feudalism in a period of social transformation that generally emerged in the sixteenth century in Europe.

19. In Houston, for example, fieldwork by researcher Nestor Rodriguez in the late 1980s and the 1990s found that social tension occasionally developed in public parks and playing fields where migrants played soccer and tempers flared during games between teams from different Latin American countries. Sometimes brawls broke out between different fan groups and the tension between teams lasted for weeks.

20. Mead did not elaborate on spatial settings as significant symbols, but his discussion of these symbols is clearly relevant for an analysis of how spatial conditions affect social interaction.

21. The enactment of IIRIRA in 1996 greatly increased the risk of removal. Moreover, the reorganization of the Immigration and Naturalization Service into bureaus of the new Department of Homeland Security in 2003 also enhanced the risk of removal, as one bureau, Immigration and Customs Enforcement, took on the role of a national deportation police force.

Chapter Two

1. The estimates given by ACS are midpoints of intervals of estimate with a 90 percent level of confidence.

2. Applications for immigrant visas are normally made by sponsors (family members or employers) who are citizens or immigrants who are legal permanent residents in the United States.

3. The interpolation consists of multiplying the total number of Guatemalan apprehensions reported by DHS for each year after 2003 by the percentage of Border Patrol apprehensions at the southwestern border each year.

4. The Border Patrol estimates that its apprehension rate increased from 50 percent to about 75 percent from 2005 to 2011, respectively, of estimated "known illegal entries." The Border Patrol includes in its estimate a "turned back" portion in addition

to a "got away" percentage. According to a GAO report (2012), the Border Patrol bases its estimates of known illegal entries on visual sightings, trail signs, cameras, and credible sources. The Border Patrol does not estimate "unknown illegal entries," that is, illegal entries for which it does not have reliable information.

5. The most recent DHS data available for the count of deportable Guatemalan migrants located during the writing of this book was for 2011; thus we cannot determine statistically whether phase 5 continues beyond 2011 until newer data are available.

6. Many peasants lived a semiproletarian existence as part of the year they migrated to work on the agricultural lands of large landowners.

7. Guatemala's leftist insurgency was in many respects a response to the country's prior history of the national democratic, reformist (nonsocialist) "revolution" of 1944–1954, and its overthrow through the CIA's direct intervention in June 1954, followed by the U.S. attempt to reverse all social and democratic gains from the 1944–1954 era. These events left Guatemalans seeking social justice with no legal means to achieve their objectives "within the system" and played an important role in sparking the rise of an armed insurgency in 1960. The U.S. government viewed this insurgency as the threat of a "second Cuba" and developed a comprehensive counterinsurgency strategy in Guatemala during 1966–1968, transforming Guatemala's armed forces into a disciplined killing machine (see Jonas 1991).

8. The Immigration Reform and Control Act of 1986 created the new category of "authorized worker"; it also defined the penalties against hiring undocumented workers.

9. The U.S. government uses the phrase "port of entry" to refer to officially designated places, i.e., designated airports, borderland facilities, and seaports, where persons can legally enter the country from abroad and be inspected for citizenship or visa status.

10. Early reports of this new Central American migration pattern can be found in Aguayo (1985), Rodriguez (1987), and Aguayo and Fagen (1988).

11. For details regarding the numbers of victims and refugees of political and military violence, see, to name a few examples, Falla (1994), Manz (1988), Jonas (1991), and Doyle (2005), and numerous annual reports by the U.N. and the Inter-American Commission on Human Rights of the Organization of American States, as well as reports by international and Guatemalan nongovernmental organizations. The figures of up to 150,000 unarmed civilians (primarily highlands Mayas) killed or "disappeared" between 1981–1983 alone, and at least 200,000 during the period from 1954 to 1996, are used by, and represent a virtual consensus among, experts and sources of record in Guatemala and internationally—even including some defenders of U.S. policy, who supported the Guatemalan government (e.g., Marc Falcoff in *Wall Street Journal*, March 3, 1999).

12. Fuchs (1968, 2) states that in 1967, 55 percent of total U.S. employment was in the service sector. According to U.S. Census Bureau (1991, Table 657), in 1970, 48 percent of the U.S. labor force worked in service industries, and by 1985 this figure had increased to 55 percent. To be sure, the transformation was generally relative. The decline of the large, goods-producing sector was in percentage points and not in absolute numbers; moreover, the large influx of women into the labor force through the service sector in the 1970s bolstered the prevalence of service employment (Urquhart 1984).

13. Reaganomics reduced the power of labor in a number of ways. As Harrison and Bluestone (1988) describe, these included major reductions in federal spending for social programs that helped lower-income earners and unemployed workers by cutting federal taxes, increased deregulation of industries, increased privatization of government work, the firing of air traffic controllers organized into a union, and the appointment of conservative members to the National Labor Relations Board.

14. Elliot Abrams, a strong supporter of the Reagan policy, headed BHRHA in the 1981–1985 period during the Reagan administration, and in an opinion piece, he publicly characterized Salvadoran migrants as "not refugees fleeing persecution but would-be immigrants who want to live here *(New York Times,* August 5, 1983)." These statements were used to support the Salvadoran government. Abrams was indicted in 1991 under the charge of providing false information to Congress in 1987 regarding involvement in the Iran-Contra scandal. He pleaded guilty to lesser charges.

15. In the 1980s and through the mid-1990s, many families in Guatemala still had to travel to nearby towns for telephone service (GUATEL) to speak with migrant family members in the United States. Moreover, calls to the United States were costly, in some cases about $3.00 per minute.

16. Paula Worby (1999), who was a staff member of UNHCR-Guatemala, states that UNHCR registered and assisted some 46,000 Guatemalan refugees in southern Mexico after the start of the counterinsurgency war waged by the Guatemalan governments in the early 1980s. The total number of Guatemalan refugees in the southern Mexican region, however, was greater than 46,000, since a large majority of Guatemalan refugees settled in localities outside the refugee camps (Aguayo 1985).

17. A department *(departamento)* is a regional province, Guatemala's basic administrative unit, the equivalent of a U.S. state.

18. In Guatemala, a *municipio* is a municipality, usually a town and surrounding villages with a local government.

19. Border Patrol apprehension statistics give a rough indication of the surge of Mexican undocumented immigration that developed after the Bracero Program was terminated. The number of "deportable aliens," who were mainly Mexican, apprehended by the Border Patrol rose from 110,371 in 1965 to 1,042,215 by 1977 (U.S. DHS 2006, table 34). The number of undocumented migrants who successfully crossed the border is considered to have been considerably greater than the number that was apprehended (Espenshade and Acevedo 1995).

20. IRCA introduced the category of "authorized worker" into federal law to refer to U.S.-born workers or to foreign-born persons with visas who were authorized to work. IRCA also required all employers to have an Employment Eligibility Verification form (I-9) on file for each worker.

21. According to Hagan (1994), the migrant men participated in social networks in neighborhoods, large workplaces, churches, and soccer leagues, while migrant women participated mainly in social networks in small household clusters, places of worship, and in their usually small workplaces.

22. The application fee for amnesty was $185 per adult and $50 per child, or a nuclear family cap of $450.

23. This practice endured for decades. For example, in March 2005, Wal-Mart agreed to pay $11 million to settle a case of hiring hundreds of undocumented migrants to clean its stores. Twelve businesses that provided cleaning services to Wal-Mart also

were fined ($4 million) after pleading guilty to criminal charges for hiring undocumented migrant workers (*New York Times*, March 19, 2005).

24. The 1,000-mile journey took migrants to the southern reaches of Texas. Migration to other Texas sites or states required longer travel.

25. Some years later, in 2003, Guatemalan migrants were among the casualties of the worst smuggling disaster in the U.S. southwestern region when 19 migrants died as a consequence of being smuggled in the back of a tractor-trailer truck. Seventeen migrants died near Victoria, Texas, inside the truck from lack of water and heat, and two more died later at a local hospital (Ramos 2005).

26. CACIF was the Coordinating Committee of Agricultural, Commercial, Industrial, and Financial Associations.

27. A consequence of the softening of labor policy was that for the first time in eight years, the U.S. minimum wage was increased, from $3.35 to $3.80 per hour.

28. TPS provides work authorization to the designated migrants while their deportations are temporarily suspended.

29. A small number of Guatemalan migrants in the United States are Afro-Caribbeans from the Caribbean coastal area of Puerto Barrios in Guatemala. It is likely that some of their U.S.-born children have skills in Spanish, English, and their language of Garifuna.

30. By comparison, the U.S. mortality rate for children under age 5 went from 10 to 8 in the same time period of 1992–2003 (World Bank 2011b).

31. As part of the peace accords finalized in December 1996, an agreement signed in Oslo in June 1994 contained provisions for managing the return and integration of persons who had been displaced (see Jonas 2000b). The conditions in the agreement (e.g., full respect for human rights), did not weigh heavily in the actual return experiences.

32. Operation Wetback was enacted in 1954 during the Bracero Program. More than a million Mexicans were repatriated to Mexico as the campaign covered the Southwest (see García 1980). An earlier repatriation operation during the Great Depression also had sent hundreds of thousands of Mexican immigrants and Mexican American citizens back to Mexico (see Hoffman 1974).

33. Two other restrictive laws enacted in this vein in 1996 were the Personal Responsibility and Work Opportunity Reconciliation Act, which reorganized federal assistance to the poor and initially excluded most immigrants from federal income aid, and the Anti-Terrorism and Effective Death Penalty Act, which made mandatory the detention and deportation of noncitizen immigrants convicted of drug-related offenses and greatly reduced the right to judicial review for migrants facing deportation.

34. Although having U.S. citizenship is the only absolute protection against deportation, Guatemalans who were arrested and ordered deported for being undocumented, and who had not committed "aggravated felonies," could have their removal proceedings suspended if they had applied for asylum under the ABC agreement of 1990 (see Chapter 3) and were waiting for the outcome of their application. In addition, all migrants who are in deportation proceedings have the right to apply for "defensive asylum" if they fear that they will face life-threatening persecution in their home country after being deported. The U.S. government grants defensive asylum to only about 2–3 percent of all migrants ordered deported each year.

35. At the time this manuscript was submitted for publication, DHS had released

the 2012 figures for Guatemalans legally admitted but not the counts for deportable migrants located by countries of birth other than Mexico.

36. See note 4 above concerning Border Patrol estimations of undocumented migrant counts.

37. Information obtained through personal communications with sociologists Jacqueline Hagan and Cecilia Menjívar. Media sources report that Central American migrant women prepare for the risk of rape in the journey to the United States by getting on a regimen of contraception prior to their migration (El Universal.com.mx, http://www.redpolitica.mx/nacion/migrantes-se-protegen-contra-violaciones-toman-anticonceptivos; diariodechiapas.com, http://www.diariodechiapas.com/201205284 4632/metropoli/migrar-no-es-aventura).

38. For accounts of the event, see *The Daily Utah Chronicle*, June 6, 2005.

39. The legalization proposal offered by the Bush administration included a "touch base" requirement in which undocumented migrants had to return to their home country to apply for legal status. For some immigrant advocates, the "touch base" requirement disqualified the proposal as a real legalization program (Immigrant Communities in Action 2007).

40. Section 287(g) of IIRIRA already provided a measure for state and local police officers to receive federal training and become certified for immigration enforcement (U.S. ICE 2012a).

41. SBI had the goal of completing 652 miles of fencing at the U.S.-Mexico border and completed 646 miles by 2010 (U.S. GAO 2010). Lawsuits filed by landowners, problems with newer detection technology, and concerns about environmental impacts have delayed the completion of all SBI components, which as of 2009 were not expected to be completed until 2016 (U.S. GAO 2009).

42. Among other factors was the significant national publicity about the methods used in this raid—first exposed by a court translator in July 2008 (see Camayd-Freixas 2009 and 2013). The aftermath of the raid was maintained in the national public view for several years by the *New York Times* and other media, in both news coverage and editorials.

Chapter Three

1. One example of migration research on political generations is the work of Susan Eckstein (on Cuban exiles in Miami). She explicitly focuses on "generations [that] are historically and contextually grounded" (Eckstein and Barberia 2002)—grounded in experiences, in that case, the Cuban Revolution, that "are not necessarily left behind when people uproot" (Eckstein 2004).

2. Although the civil war in Guatemala lasted from 1960 through 1996, its 1960s phase culminated in a fierce 1966–1968 counterinsurgency campaign by the army, trained and supervised by U.S. military advisers, in Eastern (ladino) Guatemala; this campaign also included targeted assassinations and "disappearances" of opposition leaders in Guatemala City. During that first phase, there was no sizeable exodus of exiles to the United States. Rather, these events sparked a trickle of individual political emigrants to Mexico, where they joined a preexisting diaspora (from the 1954 U.S.

intervention against the progressive government of Jacobo Arbenz) of largely professional, middle-class Guatemalan political exiles. Some individuals went to Europe.

3. We use the word "refugee" not in the formal sense of those very few who were granted refugee status by the U.S. government before arriving in the United States, but rather to refer to the self-identification of the thousands who fled the violence of the Guatemalan civil war.

4. See, for example, Hagan (1994) on Guatemalans, Menjívar (2000) on Salvadorans, and Kearney (1995) on Mixtec Mexicans, among others. Massey et al. (1993) focused on family and community network activities generating resources and access to jobs for new Mexican migrants.

5. See García (2006), Coutin (2000), and a plethora of books from the 1980s, among them McEoin (1985), Crittenden (1988), Golden and McConnell (1986), Aguayo and Fagen (1988), and Torres-Rivas (1985).

6. García (2006, 87, 202n11) cites a specific U.S. policy memorandum of 1985 referring to the U.N. refugee camps established during the early 1980s in southern Mexico. Largely because of the U.N. presence there, southern Mexico had been a haven for Guatemalan Maya fleeing the army's scorched-earth counterinsurgency campaign in the early 1980s, with 45,000 in U.N.-run camps and some 150,000 outside the camps—although none with official status as refugees. As shown by García (2006, Chapter 2), even in the early 1980s, rough treatment and even some repression were mixed in with the protective elements of Mexican government treatment of the Guatemalans—mixed messages. By the late 1980s, early 1990s, and subsequently, in part because of U.S. pressure, Mexican policies leaned more clearly toward detentions and deportations of Central Americans. Yet in the late 1990s, Mexico allowed some of the Guatemalan refugees who chose not to return to Guatemala to regularize their status or to naturalize as Mexican citizens.

7. The date is often cited as January 1991, when the United States District Court in San Francisco approved the settlement (e.g., García 2006; Gzesh 2006), but many of those affected remember the date in December 1990, when it was first announced. Under the terms of the settlement, the INS affirmed that "foreign policy and . . . the fact that an individual is from a country whose government the United States supports . . . [and] whether or not the U.S. government agrees with the political or ideological beliefs of the individual [are] not relevant to the determination of whether an applicant for asylum has a well-founded fear of persecution" (USCR 1990).

8. According to Batalova and Terrazas (2007), based on data from the 2005 American Community Survey, 37 percent of Guatemalans arrived before 1990, 33 percent during the 1990s, and 30 percent between 2000–2005 (in contrast with 19 percent for Salvadorans during that last period).

9. In this particular respect, Guatemalans have had more in common with Mexicans than Salvadorans, insofar as Mexican migrant streams are also ethnically diversified, with migrants from southern Mexico coming from the same cross-border Mayan "people-nation" as Guatemalan Maya.

10. Regarding their prior stay in Mexico, see, for example, Burns (1993, 29) and Olivia Carrescia's 1994 documentary film "Mayan Voices, American Lives"—both about Guatemalan Maya in Indiantown, Florida. See also various articles in Loucky and Moors (2000) and Kauffer (2005).

11. The Welfare Reform Act of 1996 (PRWORA) denied all public services and benefits to all noncitizens—that is, to long-term LPRs as well as undocumented immigrants—hence moving the line far beyond California's Proposition 187. The "Antiterrorism" Act of 1996 (AEDPA) had already been passed to commemorate the victims of the 1995 Oklahoma bombing by a native-born white American and therefore should have had nothing to do with immigrants. However, severely punitive anti-immigrant provisions were inserted during the Republican-dominated House-Senate Conference Committee—provisions that Democratic President Clinton promised to repeal but never did. Specifically, these provisions, strengthened by those of IIRIRA, meant that any immigrant, regardless of status, could be deported if she or he had been convicted of a crime carrying a sentence of one year or more (whether or not he or she was actually sentenced to prison time), and even if that crime had been committed 15–20 years earlier, with the immigrant subsequently living an exemplary life. Most immediately, LPRs who now went to naturalize as citizens could find themselves in deportation proceedings instead.

12. Rather disingenuously, the opponents of NACARA parity—many of them the very same Congressmen who had approved NACARA amnesty for Cubans and Nicaraguans—used the argument that exceptions should not be made for nationals of particular countries—in this case, Guatemalans, Salvadorans, Hondurans and Haitians (Senator Orrin Hatch [R, UT], quoted in *New York Times*, December 13, 2000).

13. In the late 1990s, Clinton was unable to gain Congressional Republican support for parity, but during the phase of writing the rules for NACARA implementation, the White House negotiated the somewhat more favorable interpretation for ABC Central Americans. See Giovagnoli (2011) for a detailed account of the negotiations.

14. Both the AFL-CIO and the big business community, each for its own reasons, began to support legalization measures. Some Congressional Democrats spoke of the need to "Fix 96." The Clinton administration in its last year pushed for some changes in the 1996 laws, but its efforts were insufficient and were systematically stymied by the Republican majority in Congress. In the spring of 2001, the Supreme Court ruled that a few provisions of the 1996 laws went too far and were unconstitutional.

During its first eight months in office (2001), the George W. Bush administration engaged in negotiations with the Vicente Fox government of Mexico about a proposed new guest worker program, with the Mexican government calling for "earned legalization." Although the Bush administration never accepted any immediate legalization component (insisting that applicants would have to go to their home country to apply), this debate did push some Democratic Congressional leaders to suggest the need to extend "earned legalization" beyond Mexicans, to other Latin Americans who had been living and working in the United States for 15–20 years. Guatemalans and Salvadorans would doubtless have been among the beneficiaries.

15. For fiscal years 1991–1992, the funds came from the INS; for fiscal year 1993, according to Congressional documents, the U.S. Congress approved $350,000 to the Mexican government "for the repatriation of third-country nationals directly from Mexican custody to their home nations" (USCR 1992; see also Frelick 1991b; Gzesh 1995). The Congressional inquiry about the use of funds against Central Americans came from Senator Barbara Mikulski (D, MD) in 1993 and was answered by the State Department in early 1994.

16. Ironically, according to knowledgeable Guatemalan sources, the government of Alvaro Arzú in Guatemala did not ask for TPS at that time.

17. Another effect of Hurricane Mitch was to highlight the importance of remittances from Central American migrants in reconstructing the home-country economies, providing a practical, not simply moral, argument for their regularization.

18. There is a clear distinction between deprivation of rights (punitive) and reducing numbers (restrictionist). In fact, analysts Ruhs and Martin (2008) have argued that there is a "trade-off" between the two categories.

19. Uniting and Strengthening America by Providing Appropriate Tools Required to Intercept and Obstruct Terrorism.

20. In addition, while many provisions of the PATRIOT Act were subject to re-evaluation in 2005, the anti-immigrant provisions were excluded from that review, as they had been deliberately designed to be permanent.

21. An "aggravated felony" would be a criminal violation punished far more harshly than a nonviolent civil offense, as was previously the case for undocumented immigration. Additionally, anyone or any organization assisting or hiring undocumented immigrants would have been brought up on criminal charges.

22. This information was provided to us by the Immigrant Legal Resource Center, based in San Francisco. See also Silverman and Joaquín (2005).

23. This meeting featured a series of presentations from national immigrant rights legal and advocacy organizations (e.g., American Immigration Lawyers Association, National Immigration Law Center, National Council for La Raza), and addressed upcoming actions such as the (fall 2003) Immigrant Workers' Freedom Ride and the Congressional "AgJobs and "DREAM Act" initiatives.

24. To give a few examples of nontraditional sites: various cities in New Jersey, New York, Nevada, North Carolina, South Carolina, and Oklahoma, and including Lynn, Massachussetts, Provincetown, Rhode Island, and Stockton, California.

25. To cite a striking example from Guatemala: during the pre-election upheavals in July 2003, when extreme rightist presidential aspirant Efraín Ríos Montt mobilized his followers to literally invade and terrorize Guatemala City, the Sunday edition of *Prensa Libre*, the leading newspaper, dedicated its front page to the outrage and shame of Guatemalans in the United States at seeing such retrograde events occurring in Guatemala. Even if press coverage in the home country was primarily symbolic, it raised the profile of migrant leaders and communities.

26. Regarding these deportation programs and quotas, sources include, among many others: ICE officials and memoranda quoted in the PBS television *Frontline* program "Lost in Detention" (October 17, 2011)—Young 2011; Elmi and McCabe 2011; *Washington Post*, March 27, 2010; *New York Times*, September 16, 2011; *Los Angeles Times*, May 26, 2012. The deportation numbers for fiscal years 2009 through 2011 are in U.S. DHS 2012a, Table 41.

27. The Secretarías Técnicas (administrative secretariats) were held respectively by Manuel Angel Castillo in Mexico and Irene Palma in Guatemala. When GGMMD was formed in 2003, Palma was still at FLACSO/Guatemala, but she subsequently became the founder and Executive Director of INCEDES.

28. Given the politicization of immigration policies in the United States, one high-level Guatemalan official we interviewed expressed the possibility that Guate-

mala's lack of influence was partly a result of not doing "favors" for the United States such as sending troops to Iraq—in contrast to successive Salvadoran governments under ARENA. More structurally, Guatemalan governments of the early 2000s never achieved the synergy that existed between successive rightist ARENA governments and the Bush administration—and subsequently, between the center-left FMLN-supported government of Mauricio Funes and the Obama administration.

29. Tensions over these issues became quite evident during U.S. President George W. Bush's state visit to Guatemala in March 2007, when migration was a major concern raised by Guatemalans at all levels, including government officials; Bush responded that the deportations would continue.

30. CONAMIGUA was structured to have representation from Congress, Bank of Guatemala, Ministry of Foreign Affairs (presiding) and Labor Ministry, Ombudsman for Human Rights, Planning Office, Office of the Presidency—and representatives from nonstate migrant advocacy organizations in various U.S. cities with sizeable Guatemalan communities.

31. These practices, including restrictions on entry to Guatemala, created tension with the other Central American governments, threatening to thwart plans to develop a Central America-wide zone of free mobility across borders, including Guatemala, El Salvador, Nicaragua, and Honduras, the group of "CA-4." This agreement was eventually adopted in 2006.

Guatemalan officials sometimes linked Guatemalan measures to the Mexican practice, during the 1990s and the early 2000s, of dumping thousands of non-Guatemalan Central Americans on the Guatemalan side of the border (e.g., Foreign Minister Eduardo Stein cited in *Prensa Libre*, March 18, 1999; see also Smith 2006). Eventually, this practice was stopped, with Mexico carrying out deportations to the actual country of origin and signing agreements with the other Central American governments to gain their cooperation in "appropriate, orderly, efficient, and secure" repatriations (Castillo et al. 2011, 246–247). According to Castillo et al. (2011) and Ogren (2007, 211), it was widely believed that the U.S. government helped fund these arrangements, including the costs of delivering Salvadorans and Hondurans to their home countries, but the information was not public and could not be definitively corroborated.

32. As another example, Panama was not considered politically part of Central America until the 1990s, after the U.S. invasion of December 1989; during the 1980s civil wars in other countries, Panama was a *Contadora* country (bordering on Central America). Belize was not part of Central America until independence from Great Britain in 1981, and even subsequently is often seen culturally as more Caribbean than Central American.

33. To mention only a few prominent examples of studies on Salvadorans and/or Guatemalans that emphasize transnational practices, see Hamilton and Chinchilla (2001), Loucky and Moors (2000), Mahler (2000), Landolt et al. (1999). In a region-wide summary, Mahler (2000, 36) went back to the original formulation by Glick Schiller et al. (1992) of transnational migration as the processes through which migrants maintain and promote ties between the countries where they reside and their homelands and home communities. Itzigsohn (2000) included Salvadorans in his comparative study of "political transnationalism." Regarding Guatemalans, see Popkin (1999), Palma et al. (2007), and other works cited in the bibliography.

34. To give one example, Seminario Permanente de Estudios Chicanos y de Fronteras (SPEChF—Permanent Seminar of Chicano and Border Studies).

35. As with all the migrant rights advocacy spaces discussed in this chapter, RROCM was not the only transregional network. A lower-profile network was Grupo Regional de Organizaciones Protectoras de los Derechos Humanos de los Migrantes (GREDEMIG—Regional Network for the Defense of the Human Rights of Migrants). GREDEMIG was a project of the Canadian-based Project Counseling Service of Inter Pares, which brought together migrant rights organizations from Honduras, Guatemala, El Salvador, and Mexico.

36. According to interviews with key leaders and the written *Memoria* (Report) from RROCM's September 2005 annual assembly, RROCM itself went through a difficult period of reduced activity and less contact with constituent networks/organizations during 2003–2005. This was partly a result of limited financial and human resources—and politically of being taken less seriously by governments at CRM meetings in the post-9/11 climate.

37. An extreme example was the indirect U.S. role in the 2004 Salvadoran election, in which voters were inundated by an intense media campaign with the message that they would no longer be receiving remittances from relatives in the United States if the leftist FMLN were to win the election—see Grigsby (2004), reports from Univisión Noticiero, March 17, 2004, *BBC Mundo*, May 10, 2004). This was acknowledged by the next U.S. ambassador in the lead-up to the Salvadoran presidential election of 2009, according to an interview and press release of the Committee in Solidarity with the People of El Salvador (CISPES), July 14, 2008.

38. Bustamante, a leading Mexican expert on migration, was the founder and, for many years, president of the major research institution Colegio de la Frontera Norte.

39. One major reason was that the *pacto fiscal* (tax agreement) programmed in the 1996 Peace Accords, under which taxes would contribute 12 percent to gross domestic product (still a low rate), was never implemented and the economic elites still paid virtually the lowest tax rates in the hemisphere. This is documented in Juan Alberto Fuentes Knight's extraordinary book (2011) based on his experiences in public service, most recently as finance minister for the Colóm government, from 2008 through mid-2010. The book recounted the struggles over tax reform—a continuation of the late 1990s struggles to implement the Peace Accords through a *pacto fiscal* (Jonas 2000b, Chapter 7). In fact, the battles over taxes dated back to prior decades, when his father, Alberto Fuentes Mohr, was the finance minister responsible for a progressive tax reform in the late 1960s; the reform was soon repealed, he was dismissed from the government, and he was subsequently assassinated by right-wing forces in 1979.

40. Among the various forces that collaborated with the Zetas, for example, were former officers and soldiers from the elite and particularly brutal Kaibil unit of Guatemala's counterinsurgency army during the civil war—especially but not only in the northern Petén region bordering on Mexico (Smyth 2012; López 2011, both citing well-informed Guatemalan and U.S. sources).

41. In El Salvador, 20 years of right-wing ARENA civilian-military governments (1989–2009) had polarized the society and destroyed state legitimacy and authority. The reformist government that took office in June 2009 negotiated a gang truce in 2012 that significantly reduced the homicide rate, although its long-range sustainability was not yet clear.

Meanwhile, in the aftermath of the June 2009 military coup, Honduras underwent several months in 2009 with no elected government, followed by an elected government whose legitimacy was widely questioned. Unable to control rampant social violence, it was also accused of fomenting violence in the form of ongoing human rights abuses. Certainly it was in no position to take proactive migrant-protective measures.

42. Nicaragua, by contrast, was less impacted by Mexico, as many Nicaraguans migrated to Costa Rica. In addition, the Nicaraguan and Costa Rican governments proved to be somewhat stronger in controlling the above-mentioned sources of violence, including the drug trade. Regarding Nicaragua, see, for example, Shifter 2012 and *Latin American Weekly Report*, April 19, 2012.

43. As a contrast, Falla (2008) wrote a case study of young Mayan adults, whose return to the town of Zacualpa in Quiché, Guatemala, was truly voluntary; they had a positive identity as "generators" of social change and had an easier time reintegrating into their home community.

44. This was somewhat less true of successive postwar Salvadoran governments, which maintained a closer relationship with the U.S. government and were better able than neighboring countries to protect the significant numbers of Salvadorans living abroad, primarily in the United States.

45. A 2008 campaign, for example, pressured the Mexican government to fully implement the provisions of the reformed LGP. Subsequently, M3 demanded that the Mexican government protect transmigrants, e.g., by issuing a visitors' visa during their transit journey. By 2011, M3 was pressuring the government through PRD congressional representatives to implement the new Ley de Migración.

46. On paper, the creation of CONAMIGUA in 2007 appeared to be an advance, but in practice, its accomplishments were limited by partisan infighting, alleged corruption, and insufficient long-range vision or resources to make a real difference in the lives of migrants and deportees. Various analysts, including Alba and Castillo (2012), suggested that some of the necessary Guatemalan governmental structures appeared to exist but did not function adequately.

Chapter Four

1. Jacqueline María Hagan (1994) presents a case study of the migration to Houston from the municipio of San Cristóbal Totonicapán in her book, *Deciding to be Legal*. As stated in note 18 of Chapter 2, in Guatemala, a municipio is a municipality, usually a town and surrounding villages with a local government. They are the local government administrations of the 21 departments in the country. Departments usually have a dozen or more municipios.

2. In his first trip to the muncipio in 1988, Nestor Rodriguez was quickly instructed by town residents to substitute the word *problems* for *politics* in his interviews of municipio residents.

3. Fifty-five percent of the Houston workforce in 1980 was employed in oil- and gas-related related manufacturing and services or in jobs dependent on the oil and gas industry (Feagin 1988).

4. In contrast to Mexican migrants, who had a history of migration to the Hous-

ton area since the early 1900s, the Guatemalans and other Central Americans started their initial sizeable migrations to the Houston area in the early 1980s and thus had no preestablished Central American communities on which to draw for support for their settlement.

5. We use the phrase "household turnover rate" to refer to the number of times a migrant has changed households in a one-year period. The reported household survey was conducted by Nestor Rodriguez.

6. A few women had immigrated in the 1960s from the municipio to work as domestics, but their migration did not lead to a migrant stream as occurred with the migration in the early 1980s.

7. As described in Chapter 2, IRCA was enacted in 1986 to provide amnesty and legalization to undocumented migrants who had been in the country since before 1982.

8. Top pay was the highest wage paid in the different occupations in the supermarket chain.

9. From the early 1980s to 2010, the weekly salaries of the sancristobalense live-in maids increased from about $100 to about $250, an increase of 150 percent, while the Consumer Price Index of urban consumers increased by about 130 percent in the same time period (U.S. BLS 2012b).

10. Christian-based communities consisted mainly of Catholics and pursued principles of Liberation Theology.

11. As explained in Chapters 2 and 3, the U.S. government may grant TPS to undocumented migrants to delay their removal if their home country is experiencing a national calamity, such as that caused by a natural disaster or political conflict. The granting of TPS also provides work authorization to migrants who qualify for the status.

12. A complete sociological analysis as to why the social division between the Maya and ladinos in Guatemala has not been reproduced in Houston would require surveys of interactional predispositions before and after the migration experience, controlling for selectivity among migrants.

13. While the majority of municipio residents in Guatemala remained Catholic and attended the main Catholic Church at the center of town or one of a couple of Catholic chapels in the town neighborhoods, Protestant churches, including fundamentalist sects, made strong inroads in the municipio. These churches and groups included Seventh Day Adventists and Church of God followers among the more than ten Protestant churches that were organized by the end of the 1980s (Hagan 1994).

14. For a discussion of the role of imagination for forming concepts of communities, including nations, see Anderson (1983).

15. The *reina indígena* (indigenous queen) contest is part of the annual patron saint festival of municipios in the highlands of Guatemala, in which a Mayan young woman is selected in a contest to represent the municipio in other *reina indígena* contests of their departments.

16. The informal couriers were Guatemalans who traveled on a monthly basis between Houston and Guatemala to take packages from Guatemalan migrants to their families back home for a fee. By the 1990s, about half a dozen informal couriers worked transporting packages between Houston and Guatemala, and they continued to operate in the 2000s. It is a risky trade because bandits sometimes rob and assault the couriers, who carry truckloads of packages.

17. See Piedrasanta (2007) for pictures of new homes built with migrant remittances in the highland municipio of San Mateo Ixtatán.

18. More than just becoming the new rich of the municipio, they have become the new rich of the *town*, which is the most valued space of the municipio. This is a major social achievement, as many of the migrants who have built new homes in the town originated from surrounding poor, peasant villages. Indeed, from the perspective of the migrants who plan to one day retire in the town, the more than 1,000-mile migration to Houston was a strategy to simply relocate one or two miles from the village to the town.

19. Migrants from Guatemalan war zones sometimes had tense moments in Houston when they recognized individuals they had fought against in the civil war. Yet, this did not develop into a pattern of conflict in Houston. A comparison with a Los Angeles, California, experience can be found in Héctor Tobar's novel *The Tattooed Soldier* (1998) about a revenge encounter in the Guatemalan community in the city.

20. The Spanish terms *gente natural* or *naturales* used by the Maya to describe themselves are laden with interpretive possibilities as the terms seem to imply that non-Mayan people are not natural or authentic, or not derived from a natural source.

21. Smuggling prices from Guatemala to the United States vary by smuggler and smuggling networks, and also by the migrant (man, woman, or child) who is smuggled. In the summer of 2010, some families reported that relatives in San Cristóbal Totonicapán were paying as much as $7,000 to be taken by smugglers to the United States.

22. Fiscal years of the U.S. Department of Homeland Security, which houses the bureau of Immigration and Customs Enforcement, run from October 1 to September 30 of consecutive years. The TRAC Immigration Project at Syracuse University tracks and stores deportation data for all states, immigrant nationalities, and immigration courts across the United States.

23. Houston had the first privately operated migrant detention center in the country. It opened in 1984.

24. After the passage of IIRIRA, which accelerated deportations, the city government of Houston initially was hesitant to cooperate with federal immigration officials in identifying undocumented migrants among persons arrested and booked in jail. After three separate killings of police officers by undocumented migrants in the Houston area, however, by early 2009 the city of Houston made a special effort to participate in the federal Secure Communities program to identify suspected undocumented migrants who are arrested and booked into the city jail.

25. U.S. DHS estimates the number of Guatemalan undocumented migrants to have been 520,000 in January 2011 (U.S. DHS 2012b, Table 3).

26. The enforcement against the hiring of undocumented migrant workers that started in 1986 under IRCA was not fully implemented. It was not until 1997 that the federal government introduced the system of E-Verify to help employers check the eligibility of potential employees. It was the creation of ICE in 2003, however, that began a systematic effort to make employers comply with federal employment law.

27. In the 1990s, Houston became a major hub of bus transportation between the city and Mexico and Central America as U.S. investors bought bus lines that had been started as small neighborhood businesses by Latino migrants.

Chapter Five

1. Although we focus on the three counties that constitute the San Francisco area, we mention the broader "city-region"—often the equivalent of Consolidated Metropolitan Area (Ellis 2001), or, less formally, the San Francisco Bay Area—because "city-region" has come to be widely used in the literature, particularly in comparative studies. Ellis and Almagren (2009) argue that city-regions are a useful context for analyzing the integration of immigrants and their children.

More generally regarding scale of analysis, these and other scholars (e.g., Scott 2001; Smith 2001; Wells 2004), argue that subnational and local spatial units analyze immigrant experiences and interactions with other sectors at a more specific level, more useful for some purposes (e.g., comparing wage levels, poverty, and overall economic well-being) than the nation as context of reception. Holston (2001) adds that this is particularly the case for culturally heterogeneous metropolitan areas or spaces that contain multiple immigrant populations—certainly the case in the San Francisco area.

2. This chapter includes only occasional references to more rural Bay Area counties (Marin, Solano, Sonoma, Napa, Contra Costa), although most do have Guatemalan communities. It does not include San Jose or Silicon Valley, the center of the high-tech industry (located primarily in Santa Clara County), except as it has impacted the economy of the San Francisco area. Finally, it does not include northern or central California centers outside the Bay Area, such as Sacramento/Davis and environs, Fresno, Stockton, nor other cities or semirural towns, some of which do have Guatemalan communities, but with very different dynamics.

3. The need to analyze the interactions was stated clearly by Waldinger (1989, 211) as follows: "much of the sociological research on the new immigration to the United States is about people who just happen to live in cities, but how the particular characteristics of the immigrant receiving areas impinge on the newcomers is a question immigration researchers rarely raise." See also Brettell (2000, 2003).

4. The "Inner Mission District," as we shall refer to it in this chapter, is the area (the census tracts) where the Latino population has been most heavily concentrated. The Mission District as a whole, as defined by Census tracts, is bounded by Cesar Chavez Street to the south, the 101 Freeway to the east and north, Market Street in the northwest corner, and Dolores Street to the west; it includes, in addition to the Inner Mission District, the upscale Western area between Valencia and Dolores Streets, as well as the more industrial/mixed Northern area from 17th Street north to 101. The Inner Mission District is bounded by Cesar Chavez to the south, the 101 Freeway to the east, 17th Street to the north, and Valencia Street to the east. For our purposes, the "core" or "*micro-barrio*" refers to the smaller area in and around lower 24th Street, between Mission Street and Potrero Avenue.

5. The San Francisco-Oakland-Fremont Metropolitan Area ranked #6 in 2000 and #4 in 2010 in regard to the highest concentration of immigrants, according to Wilson and Singer (2011), using Census 2000 and ACS 2010 data.

6. In the words of Smith (2001, 168), ". . . the local often reconstitutes the meaning of globalization . . . local cultural practices and political understandings mediate global power relations. . . . Because local social constructions of 'immigrants' may differ from one city to the next, it matters whether migrants from Latin America and

the Pacific Rim move to New York or Miami, Los Angeles or San Francisco. . . ." See also Mollenkopf (1983), Davis (1990), and Glick Schiller and Caglar (2009). Arreola (2004, 2) specifies "sensitivity to time of settlement and the percentage of the ethnic population in a place," and continuity or discontinuity of the particular community, as key variables.

In editing a thematic issue of *Journal of Ethnic and Migration Studies* (2009, 1063–1064), Ellis and Almgren emphasize "the roles of local contexts in mediating processes of integration" and the "variations in how the host society accommodates or changes in response to immigrants." "*[L]ocal contexts of integration*," they continue (p. 1065), refer to "institutional structures, labour market conditions, and other relevant factors which affect immigrants and which vary sub-nationally." Specific neighborhoods have their own attributes and "are situated within urban spaces where their location confers variable degrees of access to resources including jobs and schools." Similar themes are emphasized by Brettell (2003) as "bringing the city back in."

7. As Price and Benton-Short (2007) pointed out, definitions of "urban center" are somewhat variable. Another measure of immigrant impact is the very high share of the foreign born in 2010 in several counties within the greater San Francisco Bay Area: Santa Clara County (at 37 percent), San Francisco County (at 36 percent), and San Mateo County (at 35 percent)—among the top ten counties nationally of those counted by ACS 2010 (Batalova and Lee 2012). All three have been in the top ten counties in share of the foreign born for several previous years.

8. Regarding the "urban growth machine" literature, see also Logan and Molotch (1987), Domhoff (2005), and Jonas and Wilson (1999).

9. The most striking, paradigmatic case of redevelopment was the transformation of the "South of Market" area into the Yerba Buena Center in the 1960s (Hartman 1974), along with the redevelopment in the traditionally African American "Western Addition." Both cases led to the economic displacement of significant numbers of previous residents and small businesses.

10. San Francisco as "Left Coast City" achieved renewed national attention both in late 2002, when Congresswoman Nancy Pelosi became head of the Democratic Party delegation in the U.S. House of Representatives, and in 2006, with her subsequent ascent to Speaker of the House.

11. In the early 1990s, when that office invited this author (a longstanding critic of U.S. policies in Central America) as the expert to testify about the "country conditions" in Guatemala, the legal staff was a striking mix of old-style INS bureaucrats and young lawyers, with many of the latter being members of pro-immigrant rights organizations.

12. According to one Guatemalan-American resident who knew the community well, a limited number of middle-class, university-educated Guatemalans came to the San Francisco area after having fought in the Korean and Vietnam wars, but there was no "community." As seen in Chapters 2 and 3, there was no visible stream of Guatemalans to the United States after the 1954 overthrow of the Arbenz government, nor after the first wave (1960s) of the guerrilla insurgency and the army's counterinsurgency campaign of 1966–1968 in Eastern Guatemala.

13. More recent figures released in 2011 projected 4,423 foreign-born Guatemalans in San Francisco City/County, 5,995 in Alameda County, and 5,051 in San Mateo County (U.S. Census Bureau 2011). These numbers, released by the ACS for 2010,

using three years of data (2008–2010), showed larger numbers of foreign-born Guatemalans in all three counties than for 2009; however, this population difference was considered by some experts to reflect a new ACS procedure for making these estimates, rather than an actual population growth (Batalova 2011).

14. Technically, the survey included 12 of the 98 Guatemalan respondents (one missing value or m.v. for this question) from counties outside the San Francisco area, in the larger San Francisco Bay Area; but since the vast majority lived in the San Francisco area, we will use that category.

15. This survey was part of a two-stage multiyear project conducted in the San Francisco and Los Angeles areas by a two-person team in each of the two locations. The other participants were Nora Hamilton and Norma Stoltz Chinchilla in Los Angeles, and Carlos Córdova and this author in San Francisco. The first stage of the project (the survey of around 200 Salvadorans and 100 Guatemalans, following 1990 Census approximations, in each venue) was funded by a grant from the University of Miami's North-South Center. Some of the San Francisco results concerning Salvadorans were published in Córdova (2005). The Los Angeles results were comprehensively published in Hamilton and Chinchilla (2001). In both venues, since the survey was based on a snowball sample, the results are illustrative rather than generalizable to Guatemalans and Salvadorans in these two venues.

San Francisco–area participants in the survey were identified through contacts and collaboration with cultural organizations, churches, immigrant and refugee rights organizations serving those populations, soccer clubs, and a variety of other organizations and networks. The questionnaire consisted of both coded and open-ended questions; quantitative answers were initially coded by a team at San Francisco State University headed by Carlos Córdova working with José Mauro Barrón, and the Guatemalan responses were subsequently refined by this author working with Angela Peña. The open-ended questions for San Francisco area Guatemalans were summarized by Aura Aparicio.

16. This result is consistent with the findings of Ellis (2001, 137) and Bohn (2009, 11, 24) about immigrants to San Francisco, compared with the national norm. But this higher educational level did not protect them from a growing wage gap as compared with native-born workers, especially among males.

17. We refer to these links as "transnational," i.e., direct ties with their families in Guatemala. However, it is possible that they were also "transregional": although our survey did not include questions about their experience in Mexican refugee camps before coming to the United States or their ties to family members still in Mexico, other studies (e.g., Castañeda, Manz, and Davenport 2002) maintain that many of the Maya in the East Bay had spent time in the camps and for a variety of reasons had adopted a deliberate strategy of "Mexicanization" (being identified as Mexican rather than Guatemalan). Regarding the experiences of Central American migrants in Mexico as part of a "trinational region," see Jonas 1996.

18. In respect to the scarcity of hometown associations, Guatemalans in San Francisco differed from those in Los Angeles, as described, for example, in Hamilton and Chinchilla (2001) and Popkin (1999).

19. Phase 2 of the study, funded by the Ford Foundation, involved targeted interviews by each of the two project participants in the San Francisco area and were taped and subsequently transcribed by Salvador Enríquez. Phase 2 also included research

teams in Guatemala and El Salvador focusing largely on the impact on sending communities—see Gellert et al., 1997, and Lungo and Kandel, 1999, respectively.

20. One Guatemalan female migrant we interviewed in 1998 had been a professional (assistant to an occupational therapist) in Guatemala but was unable to find professional work in the San Francisco area. Leaving behind the rest of her family in Guatemala, she had come by herself in 1984, even as she was in the early stages of being pregnant. Because of the pregnancy, she was fired from her initial job doing housework for an American. She went to live in Casa de Refugiados and was assisted in having her baby by an organization of the Sanctuary movement. Meanwhile, she worked with the Sanctuary movement and emerged as one of the first women to speak out publicly about political issues, denouncing human rights and social justice violations in Guatemala. For some time, she worked with a group of students at the University of California, Berkeley, and became involved in a community mental health organization treating victims of post-traumatic stress. She participated in the founding of the Comité de Unidad Guatemalteca in the late 1980s and of the Asociación de Guatemaltecos Unidos (AGU) in the late 1990s. She also worked with Mujeres Unidas y Activas (MUA), a major pan-Latino organization for the support and empowerment of immigrant Latina women, and against domestic violence. During all these years, meanwhile, she brought up her own daughter and maintained/financed her own household by cleaning other families' homes and taking care of other families' babies, a phenomenon widely referred to as "transnational motherhood" (Hondagneu-Sotelo 2001).

21. For example, its main organizers in the late 1990s and subsequently in the early 2000s participated individually in the activities of political immigrant rights organizations and coalitions.

22. At the 1998 CCG Valentine's Day fiesta, activists from the refugee community were sitting together at the same table with the vice-Consul, exchanging jokes and *chismes* (gossip)—a previously unimaginable scenario. The May 1998 Mother's Day celebration brought together many Guatemalans who had not come to the explicitly political memorials for Monseñor Juan Gerardi, assassinated in April 1998; but within this social context, people began speaking about it.

23. As an annual event for expression of popular criticisms/satire/gallows humor directed primarily against public officials, the Huelga is a uniquely Guatemalan way to cope with a repressive and exclusionary political system. The event in the United States featured distribution of the Huelga bulletin, "*No Nos Tientes*," sent up by courier the same day from Guatemala. Referring mainly to internal events in Guatemala, the celebration served to inform/remind California Guatemalans about events and cultural traditions in the home country—although in 2003, the U.S. Iraq war was a major target of protest/ridicule in Guatemala's Huelga and in *No Nos Tientes*.

24. For an analysis of sociocultural transnational practices among other national-origin immigrant groups (Dominican, Salvadoran, Colombian), see Itzigsohn and Giorguli 2002.

25. Examples included displays of the work by indigenous artists and weavers who had been brought up from Guatemala, and displays for the Guatemalan Día de los Muertos (Day of the Dead), held one year at San Francisco's prestigious Mexican Museum. Marimba groups were also brought up from Guatemala, and several marimba groups were permanently based in the Bay Area, performing and teaching.

26. MUA has operated in Oakland as well as San Francisco. Other women worked

with a mental health coalition providing services to the broader Latino community, and with the pan-Latino Clínica de la Raza in Oakland.

27. The San Francisco meeting featured representation from the Guatemalan Consulate, the office of San Francisco Congresswoman Nancy Pelosi, the major Guatemalan newspaper *Prensa Libre*, and the Guatemalan Ambassador to the United States. The critical mass of political lobby activity had already gained support from forces outside the Guatemalan community. For example, after making a 1998 fact-finding visit to Guatemala, Congresswoman Pelosi met with a broad range of Guatemalan organizations for a "report back" event, covering both the situation in Guatemala and community needs.

28. One such organization of Guatemalans that still had solidarity as its main priority, and maintained strong ties to Guatemalan politics, was the Oakland-based Grupo Quetzal, founded by male students/activists who had to leave Guatemala during the height of the military repression.

29. Solidarity activity in the Bay Area was particularly high profile after the late 1970s because of the impetus coming from the San Francisco area–based Guatemala News and Information Bureau, GNIB, with its offices alternating between Berkeley and San Francisco's Mission District. And in the early 2000s, the national-level Network in Solidarity with the People of Guatemala, NISGUA, moved from Washington, D.C. to Oakland. Along with organizations such as the Marin Interfaith Task Force on some occasions, they initiated and participated in activities emphasizing human rights and social justice in Guatemala, annually sponsoring U.S. tours for rights/justice leaders from Guatemala and organizing delegations to Guatemala.

30. Overall, *fraternidades* have been uncommon in the San Francisco area, and this one did not serve as a channel for remittances sent collectively back to Guatemala (research interviews).

31. Despite some early victories during the late 1980s and 1990s (Wells 2000), by 2008, Unite-HERE was locked in a multiyear struggle with San Francisco's major hotels to get labor contracts, and engaged in rolling strikes at these hotels. They reached settlements with some but not all of the hotels in 2010–2011. In April 2010, 475 janitors working at the building services contractor ABM in San Francisco and organized by SEIU became the target of ICE no-match letters, and many workers were fired (Bacon 2010). Since these were largely immigrant worker unions, immigrant issues (e.g., legal services as part of benefits, English classes) were among their labor demands.

32. As Varsanyi (2008) theorizes it from her work in Arizona, for undocumented day laborers, this is a way of establishing "belonging" (vs. exclusion) and a stake in the "right to the city."

33. Day labor centers such as the San Mateo Worker Resource Center (originally started by Samaritan House), as well as (since 2006) an office of the Multicultural Institute in Redwood City, serving North Fair Oaks, were run by religious and non-profit organizations. In addition to providing employment and social services, these Centers helped defuse opposition to street-corner day laborers, as expressed in a San Mateo county-wide ordinance outlawing some of their practices, which was in effect from 2006 through 2008 (*San Mateo County Times*, January 27, 2008).

34. For example, state officials opposed mandatory application of the E-Verify system and passed a California-only watered-down stand-in for the DREAM Act, A.B.

540, to help undocumented youth attend public universities—even as the 1993 law banning driver's licenses for the undocumented has been vetoed and unvetoed by different governors.

35. Even the nationwide mortgage crisis toward the end of the decade did not stop the construction of new condominium complexes and "live-work" spaces (Pamuk 2004, 295), although some buildings remained semivacant. Nor did it stop the corresponding unaffordability and displacement effects for low-income Latino and African American communities. City-wide, the *San Francisco Bay Guardian* (October 5, 2010) reported National Low Income Housing Coalition figures showing that San Francisco renters would have to earn more than $70,000 to afford rental of a two-bedroom apartment. In mid-2012, the situation reached the absurd extreme of a property management company renting a 600-square-foot apartment in the Mission District for $2,800 a month (*Bay Citizen*, June 27, 2012). It should be noted, however, that the median housing and rental prices for the Mission District overall are somewhat skewed to the higher end because they include the middle-class Western corridor between Valencia and Dolores Streets.

36. In addition to our own ethnographic observations, sources regarding these changes were the Bay Citizen and Mission Loc@l publications and websites (*baycitizen.org* and *missionloc@l.org*) as well as the *San Francisco Chronicle* and the weekly alternative newspaper *San Francisco Bay Guardian*.

37. The leader of the Comunidad Maya Mam also served for a time as the San Francisco area's representative to CONAMIGUA in Guatemala (see Chapter 3).

38. Beginning in 2007, the East Bay Sanctuary Covenant was also central in the founding and functioning of a Bay Area–wide "chapter" of the faith-based New Sanctuary Movement, modeled on the original 1980s Sanctuary Movement but now addressing such conditions as ICE raids (Freeland 2010).

39. Although Daly City, just to the south of San Francisco, was found in the 2000 Census to have the fifth-highest percent (50 percent) of foreign-born residents in the United States (*San Francisco Chronicle*, December 20, 2003) and to be the fifth most diverse city nationally, migrants were primarily Asian, particularly Filipinos (*San Francisco Chronicle*, February 27, 2011).

40. According to Wells (2004, 1316–1317), IIRIRA (1996) technically "voided state and local laws prohibiting information-sharing with the INS and allowed state and local governments to enter into agreements with the Attorney General to help enforce immigration law more broadly. Shortly thereafter, the Department of Justice's legal counsel issued an opinion opposing such agreements. As a result, few localities had pursued them" before the early 2000s, and in places such as San Francisco, local sanctuary-type ordinances preventing such collaboration prevailed.

41. Campos had come to the United States in 1982 as an undocumented Guatemalan immigrant but was able to become a citizen and graduate from Harvard Law School. He held a series of offices (Deputy City Attorney, Police Commissioner) in San Francisco before running for District 9 Supervisor and winning over two equally progressive Latino candidates in 2008. Ironically, one of these two was a U.S.-born Guatemalan-American. A Salvadoran-American activist who was close to both of them noted the fascinating contrasts—in her words, their different ways of "framing" a variety of issues on which they were in agreement—between the U.S.-

born Guatemalan-American candidate and the Guatemalan immigrant candidate. Campos's website is http://www.sfbos.org/index.aspx?page=2129.

42. This Commission sponsored a high-profile Summit on Immigrant Rights in September 2002 with participation from the INS as well as the San Francisco mayor and representatives from the offices of leading politicians.

43. Also in 2010, the commission published a report that explicitly projected "San Francisco's Role in Shaping National Policy" (City and County of San Francisco, Immigrant Rights Commission, 2010). By 2010, however, some commission participants as well as other analysts noted in interviews that while it remained an important, prestigious moral authority and community resource, by itself the commission had limited power.

44. In the 2004 vote, former San Francisco City Attorney Louise Renne was quoted as saying, "If noncitizens can vote, can Osama bin Laden vote in school elections?" (*New York Times*, August 9, 2004).

45. In addition to Northern California, the San Francisco Asylum office serviced Alaska, Oregon, Washington, and the Reno area of Nevada.

46. Other jurisdictions that were petitioning for the authority to opt out included Oakland, Santa Clara County (with the major city of San Jose), Cook County (containing Chicago), Washington, D.C., Arlington, Virginia, Taos, New Mexico, and the state governments of New York, Massachusetts, and Illinois. To the south of San Francisco, San Mateo County was requesting information about how to opt out.

47. In September 2013, the San Francisco Board of Supervisors passed an ordinance instructing local law enforcement officials not to cooperate with ICE requests for detainers of undocumented immigrant arrestees. The mayor threatened to veto the measure unless exceptions were made for those who had been convicted as violent felons or who were being charged with violent felonies. In order to pass the ordinance unanimously, the Board of Supervisors compromised and accepted those provisions. This "Due Process for All" ordinance became law in September 2013, and its implementation began in November 2013; it was considered a victory for due process rights of the majority of immigrant arrestees and a step toward equal treatment in the criminal justice system.

Meanwhile, at the California state level, in 2012, both houses of the legislature passed Assemblyman Tom Ammiano's "TRUST Act," also resisting ICE detainer requests for undocumented immigrants. The first time around, in 2012, the TRUST Act was vetoed by the governor, but he indicated being open to an amended version that would exclude felons and violent criminal arrestees. The TRUST Act was reintroduced and passed in the legislature with these amendments in 2013, and was signed by the governor in October 2013, extending the new law to the entire state. Meanwhile, Santa Clara and Los Angeles Counties had passed local versions of the TRUST Act.

48. Among these organizations were La Raza Centro Legal; San Francisco Coalition against 287(g); Bay Area Immigrant Rights Coalition; San Francisco Immigrant Legal and Education Network; Coalition of Immigrant Youth and Families; Lawyers' Committee for Civil Rights; Immigrant Legal Resource Center; American Civil Liberties Union; and a broad range of faith-based and interfaith organizations. Among this last group was a "New Sanctuary Movement" (see Freeland 2010). Alameda County organizations developed their own anti–S-Comm coalition, which

included, among others, East Bay Sanctuary Covenant, National Network for Immigrant and Refugee Rights, Black Alliance for Just Immigration, the Oakland chapter of Mujeres Unidas y Activas, and Centro Legal de la Raza. Several of these organizations were members of the Los Angeles–based National Day Laborer Organizing Network, which led mobilizations and legal challenges to S-Comm throughout the United States.

Chapter Six

1. Shortly after Independence (1821), when Central America split away from Mexico in 1823, Chiapas was briefly independent, but in 1824 it was reincorporated into Mexico (Castillo, Toussaint, and Vásquez 2006). Throughout the nineteenth and twentieth centuries, southern Mexican Mayan areas have "belonged" to Mexico. Focusing on recent decades, at times the experiences of the Mexican Maya have been "Mexican"—for example, during the 1980s, as part of the Mexico that permitted U.N. refugee camps for Guatemalan Maya fleeing the scorched-earth counterinsurgency war. But at other times, the Mexican Maya have had more in common with the Guatemalan highlands Maya than with the rest of Mexico—for example, since the 1994 Chiapas uprising, and into the early 2000s, with both groups being invaded by and resisting neoliberal economic integration schemes. For their part, Guatemala's Maya and their organizers have at times had much in common with Guatemalan ladinos and Salvadorans as subjects of state violence during the 1980s civil wars, while at other times (postwar) they share common goals with the Mexican Maya in demanding respect for indigenous rights and in migrating to improve their lives.

2. During the 36-year civil war (1960-1996), as we have argued elsewhere (Jonas 1991, 173-174), Guatemala's "centaurized" counterinsurgency state, constituted by a coalition of the wealthy classes and the army, made the state little more than a militarized repressive apparatus. As such, the state had no legitimacy among the vast majority of the population. Politically, it was a weak rather than a strong state.

3. Beginning in the mid-1990s, such conservative and frequently "neoliberal" international institutions as the World Bank and the International Monetary Fund called for the strengthening, in fact the enlargement, of the Guatemalan state, the broadening of social services, and the raising of the domestic tax base as a percentage of gross domestic product.

4. As argued by Torres-Rivas (2012), the coexistence of a weak state and a democratic (electoral) system cannot last very long, since "poverty and a high rate of inequality for the majority of citizens do not strengthen institutions and democratic practices [in Central America]. . . ."

5. In the United States, such specialized institutions as the Center for Gender and Refugee Studies, at the University of California, Hastings College of the Law, are developing the case for granting asylum to likely targets of femicide and to victims of domestic abuse and gang violence involving domestic violence against young women—see cgrs.uchastings.edu.

Bibliography

Aguayo, Sergio. 1985. *El Éxodo Centroamericano: consecuencias de un conflict.* México, D.F.: Foro 2000, Consejo Nacional de Fomento Educativo.

Aguayo, Sergio, and Patricia Weiss Fagen. 1988. *Central Americans in Mexico and the United States.* Washington, D.C.: Center for Refugee Policy and Refugee Assistance, Georgetown University.

Alba, Francisco, and Manuel Ángel Castillo. 2012. *New Approaches to Migration Management in Mexico and Central America.* Migration Policy Institute. http://www.migrationpolicy.org/pubs/RMSG-MexCentAm-Migration.pdf.

Altamirano, Teofilo. 1990. *Los que se fueron: Peruanos en los Estados Unidos de América.* Lima, Peru: Fondo Editorial PUCP.

Amnesty International. 2010. *Invisible Victims: Migrants on the Move in Mexico.* London: Amnesty International Publications. http://www.amnesty.org/en/news-and-updates/report/widespread-abuse-migrants-mexico-human-rights-crisis-2010-04-27

Anderson, Benedict. 1983. *Imagined Communities: Reflection on the Origins and Spread of Nationalism.* London: Verso.

Arreola, Daniel (ed.). 2004. *Hispanic Spaces, Latino Places.* Austin: University of Texas Press.

Bach, Robert L. 1993. *Changing Relations: Newcomers and Established Residents in U.S. Communities.* New York: The Ford Foundation.

Bacon, David. 2010. "Hundreds of Union Janitors Fired under Pressure from Feds." *Truthout.* May 7. http://www.truthout.org.

Barreto, Matt A., Sylvia Manzano, Ricardo Ramirez, and Kathy Rim. 2009. "Mobilization, Participation, and Solidaridad: Latino Participation in the 2006 Immigration Protest Rallies." *Urban Affairs Review* 44: 736–764.

Barry, Tom, and Deb Preusch. 1986. *The Central American Fact Book.* New York: Grove Press, Inc.

Batalova, Jeanne. 2011. "Immigration Population in the United States at Historic High—But Does a 'Data Illusion' Affect the Increase?" Migration Policy Institute, MPI Data Hub. October 27.

Batalova, Jeanne, and Aaron Terrazas. 2007. "The Recently Arrived Foreign Born in the United States." Migration Policy Institute, *Migration Information Source.* May 24. http://www.migrationinformation.org/USfocus/display.cfm?id=603

Batalova, Jeanne, and Alicia Lee. 2012. "Frequently Requested Statistics on Immigrants and Immigration in the United States." Migration Policy Institute. March 21. http://www.migrationinformation.org/USfocus/print.cfm?ID=886

Bohn, Sarah. 2009. "New Patterns of Immigrant Settlement in California." Public Policy Institute of California July: 1-38.

Bonacich, Edna. 1998. "Organizing Immigrant Workers in the Los Angeles Apparel Industry." *Journal of World-Systems Research* 4 (1): 10-19.

Bonilla, Frank. 1985. "Ethnic Orbits: The Circulation of Capitals and Peoples." *Contemporary Marxism.* No. 10: 148-167.

———. 1998. Preface: Changing the Americas from Within the United States. In *Borderless Borders*, edited by Frank Bonilla et al., ix-xiii. Philadelphia: Temple University Press.

Bonilla, Frank, et al. (History Task Force, Centro de Estudios Puertorriqueños). 1979. *Labor Migration under Capitalism: The Puerto Rican Experience.* New York: Monthly Review Press.

Booth, John A., and Thomas W. Walker. 1993. *Understanding Central America.* Boulder, CO: Westview Press.

Booth, John A., Christine J. Wade, and Thomas W. Walker. 2006. *Understanding Central America.* Boulder, CO: Westview Press.

Bowman, Shannon, and Lianna Marmor. 2007. "Day Labor in Northern California." Undergraduate Thesis, Latin American & Latino Studies, University of California at Santa Cruz.

Brechin, Gray. 1999. *Imperial San Francisco: Urban Power, Earthly Ruin.* Berkeley: University of California Press.

Brettell, Caroline B. 2000. "Urban History, Urban Anthropology, and the Study of Migrants in Cities." *City & Society* 12 (2): 129-138.

———. 2003. "Bringing the City Back In: Cities as Contexts for Immigrant Incorporation." In *American Arrivals*, edited by Nancy Foner, 163-196. New Mexico: School of American Research, Advanced Seminar Series.

Brown, Mary Elizabeth. 2001. "Giovanni Battista Scalabrini." *Migration World.* XXIX (4): 40-41.

Burawoy, Michael. 1976. "The Functions and Reproduction of Migrant Labor: Comparative Material from Southern Africa and the United States," *American Journal of Sociology* 81: 1049-1087.

Burke, Garance. 2002. "The Newest San Franciscans." *San Francisco Chronicle Magazine* April 28: 8-23.

———. 2004. "Yucatecos and Chiapanecos in San Francisco: Mayan Immigrants Form New Communities." In *Indigenous Mexican Migrants in the United States*, edited by Jonathan Fox and Gaspar Rivera-Salgado, 343-354. San Diego: Center for U.S-Mexican Studies and Center for Comparative Immigration Studies, University of California, San Diego.

Burns, Allen F. 1993. *Maya in Exile: Guatemalans in Florida.* Philadelphia: Temple University Press.

———. 2000. "Indiantown, Florida: The Maya Diaspora and Applied Anthropology."

In *The Maya Diaspora*, edited by James Loucky and Marilyn Moors, 152–171. Philadelphia: Temple University Press.

Caballeros, Alvaro. 2003–2011. *Voz Itinerante*. Guatemala: MENAMIG. Monthly newsletter. #1-#101, posted at www.menamig.org.gt.

Camayd-Freixas, Erik. 2009. "Interpreting After the Largest ICE Raid in U.S. History: A Personal Account." *Latino Studies* 7: 123–129.

———. 2013. *U.S. Immigration Reform and Its Global Impact: Lessons from the Postville Raid*. New York: Palgrave-Macmillan.

Camposeco, Jerónimo. 2000. "A Maya Voice: The Refugees in Indiantown, Florida." In *The Maya Diaspora*, edited by James Loucky and Marilyn Moors, 172–174. Philadelphia: Temple University Press.

Camus, Manuela (ed.). 2007. *Comunidades en movimiento: La migración internacional en el norte de Huehuetenango*. Guatemala: Instituto Centroamericano de Desarrollo y Estudios Sociales (INCEDES) and Centro de Documentación de la Frontera Occidental Guatemala (CEDFOG).

Carmack, Robert M. 1981. *The Quiché Mayas of Utatlan: The Evolution of a Highland Guatemala Kingdom*. Norman, OK: University of Oklahoma Press.

——— (ed.). 1988. *Harvest of Violence: The Mayan Indians and the Guatemalan Crisis*. Norman: University of Oklahoma Press.

Carrescia, Olivia. 1994. "Mayan Voices, American Lives." Documentary film. New York: First Run/Icarus Films.

Casillas, Rodolfo. 1995. "¿Se mueve la frontera al Suchiate?" *Este País*. Mexico. April.

———. 2006. *Una vida discreta, fugaz y anónima: Los centroamericanos transmigrantes en México*. México, D.F.: Comisión Nacional de los Derechos Humanos/Organización Internacional para las Migraciones.

Castañeda, Xóchitl, Beatriz Manz, and Allison Davenport. 2002. "Mexicanization: A Survival Strategy for Guatemalan Mayans in the San Francisco Bay Area." *Migraciones Internacionales* 3: 102–123.

Castells, Manuel. 1983. *The City and the Grassroots: A Cross-cultural Theory of Urban Social Movements*. Berkeley: University of California Press.

———. 2004. "Informationalism, Networks, and the Network Society: A Theoretical Blueprint." In *The Network Society: A Cross-Cultural Perspective*, edited by Manuel Castells, 3–45. Gloucester, England: Edward Elgar Publishing Ltd.

Castillo, Manuel Ángel. 1997. "Las politicas migratorias de México y Guatemala en el context de la integración regional." In *Las fronteras del Istmo: Fronteras y sociedades entre el sur de México y América Central*, edited by Philippe Bovin, 203–212. México: CIESAS, Cemca.

———. 2003a. "The Mexico-Guatemala Border: New Controls on Transborder Migrations in View of Recent Integration Schemes?" *Frontera Norte* 15 (Enero-Junio): 35–64.

———. 2003b. The Regional Conference on Migration: Its Evolution and Current Security Context. *Studi Emigrazione/Migration Studies* 149: 81–97.

———. 2005. "Migración, Derechos Humanos y Ciudadanía." Working Paper #05–02b, presented at The Center for Migration and Development: Princeton University.

———. 2006. "Mexico: Caught between the United States and Central America."

Migration Information Source, Migration Policy Institute. Washington, D.C. http://www.migrationinformation.org/datahub/countrydata.cfm?ID=389.

Castillo, Manuel Ángel, Mónica Toussaint, and Mario Vázquez. 2006. *Espacios Diversos, Historia en Común: México, Guatemala, Belice—La Construcción de una Frontera.* México, D.F.: Secretaría de Relaciones Exteriores, Dirección General de Acervo Histórico Diplomático.

———. 2011. *Centroamérica.* Vol. 2 of series *Historia de las Relaciones Internacionales de México, 1821–2010,* compiled by Mercedes de Vega. Archivo Histórico Diplomático. Mexico: Secretaría de Relacicones Exteriores.

Center for Gender and Refugee Studies. 2012. *Ending Deportation to Death—Developing Positive Jurisprudence for Asylum Claims Based on Gang Persecution.* San Francisco. CGRS, University of California Hastings College of the Law. San Francisco. November.

Chavez, Leo R. 1992. *Shadowed Lives: Undocumented Immigrants in American Society.* Fort Worth: Harcourt Brace Jovanovich College Publishers.

———. 1997. "Immigration Reform and Nativism: The Nationalist Response to the Transnationalist Challenge." In *Immigrants Out!: The New Nativism and the Anti-Immigrant Impulse in the United States,* edited by Juan F. Perea, 61–77. New York: New York University Press.

———. 2007. "The Condition of Illegality." *International Migration* 45 (3): 192–196.

Chavez, Leo R., Estevan T. Flores, and Marta López-Garza. 1989. Migrants and Settlers: A Comparison of Undocumented Mexicans and Central Americans. *Frontera Norte* 1: 49–75.

Chinchilla, Norma Stoltz, Nora Hamilton, and James Loucky. 1993. "The Making of an Immigrant Community: Central Americans in Los Angeles." In *In the Barrios: Latinos and the Underclass Debate,* edited by Joan Moore and Raquel Pinderhughes, 51–78. New York: Russell Sage Foundation.

City and County of San Francisco, Immigrant Rights Commission. 2010. "Are We a Nation of Immigrants? Summary Report on Comprehensive Immigration Reform: San Francisco's Role in Shaping National Policy." http://www.sfgov2.org/Modules/ShowDocument.aspx?documentid=83.

City and County of San Francisco, Planning Department. 2012. San Francisco Neighborhoods: Socio-Economic Profiles: American Community Survey 2006–2010. San Francisco. May. http://www.sf-lanning.org/modules/showdocument.aspx?documentid=8779.

City and County of San Francisco, Immigrant Rights Commission. 2013. *A City and Nation of Immigrants: 2013 Recommendations on Comprehensive Immigration Reform.* San Francisco. April.

Cleaver, Harry. 1979. *Reading Capital Politically.* Austin, TX: University of Texas Press.

Cohen, Robin. 1987. *The New Helots: Migrants in the International Division of Labor.* Brookfield, VT: Avebury.

Coll, Kathleen. 2004. "Necesidades y Problemas: Immigrant Latina Vernaculars of Belonging, Coalition, & Citizenship in San Francisco, California." *Latino Studies* 2: 186–209.

———. 2010. *Remaking Citizenship: Latina Immigrants and New American Politics.* Stanford: Stanford University Press.

Comisión Económica para América Latina y el Caribe (CEPAL). 2012. Bases de Datos y Publicaciones Estadisticas. http://websie.eclac.cl/infest/ajax/cepalstat.asp?carpeta=estadisticas.

Comisión para el Esclarecimiento Histórico (CEH). 1999. *Guatemala: Memoria del silencio*. Guatemala: Comisión para el Esclarecimiento Histórico.

Committee in Solidarity with the People of El Salvador (CISPES). 2008. Press Release. July 14.

Conover, Ted. 1987. *Coyotes: A Journey through the Secret World of America's Illegal Aliens*. New York: Random House.

Córdova, Carlos. 2005. *The Salvadoran Americans*. Westport, CT: Greenwood Press.

Coutin, Susan Bibler. 2000. *Legalizing Moves: Salvadoran Immigrants' Struggle for U.S. Residency*. Ann Arbor: University of Michigan Press.

Cranford, Cynthia. 2004. "Economic Restructuring, Immigration, and the New Labor Movement: Latina/o Janitors in Los Angeles." The Center for Comparative Immigration Studies. Working Paper No. 9. University of California San Diego.

Crittenden, Ann. 1988. *Sanctuary: A Story of American Conscience and the Law in Collision*. London: Weidenfeld & Nicolson.

Cruz, Hugo Ángeles. 2009. "Caracteristicas de los trabajadores agrícolas guatemaltecos en México según la EMIF GUAMEX." In *Flujos migratorios en la frontera Guatemala-México*, edited by Maria Eugenia Anguiano Téllez and Rodolfo Corona Vazquez, 157–198. México, D.F.: Centro de Estudios Migratorios, Instituto Nacional de Migración.

Dardón, Jacobo. 2009. "Dos rostros de un mismo vuelo: Las personas guatemaltecas deportadas desde Estados Unidos." In *Flujos migratorios en la frontera Guatemala-México*, edited by María Eugenia Anguiano Téllez and Rodolfo Corona Vásquez, 333–369. México: Centro de Estudios Migratorios, Instituto Nacional de Migración, SEGOB, and El Colegio de la Frontera Norte A.C.; DGE Ediciones S.A. de C.V.

Davidson, Miriam. 1988. *Convictions of the Heart: Jim Corbett and the Sanctuary Movement*. Tucson, AZ: University of Arizona Press.

Davis, Mike. 1990. *City of Quartz: Excavating the Future of Los Angeles*. London: Verso.

Davis, Shelton H. 2007. "Migration, Remittances, and Ethnic Identity: The Experience of Guatemalan Maya in the United States." In *Moving Out of Poverty: Cross-Disciplinary Perspectives on Mobility*, edited by Deepa Narayan and Patti Petesch, 333–354. New York: Palgrave Macmillan.

De Leon, Arnoldo. 2001. *Ethnicity in the Sunbelt: Mexican Americans in Houston*. College Station, TX: Texas A&M Press.

DeLeon, Richard. 1992. *Left Coast City: Progressive Politics in San Francisco 1975–1991*. Lawrence, KS: University Press of Kansas.

Díaz, Gabriela, and Gretchen Kuhner. 2007. "Women Migrants in Transit and Detention in Mexico." Migration Policy Institute, *Migration Information Source*, March 1. http://www.migrationinformation.org/Feature/display.cfm?id=586.

———. 2008. "Women Migrants in Detention in Mexico: Conditions and Due Process." Migration Policy Institute, *Migration Information Source*, June 2. http://www.migrationinformation.org/Feature/display.cfm?id=684

Dirección General de Estadistica (Guatemala). 1984. *Censos Nacionales: IV Habitacion-IX Poblacion, 1981*. Febrero. Ministerio de Economia, Republica de Guatemala.

Domhoff, G. William. 2005. "Power at the Local Level: Growth Coalition Theory" and "Why San Francisco Is Different: Progressive Activists and Neighborhoods Have Had a Big Impact." http://sociology.ucsc.edu/whorulesamerica/power/local .html.

Donato, Katherine M., Brandon Wagner, and Evelyn Petterson. 2008. "The Cat and Mouse Game at the Mexico-U.S. Border: Gendered Patterns and Recent Shifts." *International Migration Review* 42: 330–359.

Doyle, Kate. 2005. *The Guatemalan Police Archives*. National Security Archive Electronic Briefing Book, No. 170. November 21. *http://www.gwu.edu/~nsarchiv/NSAEBB /NSAEBB170/index.htm.*

Dreier, John, John Mollenkopf, and Todd Swanstrom. 2001. *Place Matters: Metropolitics for the Twenty-First Century.* Lawrence, KS: University Press of Kansas.

Durand, Jorge, and Douglas S. Massey. 2006. *Crossing the Border: Research from the Mexican Migration Project.* New York: Russell Sage Foundation.

Eckstein, Susan. 2004. "On Deconstructing Immigrant Generations: Cohorts and the Cuban Émigré Experience." Working Paper #97, presented at The Center for Comparative Immigration Studies (CCIS). University of California, San Diego.

Eckstein, Susan, and Lorena Barberia. 2002. "Grounding Immigrant Generations in History: Cuban Americans and Their Transnational Ties." *International Migration Review* 36: 799–837.

ECLAC. 2007. "Growth, Poverty, and Inequality in Central America." Social Development Unit, United Nations. Mexico, D.F. http://www.eclac.org/publicaciones /xml/0/30240/Serie_88.pdf.

———. 2006. *2005 Statistical Yearbook for Latin America and the Caribbean.* United Nations. http://www.eclac.org/publicaciones/xml/1/26531/LCG2311B_1.pdf.

———. 2010. *2009 Statistical Yearbook for Latin America and the Caribbean.* United Nations. http://www.eclac.org/publicaciones/xml/9/38409/LCG2430b_1.pdf.

———. 2011. CEPALSTAT. United Nations. http://www.eclac.org/estadisticas/de fault.asp?idioma=IN.

Ellis, Mark. 2001. "A Tale of Five Cities? Trends in Immigrant and Native-Born Wages." In *Strangers at the Gates: New Immigrants in Urban America*, edited by Roger Waldinger, 117–158. Berkeley: University of California Press.

Ellis, Mark and Gunnar Almgren. 2009. "Local Context of Immigrant and Second Generation Integration in the United States." *Journal of Ethnic and Migration Studies* 35: 1059–1076.

Elmi, Sheida, and Kristen McCabe. 2011. "Immigration Enforcement in the United States." Migration Policy Institute, *Migration Information Source*. October 25. http://www.migrationinformation.org/USFocus/display.cfm?ID=858.

England, Sarah. 2006. *Afro Central Americans in New York City: Garifuna Tales of Transnational Movements in Racialized Space.* Gainsville, FL: University Press of Florida.

Eschbach, Karl, Jacqueline Hagan, Nestor Rodriguez, Ruben Hernandez Leon, and Stanley Bailey. 1999. "Death at the Border." *International Migration Review* 33: 430–454.

Escobar Sarti, Carolina. 2008. "Los pequeños pasos en un camino minado: Migración, niñez y juventud en Centroamerica y el sur de México." Oxford, England: Project Counseling Service.

Espenshade, Thomas J., and Dolores Acevedo. 1995. "Migrant Cohort Size, Enforcement Effort, and the Apprehension of Undocumented Aliens." *Population Research and Policy Review* 14 (2): 145–172.

Falla, Ricardo. 1978. *Quiché Rebelde.* Guatemala: Editorial Universitaria.

———. 1984. "We Charge Genocide." In *Guatemala: Tyranny on Trial, Testimony of the Permanent People's Tribunal.* Edited by Susanne Jonas, Ed McCaughan, and Elizabeth Sutherland Martinez, 112–119. San Francisco: Synthesis Publications.

———. 1994. *Massacres in the Jungle: Ixcán, Guatemala, 1975–1982.* Boulder: Westview Press.

———. 2008. *Migración transnacional retornada: Juventud indígena de Zacualpa, Guatemala.* Guatemala: Asociación para el Avance de las Ciencias Sociales (AVANCSO) and Editorial Universitaria, Universidad de San Carlos de Guatemala.

Feagin, Joe R. 1988. *Free-Enterprise City: Houston in Political and Economic Perspective.* Piscataway Township, NJ: Rutgers University Press.

Fink, Leon. 2003. *The Maya of Morgantown: Work and Community in the Nuevo New South.* Chapel Hill: The University of North Carolina Press.

Flynn, Michael. 2002. "U.S. Anti-Migration Efforts Move South." Americas Program, Interhemispheric Resource Center, August 7. http://www.cipamericas.org/archives/1066.

Fox, Jonathan, and Gaspar Rivera-Salgado. 2004. *Indigenous Mexican Migrants in the United States.* Boulder, CO: Lynne Rienner Publishers.

Freeland, Gregory. 2010. "Negotiating Place, Space and Borders: The New Sanctuary Movement." *Latino Studies* 8: 485–508.

Frelick, William. 1991a. *Running the Gauntlet: The Central American Journey through Mexico.* Issue Paper. Washington: U.S. Committee for Refugees. January.

———. 1991b. "Update on Interdiction of Central Americans in Mexico." Washington: U.S. Committee for Refugees. July 16.

Fuchs, Victor R. 1968. *The Service Economy.* New York: National Bureau of Economic Research.

Fuentes Knight, Juan Alberto. 2011. *Rendición de cuentas.* Guatemala: FyG Editores.

Gallardo, María Eugenia, and José Roberto López. 1986. *Centroamérica: la crisis en cifras.* San José, Costa Rica: IICA-FLACSO.

Gans, Herbert J. 1962. *The Urban Villagers: Group and Class in the Life of Italian Americans.* New York: The Free Press.

García, Gabriel. 2012. "Análisis: Seguridad regional a paso de tortuga." *Contrapunto* (El Salvador). February 16. www.contrapunto.com.

García, Juan Ramon. 1980. *Operation Wetback: The Mass Deportation of Mexican Undocumented Workers in 1954.* Westport, CT: Greenwood Press.

García, María Cristina. 2006. *Seeking Refuge: Central American Migration to Mexico, the United States, and Canada.* Berkeley: University of California Press.

García Zamora, Rodolfo. 2005. Migracion, Remesas y Desarrollo: Los retos de las organizaciones migrantes mexicanas en Estados Unidos. Doctorado de Estudios del Desarrollo, Universidad Autonoma de Zacatecas. Mexico.

Gaynor, Tim. 2007. "Illegal Immigrants 'Self-Deport' as Woes mount." Reuters, December 24. http://www.reuters.com/article/2007/12/24/us-usa-immigration-selfdeport-idUSN2126758320071224.

Gellert, Gisela, Sílvia Irene Palma, and Antonio Vásquez. 1997. Transformaciones sociopolíticas a causa de la migración a EEUU en comunidades seleccionadas del Altiplano Occidental de Guatemala. Guatemala: FLACSO/Guatemala. Monograph.

Gibson, Campbell, and Kay Jung. 2006. "Historical Census Statistics on the Foreign-Born Population of the United States: 1850–2000." Working Paper No. 81, Population Division, U.S. Bureau of the Census. Washington, D.C. http://www.census .gov/population/www/documentation/twps0081/twps0081.pdf.

Giddens, Anthony. 1986. *The Constitution of Society*. Berkeley: University of California Press.

Giovagnoli, Mary. 2011. "Using All the Tools in the Toolbox: How Past Administrations have used Executive Branch Authority in Immigration." Washington, DC: American Immigration Council/Immigration Policy Center. www.migra tionpolicy.org.

Glick Schiller, Nina, Linda Basch, and Cristina Blanc-Szanton. 1992. *Towards a Transnational Perspective on Migration*. Vol. 645. New York: Annals of the New York Academy of Sciences.

Glick Schiller, Nina, and Ayşe Çağlar. 2009. "Towards a Comparative Theory of Locality in Migration Studies: Migrant Incorporation and City Scale." *Journal of Ethnic and Migration Studies* 35 (2): 177–202.

Godfrey, Brian. 1988. *Neighborhoods in Transition: The Making of San Francisco's Ethnic and Nonconformist Communities*. Berkeley: University of California Press.

———. 2004. "Barrio Under Siege: Latino Sense of Place in San Francisco, California." In *Hispanic Spaces, Latino Places*, edited by Daniel Arreola, 79–102. Austin: University of Texas Press.

Golden, Renny, and Michael McConnell. 1986. *Sanctuary: The New Underground Railroad*. Maryknoll, NY: Orbis Books.

Gonzalez, Nancy. 1988. *Sojourners of the Caribbean: Ethnogenesis and Ethnohistory of the Garifuna*. Urbana, IL: University of Illinois Press.

Gordon, David M. 1972. *Theories of Poverty and Unemployment: Orthodox, radical, and dual labor market perspectives*. Lexington, MA: Lexington Books.

Gorney, Cynthia. 2008. "Mexico's Other Border." *National Geographic*. February. 60–79.

Gottdiener, Mark. 1985. *The Social Production of Urban Space*. Austin: University of Texas Press.

———. 1994. *The New Urban Sociology*. New York: McGraw-Hill.

Greene, Joseph R. 2001. "U.S. and Multinational Coalition Disrupts Migrant Smuggling Operations." IWS (Information Warfare Site). http://www.iwar.org.uk/eco espionage/resources/transnational-crime/gj04.htm.

Grigsby, William. 2004. "Did the FMLN Lose, or Did Fear Win the Day?" *Envio*. April. 39–40. Managua, Nicaragua.

Grupo Guatemala-México Migración y Desarrollo (GGMMD). 2005. "Un puente entre migración y desarrollo." *Diálogo Extraordinario*. Guatemala: Facultad Latinoamericana de Ciencias Sociales (FLACSO)/Guatemala. September. 2–6

———. 2009. *Las políticas migratorias de México y Guatemala: Una primera aproximación*. Guatemala: Instituto Centroamericano de Estudios Sociales y Desarrollo (INCEDES). May.

Gzesh, Susan. 1995. "So Close to the United States, So Far from God: Refugees and Asylees under Mexican Law." *World Refugee Survey: 1995*. 34–40.

————. 2000. "Advocacy for Human Rights in an Intergovernmental Forum: The Puebla Process from the Perspective of Nongovernmental Organizations." In *In Defense of the Alien*, edited by Lydio Tomasi. 207–222. New York: Center for Migration Studies.

————. 2006. "Central Americans and Asylum Policy in the Reagan Era." *Migration Information Source*. April. Washington, D.C.: Migration Policy Institute. www.migrationinformation.org/USfocus/display.cfm?ID=384.

Hagan, Jacqueline Maria. 1987. "The Politics of Numbers: Central American Migration during a Period of Crisis, 1978–1985." Master's thesis, The University of Texas at Austin.

————. 1994. *Deciding to be Legal: A Maya Community in Houston*. Philadelphia: Temple University Press.

————. 1998. "Social Networks, Gender and Immigrant Settlement: Resource and Constraint." *American Sociological Review* 63: 55–67.

————. 2006. "Making Theological Sense of the Migration Journey from Latin America: Catholic, Protestant, and Interfaith Perspectives." *American Behavioral Scientist* 49: 1554–1573.

————. 2008. *Migration Miracle: Faith, Hope, and Meaning on the Undocumented Journey*. Cambridge, MA: Harvard University Press.

Hamilton, Nora, and Norma Stoltz Chinchilla. 1991. "Central American Migration: A Framework for Analysis." *Latin American Research Review* 26: 75–110.

————. 2001. *Seeking Community in a Global City: Guatemalans and Salvadorans in Los Angeles*. Philadelphia: Temple University Press.

Handlin, Oscar. 1974. *Boston's Immigrants: A Study in Acculturation*. New York: Atheneum.

Handy, Jim. 1984. *Gift of the Devil: A History of Guatemala*. Cambridge, MA: South End Press.

Harris, Nigel. 1995. *The New Untouchables: Immigration and the New World Order*. London: I. B. Tauris.

Harrison, Bennett, and Barry Bluestone. 1988. *The Great U-Turn: Corporate Restructuring and the Polarizing of America*. New York: Basic Books.

Hartman, Chester. 1974. *Yerba Buena: Land Grab and Community Resistance in San Francisco*. A Publication of the National Housing and Economic Development Law Project, Earl Warren Legal Institute, University of California, Berkeley. San Francisco: Glide Publications.

Hartman, Chester, with Sarah Carnochan. 2002. *City for Sale: The Transformation of San Francisco*. Berkeley: University of California Press.

Harvey, David. 2006. *Spaces of Global Capitalism: A Theory of Uneven Geographical Development*. London: Verso.

Haupt, Arthur, and Thomas T. Kane. 1998. *Population Handbook*, 4th International Edition. Washington, D.C.: Population Reference Bureau.

Hayden, Dolores. 1995. *The Power of Place: Urban Landscapes as Public History*. Cambridge, MA: The MIT Press.

Hayes, Margaret D. 1989. "The U.S. and Latin America: A Lost Decade?" in *Foreign Affairs* 68 (1): 180–198.

Hernández-León, Rubén. 2008. *Metropolitan Migrants: The Migration of Urban Mexicans to the United States*. Berkeley: University of California Press.

Hernández-León, Rubén, and Victor Zúñiga. 2002. "Appalachia Meets Aztlán: Mexican Immigration and Inter-Group Relations in Dalton, Georgia." In *New Destinations: Mexican Immigration in the United States*, edited by Victor Zúñiga and Rubén Hernández-León, 244–273. New York: Russell Sage Foundation.

Hoffman, Abraham. 1974. *Unwanted Mexican Americans in the Great Depression: Repatriation Pressures*, 1929–1939. Tucson: University of Arizona Press.

Holston, John. 2001. "Urban Citizenship and Globalization." In *Global City-Regions*, edited by Allen J. Scott, 325–348. Oxford: Oxford University Press.

Hondagneu-Sotelo, Pierette. 2001. *Doméstica: Immigrant Workers Cleaning and Caring in the Shadows of Affluence*. Berkeley: University of California Press.

Horowitz, Roger and Mark Miller. 1998. "Migration to Delaware: The Changing Face of Georgetown, DE, and Environs." *MigrationWorld*, 26 no. 5. September. 15–18.

Howell, Jude, and Jenny Pearce. 2001. *Civil Society and Development: A Critical Exploration*. Boulder, CO: Lynne Rienner Publications.

Huntington, Samuel P. 2004. "The Hispanic Challenge." *Foreign Policy* 141: 30–45.

Immigrant Communities in Action. 2007. "Millions of Immigrants Did Not March Last Year to Settle for the 'STRIVE' ACT." http://immigrantcommunitiesinaction .blogspot.com/2007_04_01_archive.html.

Instituto de Estudios y Divulgación sobre Migración, A.C. (INEDIM, Mexico) and Instituto Centroamericano de Estudios Sociales y Desarrollo (INCEDES, Guatemala). 2011. *Seguridad para el Migrante: Una agenda por construir*. Documento de Trabajo no. 2. Julio. Mexico.

Instituto Nacional de Migración (INM). 2003. "Boletín de Estadísticas Migratorias 2003: Extranjeros Alojados y Devueltos." Secretaría de Gobernación, México. http://www.politicamigratoria.gob.mx/es_mx/SEGOB/Extranjeros_alojados_y _devueltos_2003.

Instituto Nacional de Migración (INM), Secretaría de Gobernación (SEGOB) (Mexico). 2011. *Boletínes Estadísticos Anuales* for 2004–2006, 2011. http://www .inm.gob.mx/index.php/page/Boletínes Estadísticos.

Inter-American Development Bank. 2010. *Guatemala*. April. http://idbdocs.iadb.org /wsdocs/getdocument.aspx?docnum=35434997.

———. 2012. *2011 Report: Remittances to Latin America and the Caribbean*. Washington, D.C. http://idbdocs.iadb.org/wsdocs/getDocument.aspx?DOCNUM=3672 3460.

Itzigsohn, José. 2000. "Immigration and the Boundaries of Citizenship: The Institutions of Immigrants' Political Transnationalism." *International Migration Review* 34: 1126–1154.

Itzigsohn, José and Silvia Giorguli Saucedo. 2002. "Immigrant Incorporation and Sociocultural Transnationalism." *International Migration Review* 36 (3): 766–798.

Jáuregui, José Alfredo, y María de Jesús Ávila. 2009. "México, país de transito para migrantes guatemaltecos camino a Estados Unidos." In *Flujos migratorios en la frontera Guatemala-México*, edited by Maria Eugenia Anguiano Téllez y Rodolfo Corona Vazquez, 247–279. México, D.F.: Centro de Estudios Migratorios, Instituto Nacional de Migración.

Jonas, Andrew and David Wilson (eds.) 1999. *The Urban Growth Machine: Critical Perspectives 2 Decades Later*. New York: State of New York Press.

Jonas, Susanne. 1990. "'New Thinking' or More of the Same? Bush Administration Policy in Central America." *New Political Science* no. 18/19: 165–180.

———. 1991. *The Battle for Guatemala: Rebels, Death Squads, and U.S. Power*. Boulder, CO: Westview Press.

———. 1996. "Transnational Realities and Anti-Immigrant State Policies: Issues Raised by the Experiences of Central American Immigrants and Refugees in a Trinational Region." In *Latin America in the World Economy*, edited by Roberto Korzeniewicz and William Smith, 117–132. Westport, CN: Greenwood Press.

———. 1999. "'National Security,' Regional Development, and Citizenship in U.S. Immigration Policy: Reflections from the Case of Central American Immigrants and Refugees." In *Free Markets, Open Societies, Closed Borders? Trends in International Migration and Immigration Policy in the Americas*, edited by Max Castro, 175–195. Miami: North-South Center Press.

———. 2000a. "Democratization through Peace: The Difficult Case of Guatemala." *Journal of Interamerican Studies and World Affairs* 42: 9–38.

———. 2000b. *Of Centaurs and Doves: Guatemala's Peace Process*. Boulder, CO: Westview Press.

———. 2005. "Reframing the Immigration Debate: The Post-Election Challenge to Public Intellectuals," *LASA Forum* (Latin American Studies Association). Winter, 11–13.

———. 2007. "Dinámicas de las redes transregionales de defensa de los derechos de migrantes guatemaltecos y salvadorenos: Una exploración preliminar." In *Redes sociales en la Cuenca de los Huracanes: nueva perspectiva sobre las relaciones interamericanas*, edited by Francis Pisani, Natalia Saltalamaccchia, Arlene Tickner, and Nielan Barnes, 165–192. México: Porrúa.

———. 2013. *Guatemalan Migrants in Times of Civil War and Post-War Challenges*. Country Profiles, Migration Policy Institute. March. http://www.migrationinformation.org/USfocus/display.cfm?id=939.

Kauffer, Edith. 2005. "La política de integración de los refugiados guatemaltecos a la sociedad mexicana: De una orientación casi integral en Campeche a un enfoque minimalista en Chiapas." In *La población en el sureste de México*, edited by Hugo Angeles Cruz, 101–124. Tapachula: El Colegio de la Frontera Sur and México: Sociedad Mexicana de Demografía.

Kearney, Michael. 1995. "The Effects of Transnational Culture, Economy, and Migration on Mixtec Identity in Oaxacacalifornia." In *The Bubbling Cauldron: Race, Ethnicity, and the Urban Crisis*, edited by Michael Peter Smith and Joe Feagin, 226–243. Minneapolis: University of Minnesota Press.

Keck, Margaret and Kathryn Sikkink. 1998. *Activists Beyond Borders: Advocacy Networks in International Politics*. Ithaca, NY: Cornell University Press.

Keely, Charles. 1995. "The Effects of International Migration on U.S. Foreign Policy." In *Threatened Peoples, Threatened Borders*, edited by Michael Teitelbaum and Myron Weiner, 215–243. New York: Norton.

Kerwin, Donald M. 2010. *More than IRCA: U.S. Legalization Programs and the Current Policy Debate*. Washington, D.C.: Migration Policy Institute, December. http://www.migrationpolicy.org/pubs/legalization-historical.pdf.

Kochhar, Rakesh. 2009. "Unemployment Rises Sharply Among Latino Immigrants in 2008." Report of the Pew Hispanic Center, February 12. Washington, D.C.

Kohli, Aarti, Peter Markowitz, and Lisa Chavez. 2011. "Secure Communities by the Numbers: An Analysis of Demographics and Due Process." Berkeley: The Chief Justice Earl Warren Institute on Law and Social Policy, University of California, Berkeley Law School. www.warreninstitute.org.

Kyle, David. 2000. *Transnational Peasants: Migrations, Networks, and Ethnicity in Andean Ecuador.* Baltimore: The Johns Hopkins University Press.

Landolt, Patricia, Lillian Autler, and Sonia Baires. 1999. "From Hermano Lejano to Hermano Mayor: The Dialectics of Salvadoran Transnationalism." *Ethnic and Racial Studies* 22: 290–315.

Lefebvre, Henri. 1991. *The Production of Space.* Translated by Donald Nicholson-Smith. Cambridge, MA: Basic Blackwell, Inc.

Li, Peter S., and Chunhong Dong. 2007. "Earnings of Chinese immigrants in the Enclave and Mainstream Economy." *Canadian Review of Sociology* 44 (1): 65–99.

Logan, John, and Harvey Molotch. 1987. *Urban Fortunes: The Political Economy of Place.* Berkeley: University of California Press.

López, Julie. 2011. "Guatemala's Crossroads: The Democratization of Violence and Second Chances." In *Organized Crime in Central America: The Northern Triangle, Report on the Americas #29,* edited by Cynthia Arnson *et al.,* 140–233. Washington: Latin American Program, Woodrow Wilson Center.

Lopez, Mark Hugo, and Susan Minushkin. 2008. "2008 National Survey of Latinos: Hispanic Voter Attitudes." Pew Hispanic Center. http://www.pewhispanic.org /files/reports/90.pdf.

López-Garza, Marta, and David Diaz (eds.). 2001. *Asian and Latino Immigrants in a Restructuring Economy: The Metamorphosis of Los Angeles.* Palo Alto: Stanford University Press.

Loucky, James. 1987. "Maya Migrants and Musical Tradition in Los Angeles." In *Cityroots: New Immigrant Cultures in Los Angeles,* edited by Susan Auerbach, 8–11. Los Angeles: Cultural Affairs Department.

———. 2000. "Maya in a Modern Metropolis: Establishing New Lives and Livelihoods in Los Angeles. In *The Maya Diaspora: Guatemalan Roots, New American Lives,* edited by James Loucky and Marilyn M. Moors, 214–222. Philadelphia: Temple University Press.

———. 2005. Personal communication with Nestor Rodriguez.

Loucky, James, and Marilyn M. Moors (eds.). 2000. *The Maya Diaspora: Guatemalan Roots, New American Lives.* Philadelphia: Temple University Press.

Louie, Miriam Ching Yoon. 2001. *Sweatshop Warriors: Immigrant Women Workers Take on the Global Factory.* Cambridge, MA: South End Press.

Lungo, Mario (ed.). 1997. *Migracion internacional y desarrollo.* Tomo I, Tomo II. Fundacion Nacional para el Desarrollo (FUNDE). El Salvador.

———. 2004. "Las migraciones salvadoreñas y la sombra del tratado de libre comercio con Estados Unidos." *Estudios Centroamericanos (ECA)* July/August: 695–710.

Lungo, Mario, and Susan Kandel. 1999. *Transformando El Salvador: Migración, Sociedad y Cultura.* San Salvador: Fundación Nacional para el Desarrollo (FUNDE).

Mahler, Sarah. 2000. "Migration and Transnational Issues." *Central America 2020, Working Paper #4.* Hamburg: Institut fur Iberoamerika-Kunde.

Mancina, Peter. 2012. "The birth of a sanctuary-city: A history of governmental sanctuary in San Francisco." In *Sanctuary Practices in International Perspectives: Migra-*

tion, Citizenship and Social Movements, edited by Randy Lippert and Sean Rehaag, 205–218. London: Routledge.

Mannheim, Karl. 1952. "The Problem of Generations." In *Essays on the Sociology of Knowledge*, edited by Paul Kecskemeti, 276–322. New York: Oxford University Press.

Manz, Beatriz. 1988. *Refugees of a Hidden War: The Aftermath of the Counterinsurgency in Guatemala.* Albany: State University of New York Press.

———. 2004. *Paradise in Ashes: A Guatemalan Journey of Courage, Terror, and Hope.* Berkeley: University of California Press.

Manz, Beatriz, Xochitl Castañeda, Allison Davenport, Ingrid Perry-Houts, and Cécile Mazzacurati. 2000. "Guatemalan Immigration to the San Francisco Bay Area." University of California, Berkeley, Center for Latino Policy Research Working Paper 6 (1).

Marcus, George E., and Michael M. J. Fischer. 1986. *Anthropology as Cultural Critique: An Experimental Moment in the Human Sciences.* Chicago: University of Chicago Press.

Marx, Karl. [1847] 1955. *The Poverty of Philosophy.* Moscow: Progress Publishers.

———. [1887] 1967. *Capital*, vol. 1. New York: International Publishers.

Massey, Douglas. 1990. "Social structures, household strategies, and the cumulative causation of migration." *Population Index* 56: 3–26.

Massey, Douglas, Rafael Alarcón, Jorge Durand, and Humberto González. 1987. *Return to Aztlan: The Social Process of International Migration from Western Mexico.* Berkeley: University of California Press.

Massey, Douglas, Joaquín Arango, Graeme Hugo, Ali Kouaouci, Adela Pellegrino, and J. Edward Taylor. 1993 "Theories of International Migration." *Population and Development Review* 19: 431–466.

Massey, Douglas S., Jorge Durand, and Nolan J. Malone. 2002. *Beyond Smoke and Mirrors: Mexican Immigration in an Era of Economic Integration.* New York: Russell Sage.

McBride, Keally. 2009. "Sanctuary San Francisco." *Theory and Event*, 12 (4). Project MUSE. Web. 5 Sep. 2012. http://muse.jhu.edu/.

McEoin, Gary (ed.). 1985. *Sanctuary: A Resource Guide for Understanding and Participating in the Central American Refugees' Struggle.* San Francisco: Harper and Row.

McGovern, Stephen J. 1998. *The Politics of Downtown Development: Dynamic Political Cultures in San Francisco and Washington, D.C.* Lexington: University Press of Kentucky.

Mead, George Herbert. [1934] 1974. *Mind, Self, & Society.* Chicago, IL: University of Chicago Press.

Menjívar, Cecilia. 2000. *Fragmented Ties: Salvadoran Immigrant Networks in America.* Berkeley: University of California Press.

———. 2006. "Global Processes and Local Lives: Guatemalan Women's Work at Home and Abroad." *International Labor and Working Class History* 70 (1): 86–105.

Meyer, Peter J., and Clare Reibando Seelke. 2012. "Central America Regional Security Initiative: Background and Policy Issues for Congress." CRS Report for Congress, February 21. https://www.hsdl.org/?view&did=702799.

Migration Policy Institute Data Hub. 2007. "Global City Migration Map." July. http://www.migrationinformation.org/datahub/gcmm.cfm.

Milkman, Ruth. 2007. "Labor and the Immigrants' Rights Movement." Labor and Employment Relations Association. http://www.leraweb.org/publications/persp ectives-online-companion/perspectives-labor-and-immigrant-rights-movement.

Miller, Mike. 2009. *A Community Organizer's Tale: People in Power in San Francisco.* Berkeley: Hayday Books.

Mirabal, Nancy R. 2009. "Geographies of Displacement: Latina/os, Oral History, and The Politics of Gentrification in San Francisco's Mission District." *The Public Historian* 31 (2): 7–31.

Molina, Raúl. 2005. "Los guatemaltecos en el exterior deben ejercer sus derechos cívicos." *Diálogo Extraordinario* July. Guatemala: Facultad Latinoamericana de Ciencias Sociales (FLACSO). http://www.flacso.edu.gt/dialogo/extra12/dialogo.htm.

Mollenkopf, John H. 1983. *The Contested City.* Princeton, NJ: Princeton University Press.

Molotch, Harvey. 1976. "The City as a Growth Machine: Toward a Political Economy of Place." *American Journal of Sociology* 82 (2): 309–332.

Montejo, Victor. 1987. *Testimony: Death of a Guatemalan Village.* Willimantic, CT: Curbstone Press.

Morales, Rebecca. 1983. "Transitional Labor: Undocumented Workers in the Los Angeles Automobile Industry." *International Migration Review* 17: 570–596.

Nash, June. 2008. "Development to Unite Us: Autonomy and Multicultural Coexistence in Chiapas and Guatemala." *New Proposals: Journal of Marxism and Interdisciplinary Inquiry* I (2): 9–28.

Nazario, Sonia. 2006. *Enrique's Journey: The Story of a Boy's Dangerous Odyssey to Reunite with his Mother.* New York: Random House.

Nolin Hanlon, Catherine L., and W. George Lovell. 2000. "Flight, Exile, Repatriation, and Return: Guatemalan Refugee Scenarios, 1981–1998." In *The Maya Diaspora: Guatemalan Roots, New American Lives,* edited by James Loucky and Marilyn M. Moors, 35–55. Philadelphia: Temple University Press.

O'Brien, Matt. 2007. "The Mayan Way." Five-part series, Bay Area News Group. *San Mateo County Times.* December 23–27. http://insidebayarea.com/ci_7777307.

Odem, Mary E., and Elaine Lacy (eds.). 2009. *Latino Immigrants and the Transformation of the U.S. South.* Athens: The University of Georgia Press.

Ogren, Cassandra. 2007. "Migration and Human Rights on the Mexico-Guatemala Border." *International Migration* 45 (4): 203–242.

Olivas, Michael. 2012. *No Undocumented Child Left Behind: Plyler v. Doe and the Education of Undocumented Schoolchildren.* New York: New York University Press.

Organización Internacional para las Migraciones. 2009. *Encuesta sobre Remesas para 2009, Niñez y Adolescencia.* Cuadernos de Trabajo sobre Migración 27. Octubre. Ciudad de Guatemala: Serviprensa.

Organización Internacional para las Migraciónes (OIM)/Fondo de las Naciones Unidas para la Infancia (UNICEF). 2011. *Encuesta sobre Remesas 2010, Protección de la Niñez y Adolescencia.* Guatemala: OIM (International Migration Organization)/ UNICEF (United Nations International Childrens' Fund).

Ortíz Martínez, Lesbia. 2005. "Reseña Histórica de la Producción del Café en Guatemala y la Migración de Trabajadores Temporales Agrícolas, 1774–2000." *Revista Estudios.* 79–1007. Instituto de Investigaciones Históricas, Antropológicas, y Arqueológicas. Escuela de Historia, Universidad de San Carlos de Guatemala.

Padgett, Humberto. 2011. "Los Desaparecidos en Tamaulipas." *emeequis*, May 2, 30–42.

Palma, Sílvia Irene, Carol Girón, and Timothy Steigenga. 2007. "De Jacaltenango a Júpiter: negociando el concepto de familia en el espacio transnacional y el tiempo." In *Comunidades en movimiento: La migración internacional en el norte de Huehuetenango, Guatemala*, edited by Manuela Camus, 171–204. Guatemala: Instituto Centroamericano de Desarrollo y Estudios Sociales (INCEDES) and Centro de Estudios y Documentación de la Frontera Occidental de Guatemala (CEDFOG).

Palma, Sílvia Irene, and Alfredo Danilo Rivera. 2012. "Movilidad forzosa: buscando la inclusión 'al otro lado'." En: Programa de las Naciones Unidas para el Desarrollo (PNUD). *Guatemala: ¿un país de oportunidades para la juventud? Informe Nacional de Desarrollo Humano 2011–2012*. 189–202. Guatemala: PNUD/United Nations Development Program.

Pamuk, Ayse. 2004. "Geography of Immigrant Clusters in Global Cities: A Case Study of San Francisco, 2000." *International Journal of Urban and Regional Research* 28 (2): 287–307.

Papademetriou, Demetrios, Doris Meissner, and Eleanor Sohnen. 2013. *Thinking Regionally to Compete Globally: Leveraging Migration & Human Capital in the U.S., Mexico, and Central America*. Washington, D.C.: Migration Policy Institute.

Passel, Jeffrey S., and D'Vera Cohn. 2008. "Trends in Unauthorized Immigration: Undocumented Inflow Now Trails Legal Inflow." October 2. Washington, D.C.: Pew Hispanic Center.

Pearce, Jenny. 2005. "Towards a Post Representational Politics? Participation in the Twenty First Century." Presentation to workshop HEGOA. Bilbao, Spain: September 28. Manuscript, cited by permission of author.

Perea, Juan F. (ed.). 1997. *Immigrants Out!: The New Nativism and the Anti-Immigrant Impulse in the United States*. New York: New York University Press.

Pérez Saínz, Juan Pablo. 2001. "Exclusion y Mercado Laboral en Guatemala." *Cuadernos de Desarrollo Humano* No. 2001-2. Guatemala: Sistema de Naciones Unidas.

Piedrasanta Herrera, Ruth. 2007. "Apuntes sobre transmigración y remesas entre los chuj de Huehuetenango." In *Comunidades en movimiento: La migración internacional en el norte de Huehuetenango*, edited by Manuela Camus, 95–112. Antigua, Guatemala: Instituto Centroamericano de Desarrollo y Estudios Sociales (INCEDES) and Centro de Documentación de la Frontera Occidental de Guatemala (CEDFOG).

Piore, Michael. 1979. *Birds of Passage: Migrant Labor and Industrial Societies*. Cambridge: Cambridge University Press.

Pisani, Francis. 2005. "Redes Transnacionales en la Cuenca de los Huracanes: Marco de Referencia." (manuscript)

Pisani, Francis, and John Arquilla. 2004. "Global Dislocations, Network Solutions." *Nautilus Institute*, March 7.

Popkin, Eric. 1999. "Guatemalan Mayan Migration to Los Angeles: constructing transnational linkages in the context of the settlement process." *Ethnic and Racial Studies* 22: 267–289.

Portes, Alejandro, and Kelly Hoffman. 2003. "Latin American Class Structures: Their Composition and Change during the Neoliberal Era." *Latin American Research Review* 38: 41–82.

Portes, Alejandro and Rubén Rumbaut. 2001. *Legacies: The Story of the Immigrant Second Generation.* Berkeley: University of California Press.

Price, Marie, and Lisa Benton-Short. 2007. "Counting Immigrants in Cities across the Globe." Washington: Migration Policy Institute. January 1. http://www.migrationinformation.org/Feature/display.cfm?ID=567.

Programa de las Naciones Unidas para el Desarrollo (PNUD)/Guatemala. 2008. *Guatemala ¿Una Economía al Servicio del Desarrollo Humano? Informe Nacional de Desarrollo Humano (INDH) 2007–2008.* Guatemala: PNUD/United Nations Development Program.

———. 2010. *Guatemala: hacia un Estado para el desarrollo humano: Informe Nacional de Desarrollo Humano 2009–2010.* Guatemala: PNUD/United Nations Development Program.

———. 2012. *Guatemala: ¿Un País de Oportunidades para la Juventud? Informe Nacional de Desarrollo Humano 2011–2012.* Guatemala. PNUD/United Nations Development Program.

Quesada, James. 1999. "From Central American warriors to San Francisco Latino day laborers: Suffering and exhaustion in a transnational context." *Transforming Anthropology* 8 (1/2): 162–185.

Ramos, Jorge. 2005. *Dying to Cross: The Worst Immigrant Tragedy in American History.* New York: HarperCollins Publisher.

Red Regional de Organizaciones Civiles para las Migraciones (RROCM). 2005. "Asamblea General Anual, Documento Memoria." Report from Annual General Assembly. Unpublished document. September.

Reding, Andrew. 2002. "Groups at Risk in Guatemala." Question and Answer Series (QA/GTM/02.001), June. Washington: Immigration and Naturalization Service Resource Information Center.

REHMI/ODHA (Proyecto Interdiocesano para la Recuperación de la Memoria Histórica/Ofecina de Derechos Humanos del Arzobispado). 1998. *Guatemala: Nunca Más.* Tomos I, II, III, y IV. Guatemala.

Rhomberg, Chris. 2004. *No There There: Race, Class and Political Community in Oakland.* Berkeley: University of California Press.

Ridgley, Jennifer. 2008. "Cities of Refuge: Immigration Enforcement, Police, and the Insurgent Genealogies of Citizenship in U.S. Sanctuary Cities." *Urban Geography.* 29 (1): 53–77.

Rodríguez, Luisa. 2000. "Reporte Especial: Guatemaltecos en Estados Unidos." *Prensa Libre.* September 10–23. Guatemala: www.prensalibre.com.gt.

Rodriguez, Nestor. 1986. "Chicano-Indocumentado Relations in the Workplace." In *Chicano-Mexicano Work Relations,* edited by Tatcho Mindiola, Jr. and Max Martinez, 72–84. Mexican American Studies Center, University of Houston.

———. 1987. "Undocumented Central Americans in Houston: Diverse Populations." *International Migration Review* 21: 4–25.

———. 1997. "The Social Construction of the U.S.-Mexico Border." In *Immigrants Out!: The New Nativism and the Anti-Immigrant Impulse in the United States,* edited by Juan F. Perea, 223–243. New York: New York University Press.

———. 2007. "Comparing Mexicans and Central Americans in the Present Wave of U.S. Immigration." In *The Other Latinos: Central and South Americans in the United*

States, edited by Jose Luis Falconi and Jose Antonio Mazzoti, 81–100. Cambridge, MA: Harvard University David Rockefeller Center for Latin American Studies.

Rodriguez, Nestor, and Joe R. Feagin. 1986. "Urban Specialization in the World-System: An analysis of Historical Cases." *Urban Affairs Quarterly*, 22 (December): 187–220.

Rodriguez, Nestor, and Jacqueline Maria Hagan. 1992. "Aparment Restructuring and Latino Immigrant Tenant Struggles: A Case Study of Human Agency." *Comparative Urban and Community Research* 4: 164–180.

Rodriguez, Nestor, and Jacqueline Hagan. 2004. "Fractured Families and Communities: Effects of Immigration Reform in Texas, Mexico, and El Salvador." *Latino Studies* 2: 328–351.

Roque Ramírez, Horacio. 2005. "Claiming Queer Cultural Citizenship: Gay Latino (Im)Migrant Acts in San Francisco." In *Queer Migrations: Sexuality, U.S. Citizenship and Border Crossings*, edited by Eithne Luibhéid and Lionel Cantú. 161–188. Minneapolis: University of Minnesota Press.

Ruhs, Martin and Philip Martin. 2008. "Numbers vs. Rights: Trade-Offs and Guest Worker Programs." *International Migration Review* 42: 249–265.

Ruíz, Olivia. 2006. "Migration and Borders: Present and Future Challenges." *Latin American Perspectives*. Issue 147. 33:2. 46–55.

Sassen, Saskia. 1988. *The Mobility of Labor and Capital: A Study in International Investment and Labor Flow.* Cambridge: Cambridge University Press.

———. 1991. *The Global City.* New Jersey: Princeton University Press.

———. 1992. "Why Migration?" *NACLA Report on the Americas.* XXVI (1): 14–19.

———. 2001. "Global Cities and Global City-Regions: A Comparison." In *Global City-Regions*, edited by Allen Scott, 78–95. Oxford: Oxford University Press.

———. 2006. *Cities in a World Economy.* 3rd edition. Thousand Oaks, CA: Pine Forge Press.

Sassen Koob, Saskia. 1984. "The New Labor Demand in Global Cities." In *Cities in Transformation: Class, Capital, and the State*, edited by Michael Peter Smith, 139–171. Beverly Hills, CA: Sage.

Schoultz, Lars. 1992. "Central America and the Politicization of U.S. Immigration Policy." In *Western Hemisphere Immigration and United States Foreign Policy*, edited by Christopher Mitchell, 157–219. University Park, PA: Pennsylvania State University Press.

Schwartz. Rachel. 2012. "Central America Moves Toward a Truly Regional Stance on Drugs." *World Politics*. March 23. www.thedialogue.org.

Scott, Allen (ed.). 2001. *Global City-Regions.* Oxford: Oxford University Press.

Shifter, Michael. 2012. *Countering Criminal Violence in Central America.* Washington, D.C., and New York: Council on Foreign Relations Press. Special Report no. 64. April.

Silverman, Mark and Linton Joaquín. 2005. "NACARA for Guatemalans, Salvadorans, and Former Soviet Bloc Nationals." In *Winning NACARA Suspension Cases.* San Francisco: Immigrant Legal Resource Center.

Sin Fronteras I.A.P. (Mexico). 2005. *México y su Frontera Sur.* Mexico: Sin Fronteras.

Singelmann, Joachim. 1978. *From Agriculture to Services: The Transformation of Industrial Employment.* Beverly Hills, CA: Sage.

Singer, Audrey, and Douglas S. Massey. 1998. "The Social Process of Undocumented Border Crossing Among Mexican Migrants." *International Migration Review* 32: 561–592.

Sklair, Leslie. 1995. *Sociology of the Global System.* 2nd edition. Baltimore, MD: The Johns Hopkins University Press.

Smith, Barton. 1986. *Handbook on the Houston Economy.* Houston: Center for Public Policy, University of Houston.

Smith, Carol A. 1988. "Destruction of the Material Bases for Indian Culture: Economic Changes in Totonicapán." In *Harvest of Violence: The Mayan Indians and the Guatemalan Crisis,* edited by Robert M. Carmack, 206–231. Norman: University of Oklahoma Press.

Smith, James. 2006. "Guatemala: Economic Migrants Replace Political Refugees" in MPI, *Migration Information Source.* April. http://www.migrationinformation.org /Profiles/display.cfm?ID=392.

Smith, Michael Peter. 2001. *Transnational Urbanism: Locating Globalization.* Malden, MA: Blackwell Publishing.

Smyth, Frank. 2012. "Guatemala's Cycle of Crime." In *World Policy* blog. January 13. http://www.worldpolicy.org/blog/2012/01/13/guatemala%E2%80%99s-cycles -crime.

Soja, Edward W. 1989. *Postmodern Geographies: The Reassertion of Space in Critical Social Theory.* New York: Verso.

Solnit, Rebecca, and Susan Schwartzenberg. 2000. *Hollow City.* London: Verso.

Spatial Structures in the Social Sciences. 2005. "Sortable list for Guatemalan Population Total." 2000. Brown University. http://mumford1.dyndns.org/cen2000/His panicPop/HspSort/guaSort.htm.

Spener, David. 2009. *Clandestine Crossings: Migrants and Coyotes on the Texas-Mexico Border.* Ithaca, NY: Cornell University Press.

Stone, Michael. 2000. "Becoming Belizean: Maya Identity and the Politics of Nation." In *The Maya Diaspora: Guatemalan Roots, New American Lives,* edited by James Loucky and Marilyn M. Moors, 118–140. Philadelphia: Temple University Press.

Susser, Ida (ed.). 2002. *The Castells Reader on Cities and Social Theory.* Malden, MA: Blackwell Publishers.

Taylor, Clark. 2000. "Challenges of Return and Reintegration." In *The Maya Diaspora: Guatemalan Roots, New American Lives,* edited by James Loucky and Marilyn M. Moors, 93–111. Philadelphia: Temple University Press.

Teitelbaum, Michael, and Myron Weiner, eds. 1995. Editors. *Threatened Peoples, Threatened Borders.* New York: Norton.

Tobar, Héctor. 1998. *The Tattooed Soldier.* New York: Penguin Group.

Torres-Rivas, Edelberto. 1985. *Report on the Condition of Central American Refugees and Migrants.* July. Washington, D.C.: Center for Immigration Policy and Refugee Assistance, Georgetown University.

———. 1989. *Repression and Resistance: The struggle for democracy in Central America.* Boulder, CO: Westview Press.

———. 1993. *History and Society in Central America.* Translated by Douglass Sullivan-González. Austin: University of Texas Press.

———. 1996. "Los desafíos del desarrollo democrático en Centroamérica." *Annuario de Estudios Centroamericanos* 22: 7–40.

————. 2012. "Centroamérica: ¿Estado débil y democrático?" In Instituto Centroamericano de Estudios Fiscales. *Lente fiscal centroamericano* no. 4. http://www.icefi .org/lente-fiscal-centroamericano-no-4.

Torres, M. Gabriela, and David Carey Jr. 2010. "Precursors to Femicide: Guatemalan Women in a Vortex of Violence." *Latin American Research Review* 45: 142–164.

TRAC Immigration Project. 2012. Immigration Court Backlog, Pending Cases. http://trac.syr.edu/phptools/immigration/court_backlog/.

Trudeau, Robert H. 1993. *Guatemalan Politics: The Popular Struggle for Democracy.* Boulder, CO: Lynne Rienner Publishers.

Urquhart, Michael. 1984. "The Employment Shift to Services: Where did it come from?" *Monthly Labor Review* 107: 15–22.

Urrea, Luis Alberto. 2005. *The Devil's Highway: A True Story.* New York: Little Brown and Company.

Urrutia-Rojas, Ximena, and Nestor Rodriguez. 1997. "Unaccompanied Migrant Children from Central America: Sociodemographic Characteristics and Experiences with Potentially Traumatic Events." In *Health and Social Services among International Labor Migrants: A Comparative Perspective*, edited by Antonio Ugalde and Gilberto Cardenas, 151–166. Austin: Center for Mexican American Studies, University of Texas Press.

U.S. Bureau of Labor Statistics (BLS). 2012a. "Economic News Release: Median usual weekly earnings of full-time wage and salary workers for the foreign born and native born by selected characteristics, 2010–2011 annual averages." http://www.bls .gov/news.release/forbrn.t05.htm.

————. 2012b. Consumer Price Index for All Urban Consumers: All Items. http:// research.stlouisfed.org/fred2/data/CPIAUCSL.txt.

U.S. Census Bureau. 1983a. *1980 Census of Population: Detailed Population Characteristics, Texas*, Section 1 of 2, PC80-1-D45. Washington, D.C.: Government Printing Office.

————. 1983b. *1980 Census of Population and Housing: Census Tracts, Houston, Texas SMSA*, PHC80-2-184. Washington, D.C.: Government Printing Office.

————. 1983c. *1980 Census of Population: Characteristics of Population, Detailed Population Characteristics*, California, PC80-1-D6. Washington D.C.: Government Publishing Office.

————. 1991. *Statistical Abstract of the United States: 1991* (111th edition). Washington, D.C.: Government Publishing Office.

————. 1992. *Statistical Abstract of the United States: 1992* (112th edition.) Washington, D.C. Government Printing Office.

————. 1993a. *1990 Census of Population: Social and Economic Characteristics, Texas*. Section 2 of 3. 1990 CP-2-45. Washington, D.C.: Government Printing Office.

————. 1993b. *1990 Census of Population: Social and Economic Characteristics, Metropolitan Areas*, 1990 CP-2-1B, Section 2 of 6. Washington D.C.: U.S. Government Printing Office.

————. 2000. Fact Finder Customs Tables, Houston metropolitan area.

————. 2002. 2000 Census of Population and Housing, FactFinder.

————. 2009. 2008 American Community Survey. Factfinder.

————. 2010a. 2009 American Community Survey. Factfinder.

————. 2010b. 2010 Census. Factfinder.

———. 2011a. American Community Survey. Factfinder.

———. 2011b. International Data Base (IDB). http://www.census.gov/population /international/data/idb/informationGateway.php.

———. 2012. 2011 American Community Survey. Factfinder.

U.S. Citizenship and Immigration Services (CIS). 2013. "Deferred Action for Childhood Arrivals." http://www.uscis.gov/USCIS/Resources/Reports%20and%20Stu dies/Immigration%20Forms%20Data/All%20Form%20Types/DACA/daca-13 -3-15.pdf.

U.S. Committee for Refugees (USCR). 1990. *Refugee Reports: 1990 Statistical Issue.* Washington: USCR. XI: 12. December 21.

———. 1991. "New Lease on Life for Salvadorans and Guatemalans in the United States." *Refugee Reports.* Washington: USCR. XII: 1. January 25.

———. 1992. "U.S. pays Mexico to Deport Aliens in Absence of Basic Refugee Rights Protections." Press Release. Washington: USCR. September 11.

U.S. Department of Homeland Security (DHS). 2003. *2001 Yearbook of Immigration Statistics.* Washington, D.C.

———. 2004. *2003 Yearbook of Immigration Statistics.* Washington, D.C.

———. 2006. *2005 Yearbook of Immigration Statistics.* http://www.dhs.gov/files/statis tics/publications/LPR05.shtm.

———. 2007. *2006 Yearbook of Immigration Statistics.* http://www.dhs.gov/xlibrary /assets/statistics/yearbook/2006/OIS_2006_Yearbook.pdf.

———. 2011a. *2010 Yearbook of Immigration Statistics.* http://www.dhs.gov/files/statis tics/publications/LPR10.shtm.

———. 2011b. Estimates of the Unauthorized Immigrant Population Residing in the United States: January 2010. http://www.dhs.gov/xlibrary/assets/statistics/publi cations/ois_ill_pe_2010.pdf.

———. 2012a. *2011 Yearbook of Immigration Statistics.* http://www.dhs.gov/yearbook -immigration-statistics.

———. 2012b. "Estimates of the Unauthorized Immigrant Population Resident in the United States: January 2011." Washington, D.C. March. http://www.dhs.gov /xlibrary/assets/statistics/publications/ois_ill_pe_2011.pdf.

———. 2012c. Deferred Action. June 15. http://www.dhs.gov/deferred-action.

———. 2013. *U.S. Border Patrol Fiscal Year 2012 Profile.* http://www.cbp.gov/xp/cgov /border_security/border_patrol/usbp_statistics/usbp_fy12_stats/.

U.S. Department of Justice. 1992. *Immigration Reform and Control Act: Report on the Legalized Alien Population.* Washington, D.C.

U.S. Government Accountability Office (GAO). 1984. *Central American Refugees: Regional Conditions and Prospects and Potential Impact on the United States.* GAO/ NSIAD-84-106 (July 20). Washington, D.C.

———. 2007. *Secure Border Initiative: SBInet Expenditure Plan Needs to Better Support Oversight and Accountability.* February, GAO-A7-309. Washington, D.C. http:// www.gao.gov/new.items/d07309.pdf.

———. 2009. *Secure Border Initiative: Technology Deployment Delays Persist and the Impact of Border Fencing Has Not Been Assessed.* GAO-09-896 (September). Washington, D.C. http://www.gao.gov/new.items/d09896.pdf.

———. 2010. *Secure Border Initiative: DHS Has Faced Challenges Deploying Techonology and Fencing Along the Southwest Border.* GAO-10–651T (May). Washington, D.C. http://www.gao.gov/new.items/d10651t.pdf.

—. 2012. *Border Patrol: Key Elements of New Strategic Plan Not Yet in Place to Inform Border Security Status and Resource Needs.* GAO-13-25 (December 10). http://www.gao.gov/products/GAO-13-25.

—. 2013. *Border Security: DHS's Progress and Challenges in Securing U.S. Borders.* GAO-13-414T. March 14. http://www.gao.gov/assets/660/653037.pdf.

U.S. Immigration and Customs Enforcement (ICE). 2003. *Endgame: Office of Detention and Removal Strategic Plan, 2003–2012.* August 15. http://cryptogon.com/docs/endgame.pdf.

—. 2009. "Secure Communities: Crash Course." U.S. Department of Homeland Security. Washington, D.C. http://www.ice.gov/doclib/foia/secure_communities/securecommunitiespresentations.pdf.

—. 2012a. "Fact Sheet: Delegation of Immigration Authority Section 287(g) Immigration and Nationality Act." December 31. http://www.ice.gov/news/library/factsheets/287g.htm.

—. 2012b. "Secure Communities: Activated Jurisdictions." August 22. http://www.ice.gov/doclib/secure-communities/pdf/sc-activated2.pdf.

U.S. Immigration and Naturalization Service (INS). 1972. *Statistical Yearbook of the Immigration and Naturalization Service, 1972.* Washington, D.C.: Government Printing Office.

—. 1975. *Statistical Yearbook of the Immigration and Naturalization Service, 1975.* Washington, D.C.: Government Printing Office.

—. 1977. *Statistical Yearbook of the Immigration and Naturalization Service, 1977.* Washington, D.C.: U.S. Government Printing Office.

—. 1983. *Statistical Yearbook of the Immigration and Naturalization Service, 1983.* Washington, D.C.: Government Printing Office.

—. 1984. *Statistical Yearbook of the Immigration and Naturalization Service, 1984.* Washington, D.C.: Government Printing Office.

—. 1985. *Statistical Yearbook of the Immigration and Naturalization Service, 1985.* Washington, D.C.: Government Printing Office.

—. 1986. *Statistical Yearbook of the Immigration and Naturalization Service, 1986.* Washington, D.C.: Government Printing Office.

—. 1992a. *1991 Statistical Yearbook of the Immigration and Naturalization Service.* Washington, D.C.: Government Printing Office.

—. 1992b. *Immigration Reform and Control Act: Report on the Legalized Alien Population.* Washington, D.C.: Government Printing Office.

—. 1993. *Statistical Yearbook of the Immigration and Naturalization Service, 1992,* Table 30. Washington, D.C.: Government Printing Office.

—. 1997. *Statistical Yearbook of the Immigration and Naturalizations Service, 1996.* Washington, D.C.: Government Printing Office.

Varsanyi, Monica W. 2008. "Immigration Policing through the Backdoor: City Ordinances, the 'Right to the City' and the Exclusion of Undocumented Day Laborers." School of Justice and Social Inquiry, Arizona State University.

Villacorta Escobar, Manuel. 1984. *Recursos Economicos de Guatemala.* Guatemala: Editorial Piedra Santa.

Vlach, Norita. 1992. *The Quetzal in Flight: Guatemalan Refugee Families in the United States*. Westport, CT: Praeger.

Waldinger, Roger. 1989. "Immigration and Urban Change." *Annual Review of Sociology* 15: 211–232.

———. 2001. "Up from Poverty? 'Race,' Immigration, and the Fate of Low-Skilled Workers." In *Strangers at the Gates: New Immigrants in Urban America*, edited by Roger Waldinger, 80–116. Berkeley: University of California Press.

Walker, Dick, and The Bay Area Study Group. 1990. *The Playground of U.S. Capitalism? The Political Economy of the San Francisco Bay Area in the 1980s*. (*The Year Left*, vol. 4). New York: Verso.

Wallerstein, Immanuel. 1974. *The Modern World-System: Capitalist Agriculture and the Origins of the European World-Economy in the Sixteenth Century*. New York: Academic Press.

Wells, Miriam. 2000. "Immigration and Unionization in the San Francisco Hotel Industry." In *Organizing Immigrants*, edited by Ruth Milkman, 109–129. Ithaca, NY: Cornell University Press.

———. 2004. "The Grassroots Reconfiguration of U.S. Immigration Policy." *International Migration Review*. 38 (4): 1308–1347.

Wilson, Jill, and Audrey Singer. 2009. "How the Recession is Affecting Immigration." *The New Republic* (November 18). http://www.tnr.com/blog/how-the-recession's-affecting-immigration.

———. 2011. "Immigrants in 2010 Immigrant America: A Decade of Change." Brookings Institution. Metropolitan Policy Program. Washington.

Wilson, Kenneth L., and Alejandro Portes. 1980. "Immigrant Enclaves: An Analysis of the Labor Market Experiences of Cubans in Miami." *American Journal of Sociology* 86 (2): 295–319.

Wirt, Frederick. 1974. *Power in the City: Decision Making in San Francisco*. Berkeley: University of California Press. Published for the Institute of Governmental Studies.

Wolch, Jennifer, and Michael Dear (eds.). 1989. *The Power of Geography: How Territory Shapes Social Life*. Boston: Unwin Hyman.

Wolf, Eric. 1959. *Sons of the Shaking Earth*. Chicago: University of Chicago Press.

Women's Refugee Commission. 2012. *Presentations to Migration Policy Institute. Unaccompanied Minors and their Journey through the U.S. Immigration System*. July 30. Washington.

Worby, Paula. 1999. "Lessons learned from UNHCR's involvement in the Guatemala refugee repatriation and reintegration programme (1987–1999)." http://www.crid.or.cr/digitalizacion/pdf/eng/doc13135/doc13135.pdf.

World Bank. 1990. *World Development Report 1990*. Washington, D.C.: International Bank for Reconstruction and Development.

———. 1992. *World Development Report 1992*. Washington, D.C.: International Bank for Reconstruction and Development.

———. 2004. *Poverty in Guatemala*. Washington, D.C.: World Bank.

———. 2011a. Data. GTM_Country_MetaData_en_EXCEL-1.xls. http://data.worldbank.org/country/guatemala.

———. 2011b. Data. Mortality rate under –5 (per 1,000). http://data.worldbank.org/indicator/SH.DYN.MORT.

Wright, Richard, and Mark Ellis. 2000. "The Ethnic and Gender Division of Labor Compared Among Immigrants to Los Angeles." *International Journal of Urban and Regional Research*, vol. 24, no. 4 (September): 583–600.

Young, Rick. 2011. "Lost in Detention." Public Broadcasting Service, *Frontline and Investigative Reporting Workshop*. María Hinojosa, correspondent. October 18.

Zimmerman, Warren. 1995. "Migrants and Refugees: A Threat to Security?" In *Threatened Peoples, Threatened Borders*, edited by Michael Teitelbaum and Myron Weiner, 88–116. New York: Norton.

Zolberg A., A. Suhrke, S. Aguayo. 1989. *Escape from Violence: Conflict and the Refugee Crisis in the Developing World*. New York: Oxford University Press.

Zúñiga, Victor, and Rubén Hernández León. 2005. *New Destinations: Mexican Immigration in the United States*. New York: Russell Sage Foundation.

Index

Locators for entries in the unnumbered illustration section are in boldface type. Tables are denoted by the page number followed by *t*.

Garifuna, 213n29
gay/lesbian rights, 96
gender: among Guatemalan respondents to 1995 survey, 169, 174; and CONGUATE, 95; and gentrification, 191; and Guatemalan communities of origin, 24; and Guatemalan migration patterns, 9; and relations, 123–124; and sancristobalense migrants in Houston, 134; and San Francisco–area organizing efforts, 159, 186; and social recomposition, 15, 206; as social status, 22. *See also* women
gente natural (self-identifying term for Mayan people), 222n20
gentrification, 228n35; in Mission District, 163–165, 167, 188–191; and Oakland, 192; in San Francisco, 25, 160, 196. *See also* redevelopment
Georgia, 68. *See also* anti-immigrant measures
Gerardi, Juan, 182, 226n22
globalization, 223–224n6
Global Reach, 59. *See also* Operation Disrupt
Gracias Madre, I:14, 190
grassroots communities, 92
grassroots participation, 108, 179
Great Depression, 213n32
Great Recession, 187, 188
Great U-Turn, 33, 37. *See also* service economy
Grupo Folklórico Rabinal Achí (Oakland), 82
Grupo Guatemala-México Migración y Desarrollo (GGMMD), 100, 109, 217n27
Grupo Guatemalteco de Delaware, 82
Grupo Maya Qusamej Junam (San Francisco/Oakland), 82, 94, 163, 176, 178–179, 181, 182
Grupo Quetzal, 227n28
Grupo Regional de Organizaciones Protectoras de los Derechos Humanos de los Migrantes (GREDEMIG—Regional Network for the Defense

of the Human Rights of Migrants), 219n35
Guatemala City: and Casas del Migrante, 97; and counterinsurgency campaign (1966–1968), 214n2; as destination for Mayan migrants (1970s), 18; and emigration in phase 2, 44; and Immigrant Spring protests, 101; and labor organizing, 4; as only experience of travel for some Mayan migrants, 117; and Ríos Montt campaign terror (2003), 217n25; as source of ladino migrants to Houston, 121; and threat from URNG (1980s), 49
Guatemala-Mexico border, I:4, 14, 24, 61, 97, 103, 109–110, 201
Guatemalan activists/advocates, 71–73, 81, 178, 197. *See also specific groups*
Guatemalan American Chamber of Commerce, 81, 82, 83
Guatemalan Americans, 53, 81–83, 90, 96. *See also specific communities*
Guatemalan army, 35, 42, 43, 49, 116
Guatemalan Bishops' Conference, 97
Guatemalan civil society, 12
Guatemalan Congress, 88, 102, 204
Guatemalan Consulate in San Francisco, 180–182, 227n27
Guatemalan Consulates, 88, 101–102
Guatemalan economy (1970s-1980s), 36
Guatemala News and Information Bureau (GNIB), 182, 227n29
Guatemalan-owned enterprises, 164–165, 183–184. *See also specific businesses*
Guatemalan Unity Information Agency (GUIA), 81–82, 84, 88, 93. *See also* CONGUATE
GUATENET, 81–82, 94
"guest worker" programs, 90, 91
Gulfton Neighborhood Organization (GANO), Houston, 140–141

Haitians, 216n12
hambruna (famine), in Guatemala, 62
health clinics, 192

109; and Mayan people in Chiapas and Guatemala, 230n1; and migration, 14, 99; and migration region, 11–12; and political generations, 96; and weak states, 203, 230n3
Network in Solidarity with the People of Guatemala (NISGUA), 227n29
networks, 11–13, 73, 100, 108–109. *See also specific networks*
networks of women, 135, 136
New Sanctuary Movement, 228n38, 229–230n48
New York, 160
NGOs (nongovernmental organizations): and advocacy, 11, 70, 97–98, 103, 105, 114; and data on political and military violence, 211n11; dynamics of, 81, 90, 93, 100–101, 108; and Immigrant Spring protests, 92; and lack of community accountability, 95; in San Francisco, 166, 177. *See also specific organizations*
Nicaragua, 70–71, 220n42
Nicaraguan Adjustment and Central American Relief Act. *See* NACARA
Nicaraguan immigrants, 80, 168, 216n12
9/11, 85–86
1980 Census, 26, 121, 121t, 139, 168
1990 Census, 121t, 139, 168, 225n15
1970 Census, 26, 35, 139, 211–212n12
1960 Census, 35
North Carolina, 20
Northern Triangle, 1, 111–114, 202–205. *See also* sub-regions of Central America
North Fair Oaks, 193
Notisiete, 97
"nuestra gente" ("our people"), 150
Nunca Más (Never Again), 182

Oakland: and advocacy organizations, 82, 178, 183, 226–227n26, 227n28, 227n29, 229–230n48; and concentration of immigrants (2000 and 2010), 223n5; and day labor centers, 185; and gentrification, 187–

188, 191–193; and micro-barrios, 162–163; and numbers of foreign-born Guatemalans, 168; and re-socialization by immigrants, 157; and Sanctuary City ordinance, 180; and Secure Communities initiative, 229n46; and St. Peter's Church, 178. *See also* Alameda County; San Francisco–Bay Area
Oakland Catholic Worker, 180
Obama, Barack, 67–69
Obama administration, 196, 217–218n28
Office of Detention and Removal (DRO) within ICE, 86. *See also* deportation; ICE
Operation Blockade, 56
Operation Community Shield, 64
Operation Disrupt, 59
Operation Gatekeeper, 56
Operation Hold the Line, 56
Operation Safeguard, 56
Operation Wetback, 56, 213n32
Orden de Franciscanos de Manhattan, 82
Organización de los Pueblos Maya en el Exilio, 84–85
Organización Internacional para las Migraciones, 26–27
Organización Maya Quetzal (West Palm Beach), 82
Organización Negra Centroamericana (ONECA), 89
organizations, 174–175, 175t, 176, 198–199. *See also specific organizations*
organized crime, 111
"organized sectors," 72
out-migration, 191. *See also* gentrification

Pacto Fiscal (tax agreement), 219n39
Palacio Latino, I:14, 183
Palma, Irene, 217n27
Panama, 50, 202, 218n32
pan-Latino organizing, 91
Parlamento Centroamericano